Petersonspublishingcom/publishing updates

Check out our website at www.petersonspublishing.com/publishingupdates to see if there is any new information regarding the test and any revisions or corrections to the content of this book. We've made sure the information in this book is accurate and up-to-date; however, the test format or content may have changed since the time of publication.

OTHER RECOMMENDED TITLES

Peterson's Master the™ AP® English Language and Composition Exam

Peterson's Master the™ AP® English Literature and Composition Exam

Contents

PART III: AP® U.S. HISTORY REVIEW

PART IV: THREE PRACTICE TESTS

Before You Begin

HOW THIS BOOK IS ORGANIZED

Whether you have five months, nine weeks, or just two short weeks to prepare for the exam, Peterson's *Master the™ AP® U.S. History Exam* will help you develop a study plan that caters to your individual needs and timetable. These step-by-step plans are easy to follow and remarkably effective.

- **Top 10 Strategies to Raise Your Score** gives you tried and true test-taking strategies.
- **Part I** includes the basic information about the AP® U.S. History Exam that you need to know.
- **Part II** provides the review and strategies for answering the multiple-choice questions and opportunities to practice what you are learning. It is a good idea to read the answer explanations to all of the questions because you may find ideas or tips that will help you better analyze the answers to questions in the next Practice Test you take. You will also find strategies for writing high-scoring responses to short-answer, document-based, and long essay questions. Use the walk-throughs and analyses to guide you through the composition process of each of the three free-response question types.
- **Part III** provides a comprehensive review of U.S. history from discovery, settlement, and expansion to the present.
- **Part IV** includes three practice tests. Remember to apply the test-taking system carefully, work the system to get more correct responses, and be careful of your time in order to answer more questions in the time period.

SPECIAL STUDY FEATURES

Peterson's *Master the™ AP® U.S. History Exam* was designed to be as user-friendly as it is complete. It includes several features to make your preparation easier.

Overview

Each chapter begins with a bulleted overview listing the topics that will be covered in the chapter. You know immediately where to look for a topic that you need to work on.

Summing It Up

Each strategy chapter ends with a point-by-point summary that captures the most important points. The summaries are a convenient way to review the content of these strategy chapters.

Bonus Information

You will find two types of notes in the margins of the *Master the™ AP® U.S. History Exam* book to alert you to important information.

NOTE

Margin notes marked "Note" highlight information about the test structure itself.

TIP

Tips draw your attention to valuable concepts, advice, and shortcuts for tackling the exam. By reading the tips, you will learn how to approach different question types, pace yourself, and remember what was discussed previously in the book.

HOW TO PLAN FOR YOUR TEST USING THIS BOOK

This books consists of a section on the content, structure, scoring of as well as useful strategies for success on the exam followed by three chapters of content review and three full-length practice tests with full explanations. Each content chapter also provides review exercises and walkthroughs designed to help you get up to speed.

You may already know what you know and don't know. If not, and frankly even if you think you do, we'd recommend taking any of the three full-length tests first, without studying, as a "diagnostic test" (with the proper timing, using a bubble sheet, at 8AM, in a test-like environment, etc.) in order to see where your weaknesses lie. Let your results guide your use of this book. After reviewing your test results, note what content you need to work on and study for first.

For more specific test-prep timeline information, see our "Building an Effective Study Plan" section on page 14.

YOU'RE WELL ON YOUR WAY TO SUCCESS

Remember that knowledge is power. You will be studying the most comprehensive guide available, and you will become extremely knowledgeable about the exam. We look forward to helping you raise your score.

GIVE US YOUR FEEDBACK

Peterson's publishes a full line of books—test prep, education exploration, financial aid, and career preparation. Peterson's publications can be found in high school guidance counselor offices, college libraries and career centers, and your local bookstore and library.

We welcome any comments or suggestions you may have about this publication. Please call our customer service department at 800-338-3282 ext. 54229 or send an email to custsvc@petersons.com.

TOP 10 STRATEGIES TO RAISE YOUR SCORE

When it comes to taking an AP® Exam, some test-taking skills will do you more good than others. There are concepts you can learn and techniques you can follow that will help you do your best. Here are our picks for the top 10 strategies to raise your score:

1. **Create a study plan and follow it.** The right study plan will help you get the most out of this book in whatever time you have.

2. **Choose a place and time to study every day,** and stick to your routine and your plan.

3. **Complete the practice tests in this book.** They will give you just what they promise: practice—practice in reading and following the directions, practice in pacing yourself, practice in understanding and answering multiple-choice questions, and practice in writing timed essays.

4. **Complete all of your assignments for your regular AP® U.S. History class.** Ask questions in class, talk about what you read and write, and enjoy what you are doing. The test is supposed to measure your development as an educated and thinking reader.

5. **If the question is a *main idea* or *theme* question,** look for the answer that is the most general and can be supported by evidence in the selection.

6. **Remember that all** elements in an answer must be correct for the answer to be correct.

7. **For the free-response questions, go with what you know.** The short-answer question (Section I, Part B) and long essay (Section II, Part B) sections give you the option of choosing which question to answer. In making your decisions, look for the questions that you know the most about and can provide the most outside information to answer.

8. **With *not/except* questions, ask yourself if an answer choice is true about the selection.** If it is, cross it out, and keep checking answers.

9. **If you aren't sure about an answer but know something about the question, eliminate what you know is wrong and make an educated guess.** Ignore the answers that are absolutely wrong, eliminate choices in which part of the answer is incorrect, check the time period of the question and of the answer choices, check the key words in the question again, and revisit remaining answers to discover which seems more correct.

10. **Finally, don't cram.** Relax. Go to a movie, visit a friend—but not one who is taking the test with you. Get a good night's sleep.

PART I
AP® U.S. HISTORY BASICS

All About the AP® U.S. History Exam

OVERVIEW

- **The AP® U.S. History Exam: An Overview**
- **Registration Essentials for the AP® U.S. History Exam**
- **Getting Ready for Exam Day**
- **Building an Effective Study Plan**
- **Summing It Up**

We understand *exactly* why you're here and why you're reading this book—you're a high-achieving student with a goal to get your best possible score on the AP® U.S. History Exam. Your reasons for setting this goal are likely two-fold:

1. Getting a good exam score (typically a score of 3 or higher out of a range from 1 to 5) will help you earn valuable college credit while still in high school, allowing you to potentially place out of introductory-level undergraduate courses in that subject area.

2. A good exam score looks great on your college application and will allow you to be more competitive and stand out among the pool of qualified applicants to the schools you're applying.

These are great reasons to take your AP® exams *seriously*—which means making the most of your preparation time between now and exam day to ensure that you do your best.

You've undoubtedly taken your academic career seriously thus far, which is why you decided to take this AP®-level course in the first place. The last thing you want to have happen now is to get this close to your goal of acing the AP® U.S. History Exam and not do your absolute best because of a failure to plan appropriately!

We *completely* get it—and if this description sounds like you, then here's some great news: you have already made an excellent decision and have taken a wise step forward in your AP® exam preparation by deciding to purchase this book. We're here to help make your goal of a great score on the AP® U.S. History Exam a reality. So keep reading!

Peterson's Master™ the AP® U.S. History Exam is your comprehensive study resource, all-in-one test-prep coach, effective preparation guide, and indispensable companion on your journey to getting a great AP® U.S. History Exam score. Every facet of this book is designed by AP® Exam experts with one singular purpose: to help you achieve your best possible score on test day.

This effective test-prep tool contains all of the following helpful resources—and more:

- **Complete coverage of the AP® U.S. History Exam:** You'll get a thorough insight into every aspect of this important exam—from structure and scoring to what to expect on exam day and how to effectively tackle every question type. After reading this book, there will be no confusion or surprises about the exam, and you'll have a great head start on the test-taking competition!

- **Comprehensive AP® exam review:** This study guide will take you step-by-step through the entire AP® U.S. History Exam, with a rigorous analysis of each section of the exam, along with helpful sample passages and questions that mirror those you'll encounter on test day.

- **Proven AP® exam practice to build your test-taking skills:** This book provides sample questions for every section and question type you're likely to encounter on test day, along with comprehensive answer explanations that will help you learn from your mistakes, build your skills, and get you in test-taking shape.

- **Practice tests that mirror the actual exam:** Chapters 14, 15, and 16 of this book are full-length practice exams with detailed answer explanations that look and feel just like the exam you'll take in May. You'll be more than ready to take the real thing after you've made your way through these practice tests and read over the detailed explanations for every answer choice.

We know how important doing well on this high-stakes exam is to you—and we're here to help. Rest assured, you've come to the right place to prepare for this exam and we are right here with you along this journey. The tools you need for test-day success are in the helpful pages that follow—so let's get started!

THE AP® U.S. HISTORY EXAM: AN OVERVIEW

It's perfectly understandable if you're eager to skip over this chapter and get straight to the test prep. However, we suggest that you take some time to review the information here. Gaining a clear understanding of test fundamentals and of the structure and format of the AP® U.S. History Exam is an important first step along your journey to exam success.

EXAM ESSENTIALS

Test Focus: This exam is designed to test your ability to effectively analyze significant events, individuals, developments, and processes in nine historical periods in United States history, from approximately 1491 to the present; to compose written essay responses that analyze primary and secondary sources; develop historical arguments; make historical comparisons; and utilize reasoning about contextualization, causation, and continuity and change over time.

Length: 3 hours and 15 minutes (with a break between Sections I and II of the exam)

Format: 2 sections, two parts each:

Section I, Part A–Multiple-Choice (55 minutes; 55 questions): 40% of your exam score

- The multiple-choice questions are organized into sets of between two and five questions.
- Each set of questions asks students to analyze and respond to primary or secondary sources, such as written texts, images, charts, graphs, or maps.

Section I, Part B–Short Answer (40 minutes; 3 questions): 20% of your exam score

- This part of the test consists of answering three out of four short-answer questions. Students are required to answer the first and second questions and then are allowed to choose to answer either the third or the fourth question.
  - Question 1 assesses the ability to analyze a secondary source and covers Periods 3–8.
  - Question 2 assesses comparison or causation skills based on a primary source text or visual source and covers Periods 3–8.
  - Question 3 assesses comparison or causation skills without a stimulus and covers Periods 1-5.
  - Question 4 assesses any skill (other than comparison or causation) without a stimulus and covers Periods 6-9.

Section II, Part A–Document Based (60 minutes, 1 question): 25% of your exam score

- The document-based question (DBQ) focuses on topics from Periods 3–8 of the AP® U.S. History course. Students will write a response to a question based on seven documents.
  - The seven DBQ documents may include charts, graphs, cartoons, and pictures, in addition to written materials of varying length.
- Time includes a 15-minute reading period.

Section II, Part B–Long Essay (40 minutes, 1 question): 15% of your exam score

- The long essay question requires students to write an essay using historical evidence to build a sound argument that analyzes and explains a significant historical issue.
- The three question choices focus on the same theme and skill, but each one focuses on a different time period range:
  - Periods 1–3
  - Periods 4–6
  - Periods 7–9

Now that you know that you'll have 3 hours and 15 minutes to complete the two sections that comprise the AP® U.S. History Exam, we recommend that you devote some time between now and test day to get comfortable with the timing, in order to develop an effective test-taking pace.

A great way to do this is to take the practice tests in this book under simulated and timed test-like conditions, in order to get comfortable with completing each exam section in the time provided. You certainly don't want to be caught by surprise and hear "Time's up!" on test day before you've had the chance to finish!

What's Tested on the Exam

The AP® U.S. History Exam is designed to assess the three primary approaches to instruction presented in the course: historical reading practices and reasoning skills, content by theme, and content by period.

AP® Historical Reading Practices and Reasoning Skills

In general, the historical disciplinary reading practices and reasoning skills on which you will be assessed are your ability to analyze and interpret historical sources and evidence, reason chronologically and by making historical connections; and create and support a reasonable argument. More specifically, you should be able to demonstrate the ability to perform the following skills:

- Analyze and interpret the content and sources of historical evidence, whether primary or secondary
- Make historical comparisons
- Contextualize, synthesize, and discuss causation
- Note patterns of continuity and change over time
- Understand the flexibility, pros, and cons of various historical processes
- Create and support a sound argument

Thematic Learning Objectives

The thematic learning objectives assessed on the exam are seven themes that focus on the issues and changes and developments and processes throughout history resulting in what has now become the United States. The seven themes are as follows:

1. American and National Identity
2. Politics and Power
3. Work, Exchange, and Technology
4. Culture and Society
5. Migration and Settlement
6. Geography and the Environment
7. America in the World

Historical Periods

The historical periods into which the course is divided provide a chronological framework upon which the weighting of exam questions is built. The coverage of the periods in the exam as a whole will reflect the approximate period weightings as they are presented in the course, as shown in the table below:

Period	Dates	Percentage of AP® Exam (Approximate)	Percentage of Course Instruction (Approximate)
1	1491-1607	5%	5%
2	1607-1754		10%
3	1754-1800		12%
4	1800-1848	45%	10%
5	1844-1877		13%
6	1865-1898		13%
7	1890-1945	45%	17%
8	1945-1980		15%
9	1980-Present	5%	5%

For more details about the instructional approaches and how they are assessed, you can refer to the "AP U.S. History Instructional Approaches" section in the *AP® United States History Course and Exam Description* (*https://secure-media.collegeboard.org/digitalServices/pdf/ap/ap-us-history-course-and-exam-description.pdf*.).

AP® Exam Question Types—A Closer Look

Now you know that on exam day you'll be tasked with utilizing what you've learned throughout your academic year—along with the breadth and scope of knowledge you've acquired throughout your academic career—to demonstrate that you've successfully mastered the skills covered in your AP® course.

As mentioned, the exam consists of two sections—one containing a multiple-choice section and a short-answer section, and the other containing a document-based question and a long essay question. Subsequent chapters will delve deeply into each section and will provide review, practice, strategies, and advice for earning your best possible score on exam day. Here, we'll provide some tips for dealing with each question type, to help you start to develop your test strategy.

Section I, Part A—Multiple Choice

Section I, Part A, of the exam will consist of fifty-five multiple-choice questions based on a variety of primary or secondary sources, such as written texts, images, charts, graphs, or maps that reflect the content and concepts presented in the AP® U.S. History course. You will have 55 minutes to complete this part, and you will need to use your knowledge of United States history and thinking abilities to full effect.

You will *not*
lose points for
incorrect answers
and you will *not*
earn points for
unanswered
questions!

Answer All Multiple-Choice Questions!

Your score on the multiple-choice section of the AP® exam will be based on the number of correct answers you provide.

This means that you should make *every effort* to answer each question on exam day. If you're stumped by a question, use effective strategies, including eliminating incorrect choices and educated guessing, in order to increase your chances of answering it correctly—and to increase your score.

Use What You *Don't* Know!

Use the questions in this book—especially the ones you answer *incorrectly*—to help you focus and refine your study plan as you prepare for test day. Incorrect answers will help you determine the subject areas in which you need more practice.

Be sure to make careful note of any possible test weaknesses you may have as you answer the sample practice questions in this book; make time in your study plan to address those weaknesses and build your skills!

You Don't Need to Go in Order

Skip around, doing those item sets you think you're most likely to answer both quickly (i.e., in a minute or less) and correctly. Read or skim the associated document—a passage of text, a map, an image, a graph or chart—or just note which question sets seem to require a higher investment of reading or other kinds of interpretation: shorter and fewer are better. Also note the topic: how confident do you feel about it? If confident, dive right in. If not so confident, save it for later, along with all those item sets you think you can figure out but which will take more time. Leave for last those that you either have to really think through or for which you must simply guess (since you won't be leaving any blank).

Predict the correct answer before you look at the answer choices

Here's a little secret: the official psychometric name for what we call "an incorrect answer choice" is *distractor*. That tells you all you need to know: there's no better way to camouflage the correct answer, which is staring all test takers right in the face. So, in order not to be distracted, cover up the answer choices when you read the question stem. Predict an answer; then, with that "search image" in mind, compare it to the answer choices.

Prediction helps with time-management and cognitive load, too. If you read the stem and then immediately predict an answer, all you need to do is compare that prediction to the answer choices. If you can't predict an answer, you've just learned that you should probably skip the item for now.

What if you don't predict an answer? First, you allow the possibility that you don't really understand the question. Second, you couple that perhaps half-understood question with trying to understand and evaluate each of the four answer choices. It's far better for time management and mental endurance to get on top of each item (or quickly determine whether that item should be left for later) by forcing yourself to answer it in your head (or on scratch paper, if you prefer). Then compare your prediction to the answer choices, looking for which one matches. If none match, you may have misunderstood the question and should 1) skip it, 2) guess, or 3) if you have time, reread the passage and question more carefully and reevaluate the answer choices.

Use Process of Elimination

Any answer choice you can reject with high confidence increases your chance of guessing correctly even when you don't know the answer. And, honestly, the worst chance you have of getting a question right about which you have literally no clue is 25 percent, so leave no question blank.

Section I, Part B—Short Answer

Section I, Part B, of the exam consists of answering three out of four short-answer questions. You will be required to answer the first and second questions and then are allowed to choose to answer either the third or the fourth question, one of which will focus on the time period before 1877 and the other after 1877. You'll have 40 minutes to answer the three questions.

Each of the short-answer items is often attached to some document as well, just like the multiple-choice items. You have to write in prose—full sentences, paragraphs, etc. Treat them as mini-essays. Feel free, as with all the free-response items, to scratch out a little outline or plan before you start writing. Answer all parts: these are graded on how well you answer each of the usually three different little points. Better to cover all relatively thinly than to bulk up on one or two of the three parts and leave the rest unaddressed.

As with the multiple-choice section, skip around. First, do whichever of the four you can answer quickest and best and then move on. Content knowledge aside, consider also going for the lower-investment items first. For example, all other things being equal, if you have a choice between an item that lacks an associated document and one that requires you read two long excerpts in order to answer, go with the former.

Section II, Part A—Document-Based Question

Section II, Part A, of the exam is called the Document-based Question (DBQ). Technically speaking, most of the items on this test are document-based, but this essay question is actually based on several documents as opposed to one or two. It's worth more than the other, non-document-based long essay (Section II, Part B), so resist the temptation to skip to the long essay question unless you're absolutely certain you can crush it fast enough to leave plenty of time for the DBQ. You will have 60 minutes to read the documents (15 minutes) and write your essay (45 minutes).

For both essays (that is, the DBQ and long essay question), do NOT skimp on planning your response before writing. It's better to first figure out if your initial idea is good, via a scratched-out outline when you have plenty of time to readjust, rather than halfway through writing it, when you won't. Furthermore, you're judged primarily on organization, not your writing, per se. Of course, the essay needs to be in Standard Written English, but the AP® Exam Readers realize you're writing off the cuff: the main role of your writing is to be as clear a window as possible through which to look at your argument.

For the DBQ in particular, you'll be expected to present and develop a thesis, taking into account as much complexity as you can. You'll have to refer to at least six of the documents while discussing the point of view, intended audience, or historical context of at least four of them. Make sure to contextualize your argument by stepping back a bit to make a more general point about the larger context, one which must include at least one piece of outside evidence that you supply. Finally, in your conclusion you will need to step back even further than your chosen contextualization in order to extend your argument in some fashion, whether to another period of American history, to the history of some other culture or society, or to a mode of historical explanation different from the one you selected. For example, if you've written in a mostly political-historical mode, consider extending to social or cultural or geographical history.

Make sure to leave a few minutes at the end of the process to edit a bit. You'll find something, and, while you're not massively downgraded for minor grammatical or spelling errors, it doesn't hurt to show that you proofread your work.

Section II, Part B—Long Essay Question

Section II, Part B, of the exam is the long essay question (LEQ). You will have 40 minutes to address one of the three prompts presented. There will be one essay for each of the following periods:

> Periods 1-3 (1491-1800)
>
> Periods 4-6 (1800-1898)
>
> Periods 7-9 (1890-Present)

As with the DBQ, don't just start writing. Plan it out first: use a T-chart, outline, concept map, whatever you normally would do in order to have and judge a plan. When deciding on which period to choose, go with the essay that will highlight your strengths. If it's not obvious which of the three essays you should choose, do a T-chart for each and take the one about which you have more to say. Then, and only then, begin to write. Leave yourself a couple of minutes to edit.

The prompts are very well-formed, specific, and tell you exactly what you need to do. Recently, they've all related to potential turning points in history, but that may not always be the case. You must discuss both why you think X is or isn't a turning point, and, no matter whether you think it is or isn't, what changed and what remained the same. The responses must be well organized, with a clear, relevant, well-supported thesis that, like the DBQ, is extended to some other historical period, culture, or mode of historical writing.

Your written responses for Section II of the AP® U.S. History Exam will be evaluated by expert exam readers based on rubrics for your **thesis/claim**, **contextualization**, **evidence**, and **analysis and reasoning**. Your essay must demonstrate historically accurate and defensible content. Exam essays are considered as first drafts and may contain grammatical errors that will not count against you unless they negatively affect the clarity of the information you are presenting in your essay.

A high-scoring DBQ essay will offer an effective, well-constructed, and persuasive argument with a thesis which makes a claim that responds to rather than restates the prompt. The essay should relate the topic of the prompt to broader historical events that occur before, during, or after the time period to which the prompt refers. It should accurately describe and use the content of at least six of the documents provided to support the argument in response to the prompt, and it should explain how or why at least three of the documents' points of view, purpose, historical situation, and/or audience is relevant to the argument. The essay should use evidence to corroborate, qualify, or modify an argument that addresses the prompt. It should demonstrate a thorough understanding of the historical development that provides the focus for the prompt.

A high-scoring LEQ essay will offer an effective, well-constructed, and persuasive argument with a thesis which makes a claim that responds to rather than restates the prompt; relates the topic of the prompt to broader historical events that occur before, during, or after the time period of the prompt; and uses specific and relevant examples of evidence to support an argument in response to the prompt. The essay should use evidence to corroborate, qualify, or modify an argument that addresses the prompt. It should demonstrate a thorough understanding of the historical development that provides the focus for the prompt.

Scoring

Your AP® U.S. History Exam score is designed to reflect the knowledge you've acquired as a result of taking this college-level course and how well you can apply this knowledge to the questions you encounter on the exam. Your score will be a weighted combination of the scores you achieve on the two exam sections and will be based on the following five-point scale:

    1 = no recommendation

    2 = possibly qualified

    3 = qualified

    4 = well qualified

    5 = extremely well qualified

The multiple-choice questions in Section I of the exam will be machine scored; the other portions of the test will be scored by expert AP® exam readers.

So, what exactly do these scores mean? The colleges you have decided to apply to, and to which you'll send your official AP® score, will use your score to determine whether or not you qualify for course credit and have achieved advanced placement—allowing you to skip over the equivalent college course.

Typically, a score of 3 or higher indicates that you have achieved a sufficient level for advanced placement and course-credit consideration.

Earn an AP® Scholar Award!

The College Board and the AP® Program have created the AP® Scholar Awards in an effort to recognize talented students who have demonstrated exemplary levels of achievement by doing well in AP® courses and exams. For more information, visit the official AP® exam website.

Register for a College Board account via the official website in order to access your score, which will only be available online. You'll receive an email update regarding when you can access and review your score, typically in July of the year you take the exam.

NOTE

AP® score reports are cumulative, which means that they will include all scores from every AP® exam you've taken, unless you have specifically requested that one or more scores be withheld or canceled.

Once you access your score report via your account, you'll have the option to view and send your score to the college indicated on your answer sheet. You can also select additional colleges to send your score report to, for a fee.

You will have several options for reporting your scores to the schools and scholarship programs you hope to pursue. In addition, each college has its own set of criteria for granting course credit and advanced placement. For a complete set of guidelines, options, and fees for score reporting and earning college credit, visit the official AP® website.

REGISTRATION ESSENTIALS FOR THE AP® U.S. HISTORY EXAM

We know that you're undoubtedly focused on making sure your history and test-taking skills are at peak form for test day. However, you also need to have a good handle on the test essentials—from registering to fees to what you can and cannot bring on test day and everything in between—in order to be fully prepared.

This section provides a comprehensive rundown of exactly what you need to know, so keep reading.

Registration

AP® exams are typically administered in May each year. The 2018 exam date for the U.S. History Exam is Friday, May 11.

NOTE

Currently, there is no limit to the number of AP® exams you can take, and you are not required to take an AP® course prior to taking an AP® exam—although it is strongly encouraged for test-day success.

Once you register for an AP® course at your school, it is the responsibility of your school's AP® exam coordinator to keep you informed regarding exam essentials and to notify you when and where to report for the official exam. Your AP® exam coordinator is also responsible for collecting all exam fees and ordering the exams. He or she will also help with scheduling if you are planning to take multiple AP® exams that are scheduled for the same time period.

Speak to your AP® exam coordinator or visit the official AP® website for additional information if you have special circumstances that need to be addressed or accommodated, including a disability or if you are home-schooled or are an international student.

Fees

The current basic fee for taking an AP® exam in the United States is $93. There are options available for fee reductions and waivers, typically based on financial need.

To determine if you're eligible for a fee adjustment, contact your school's AP® coordinator. For a comprehensive list of fees, guidelines, and available options, please visit the official College Board website for AP® students.

GETTING READY FOR EXAM DAY

We know that after preparing diligently and making the most of this study guide you'll be totally ready to tackle every AP® test section and question. But this book doesn't just take you halfway along the journey to test-day success—we take you all the way. Knowing test-day fundamentals, including what to expect when you arrive for the exam, what to bring, and what to leave home, will help you avoid surprises, reduce anxiety, and stay ahead of the competition.

First Steps

Make sure you arrive for the test early, with plenty of time to spare in case there are any unforeseen delays. When you arrive on exam day, you'll be asked to review the policies and procedures regarding test security and administration—which includes everything from maintaining exam integrity and good conduct to your right to have a fair and equal testing experience, and more. You'll be asked to complete and sign your registration answer sheet, indicating that you have reviewed and agree to all of the AP® exam policies and procedures.

Test-Day Checklist: What to Bring on Exam Day

Use this helpful checklist to know what you should bring with you on the day of your AP® U.S. History Exam:

- [ ] Your AP® Student Pack, which you should receive from your AP® exam coordinator
- [ ] A school-issued or government-issued photo ID (if you are taking the exam at a school you do not currently attend)
- [ ] Your Social Security card or Social Security number (used by some colleges as a primary student identification tool)
- [ ] A few sharpened No. 2 pencils, with erasers
- [ ] A few pens with dark blue or black ink
- [ ] A watch (*optional*)—not a smartwatch or a watch that beeps, makes noise, or has an alarm set to go off during the exam
- [ ] Your 6-digit school code
- [ ] If you've requested a specific testing accommodation, your SSD Student Accommodation Letter

What Not to Bring on Exam Day

Just as important as what you should bring on test day, here's a list of items that you should *not* bring to the test room, in order to avoid any issues or delays that could negatively affect your testing experience:

- A computer
- Books or reference materials of any kind
- Scratch paper or note paper

- Phones of any kind
- Portable listening devices or headphones
- Electronic equipment or recording devices of any kind
- Cameras or photographic equipment
- Any device that can access the Internet
- Food or drink of any kind
- Earplugs
- Smartwatches, or watches that beep or have alarms
- Clothing with subject-related information
- Office supplies, including compasses, protractors, mechanical pencils, correction fluid, highlighters, or colored pencils

BUILDING AN EFFECTIVE STUDY PLAN

We know you're on the hunt for your best possible score on exam day, and we're here to help you develop an effective study plan for making that goal a reality.

Making sure that your writing skills are in peak form on exam day is essential—remember, the writing and essay sections of the exam will count for 55 percent of your total exam score. Here are a few tips for making sure your writing skills are where they need to be:

- **Practice:** Make sure you practice writing persuasive essays on a wide variety of literary genres and texts. For most things in life—including writing—the best way to build your skills is through practice and repetition.

- **Remember the fundamentals:** Topics, focus, and points of view may vary, but some things that don't shift are the core tenets of essay writing—content, style, organization, and mechanics—on which the exam readers will be grading you. Make sure that your essay effectively delivers in all of these fundamental areas.

- **Get feedback:** It can be tough to judge the merits of your own writing. Your best approach as you practice for exam day is to have someone whose writing abilities you respect review and provide critical feedback on your work.

- **Target your weak areas:** As you practice for exam day, look critically at your writing and identify the areas that you need to focus on in order to get your writing skills in peak condition. Then, make sure your subsequent writing attempts address these weak areas—in an effort to eradicate them!

As a high-achieving student, you've likely had your fair share of successes during your academic career. You know what study habits work for you—and which don't—and you know the value of careful preparation for an important test. Make good use of this knowledge as you prepare for the exam.

AP® U.S. History: Not a Cram Exam!

Doing well on this AP® exam is *not* a race to memorize as many facts as possible between now and test day—especially since you won't know what historical documents will appear until the day of the exam.

The exam is designed to test your ability to think critically, to utilize your reading comprehension and analysis skills, and to construct effective, targeted written responses.

Your *best* tools on exam day will be the knowledge and skills you've acquired throughout your academic career and during your AP® U.S. History course.

You may already have a fully fleshed-out study plan. However, if you'd like some guidance or are open to advice for constructing an effective plan of attack, we suggest the following strategy for using this book and making the most of the time you have between now and test day.

Review Strategy

Perhaps you're short on time between now and test day—maybe you have just a few days. This quick and efficient approach helps you make the most of the small amount of time you have left to earn your best possible exam score!

- **Step 1:** Quickly read this chapter to learn the AP® U.S. History Exam basics. Don't spend too much time on it—you have some serious test preparation to get to!

- **Step 2:** Take and score the first practice test in this book. Carefully review the answer explanations for the questions you got wrong, making sure that you understand why you answered them incorrectly. Use your results to help gauge your strengths and weaknesses.

- **Step 3.** Review the book chapter material that focuses on the areas in which you are weakest, based on the results of your first practice test. Make careful use of the time that you have, spending time on the areas in which you most urgently need to build your skills.

- **Step 4:** Take and score the second practice test in this book. Carefully review the answer explanations for the questions you got wrong, making sure that you understand why you answered them incorrectly. Once again, use your results to help gauge your strengths and weaknesses. Hopefully, your list of weak areas is shorter this time!

- **Step 5.** Review the book chapter material that focuses on the areas in which you are weakest, based on the results you obtained on the second practice test. Make careful use of the time that, you have spending time on the areas in which you most urgently need to build your skills.

- **Step 6:** Take and score the third practice test in this book. Carefully review the answer explanations for the questions you got wrong, making sure that you understand why you answered them incorrectly. Once again, use your results to help gauge your strengths and weaknesses. Hopefully, your list of weak areas is now even shorter!

- **Step 7.** If time permits, review the book chapter material that focuses on the areas in which you are still showing weakness, based on the results of your third practice test. Make careful use of the time that you have left, spending time on the areas in which you most urgently need to build your skills.

A Note for Parents and Guardians

If you're the parent or guardian of a student who is planning to take the AP® U.S. History Exam, your support and encouragement can go a long way toward test-day success!

Help your student stay on track and focused with his or her study plan between now and test day, and make sure that his or her needs for effective test preparation are well met.

The path to a great score on the AP® U.S. History Exam is *not* an easy one. The knowledge and skills you've obtained in your AP® course will be fully put to the test and will need to be razor sharp on exam day. That's where this book comes in!

Consider this your indispensable guide along your test-preparation journey. It includes a comprehensive review of the most frequently-tested concepts on the exam and helpful practice for all of the question types you can expect to encounter. Make the most of the resources in the following pages as you craft your study plan and move closer to achieving an excellent score.

Best of luck!

SUMMING IT UP

- The AP® U.S. History Exam tests your knowledge of U.S. history and your ability to think historically.

  - Section I, Part A, of the exam is comprised of fifty-five multiple-choice questions analyzing historical texts, interpretations, and evidence. This part of the section lasts 55 minutes and makes up 40 percent of your exam score.

  - Section I, Part B, of the exam consists of three out of four short-answer questions. You will be required to answer the first and second questions and then allowed to choose to answer either the third or the fourth question. This part of the section lasts 40 minutes and makes up 20 percent of your exam score.

  - Section II, Part A, is the document-based question (DBQ). This essay question requires you to examine written, statistical, or illustrative material as historical evidence and develop an argument based on your analysis of the historical evidence. This part of the section lasts 1 hour and makes up 25 percent of your exam score.

  - Section II, Part B, is the long essay question (LEQ) in which you will analyze and explain a significant issue from U.S history, choosing from one of three time periods, and present an argument supported by your analysis. This part of the section lasts 40 minutes and makes up 15 percent of your exam score.

- The complete AP® U.S. History Exam is 3 hours and 15 minutes long, with a break between Sections I and II.

- Your score on Section I, Part A, of the exam is based *only* on the number of correct answers you earn. Answer every question on exam day—you will not lose points for incorrect answers.

- Your written responses in Section I, Part B, and Section II will be evaluated by expert AP® exam readers based on the revised 2017-2018 rubrics set by AP. The highest-scoring answers and essays present a well-constructed, fact-supported argument addressing the given prompt.

- Your final score will be a weighted combination of your scores on Section I and Section II and will be based on a 5-point scale:

  1 = no recommendation

  2 = possibly qualified

  3 = qualified

  4 = well qualified

  5 = extremely well qualified

- Each college has its own set of criteria for granting course credit. For a complete set of guidelines, options, and fees for score reporting and earning college credit, visit the official AP® website.

- The 2018 exam date for the U.S. History Exam is Friday, May 11.

- Your AP® exam coordinator will collect all exam fees and order your exams. He or she will also help with scheduling if you are planning to take multiple AP® exams that are scheduled for the same time period.

- Arrive early on test day. Make sure to complete your registration answer sheet completely and accurately to avoid any potential score reporting delays.
- Take the practice tests in this book under simulated and timed test-like conditions to become comfortable with the pacing and content of the exam.

PART II
AP® U.S. HISTORY
STRATEGIES

Answering Multiple-Choice and Short-Answer Questions

Chapter 2

OVERVIEW

- **About the Multiple-Choice Section**
- **Strategies for Attacking Multiple-Choice Questions**
- **Multiple-Choice Practice**
- **About the Short-Answer Section**
- **Skills Tested in the Short-Answer Section**
- **Strategies for Attacking Short-Answer Questions**
- **Short-Answer Practice**
- **Summing It Up**

This chapter is designed to get you ready to earn your best possible score on Section I of the AP® U.S. History Exam, which contains a series of multiple-choice questions that will test your understanding and mastery of the curriculum covered in your AP® U.S. History course. Remember, your best tools on test day will be your core knowledge of the material covered in your course work, along with the strategies, review, and practice in this guide. Combined, these helpful resources will get you in great test-taking shape.

ABOUT THE MULTIPLE-CHOICE SECTION

At a Glance
- **Length:** Section I, Part A, of the exam consists of 55 multiple-choice questions.
- **Time:** You will have 55 minutes to answer the multiple-choice questions in Section I, Part A, of the exam.
- **Scoring:** Section I, Part A, of the exam will count for 40% of your total AP® exam score.

The multiple-choice questions on the AP® U.S. History Exam are organized into sets that can contain between two and five questions. In each of these question sets, you'll encounter primary or secondary source material on which the questions will be based. This source material is designed to represent research material that historians typically use in historical study and can include graphs, charts, maps, images, or relevant written text.

Historical Timeframes Covered on the AP® U.S. History Exam

The AP® U.S. History Exam covers the key events, figures, and documents in American history from 1491 (North American exploration) through the present, structured around the following nine time periods:

- Period 1: 1491–1607
- Period 2: 1607–1754
- Period 3: 1754–1800
- Period 4: 1800–1848
- Period 5: 1844–1877
- Period 6: 1865–1898
- Period 7: 1890–1945
- Period 8: 1945–1980
- Period 9: 1980–Present

The following *approximate* weights are given to each time period on the exam:

- Period 1: 5 percent of the exam
- Period 2–Period 5: 45 percent of the exam
- Period 6–Period 8: 45 percent of the exam
- Period 9: 5 percent of the exam

Thematic Learning Objectives Covered on the AP® U.S. History Exam

In addition to a strong understanding of the concepts of U.S. history for each time period and an ability to effectively analyze relevant primary and secondary historical source material, the test will ask you to apply knowledge and reasoning skills across the following seven major thematic learning objectives:

- **Culture and Society:** The impact of individual and collective social mores, beliefs, creative expression, and ideas on shaping the nation, and how different values, identities, and cultures have been shaped over time and across context in American history

- **America in the World:** The influence and impact that the United States and American History has had on the global state, including other nations and world affairs

- **Geography and the Environment:** The effects of geography and environment, both natural and human-made, on society and politics in the United States

> **NOTE**
>
> Several of the periods show some degree of overlap, depending on the kinds of key concepts covered in that period. This overlap acknowledges the differences in how historians apply boundaries between distinct historical eras.

- **American and National Identity:** The development of core definitions of national and American values and identity, including foreign policy, citizenship, assimilation, American exceptionalism, and constitutionalism

- **Work, Exchange, and Technology:** Historical developments of American systems of economic exchange and the related roles of economic markets, technology, and government

- **Migration and Settlement:** The history of settlement into the United States over its history and the reflexive effects on cultural, social, and physical environments

- **Politics and Power:** The influence of various political and social groups on government and society and the evolution of political institutions and beliefs over time

For the most up-to-date information regarding the AP® U.S. History Exam, visit the official College Board website at ***https://apstudent.collegeboard.org/home.***

STRATEGIES FOR ATTACKING MULTIPLE-CHOICE QUESTIONS

On exam day, all of the knowledge you've acquired in your AP® U.S. History course will be put to the test, along with your well-honed analytical, reasoning, and comprehension skills—and your ability to manage your time and work effectively under the pressure of a ticking clock. Yes, that's a lot to juggle, but you've already made a good decision by choosing this book to prepare. Don't forget—careful and thorough practice and review, and a well-organized study plan, are great tools to help you get ready for exam day!

Let's take a look at a sample multiple-choice question and explore how to tackle it. Say the following question accompanied text from the Emancipation Proclamation:

> Which of the following was true of the Emancipation Proclamation of 1863?
> A. It immediately freed slaves in Southern states or parts of Southern states under Union occupation.
> B. It freed slaves in Southern states still at war with the Union on January 1, 1864.
> C. It freed slaves only in the border states.
> D. It guaranteed freedom for slaves who escaped into the Union lines.
> E. It freed all enslaved blacks when the war ended.

Okay, we can see clearly from the question stem that this question focuses on a very specific and easily identifiable historical event and timeframe—the Emancipation Proclamation of 1863 (Period 5). We are also signaled in the question stem that we are looking among the answer choices for information pertaining to this historical event that is *true*.

Perhaps you know the answer right off the bat—if so, that's great—select the right answer and move on. If not, try to eliminate as many incorrect choices as you can in your hunt for the correct answer.

The Emancipation Proclamation did not affect slaves in Southern states or parts of Southern states occupied by the Union, so we can eliminate choice A. We can eliminate choice C because it was very important that the Border States stay in the Union; Lincoln feared that freeing their slaves would

TIP

Be sure to read all instructions and directions *carefully* for all sections of the AP® U.S. History Exam. You'll want to make sure that you're tackling each exam section properly on your quest for your best possible score!

TIP

What works well for all multiple-choice tests works well for the AP® U.S. History Exam as well—when you run into trouble on a question, try eliminating as many incorrect answer choices as possible to help increase your chances of arriving at the correct answer.

drive them out. The Confiscation Act freed slaves who escaped into the Union lines, so choice D is also incorrect. The Thirteenth Amendment, not the Emancipation Proclamation, ended slavery, so we can eliminate choice E as well. That leaves us with choice B: The Emancipation Proclamation of 1863 did decree that slaves in states still at war with the Union on January 1, 1864, would be free. It was a proclamation without any force, but it did help to sway the British away from supporting the South. Therefore, choice B is the correct answer.

When you take the AP® U.S. History Exam, you'll want to have every advantage possible. Of course, in a perfect world you'll know the correct answers to all of the multiple-choice questions and will be able to breeze through the test with more than enough time to spare, but that doesn't always happen.

Work Smart!

Keep in mind that 55 minutes is *not* a huge amount of time to tackle this test section, so you'll need to work quickly and wisely in order to make efficient use of your time on test day.

The key is to establish an effective test-taking pace *before* test day arrives! Use the practice tests in this book under timed conditions to establish a working pace that will help you achieve your score goals. Students who show up on test day who *haven't* done this are at a real disadvantage.

Here are some effective strategies to help you reach your target exam score.

Read each question carefully.

Make sure you know precisely what the question is asking and pay attention to key words and phrases. You may find key word prompts, such as *significant; direct result of, consequence of; true, correct; most characteristic of, best known for, best describes; primarily, primary reason.* These are qualifiers or descriptors that supply clues as to what you should be looking for among the answer choices—and can help you quickly eliminate incorrect choices.

- A word like *significant* means you should be looking for why something is important in the larger context of U.S. history.
- Phrases such as *best describes* or *most characteristic of* are asking you to analyze the information and come up with an opinion based on facts.

In both of these instances, one or more of the answer choices may be correct; you need to look for the one that *best* addresses the question or is most inclusive.

A word of caution: Most of the questions you'll encounter on test day are straightforward, but there may be some NOT/EXCEPT or reverse order questions. When you encounter one of these questions, read each answer, proceed carefully, and remember what the question is asking. You are looking for the choice that is **not** true, so don't fall for any subtle traps!

Use order to your advantage.

Knowing that the questions are in chronological order can help you to eliminate answers that do not make sense for the time period. For example, identifying the Wilmot Proviso as having happened in the first half of the nineteenth century can help you eliminate any answers that refer to any other incorrect time period.

When in doubt, take an educated guess.

When you don't immediately know the correct answer to a question, one technique that is especially helpful is educated guessing. Your goal here is to eliminate as many incorrect answer choices as possible in an effort to increase your chances of choosing the correct answer:

- Ignore answer choices that are absolutely wrong.
- Eliminate choices in which only part of the answer is incorrect.
- Discard choices that are illogical or unrelated to the subject.
- Check the time period of the question and the answer choices. Discard any responses that don't fit.
- Check the key words in the question again, and see if that helps you eliminate any incorrect choices.
- Revisit the remaining answers to discover which seems most correct.
- Choose the answer that feels right. Trust yourself and your instincts!
- Be sure not to spend too much time on any one question. You don't want to run out of time before you reach the end of this test section!

MULTIPLE-CHOICE PRACTICE

One of the best strategies for getting in top test-taking shape for the AP® U.S. History Exam is to practice—getting comfortable with the types of questions you'll encounter on test day and working under timed, test-like conditions is an excellent way to get ready to earn your best possible score on test day. At the end of this book, you will find full-length practice exams that mirror the test day experience.

Practice will also help you target your strengths and weaknesses—use your results on all of the practice items and tests in this book to help you pinpoint any weak areas and focus your study time between now and test day to eliminate those weak areas. Perhaps there's a certain time period or question type you're struggling with, or a certain key historical event that you want to study further—the information you'll receive from your practice results will really help put you in a position to earn your best possible score.

Carefully read and answer the following questions, and then review the answer explanations to see how you did.

Questions 1–3 refer to the following map.

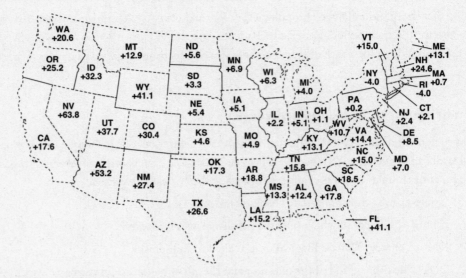

1. According to the map, which two Northeast states were the only states to lose population between 1970 and 1980?
   A. New York and Pennsylvania
   B. Massachusetts and Rhode Island
   C. New York and Rhode Island
   D. Pennsylvania and Rhode Island
   E. Massachusetts and Pennsylvania

2. Which region of the forty-eight contiguous states had the greatest percentage increase in population between 1970 and 1980?
   A. New England
   B. Middle Atlantic states
   C. Midwest
   D. Southeast
   E. Southwest

3. Which of the following states experienced the greatest percentage increase in population between 1970 and 1980?
   A. New Hampshire
   B. Florida
   C. Nevada
   D. Arizona
   E. Texas

Answer Key and Explanations

1. C	2. E	3. C

1. **The correct answer is C.** According to the map provided, the two Northeast states that were the only states to lose population between 1970 and 1980 are New York (–4.0) and Rhode Island (–4.0).

2. **The correct answer is E.** Based on the data in the map, the region of the forty-eight contiguous states that had the greatest percentage increase in population between 1970 and 1980 is the Southwest. We can see the largest concentration of high percentage increases across the states that comprise this region (i.e., Nevada, Arizona, New Mexico, Texas, etc.).

3. **The correct answer is C.** Among the states listed in the answer choices, the one that experienced the greatest percentage increase in population between 1970 and 1980 is Nevada, which experienced a 63.8 percent population increase during this decade.

ABOUT THE SHORT-ANSWER SECTION

Now, let's shift our focus to Section I, Part B, of the AP® U.S. History Exam, which consists of a series of three short-answer questions based on the historical time periods covered in your AP® U.S. History course.

At a Glance

- **Length:** Section I, Part B, of the exam consists of 4 short-answer questions—you'll be responsible for answering 3 of the 4 questions presented.

- **Time:** You'll have 40 minutes to answer the short-answer questions in Section I, Part B, of the exam. (*Note: You must complete and turn in Section I, Part A, of the exam before you'll be able to move on to Part B.*)

- **Scoring:** Section I, Part B, of the exam will count for 20% of your total AP® Exam score.

The short-answer questions on the AP® U.S. History Exam are organized as follows.

You are *required* to answer **Questions 1 and 2**, which will be based on subject matter from any of the following time periods:

- Period 3: 1754–1800
- Period 4: 1800–1848
- Period 5: 1844–1877
- Period 6: 1865–1898
- Period 7: 1890–1945
- Period 8: 1945–1980

Then, you must choose *one* of the following questions to answer.

Question 3: Based on subject matter from any of the following time periods:

- Period 1: 1491–1607
- Period 2: 1607–1754
- Period 3: 1754–1800
- Period 4: 1800–1848
- Period 5: 1844–1877

Question 4: Based on subject matter from any of the following time periods:

- Period 6: 1865–1898
- Period 7: 1890–1945
- Period 8: 1945–1980
- Period 9: 1980–Present

NOTE

Students who do well on test day are comfortable with the material covered in their AP® U.S. History course for all the time periods tested. If you're strong in a few specific time periods but feel less confident in others, make sure to target your weak areas as you build your study plan between now and test day!

SKILLS TESTED ON THE SHORT-ANSWER QUESTIONS

Each of the short-answer questions on the AP® U.S. History Exam is designed to assess your ability in a specific primary practice or skill area, involving a specific source type, within the specified historical timeframe. You will be asked to provide relevant historical evidence in your written response.

- **Question 1**, which you will be required to answer, will ask you to respond to a specific historian's argument and will gauge your ability to effectively analyze secondary source material. This question will represent historical material between 1754 and 1980.

- **Question 2**, which you will also be required to answer, will test your skills in either comparison or causation within a historical context and will gauge your ability to effectively analyze a written primary source text or visual source (i.e., a map, chart, graph, or image, etc.). This question will also represent historical material between 1754 and 1980.

- **Questions 3 and 4** (you must choose to answer either one of these questions) will each ask you to develop a written response to a general proposition rooted in United States history and will test your skills in either comparison or causation (neither of these questions will test the same skill covered in Question 2). Question 3 will represent historical material between 1491 and 1877, and question 4 will represent historical material between 1865 and the present.

Analyzing Primary and Secondary Sources

Your ability to analyze both **primary** and **secondary sources** will be tested on the exam, both in the short-answer questions and throughout the test. According to the College Board—the official test creators—your ability to analyze relevant historical evidence will be gauged as follows.

For *primary* sources, you will have to…

- Discuss the historical relevance and significance of a source's purpose, audience, point of view, and historical situation
- Analyze a source's limitations, authority, and/or credibility

- Discuss historically relevant information and/or arguments pertaining to a source
- Analyze how a specific source's audience, purpose, historical situation, and/or point of view might affect a source's meaning
- Discuss how a source provides key information regarding the broader historical setting in which it was created

For *secondary* sources, you will have to…

- Discuss how the claim or argument of a historian is supported with evidence
- Evaluate trends and patterns in non-text-based sources regarding quantitative data
- Discuss a relevant trend or pattern in quantitative data in non-text-based sources
- Describe how a historian's context influences an argument or claim
- Evaluate the argument or claim of a secondary source, along with the evidence used
- Analyze the relevant effectiveness of a historical claim or argument

Comparison and Causation Skills on the AP® U.S. History Exam

Some of the short-answer questions on the AP® U.S. History Exam will test your skills in either **comparison** or **causation** within a historical context.

- **Comparison:** Analyze and explain relevant differences and/or similarities between various historical processes or developments, and their historical significance
- **Causation:** Analyze causal relationships between various historical processes or developments, and their effects (both short-term and long-term), as well as their historical significance.

Let's take a close look at a sample short-answer question, so you can get a better idea of what to expect on test day.

"A house divided against itself cannot stand. I believe this government cannot endure, permanently, half slave and half free. I do not expect the Union to be dissolved; I do not expect the house to fall; but I do expect it will cease to be divided. It will become all one thing, or all the other. Either the opponents of slavery will arrest the further spread of it and place it where the public mind shall rest in the belief that it is in the course of ultimate extinction, or its advocates will push it forward till it shall become alike lawful in all the states, old as well as new, North as well as South."

Abraham Lincoln, excerpt from "A House Divided" speech, 1858.

"The next question propounded to me by Mr. Lincoln is, Can the people of a Territory in any lawful way, against the wishes of any citizen of the United States, exclude slavery from their limits prior to the formation of a State constitution? I answer emphatically, as Mr. Lincoln has heard me answer a hundred times from every stump in Illinois, that in my opinion the people of a Territory can, by lawful means, exclude slavery from their limits prior to the formation of a State constitution. …It matters not what way the Supreme Court may hereafter decide as to the abstract question whether slavery may or may not go into a Territory under the Constitution, the people have the lawful means to introduce it or exclude it as they please…"

Stephen Douglas, excerpt from "Freeport Doctrine" speech, 1858.

1. Using the excerpts above, answer A, B, and C.
    A. Briefly discuss ONE major difference between Lincoln's and Douglas's position on the issue of slavery in the United States.
    B. Briefly describe ONE significant historical event or development following the Lincoln-Douglas debates that suggested Lincoln's beliefs had some level of support among the citizens of the United States.
    C. Briefly describe ONE specific historical development regarding the issue of slavery that occurred in the post-debate period between 1858 and 1865.

Analyzing the excerpts and questions provided, we can quickly zero in on the relevant historical figures and events involved: Abraham Lincoln, Stephen Douglas, The Lincoln-Douglas Debates, and the issue of slavery in the United States. We must summon our knowledge of key historical facts involving each.

A close read of Lincoln's excerpt reveals his opinion regarding the existence of slavery within a nation as varied and vast as the United States—it is an "all or nothing" issue. A nation made up of collective states that are tasked with working together toward common goals cannot be divided on such an important issue. In order for the United States to move forward and progress, it must be unified regarding its decision to permit or abolish slavery.

What can be gleaned from the words in Stephen Douglas's Freeport Doctrine speech? He seems to suggest a different approach, that the decision to permit or abolish slavery can be decided upon on a much smaller scale and context—the people of a territory, such as a state, can make their own decision regarding the issue and need not have the agreement of the entire nation or a governing judicial body such as the United States Supreme Court to decide on such an important issue.

Our analysis of the information provided has already given us a starting point for responding to the short-answer questions. We can tackle question A by discussing Lincoln's belief of an "all or nothing" approach to deciding the issue of slavery vs. Douglas's contention that individual territories within the United States can make their own decisions. Questions B and C will require you to draw upon the knowledge you've acquired in your course work—one possible approach to question B would be to discuss Lincoln's rise to power following the debates, culminating in his becoming the sixteenth President of the United States in 1861. As for question C, you can discuss the ratification of the Thirteenth Amendment of the United States Constitution, which effectively abolished slavery, or any number of historical events that led up to its abolishment between 1858 and 1865.

On test day, be sure to take a similar approach to tackle the short-answer questions you'll encounter:

- Carefully read and analyze the excerpts.
- Identify all of the tasks that you must accomplish in the questions provided tasks. Indicate key historical figures, events, and developments related to the topic at hand.
- Decide upon your primary approach for each question.
- Write your responses carefully, clearly, and succinctly.

STRATEGIES FOR ATTACKING SHORT-ANSWER QUESTIONS

Use the following proven strategies on the short-answer question part of the AP® U.S. History Exam to earn your best possible score.

Before we break these strategies down step by step, let's consider perhaps the most important strategy you will need to consider when answering short-answer questions:

Divide and manage your time effectively.

Remember that you have 40 minutes to answer three of the four short-answer questions provided; be sure to utilize and divide your time accordingly, so that you have ample time to work at a comfortable pace and answer each of the questions effectively.

Carefully read and analyze each question.

This seems obvious, but you'd be surprised by how many people get nervous when they hear the clock ticking on test day and race through reading the short-answer questions and instructions—and then craft responses that are either off topic or don't answer the precise questions, which will certainly affect their score.

Choose to respond to the question you know most about.

Remember that you have a choice to answer either the third or fourth short-answer question; these two questions will be based in different time periods, as noted earlier in this chapter. Be sure to choose the question in which you have the most factual knowledge mastery and that will allow you to craft the more comprehensive and in-depth written response.

Know which skills are being primarily assessed.

As mentioned earlier in the chapter, each short-answer question on the exam is designed to primarily assess a specific skill type. Now that you know what AP® Exam readers are looking for, be sure to keep this in mind as you craft your responses.

Jot down notes.

As you read each question, it's common for ideas associated with the topic at hand to come rushing through your brain—these ideas will help form your polished and final written responses. It's a good idea to write these down quickly, so they don't get lost or forgotten as you work.

Make key historical connections.

Your responses should make significant historical connections that are relevant to the task(s) at hand, drawing on your ability to highlight differences and similarities (compare and contrast), establish cause and effect, establish historical evolution and continuity, and process key contextual evidence.

Remember
that for the
short-answer
questions—
and for all the
free-response
questions on the
AP® U.S. History
Exam—there
are no correct
or incorrect
viewpoints.
The AP® Exam
Readers are
looking to gauge
how successfully
you answered
all parts of
the questions
provided and
developed your
individual points
of view using
relevant historical
evidence, not
what you may
or may not
believe in.

Go beyond paraphrasing.

Your response to each short-answer question should go beyond merely regurgitating or paraphrasing the source material presented. Remember, your ability to successfully analyze and explain the significance and purpose of the primary or secondary source material is being evaluated, *not* your ability to merely recognize it.

Appropriately interpret the information provided.

Your short-answer question responses should demonstrate an ability to appropriately interpret and evaluate the data and source material provided within a relevant historical context.

Fulfill all the tasks outlined in each question.

Short-answer questions on the AP® U.S. History Exam typically have multiple parts; make sure that your written response appropriately addresses each part.

Check your work if time permits.

If possible, spare a few minutes to review and polish your written responses at the end of the test section. Ensuring that your responses are free from errors will help you earn your best possible exam score on test day.

SHORT-ANSWER PRACTICE

It's time to get some practice for the short-answer questions you'll encounter on the AP® U.S. History Exam. Again, one of the best strategies for getting test-ready is to get comfortable with the types of questions you'll encounter on test day and working under timed, test-like conditions.

Practice will also help you target your strengths and weaknesses as you build your study plan between now and test day and will really help put you in a position to earn your best possible score.

Carefully read and answer all parts of the following question. Use the scoring information provided in this chapter to determine how well you fulfilled the requirements of this exercise. We recommend that you use a trusted source—perhaps a fellow AP student, parent, or teacher—to review your work and provide helpful feedback.

Best of luck!

"KEEP YOUR HANDS OFF THE SCALES!"
—Chapin in the St. Louis *Republic*.

Source (Public Domain): *Literary Digest, 7/26/19. Originally from the St. Louis Republic* (Chapin). (***http://www.baruch.cuny.edu/ library/alumni/online_exhibits/digital/redscare/HTMLCODE/CHRON/RS026.HTM***)

Refer to the post-World War I cartoon (created in 1919) above and answer A, B, and C.

A. Briefly explain ONE economic concern held by the public following the events of World War I (1914–1918).

B. Briefly explain ONE way in which World War I affected the economic conditions within the United States.

C. Briefly explain ONE parallel economic condition that has remained consistent from when the cartoon was created to the present.

Question Analysis

Let's tackle this short-answer question using the steps highlighted in this chapter.

Our first step is to do a thorough read and analysis of the question and the supporting document provided.

- Here, we are presented with a political cartoon from the *St. Louis Republic* newspaper; it's significant to note the date that the cartoon was created—1919—so we know that we're dealing with an editorial viewpoint through a *post-World War I* lens.

- We also see some key labels in the cartoon: **Public, Cost of Living, High Prices, Profiteering**. Keep these in mind as we move forward.

- Let's take a closer look at the question itself, to make sure we understand all of the tasks involved. This may seem like an obvious step, but you'd be surprised by how many test takers rush ahead—thinking they have things all figured out—and then leave out some key aspect of the assignment that negatively affects their scores. Besides, this shouldn't be a time-consuming effort, just a quick review so we know what we have to accomplish:

○ **Part A** is asking us to identify an economic concern in the United States that resulted from the events of World War I.

○ **Part B** is asking us to explain one way in which World War I affected the economic conditions within the United States. This can be directly tied in to the economic concern you covered in Part A.

○ **Part C** is asking us to draw a historical parallel or **comparison** (the key skill being tested)—and identify one economic condition that has remained consistent from World War I to the present-day United States.

Okay, so now we know what the assignment is; the next step is to take some notes. The benefit of doing the previous steps is that we already have a potential direction for our short-answer response as a result of analyzing the cartoon.

The labels that we identified in our initial analysis (**Public, Cost of Living, High Prices, Profiteering**) can serve as topic headings for our notes. Consider creating a small table for your notes as follows, both for post-World War I and present-day United States:

Post World War I (1919)			
The Public	Cost of Living	High Prices	Profiteering
Present-Day United States			
The Public	Cost of Living	High Prices	Profiteering

Organizing your notes this way will help you gather information for all parts of the question. Did you notice anything else from the cartoon or question that can be helpful?

Here are a few suggestions:

- The man wearing the hat labeled "public" looks angry, and his anger seems directed towards the sneering man behind the counter—who is labeled with "high prices" and "profiteering" and who is unfairly weighing down the scale labeled "cost of living."

- We can determine that the creator of the cartoon was making a statement about how high prices and rampant profiteering in post-World War I United States unfairly affected cost of living in the country, much to the anger of the American public.

- This would seem to be a good topic to craft your responses to Part A and Part B of this question; your goal would be to draw upon your reservoir of knowledge about this issue from your AP course work to contextualize the topic within the historical framework of the United States following the war and to make key connections using relevant facts and evidence.

- As you write Parts A and B of this short-answer response, think about any historical parallels with present-day America that come to mind. Are issues of high prices and cost of living or economic class stratification still pervasive today? If you can indeed argue that that's the case, then you have a clear direction of how to proceed with the third and final part of this assignment.

Remember the fundamentals for attacking this and any short-answer question you encounter on test day, and you'll set yourself up for your best possible AP® Exam score!

SUMMING IT UP

- The multiple-choice part of the AP® U.S. History Exam consists of fifty-five multiple-choice questions.

- You'll have 55 minutes to answer the multiple-choice questions and they will count for 40 percent of your total exam score.

- Multiple-choice questions on the exam are organized into sets of two to five questions. In each question set you'll encounter primary or secondary source material, which can include graphs, charts, maps, images, or relevant written text.

- The following time periods are covered on the AP® U.S. History Exam:
  - Period 1: 1491–1607
  - Period 2: 1607–1754
  - Period 3: 1754–1800
  - Period 4: 1800–1848
  - Period 5: 1844–1877
  - Period 6: 1865–1898
  - Period 7: 1890–1945
  - Period 8: 1945–1980
  - Period 9: 1980–Present

- The following *approximate* weights are given to each time period on the exam:
  - 1491–1607: 5 percent of the exam
  - 1607–1877: 45 percent of the exam
  - 1865–1980: 45 percent of the exam
  - 1980–present: 5 percent of the exam

- The seven major thematic learning objectives tested on exam day are as follows:
  - Culture and Society
  - America in the World
  - Geography and the Environment
  - American and National Identity
  - Work, Exchange, and Technology
  - Migration and Settlement
  - Politics and Power

- The following are effective strategies to help you reach your target AP® Exam score:
  - Read each question *carefully*.
  - Use order to your advantage.
  - Not/except and reverse order questions.
  - When in doubt, take an educated guess.

- The short-answer questions on the AP® U.S. History Exam consist of four short-answer questions—you'll be responsible for answering three of the four questions presented.

- You'll have 40 minutes to answer the short-answer questions, and they'll count for 20 percent of your total AP exam score.

- The short-answer questions on the AP® U.S. History Exam are organized as follows:
  - **Question 1**, which you will be required to answer, will ask you to respond to a specific historian's argument and will gauge your ability to effectively analyze secondary source material. This question will represent historical material between 1754 and 1980.
  - **Question 2**, which you will also be required to answer, will test your skills in either comparison or causation within a historical context and will gauge your ability to effectively analyze a written primary source text or visual source (i.e., a map, chart, graph, or image, etc.). This question will also represent historical material between 1754 and 1980.
  - **Questions 3 and 4** (you must choose to answer either one of these questions) will each ask you to develop a written response to a general proposition rooted in United States history and will test your skills in either comparison or causation (neither of these questions will test the same skill covered in Question 2). Question 3 will represent historical material between 1491 and 1877, and question 4 will represent historical material between 1865 and the present.

- Your ability to analyze both **primary** and **secondary sources** will be tested.

- Some of the short-answer questions on the AP® U.S. History Exam will test your skills in either **comparison** or **causation** within a historical context.
  - **Comparison:** Analyze and explain relevant differences and/or similarities between various historical processes or developments and their historical significance.
  - **Causation:** Analyze causal relationships between various historical processes or developments and their effects (both short-term and long-term), as well as their historical significance.

- Remember the strategies for effectively tackling short-answer questions:
  - Divide and manage your time effectively.
  - Carefully read and analyze each question.
  - Choose to respond to the question you know most about.
  - Know which skills are being primarily assessed.
  - Jot down notes.
  - Make key historical connections.
  - Go beyond paraphrasing.
  - Appropriately interpret the information provided.
  - Fulfill all the tasks outlined in each question.
  - Check your work if time permits.

Writing a Winning Document-Based Question (DBQ)

OVERVIEW

- **About the DBQ**
- **Skills Tested on the DBQ**
- **The DBQ—A Closer Look**
- **Crafting an Effective DBQ Essay: Strategies**
- **DBQ Practice**
- **Summing It Up**

The next two chapters are designed to get you ready to earn your best possible score on Section II of the AP® U.S. History Exam. On Part A of Section II, you'll be tasked with crafting an effective written response to a document-based question (DBQ) rooted in United States history. Use the helpful information and strategies in this chapter to develop a memorable and high-scoring response.

ABOUT THE DBQ

At a Glance

- **Length:** Section II, Part A of the exam consists of 1 question—you'll be responsible for crafting an essay in response to the question provided.
- **Time:** You'll have 60 minutes to answer the document-based question in Section II, Part A, of the exam, which includes a 15-minute reading period.
- **Scoring:** Section II, Part A, of the exam will count for 25% of your total AP® Exam score.

The document-based question on the AP® U.S. History Exam can be rooted in any of the following historical time periods (questions can span multiple periods):

- Period 3: 1754–1800
- Period 4: 1800–1848

- Period 5: 1844–1877
- Period 6: 1865–1898
- Period 7: 1890–1945
- Period 8: 1945–1980

TIP

You will not be forced to move from Part A to Part B (the long essay question) in Section II of the exam, so effective time management is essential. Be sure to practice writing a document-based and long essay question at least once before test day, so you can get comfortable with the timing and pace you'll need to complete both writing tasks!

SKILLS TESTED ON THE DBQ

The DBQ you'll encounter on exam day will gauge your ability to analyze and synthesize the historical material provided and utilize it as contextual source evidence in a well-constructed and effective essay response. You'll encounter an interrelated set of seven documents within the question—these documents can include a wide array of relevant material, such as pictures, graphs, maps, charts, cartoons, written material, and more. The purpose of these documents is to illustrate and highlight a specific topic within the time frame indicated, including the inherent historical complexities and interactions at the heart of the topic at hand.

The documents you'll encounter on test day *may be* familiar to you—or completely new. Chances are, at least some of the seven documents you'll be confronted with on the exam will be new to you. Therefore, your analytical skills will be tested *at least* as much as your memory of historical documents. When crafting your essay, make sure you focus on the events these documents represent, drawing on your arsenal of historical knowledge that you've developed over your entire AP® U.S. History course.

You'll be tasked with developing a written argument that reflects your point of view on the topic and with using the documents provided in support of your perspective. An analysis of the historical significance, audience, events, trends, and purpose of the documents provided should be factored into your written response. Major issues and information regarding the time period(s) covered should be utilized in your work.

About the AP® Exam Readers

Who's going to read and evaluate your DBQ essay? Good question! The College Board—the official AP® Exam testing organization—utilizes highly trained, capable, and experienced AP® Exam Readers to read and evaluate the free-response portions of the AP® U.S. History Exam. These individuals are typically college faculty or expert AP® course teachers, with extensive backgrounds in the subject area, who will score your essay based on a set of specific, standardized criteria.

THE DBQ—A CLOSER LOOK

All DBQs consist of the following three parts:

1. The directions
2. The question
3. The documents

Let's take a closer look at each part. Remember—knowing what to expect on the exam *before* test day will help build your confidence, save you precious time, and put you one step ahead of the test-taking competition!

The Directions

The directions will indicate that you'll be tasked with responding to one document-based question on the AP® U.S. History Exam. You'll have 60 minutes on this part of the exam; this includes a suggested 15-minute reading period to analyze the task, review the material, and take notes and 45 minutes to craft and edit your written response.

The directions also present the purpose of the DBQ. They'll read something like this:

> **Directions:** The following question asks you to write a cohesive essay incorporating your interpretation of Documents 1 through 7 and your knowledge of the period stated in the question. To earn a high score, you must cite key evidence from the documents and use your outside knowledge of U.S. history.

The directions clearly state that you are to analyze the documents and relate information to the mainstream of U.S. history in a well-written essay that expresses your opinion about the issues the question raises. That means you must state YOUR opinion as well as refer to historical events and developments that are not found in the documents.

The Question

The second part of the DBQ is the question itself. Read it *carefully*. Examine *all* of its parts. Consider its implications. Do *not* fall into the trap of reading quickly and assuming you know what the question asks—that's a good way to miss an essential aspect of the task and lower your score.

Feel free to underline, circle, or put brackets around key words in the question to help you focus and target your written response. Don't forget—essays that thoroughly address all aspects of the question typically receive the highest scores.

The Documents

The third section of the DBQ consists of the seven source documents; your job will be to thoroughly review and analyze them in preparation for crafting your essay.

The order in which the documents appear is not random. They are usually arranged chronologically. Other times, the documents will be grouped by point of view. Not all documents will agree with one another. Often, they will present different positions on important issues and opposing interpretations of historical events. In designing the question, the examination writers want you to analyze multiple sides and opposing viewpoints when crafting your own point of view. Use this information to your advantage on test day!

NOTE

On the DBQ portion of the exam, you are not being tasked with simply recognizing the documents presented. You are also being asked to incorporate their historical purpose and significance within the broader context of the time period covered, along with key relevant historical themes.

TIP

The College Board emphasizes that students must demonstrate outside knowledge of the issues involved "if the highest scores are to be earned" on the DBQ.

CRAFTING AN EFFECTIVE DBQ ESSAY: STRATEGIES

Now that you understand what the DBQ consists of, you need a game plan. Use the following strategies for crafting an effective and high-scoring DBQ essay on test day.

Analyze the Question

As obvious as this sounds, begin with the directions. Again, read them carefully and be sure you fully understand the writing task at hand. As you read the question, consider the following:

- What is your opinion on the subject?
- What is the historical relevance of the topic at hand?
- How are the documents connected to the topic—both individually and as a collective group?
- Determine what issues to address in your written response and how best to utilize both the documents provided and your knowledge of the subject matter to craft a compelling and effective written response that fully supports your point of view.

Consider the following question:

> During the last three decades of the nineteenth century, farmers experienced severe difficulties. As the problems mounted, farmers pinned their hopes on political solutions. Using the documents provided and your knowledge of U.S. history for the period from 1870 to 1900, evaluate the effectiveness of the agrarian protest.

Examine the question and query yourself about what the DBQ asks. The first thing to do is ensure you understand specific phrases in the question. Do you understand the word *agrarian?* You may wish to define the term in your essay.

Ask yourself what are the key points of the question. Be clear about the time frame—the 1870s to the turn of the century. Highlight in some way the key words in the question: *last three decades of the nineteenth century, farmers, problems mounted, evaluate, effectiveness, agrarian protest.*

The question revolves around farmers' difficulties and their efforts to solve their problems. Then the question goes on to ask you to express your opinion regarding the success farmers had at forcing political solutions. Therefore, you must explain the political steps they took and their results. In doing this, you must, of course, include a discussion of the documents as they relate to farmers' hardships and efforts for reform. In addition, you must use your historical knowledge of the agrarian and Populist movements during the latter half of the nineteenth century.

The DBQ you just analyzed is straightforward and easy to understand. It states directly that you must evaluate a situation. Other questions may be more difficult to discern. However, if you can identify the type of question, dissecting the DBQ becomes easier. The chart that follows shows question types you might encounter in Section II of the AP® U.S. History Exam. You'll notice that certain words offer clues to the kinds of support you'll need in order to develop an appropriate answer.

This section of the exam is demanding, and you will find that some questions combine two or more question types. However, by learning the clue words, you can apply the appropriate support and development strategies.

QUESTION TYPE	WORDS THAT OFFER CLUES	REQUIRED SUPPORT
Evaluation	*Assess, evaluate, judge the validity, assess the validity*	Look for evidence from the documents and your knowledge of U.S. history that substantiates your opinion.
Compare	*Compare, common, similarities*	Look for and stress similarities with specific examples.
Contrast	*Contrast, differ, differences*	Identify and stress differences with specific examples.
Definition	*Define, explain*	Explain what something, such as a law or a policy, is or does.
Description	*Describe*	Provide the main features with specific details and examples.
Discussion	*Discuss, explain*	Make a general statement that shows you understand the concept in the question. Then support your main idea with examples, facts, and details.
Explanation	*Explain, why, what, how*	Offer examples, details, and facts that illustrate how something happened, what it is, or why it is so.
Illustration	*Illustrate, show*	Provide concrete examples and explain each one to demonstrate the truth or significance of the main idea.
Interpretation	*Significance, meaning of quotations or events, influence, analyze*	State a main idea about meaning. Give examples, facts, and reasons to explain and support your interpretation.
Opinion	*What do you think, defend an idea or position, state your opinion*	State your opinion clearly. Support and develop it with examples, facts, and reasons.
Prediction	*If . . ., then; What if . . .*	Predict and state a logical outcome based on your knowledge and evidence from the documents. Offer arguments to support your opinion.

Take Notes

This step probably seems out of place to you, but it isn't. Most students want to review the documents immediately after reading the question. However, many students experience difficulty generating their own ideas because they focus exclusively on the documents. All they can think about is what they have read.

We suggest that *before* you begin to read the documents, you brainstorm for the background and outside information you already know about the subject. Take a few minutes and jot down everything you can recall about the subject. Do not worry if it is relevant. Some of the information from your brainstorming may be included in the documents. Actually, that is a good thing because it shows your thinking is pertinent.

Review the Documents

Now you are ready to review and analyze the documents. The order in which the documents appear is important. Documents are usually arranged in chronological order. If the documents in your test are in this order, this is a hint that suggests your essay should have some sort of chronological development.

It does *not* mean that you have to include each document in this order. You should refer to the documents in the best way to support your thesis, but chronology is a useful principle of overall organization. You may find the documents in your test are grouped around points of view. While this arrangement is not as common, it tells you that the focus of your essay should be a comparison or a contrast.

As you read, look for similarities and differences among the documents. Since the purpose of the DBQ is to assess your ability to combine historical research and analytical skill with factual recall, documents will present both similar and opposing points of view, as well as complementary and contradictory explanations of events. You must recognize and discuss these similarities and differences, and their historical significance, in your analysis.

Be sure to read the source information for each document. A given writer or a time period may trigger important points to include in the DBQ. Sources can also provide insight into conflicting positions since different individuals have different perspectives. Ask yourself how gender, political beliefs, race, social class, and religion may contribute to the viewpoints expressed in the documents.

You will find that some documents are more helpful to you than others when creating your essay response. However, do *not* simply ignore those that advocate opposing positions. Look for refuting evidence and incorporate it in your essay. By acknowledging opposing sides of an issue, you show that you understand the complexities of history.

Organize Your Information

After you have finished reading and taking notes, it is time to organize your information. Review what you have written and delete repetitious or irrelevant information. Use a chart, columns, or a Venn diagram to order facts by topic or time period.

Now you are ready to create a thesis, or personal opinion, on the topic. Again, review your information. Ask yourself, "What do I think about the topic and how can I support that position?" Your

TIP

Watch out for key transition words (see chart) for DBQs and all of the free-response questions on the exam—they'll provide valuable context clues that will help you focus and craft your written responses effectively.

answers provide ideas for your thesis. Before you make a final decision, reread the question to ensure your thesis addresses all parts of the question. When you begin to write, be sure to write your thesis in your first paragraph.

Only after the reading period will you be permitted to begin your essay. If you finish your reading, notes, and thesis statement early, create an informal outline. Number each of your ideas in the order you will write about them. Be sure to save your most powerful idea for the final paragraph before the conclusion.

If the reading period ends before you have created your informal outline, you must decide if using writing time to outline is advantageous. Consider circling, numbering, or underlining your notes as a time-saver.

Let's take a close look at a sample DBQ and one supporting document (*the DBQ on the actual exam will include seven documents*), so you can get a better idea of what to expect on test day.

Evaluate the extent to which World War II was a war fought on multiple fronts—both on the battlefield and within homes across the United States.

Document 1

Source: Poster from the Office of War Information, Washington DC, 1943. *(https://freeclassicimages.com/images/rationing-food-is-a-weapon-war-poster.jpg)*

Although just one single image, this poster serves as rich source material to answer the question at hand. It is often said that wars are fought on multiple fronts—both on the battlefield and at home, and World War II was no exception to this notion in the United States. During World War II, government offices such as the Office of War Information were tasked with inspiring every American to sacrifice for the war effort—from time, money, and labor, to the very food citizens ate, as this poster so aptly reflects. All citizens were asked to be mindful of the food they purchased and consumed during World War II and to avoid unnecessary waste in order to help support the nation and the war effort.

Once you encounter the question alongside seven related documents, follow these steps to help you craft a nuanced and multifaceted written response:

- Carefully read the question.
- Analyze each source document, and consider how each relates to the question at hand.
- Identify all of the tasks that you must accomplish in the question provided.
- Indicate key historical figures, events, and developments related to the topic at hand.
- Decide upon your primary approach for the question.
- Write your response carefully, clearly, and succinctly.

Tips for Writing an Effective Essay

The following chapter, which addresses Part B of Section II, the long essay question, covers the essential rules of good essay writing—be sure to review this information as you prepare for all of the free-response questions on the exam.

The following are helpful hints for developing your DBQ essay:

- Remember that although you can argue many different points of view on any given DBQ, you should choose the one that you can defend and support most successfully.
- Identify documents as you reference them in your essay.
- Include an analysis of as many documents as you can.
- Understanding and interpreting the documents provided and analyzing how they relate to each other in a historical context are critical to writing a high-scoring essay.
- Try to summarize information from the source documents instead of simply quoting.
- Remember, you must include references to historical information from outside the documents provided.
- Write an essay that relates the documents to the events of the time period and supports your thesis.
- Be sure to adhere to the basic structure of good essay writing:
  - Introduction: Make sure your essay's introduction captures your audience's attention, highlights your topic and introduces your point of view, and contains your main thesis.
  - Body: The body paragraphs of your essay should be used to develop your thoughts on the topic and provide relevant support to your ideas as they pertain to your main thesis and point of view. Effective essays also acknowledge and directly address opposing viewpoints.
  - Conclusion: The final paragraph of your essay should wrap things up and tie together your ideas as they relate to your main thesis and, ideally, will end on a strong and memorable note.

The Elements of a High-Scoring DBQ Response

A high-scoring DBQ response will successfully accomplish each of the following:

- Establish your point of view in a clear thesis statement. Your written response should address all of the elements of the question while establishing a clearly discernible thesis that encapsulates your point of view on the topic at hand.

- Draw relevant historical parallels. Your essay should explore the relevance of the topic within a broad historical context, which includes relevant events, developments, and processes in United States history.

- Include additional historical evidence. While crafting your essay, you should consider and utilize historical documents and material beyond those provided in the question, drawing on your knowledge of U.S. history that you've acquired throughout your course work.

- Demonstrate solid historical reasoning. While making inferences, analyzing historical documents, and developing your point of view on the DBQ, you should demonstrate an ability to deploy sound reasoning—within a historical context—as you write your essay, drawing upon as many of the source materials as feasible.

- Establish historical relevance. Your written response should explore the historical significance of the documents provided and draw historical connections and relationships that support your thesis.

DBQ PRACTICE

It's time to get some practice for the DBQ portion of the AP® U.S. History Exam. Once again, practice is among your best strategies for getting comfortable with the types of questions you'll encounter on test day, targeting your strengths and weaknesses, and developing an effective study plan that will help you earn your best possible score.

Carefully read and answer all parts of the following question. Use the scoring information provided in this chapter to determine how well you fulfilled the requirements of this exercise. We recommend that you use a trusted source—perhaps a fellow AP® student, parent, or teacher—to review your work and provide helpful feedback.

When evaluating your essay, you can also refer to the official College Board/AP website for more insight into what makes a good long essay response. View or download the following documents:

- Rubrics for AP Histories+ History Disciplinary Practices and Reasoning Skills (*https:// apcentral.collegeboard.org/pdf/rubrics-ap-histories.pdf?course=ap-united-states-history*)

- AP U.S. History Student Samples Aligned to the 2018 Rubrics—Document- Based Question (*https://apcentral.collegeboard.org/pdf/ap-us-history-dbq-2018. pdf?course=ap-united-states-history*).

Best of luck!

Question 1: During the last three decades of the nineteenth century, farmers experienced severe difficulties. As the problems mounted, farmers pinned their hopes on political solutions. Using the documents provided and your knowledge of U.S. history for the period from 1870 to 1900, evaluate the effectiveness of the agrarian protest.

Document 1

Source: Resolutions of a meeting of the Illinois' State Farmer's Association, April 1873

Resolved, That the railways of the world, except in those countries where they have been held under the strict regulations and supervision of the government, have proved themselves arbitrary; extortionate and as opposed to free institutions and free commerce between states as the feudal barons of the middle ages. . .

Resolved, That we hold, declare and resolve, that this despotism, which defies our laws, plunders our shippers, impoverishes our people, and corrupts our government, shall be subdued at whatever cost. . .

Resolved, That we urge the passage of a bill enforcing the principle that railroads are public highways, and requiring railroads to make connections with all roads whose tracks meet or cross their own, and to receive and transmit cars and trains offered over their roads at reasonable rates, whether offered at such crossings, or at stations along their roads, and empowering the making of connections by municipal corporations for that purpose, and for the public use. . .

Resolved, That we indorse most fully the action of those who tender legal rates of fare upon the railroads and refuse to pay more; and that it is the duty of the Legislature to provide by law . . . the right to ride on railroads at legal rates.

Document 2

Source: Chief Justice Morrison R. Waite, *Munn v. Illinois,* in his rejection of the argument that regulation violated the Fourteenth Amendment, 1877

The question to be determined in this case is whether the general assembly of Illinois can, under the limitations upon the legislative powers of the States imposed by the Constitution of the United States, fix by law the maximum charges for the storage of grain . . .

. . . Looking, then, to the common law, from whence came the right which the Constitution protects, we find that when private property is "affected with a public interest, it ceases to be *juris privari* only" . . . Property does become clothed with a public interest when used in a manner to make it of public consequence, and affect the community at large. When, therefore, one devotes his property to a use in which the public has an interest, he, in effect, grants to the public an interest in that use, and must submit to be controlled by the public for the common good, to the extent of the interest he has thus created. He may withdraw his grant by discontinuing the use; but, so long as he maintains the use, he must submit to the control . . .

Document 3

Source: Populist Party Platform, July 4, 1892

. . . [T]he forces of reform this day organized will never cease to move forward until every wrong is righted and equal rights and equal privileges securely established for all the men and women of this country. We declare, therefore–

First—That the union of the labor forces of the United States this day consummated shall be permanent and perpetual; may its spirit enter into all hearts for the salvation of the Republic and the uplifting of mankind.

Second—Wealth belongs to him who creates it, and every dollar taken from industry without an equivalent is robbery. "If any will not work, neither shall he eat." The interests of rural and civil labor are the same; their enemies are identical.

Document 4

Source: W. H. ("Coin") Harvey, *Coin's Financial School*, 1894

The money lenders in the United States, who own substantially all our money, have a selfish interest in maintaining the gold standard. They, too, will not yield. They believe that if the gold standard can survive for a few years longer, the people will get used to it—get used to their poverty—and quietly submit.—To that end they organize international bimetallic committees and say "Wait on England, she will be forced to give us bimetallism." Vain hope! Deception on this subject has been practiced long enough upon a patient and outraged people.

With silver remonetized, and gold at a premium, not one-tenth the hardships could result that now afflict us . . .

Document 5

Source: Leonidas Polk and the Farmers' Alliance "Agricultural Depression: Its Causes -- the Remedy." Speech of L. L. Polk, President of the National Farmers' Alliance and Industrial Union, before the Senate Committee on Agriculture and Forestry, April 22, 1890 (Raleigh: Edwards & Broughton, 1890).

… After a calm, dispassionate and earnest investigation of the conditions and causes which have led to the wide-spread and alarming depression that has paralyzed the great agricultural interests of the country, they outlined what they conceived to be a measure of relief. They appointed a committee on national legislation, which, under their instructions, has formulated and presented to both houses of Congress, a bill embodying, as it believes, a safe, proper and just solution of the financial trouble which threatens the agricultural interests of the country with bankruptcy and ruin. …

… As faithful representatives, you must be satisfied as to whether the conditions and necessities of the country are such as to justify or require legislation in this direction. And whatever may be your conclusions as to the particular method here presented, of one thing I feel assured, the spectacle — unparalleled in all our history — of fifteen hundred thousand farmers — quiet, unobtrusive, law-loving, law-abiding, conservative farmers — standing at the doors of Congress demanding relief, must, at least, command your respectful, patriotic, earnest and profound consideration. …

Document 6

Source: Patrons of Husbandry speech delivered by Master Wright; published in the *Sacramento Daily Union*, Number 7034, Oct. 20, 1873.

… The farmers of Great Britain here written to our American granges to know the principles of our organization. Our ritual is being translated into German, that the farmers of Germany may enjoy the benefits which our order proposes to secure for all its members. So broad then are our principles of unity, harmony and brotherhood, so well do they meet a common want of the human race, for social mental and moral advancement, should any still doubt the excellence of our Order to meet the farmers' wants, or dread its secrecy, or fear that it is political, or may in some way interfere with their personal independence?...

… But we oppose the tyranny of all such monopolies as become oppressive. It we cannot create a monopoly without making it oppressive we say don't create it. If we cannot correct any existing monopoly so that it will cease to be oppressive, we say put it down! It can be done. We do not make war upon just freights and fair profits, but only upon those which are made exorbitant and burdensome by the men who handle our productions and supply our wants. …

… We wish always to bear in mind that we do not expect to accomplish our purposes, as producers, by our own unaided efforts, but we hope our demand will appear so just, when properly understood, that every reasonable, ungrasping capitalist banker, trader, representative of the press, railroad man, grain-buyer, warehouse-keeper, ship-owner—all who are engaged in the development of our industries—every professional and laboring man, nay, more, every uncorrupt and incorruptible politician, office-holder, will heartily aid us in our work. …

Document 7

Source: Illustration by Henry Worrall, Kansas State Historical Society, 1874. *http://www.historynet.com/1874-the-year-of-the-locust.htm*

Question Analysis

Let's tackle this document-based question using the steps highlighted in this chapter.

Our first step is to do a thorough read and analysis of the question and the supporting documents provided. Here, we're being asked to evaluate the effectiveness of the agrarian protest toward the end of the ninteenth century (1870–1900) to galvanize political solutions in an effort to combat the difficulties they faced.

Now that we know precisely what we're being tasked to handle, for DBQs, an effective next approach is to analyze each document individually and take relevant notes that pertain to the task at hand.

Document 1

- Document 1 typifies the grievances of farmers against the railroads and their demands for effective state regulation.
- Such unified action shows that farmers were becoming increasingly vocal. They organized farmers' clubs and political parties.
- During this period, the National Grange exerted its greatest power and led the battle against the railroads. For a while the Grange movement was able to effect political change.
- You should be able to easily incorporate Document 1 into an essay examining agrarian protests. This document would serve two purposes for you.
  - First, it presents the farmers' position, emphasizing their economic problems
  - Second, it states their solution.

- The resolutions also offer you the opportunity to discuss the role of railroads in agriculture and their effect on agriculture. Implicit in a discussion of farmers versus the railroads is the role of government and government regulation.

- You have probably thought of other issues related to this document. Remember, there is no one right answer. As long as you can support your thesis, you will do well!

Document 2

- Farmers, especially those in sparsely populated or newly settled regions, were overwhelmed by the high cost of shipping and grain storage.

- Railroads, grain elevators, and meat packers set their prices according to whim or monopoly rather than fair market value.

- *Munn v. Illinois* involved the right of the legislature to regulate prices for grain storage. However, the case had greater implications since it directly affected the constitutionality of state regulation of railroads. Document 2 presents the legal basis for regulating such property as grain elevators and railroads. Chief Justice Waite used a seventeenth-century English principle that property affecting the public interest is no longer affected only by private law but becomes subject to public regulation as well.

- The decision set a legal precedent for regulation.

- Document 2 relates to Document 1 in that the case involves the farmers' interests.

- You might have remembered that the dissenting opinion of Justice Stephen J. Fields influenced later court decisions limiting state and federal regulation of railroads.

- You could use this document to support an argument that farmers' organizations were influencing state politicians who passed laws favorable to agriculture.

- In addition, you could maintain that the Supreme Court was also influenced by the farmers' position.

Document 3

- Document 3 is an excellent statement of some of the goals of the Populist Party.

- This selection shows the new unity among southern and western farmers as well as radicals and reformers. All workers, whether rural or urban, shared common goals and had common adversaries.

- Document 3 opens the door to discuss many topics.
  - You could use it as a springboard to a discussion of farmers' alliances and political parties.
  - The document lends itself to a discussion of the remaining elements of the Populist platform of sweeping reform—unlimited coinage of silver, an increase in the money supply, a progressive income tax, governmental ownership of railroads and the telephone and telegraph systems.
  - Also, the excerpt suggests the possibility of including in your essay a discussion of the election of 1892 and Cleveland's second term.

Document 4

- Document 4 promotes the cause of free silver. It clearly states the demands of the free silver advocates and their hatred of the gold standard, bankers, and the British Empire.

- You will recall that the free silver concept advocated unlimited coinage of silver dollars.

- Harvey argues that those supporting the gold standard have no interest in stopping the deflation that has caused tremendous hardships for farmers and also the owners of small businesses.

- Document 4 opens up several possibilities for your essay.

  o It gives you the opportunity to discuss the plight of farmers, the switch in emphasis from government regulation to free silver, and the role of William Jennings Bryan.

  o You might choose to write about the farmers' failure to compel Congress to enact a free silver policy.

  o You could also mention that the Sherman Silver Purchase Act was repealed.

  o The Democrats repudiated Cleveland and nominated William Jennings Bryan.

Document 5

- Document 5 highlights the efforts of activist farmers in post-Civil War America who fought hard for agrarian rights and lobbied for political and legislative support.

- Polk, a modest farmer by trade, also held political positions (he was the first commissioner of the North Carolina Department of Agriculture) and founded the Progressive Farmer magazine, whose purpose was to provide support to small farmers across the United States and advocate on their behalf.

- You may recall that Polk eventually became involved with the National Farmers' Alliance, and served as its president, a group whose members fought for the advancement of farmers' interests—both for higher prices on agricultural goods and for cooperative farming efforts.

- This speech was delivered before the U.S. Senate in 1890 and did a great job of highlighting the plight of the American farmer in post-Civil War America.

- Document 5 includes a wealth of powerful key phrases that can be expounded upon in a well-developed DBQ essay response, from the "unparalleled" struggles "of fifteen hundred thousand farmers—quiet, unobtrusive, law-loving, law-abiding, conservative farmers—standing at the doors of Congress demanding relief..." to the "calm, dispassionate and earnest investigation of the conditions and causes which have led to the wide-spread and alarming depression that has paralyzed the great agricultural interests of the country..."

- Remember, a strong DBQ response will expand upon the information provided with relevant historical evidence, as well as cogent historical context.

Document 6

- The National Grange of the Order of Patrons of Husbandry, or The Grange, was a tight-knit group of mostly citizen-farmers whose mission was to help support the political and economic health of agricultural communities across the United States.

- There were several such agrarian advocacy groups across the United States in the latter half of the nineteenth century, but The Grange is the oldest and most comprehensive, with a national focus on farmers' rights.

- The Granger Laws were a key example of the fruits of their efforts and led to lower railroad rates across the midwest for transporting agricultural products, allowing farmers to remain more competitive and profitable.

- The Granger Laws resulted in some significant U.S. Supreme Court cases, such as *Munn v. Illinois*, which upheld the notion of governmental regulation in private industries.

- Document 6, an excerpt from a speech by Grange member Master Wright, poignantly spoke out against the perceived oppressive tyranny of any greedy monopolistic organization or enterprise that posed unfair burdens upon the hard-working farmers and their families.

- An effective DBQ essay response can discuss the influence that collective organizations and powerful rallying member speeches had toward galvanizing support for agrarian rights at the end of the nineteenth century.

Document 7

- The old cliché, "a picture is worth 1,000 words," is indeed sometimes true—United States history is full of powerful images that have served to encapsulate moments, highlight struggles, and stir people to action and positive change.

- As this 1874 cartoon by Henry Worrall so poignantly highlights, life was hard for nineteenth-century farmers and their families in post-Civil War America, who had to struggle against a multitude of hardships in an effort to survive and prosper—from hazardous weather and droughts to claim jumpers and bug plagues.

- An effective DBQ response could use this cartoon to highlight the fact that agrarian struggles in post-Civil War America went beyond a battle against the railroad companies, greedy competing industries, and apathetic political parties—the very forces of nature themselves often worked against them.

After you have finished reading and taking notes, it is time to organize your information and create a thesis, or personal opinion, on the topic. Ask yourself, "What do I think about the topic and how can I support that position?" Your answers provide ideas for your thesis. Before you make a final decision, reread the question to ensure your thesis addresses all parts of the question. Be sure to write your thesis in your first paragraph.

When you begin to write, remember the strategies covered in this chapter for crafting an effective DBQ response:

- Remember that although you can argue many different points of view on any given DBQ, you should choose the one that you can defend and support most successfully.

- Identify documents as you reference them in your essay.

- Include an analysis of as many documents as you can.

- Try to summarize information from the source documents instead of simply quoting.

- Understanding and interpreting the documents provided and analyzing how they relate to each other in a historical context are critical to writing a high scoring essay.

- Remember, you *must* include references to historical information from outside the documents provided.
- Write an essay that relates the documents to the events of the time period and supports your thesis.
- Be sure to adhere to the basic structure of good essay writing: Introduction, Body, Conclusion.

A high-scoring DBQ response will successfully accomplish each of the following:

- Establish your point of view in a clear thesis statement.
- Draw relevant historical parallels.
- Include additional historical evidence.
- Demonstrate solid historical reasoning.
- Establish historical relevance.

SUMMING IT UP

- The DBQ portion of the exam consists of one question—you'll be responsible for crafting an essay in response to the question provided. You'll have 60 minutes to answer the document-based question, which includes a 15-minute reading period. It will count for 25 percent of your total AP® exam score.

- The DBQ can be rooted in any of the following historical time periods (questions can span multiple periods):
  - Period 3: 1754–1800
  - Period 4: 1800–1848
  - Period 5: 1844–1877
  - Period 6: 1865–1898
  - Period 7: 1890–1945
  - Period 8: 1945–1980

- The DBQ you'll encounter on exam day will gauge your ability to analyze and synthesize the historical material provided and utilize it as contextual source evidence in a well-constructed and effective essay response.

- You'll encounter seven documents within the question—these can include pictures, graphs, maps, charts, cartoons, written material, and more. The purpose of these documents is to illustrate and highlight a specific topic within the time frame indicated, including the inherent historical complexities and interactions at the heart of the topic at hand.

- All DBQs consist of the following three parts: Directions, Question, and Documents.

- Use the following strategies for crafting an effective DBQ essay on test day:
  - Analyze the Question
  - Take Notes
  - Review the Documents
  - Organize Your Information

- Remember that although you can argue many different points of view on any given DBQ, you should choose the one that you can defend and support most successfully.

- Identify documents as you reference them in your essay.

- Include an analysis of as many documents as you can.

- Try to summarize information from the source documents instead of simply quoting.

- Understanding and interpreting the documents provided and analyzing how they relate to each other in a historical context are critical to writing a high scoring essay.

- Remember, you *must* include references to historical information from outside the documents provided.

- Write an essay that relates the documents to the events of the time period and supports your thesis.

- Be sure to adhere to the basic structure of good essay writing:

- o Introduction: Make sure your essay's introduction captures your audience's attention, highlights your topic and introduces your point of view, and contains your main thesis.

- o Body: The body paragraphs of your essay should be used to develop your thoughts on the topic and provide relevant support to your ideas as they pertain to your main thesis and point of view. Effective essays also acknowledge and directly address opposing viewpoints.

- o Conclusion: The final paragraph of your essay should wrap things up and tie together your ideas as they relate to your main thesis and, ideally, end on a strong and memorable note.

- A high-scoring DBQ response will successfully accomplish each of the following:

  - o Establish your point of view in a clear thesis statement.

  - o Draw relevant historical parallels.

  - o Include additional historical evidence.

  - o Demonstrate solid historical reasoning.

  - o Establish historical relevance.

Writing a Convincing Argumentative Long Essay

Chapter 4

OVERVIEW

- **About the Long Essay**
- **Crafting an Effective Long Essay Response: Strategies**
- **Tackling a Sample Long Essay Response**
- **Long Essay Practice**
- **Summing It Up**

ABOUT THE LONG ESSAY

On Section II, Part B, of the AP® U.S. History Exam, you'll be tasked with crafting a long essay response to a question rooted in a specific time period and topic in United States history.

At a Glance

- **Length:** Section II, Part B, of the exam consists of 1 question—you'll be responsible for crafting an essay in response to one of the three options provided on the same theme.

- **Time:** You'll have 40 minutes to fully develop your essay response.

- **Scoring:** Section II, Part B, of the exam will count for 15% of your total AP® exam score.

- **Organization:** The long essay question on the AP® U.S. History Exam can be rooted in any of the following historical time periods (questions can span multiple periods):

  - Periods 1–3: 1491–1800
  - Periods 4–6: 1800–1898
  - Periods 7–9: 1890–Present

The long essay question is the final part of your AP® U.S. History Exam and is a great opportunity for you to demonstrate both your knowledge of U.S. history and your argumentative writing skills. On the day of the test, you'll be presented with three long essay questions, one from each of the time periods previously noted, and you'll have the opportunity to choose the one you'd like to focus on for your long essay response.

The three questions you'll encounter will all address the same theme and reasoning skill (causation, continuity, comparison, change over time, or contextualization)—choose the one that you think will best allow you to showcase your abilities.

Like the DBQs, the long essay questions have no single correct answer. As you craft your long essay, keep the following in mind:

- All the information must come from your knowledge and understanding of U.S. history and your ability to develop an effective argument that contains relevant, evidence-based support and historical analysis.
- You'll also need to show historical relationships and connections and make insightful generalizations regarding the question topic if you're aiming to get a high score.

CRAFTING AN EFFECTIVE LONG ESSAY RESPONSE: STRATEGIES

You have already read a great deal about writing a high-scoring essay with the discussion of the short-answer and document-based questions. To review, utilize the following steps for structuring your long response:

- Carefully read and analyze the questions presented. You'll have three options to choose from—select the one that you feel you are best equipped to tackle effectively. The three essay options will all target the *same reasoning skills but will each focus on a different time period in history.*
- Identify which skills are being primarily assessed in your chosen question.
- Jot down notes. We suggest you don't spend time creating an extensive outline, but make a quick list by brainstorming ideas and supporting evidence as well as counterarguments that come to mind. If you need to compare and contrast data or argue pros and cons, create a table to list the information.
- Evaluate your notes and develop a thesis. Turn your notes into an informal working plan by numbering the items that you want to include in your essay in the order in which you want to include them. Do not be afraid to cross out some that no longer apply, now that you have a thesis.
- You can choose to focus your essay's argument on many different theses and points of view for a given question. Choose the one that you can defend most effectively.
- Make key historical connections, and include as many relevant facts and as much historical evidence as you can to support your essay.
- Go beyond paraphrasing.
- Appropriately interpret the information provided.
- Write an essay that clearly, logically, and coherently answers the question from your unique point of view.

- Fulfill all the tasks outlined in the question.

- Write clearly and neatly. The last thing you want is to confuse or frustrate your essay readers!

- Try to leave a few minutes (3–5 minutes is recommended) at the end to check and edit your work. If you have been following your plan to develop your thesis all along, this time should be spent making sure your grammar and mechanics are correct and your handwriting is legible.

- Manage your time well so you can have enough time to prep, organize, write, and edit your essay—this is why practice before test day is so crucial. Use your time between now and test day to build and develop an effective writing pace.

Remember—you will *not* be forced to move between Part A (DBQ question) and Part B (long essay question) of this section of the AP® U.S. History Exam, so it will be up to *you* to manage your time wisely!

The Keys to Good Essay Writing

Although you may feel the pressure from the ticking clock on test day, that doesn't mean you should go into autopilot mode and abandon everything you know about the rules of good writing. Students who score well on the free response parts of the AP® U.S. History Exam can handle the pressure *and* demonstrate their mastery of effective essay writing. Let's review some essay writing fundamentals as you prepare for test day success.

Know Your Audience

Your essay will have a clear target audience on test day—a trained and experienced AP® Exam reader who teaches high school or college U.S. history and who will undoubtedly be reading hundreds of similar papers. She or he will have a scoring guide or rubric to aid in evaluating your work. The reader will consider every aspect of your writing for its impact and effectiveness. Make sure you take this part of the AP® exam seriously, and do your best to craft a strong essay that directly addresses the task at hand.

Keep Your Main Purpose in Mind

Your purpose is likely quite simple—to get the highest score possible on test day. To do that, you need to write a unified, coherent, and consistent essay that fully answers the question. A well-written essay that misses the point of the question will not get you a good score. Stay focused and on target, and make sure your writing clearly and confidently supports your main thesis with relevant historical evidence.

While it may be perfectly acceptable to leave somewhat tangential information in a piece of writing— and excellent examples of writing often include a wealth of related but off-center ideas in an effort to provide a rich and varied layering of thoughts—your goal on test day is to zero in and focus on your core claim(s) and eliminate any redundancy or off-focus ideas.

Remember, you want to make the most of the limited time you'll have on test day to craft your essay!

Maintain a Proper Tone

Your tone is the reflection of your attitude toward the subject of the essay. A writer's tone, for example, may be lighthearted, brusque, or serious. The safest tone to adopt is formal and persuasive, since you are being asked to take a position and support it. You do not want to be stuffy and pretentious by using phrases such as "one understands" or "we can surmise."

On the other hand, do not be too casual by writing things like "you know what I mean." Most students, however, err on the side of "faux" erudition, using big words and convoluted constructions, which may introduce errors in intended meaning. When in doubt, write what you mean simply and directly.

Develop a Winning Style

How do you develop the proper tone? Through style. Your style should be your own natural style that you use for school essays. That means:

- Using proper grammar and punctuation
- Choosing words that convey your meaning in an interesting rather than an ineffective or vague way
- Avoiding the use of several words when one will do
- Avoiding hackneyed phrases and clichés

Your style adds interest to the essay. Well-chosen words and phrasing, as much as a unique point of view about a subject, can make an essay interesting to read.

Aim for Unity and Coherence

Unity is another word for clarity. A unified essay is one that is clearly developed. Each paragraph has a topic sentence, and all the sentences in the paragraph relate to each other and support the development of the topic sentence.

In the same way, each paragraph relates to every other, and every paragraph supports the overall thesis. This means, of course, that you need to have a thesis to develop.

Remember that your thesis statement contains the central argument that you have developed from brainstorming ideas to answer the essay question.

Although you can place your thesis statement anywhere in your essay, it is probably safest to put it in the first paragraph, so you can refer to it as you write to be sure that everything you are writing develops and supports it. Putting the thesis first also helps get you started writing.

Organize Your Thoughts

Effectively organizing the flow of information on the long essay portion of the AP® U.S. History Exam will help to serve your writing's intended purpose—to convince the AP® Exam Reader of the validity and effectiveness of your point of view on the topic at hand. Consider the following organization options:

- **Chronological:** information is organized by the time that the events occurred (can be forward or reverse)

TIP

Consider jotting down your long essay thesis where you wrote your notes or somewhere else in view while you write your response. This way, you can always be sure that your work is supporting your essay's central contention.

- **Sequential:** often used when describing a process, information is organized by the order in which the steps or parts occur
- **Order of importance:** information is organized by its relative value or importance (can be most to least important, or vice versa)
- **Compare and contrast:** often used when writing about two or more things, wherein one is discussed, then another to compare it with, and so on
- **Cause and effect:** often used to describe a particular result and the events or reasons behind why that result occurred
- **Issue/problem and solution:** in this type of organization, a central dilemma is discussed, followed by strategies for addressing/fixing the problem

Develop Your Thoughts

You have a limited time to read, plan, and then develop your ideas—neatly. Using the five-paragraph structure will give you a format to work with: a one-paragraph introduction, a three-paragraph middle or body, and a one-paragraph conclusion.

For your body paragraphs, develop only one idea per paragraph, and be sure to include outside information. Also, make an effort to address potentially opposing or alternative viewpoints within your body paragraphs. The body of your essay may actually be more than three paragraphs, but this format gives you direction.

Let's take a closer look at each component of a well-written essay:

Introduction: Use your essay opening to introduce your thoughts on the topic and explain why you think it's an important issue worth exploration. Also be sure to begin to discuss—or fully assert—the central idea or thesis of your essay. This should directly address the central question(s) in the prompt and make your perspective on the issue quite clear for readers.

Effective essay openings do one or more of the following:

- Use engaging words to garner interest and capture attention
- State the topic of the piece succinctly, confidently, and clearly
- Ask an intriguing or provocative question
- Deploy a point-counterpoint structure
- Use a surprising fact, theory, or bit of interesting historical information to stand out
- Deploy a poignant yet relevant quote

Body: The body paragraphs of your essay should bolster the claims made in your central thesis, through thoughtful analysis, effective idea development, and strong support. A high-scoring essay will be a comprehensive and well-organized piece of writing that fully supports your viewpoint and strengthens your central thesis. Consider deploying effective topic sentences and core claims in your essay paragraphs:

- Topic sentences: topic sentences can be considered the "thesis statements" of each of the paragraphs in which they appear—they communicate the main ideas of each of the paragraphs that make up a given piece of writing. Each paragraph—including the introduction, the

TIP

A nuanced, well-developed essay will *not* shy away from directly addressing a counterclaim—it will not only mention it, it will also have a satisfying response to it.

body paragraphs, and the conclusion—will likely have an identifiable main idea, designed to deliver its core point and purpose and support the piece as a whole. Topic sentences often appear at the beginning or early on in a paragraph, with the material that follows designed to support the central claims made in these key sentences.

- Core claims: a core claim is a point or assertion that a writer is trying to make in his or her writing, which—when delivered effectively—relates directly to both the topic sentence of the paragraph in which it appears as well as the thesis statement of the entire passage. Claims can be found in persuasive, argumentative, and informative passages and can also take the form of a counterclaim, which is an opposing point of view or assertion to that of an author's. When handled effectively, directly addressing counterclaims in a piece of writing is an effective tool for providing a multifaceted, comprehensive analysis of an issue or argument.

Conclusion: Here's where you'll "wrap up" your essay, tying up all of the ideas you've provided in your writing while reasserting your central position. Relevant, insightful ideas for further exploration and consideration can also be included here. There are several ways to approach the conclusion: rephrasing the thesis, answering the questions by summarizing the main points of your argument, referring in some way back to your opening paragraph, or adding poignant food for thought regarding the topic. It's always a good idea to end your work on a powerful concluding note—always remember, a great closing will leave a positive and lasting impression on your readers. Not surprisingly, a strong closing could include many of the same elements of a strong introduction:

- Offer a succinct, clear, and poignant message.
- Reiterate key words or phrases from the passage.
- Consider a memorable quote or question that encapsulates your main point(s).
- Redefine an important idea or detail in the passage.
- Capture your perspective or point of view regarding the topic.

TIP

How you end a piece of writing is just as crucial as how you begin it. Remember, you want your essay to have two key impacts: *an engaging first impression* and *a memorable final impression.*

TACKLING A SAMPLE LONG ESSAY RESPONSE

Now that you understand what the long essay question consists of, you need a game plan for successfully crafting a high-scoring essay. The following tactics are designed to help you craft an effective long essay response on test day.

Consider the following sample question:

> When Franklin Roosevelt became president of the United States, he took a number of steps to jump-start the economy. Some experts have suggested that the steps taken by Roosevelt would not have turned the economy around without the impact of World War II. In a coherent essay, assess the validity of that claim.

As stated earlier, begin by carefully analyzing the question. Consider the following:

- What type of question is this and what are you being asked to provide in your essay? Remember to look for relevant clue words.
- What is your opinion on the subject?

- What is the historical relevance of the topic at hand?

- What historical facts and evidence can you draw upon to answer the question?

- Determine what issues to address in your written response and how best to utilize your knowledge of the subject matter to craft a compelling and effective written response that fully supports your point of view.

Let's take a close look at the sample question. Note that this is an evaluation question; the clue words *assess the validity* in the question can help make this determination.

You are asked to identify both the steps taken by President Franklin Roosevelt to improve the economy and the economic impact of World War II. Once you have accomplished that, you need to evaluate the relative importance of the two to determine if you can establish which one was more important in improving the U.S. economy. It may be helpful to list some of the points on both sides of the question before you move on.

Here is an example of two lists of notes that you might generate while quickly brainstorming:

Steps Taken by Roosevelt:

- The New Deal

- "Fireside chats" to develop confidence

- The "Hundred Days" legislation

- "Bank holiday" to ease the pressure on the banking system

- Asked Congress for the Emergency Banking Relief Act; permitted only those banks with sufficient money to meet their customers' demands to reopen

- Created a series of programs to improve the economy on both a short-term and long-term basis: (You would select only some of the following to support your position.)
  - Civilian Conservation Corps
  - Social Security Act
  - Tennessee Valley Authority
  - Works Progress Administration
  - Federal Emergency Relief Administration
  - Rural Electrification Administration
  - Agricultural Adjustment Administration
  - Federal Deposit Insurance Corporation
  - National Recovery Administration
  - Public Works Administration
  - Fair Labor Standards Act (instituted minimum wage)
- The Second New Deal

- The Recession of 1938

Impact of World War II:

- Full employment needed to produce war goods

- Women in the work force in great numbers
- Deficit spending used to fund the costs of war
- Investment in agriculture to provide food for the Allies
- Creation of a large industrial economy to design and build the weapons of war
- Spending on military research

Using the ideas you jotted down, create a thesis to serve as the core of your essay. Then select the topics and facts that you believe you can best use to support your thesis. This is important—keep in mind that the events and ideas you select may *not* be those you know the best. You are looking for the ones that *best* support your ideas. Once you have a central thesis and focus, use the information in this chapter on writing a high-scoring essay to craft your response.

So, how do you know what AP® Exam Readers will be looking for when grading your essay? Well, that's what *we're* here for! When grading your response, these readers will be looking to ensure that your essay successfully does the following:

Establishes your point of view with a clear evaluative thesis statement

Your written response should address all of the elements of the question while establishing a clearly discernible thesis—ideally located in the introduction or conclusion of your essay—that encapsulates your point of view on the topic at hand. Your thesis claim should also address the skill indicated in the question provided.

Demonstrates a solid historical reasoning

While developing your point of view on the long essay response, you should demonstrate an ability to deploy sound reasoning—within a historical context—as you write your essay, drawing upon as many relevant historical facts as possible.

Establishes historical relevance

Your written response should explore the historical significance of the topic and discuss how a relevant historical context influenced it. It should also draw historical connections and relationships to larger historical developments, events, and processes that took place before, during, and after the time period of the question.

Your point of view is *not* being tested!

Remember, *what* your point of view is on any given essay subject is not the metric by which your work will be graded—it's *how* you develop your ideas that your grade will reflect.

Trying to craft an essay response that you think will match what an AP® Exam Reader may not think about the topic at hand is a waste of your time. Instead, focus on how to develop your thoughts into a well-developed essay that effectively represents your views and addresses the question fully.

Remembering this when taking the test will help you save time and effort!

LONG ESSAY PRACTICE

It's time to get some practice for the long essay portion of the AP® U.S. History Exam. We can't say this enough—practice is among your *best* tools for getting comfortable with the types of questions you'll encounter on test day, targeting your strengths and weaknesses, and developing an effective study plan that will help you earn your best possible score.

Carefully read and answer the following question. Use the information provided in this chapter to determine how well you fulfilled the requirements of this exercise. Also provided are some sample brainstorming notes for this question. However, we suggest that you avoid using them unless you are completely stumped by how to tackle this question on your own. We recommend that you use a trusted source—perhaps a fellow AP® student, parent, or teacher—to review your final essay and provide helpful feedback.

When evaluating your essay, you can also refer to the official College Board/AP website for more insight into what makes a good long essay response. View or download the following documents:

- Rubrics for AP® Histories+ History Disciplinary Practices and Reasoning Skills (*https://apcentral.collegeboard.org/pdf/rubrics-ap-histories. pdf?course=ap-united-states-history*)
- AP® U.S. History Student Samples Aligned to the 2018 Rubrics—Long Essay Question (*https://apcentral.collegeboard.org/pdf/ap-us-history-leq-2018. pdf?course=ap-united-states-history*).

Best of luck!

Social changes influence societies on an irregular basis. It has been said that the Jacksonian and post–World War I periods were times of great social change. Support or refute the statement that those periods were a time of great social change.

Sample Essay Brainstorming Notes

Note that this question combines two categories: compare/contrast and evaluate. You are asked to agree or disagree with the statement that the Jacksonian and post–World War I periods created significant social change. Ask yourself if you think the statement is true. Also, you might ask yourself if you think that the social changes during those periods were comparable in terms of their breadth and long-term impact.

Jacksonian Period:

- The Jacksonian period is generally considered to be the years from 1824 to 1840.
- Jackson was considered the president of the common people. He was a popular frontier hero.
- Political changes:
  - New parties—Whigs or National Republicans and Democrats
  - Caucuses replaced by nominating conventions
  - Suffrage extended to all white men whether or not they owned land
- Free African Americans were denied basic rights. Women were denied their rights.
- Settlers on the frontier were independent in thought and action.
- With the exception of the African Americans, there was a growing sense of equality among social classes.
- Jackson and his independent-minded constituents did not want a government that was too powerful.
- Jackson fought the Bank of the United States because of the concern that it had too much power. He believed that it favored the rich over the poor.
- Jackson advanced the "spoils system" in government by removing members of the Whig Party and replacing them with loyal Democrats.
- The Indian Removal Act pushed the Native Americans out of their traditional lands.
- The Panic of 1837 led to a depression and hard economic times. It also opened the door for the Whigs to win the presidency.

Post-World War I Period:

- After World War I, Americans wanted a period of calm.
- Harding was elected president on a platform calling for a return to "normalcy."
- Harding's administration was plagued with scandals involving his friends. Among the most notable was the Teapot Dome scandal.
- The end of World War I brought a booming economy.
- Much of the economy was driven by the manufacture of affordable automobiles.
- Installment sales, buy-now-pay-later, fueled consumer spending.

- The stock market rose, in part, because of buying on margin.
- Prohibition was instituted.
- Women's roles changed:
  - Won the right to vote
  - Sought equal rights
  - Continued to work in jobs held by men prior to World War I
- The movie, radio, and telephone industries developed and grew.
- African American culture expanded with the Harlem Renaissance.
- Racism was still widespread. The Ku Klux Klan achieved some political power in the South.
- Farmers had a difficult time.
- The Depression brought a halt to the free spending of the 1920s.

SUMMING IT UP

- Section II, Part B, of the exam consists of one question—you'll be responsible for crafting an essay in response to one of the three options provided on the same theme. You'll have 40 minutes to fully develop your essay response. It will count for 15 percent of your total AP® Exam score.

- Organization: The long essay question on the AP® U.S. History Exam can be rooted in any of the following historical time periods (questions can span multiple periods):
  - Periods 1–3: 1491–1800
  - Periods 4–6: 1800–1898
  - Periods 7–9: 1890–Present

- The long essay question is the final part of the AP® U.S. History Exam.

- You'll be presented with three questions, one from each of the noted time periods, and you'll have the opportunity to choose one. The three questions will all address the same theme and reasoning skill—choose the one that will best allow you to showcase your argumentative writing skills.

- All the information must come from your knowledge and understanding of U.S. history and your ability to develop an effective argument that contains relevant, evidence-based support and historical analysis.

- You'll also need to show historical relationships and connections and make insightful generalizations regarding the question topic.

- Utilize the following strategies for structuring your long essay response:
  - Carefully read and analyze the questions presented.
  - Identify which skills are being primarily assessed in your chosen question.
  - Jot down notes.
  - Evaluate your notes and develop a thesis.
  - Make key historical connections, and include as many relevant facts and as much historical evidence as you can to support your essay.
  - Go beyond paraphrasing.
  - Appropriately interpret the information provided.
  - Write an essay that clearly, logically, and coherently answers the question from your unique point of view.
  - Fulfill all the tasks outlined in the question.
  - Write clearly and neatly.
  - Try to leave a few minutes (3–5 minutes is recommended) at the end to check and edit your work.
  - Manage your time well so you have enough time to prep, organize, write, and edit your essay.

- Your goal on test day is to zero in and focus on your core claim(s) and eliminate any redundancy or off-focus ideas.

- The safest tone to adopt on test day is formal and persuasive, since you are being asked to take a position and support it.
- Your style should be your own natural style that you use for school essays. That means:
  - Using proper grammar and punctuation.
  - Choosing words that convey your meaning in an interesting rather than an ineffective or vague way.
  - Avoiding the use of several words when one will do.
  - Avoiding hackneyed phrases and clichés.
- A unified essay is one that is clearly developed. Each paragraph has a topic sentence, and all the sentences in the paragraph relate to each other and support the development of the topic sentence.
- Effectively organizing the flow of information in your essay will help to serve your intended purpose. Consider the following organization options:
  - **Chronological:** information is organized by the time that the events occurred (can be forward or reverse).
  - **Sequential:** often used when describing a process, information is organized by the order in which the steps or parts occur.
  - **Order of importance:** information is organized by its relative value or importance (can be most to least important, or vice versa).
  - **Compare and contrast:** often used when writing about two or more things, wherein one is discussed, then another to compare it with, and so on.
  - **Cause and effect:** often used to describe a particular result and the events or reasons behind why that result occurred.
  - **Issue/problem and solution:** in this type of organization, a central dilemma is discussed, followed by strategies for addressing/fixing the problem.
- Using the five-paragraph structure will give you a format to work with:
  - **Introduction:** use your essay opening to introduce your thoughts on the topic and explain why you think it's an important issue worth exploration. Also be sure to assert the central idea or thesis of your essay.
  - **Body:** the body paragraphs of your essay should bolster the claims made in your central thesis, through thoughtful analysis, effective idea development, and strong support.
  - **Conclusion:** Here's where you'll "wrap up" your essay, tying up all of the ideas you've provided in your writing while reasserting your central position.
- AP® Exam Readers will be looking to ensure that your essay establishes your point of view with a clear evaluative thesis statement, demonstrates a solid historical reasoning, and proves historical relevance.

PART III
AP® U.S. HISTORY REVIEW

Period 1 (1491–1607)

OVERVIEW

- **Learning Objectives**
- **The New World**
- **Characteristics of New World Societies**
- **The Atlantic World**
- **Key Events in Period 1: A Timeline**
- **Practice**
- **Summing It Up**

LEARNING OBJECTIVES

Upon completion of this chapter you should be able to...

- Recognize how Native Peoples developed cultural, economic, and political structures by adapting to their environment and each other

- Explain how European overseas expansion created the Columbian Exchange

- Understand how interaction between Europeans, Native Peoples, and Africans altered their worldwide views

THE NEW WORLD

America (meaning the land comprising the North and South American continents) was discovered tens of thousands of years ago by nomadic people who followed game across a temporary land bridge formed during one of the many Pleistocene ice ages that periodically lowered global sea levels. (Some also argue some of that migration might have occurred *absent* the land bridge, with the migrants ferrying themselves across in boats at least part of the way.) Having originated in East Africa about 200,000 years ago, humans had been spreading around the world, and, once on the American continent, they spread slowly but surely all the way down to the southernmost tip of South America, forming distinctive societies along the way.

In 1492, a transformation of massive importance began to occur, though technically not "the discovery of America." The two branches of the human species (Europeans and Afro-Eurasians) had been virtually isolated from one another from the end of the last ice age

NOTE

Although the period has a start date of 1491, this is just a placeholder by the College Board. Anything relevant to the course that happened before this date is still considered part of the period.

(around 10,000 BCE) up to 1492 CE. Around 1500, these two branches of humanity started to mix, often with catastrophic consequences that reverberate still. This interaction between the Old World (Europe) and New World (Americas) would result in a transfer of goods, ideas, and cultures.

However, an entire history full of rich culture, diverse languages, political structure, and complex society had already been established. The **Aztec** ruled Central America from their "city of gold" Tenochtitlan (Mexico City); the **Inca** dominated South America; **Pueblos** built settlements around the Rio Grande; the **Anasazi** could be found in regions around New Mexico; the Woodland mound builders (**Cahokia**) developed around the Mississippi River Valley as the Great Plains saw nomadic tribes such as the Sioux, and the Pawnee, who were more sedentary; and finally the **Iroquois Confederation** settled around New York. Native Peoples had built great cities, developed rich trade networks, and structured intricate societies that assigned gender roles, elevated political leaders, and practiced religious ceremonies centered on crop production. These people were adept at understanding their environment and, if necessary, moving to find ways to survive.

CHARACTERISTICS OF NEW WORLD SOCIETIES

In Mesoamerica (a region extending roughly from mid-Mexico into what is now Central America), settled life was based on the cultivation of what is sometimes referred to as **The Three Sisters**: maize (corn), squash, and beans. These crops could be rotated in such a way that didn't exhaust the soil, and their cultivation led to what would become large settlements and, eventually, great cities. These powerful empires engaged in trade and maintained political and social structure in their society.

The largest pre-Columbian civilizations—the Aztec, the Inca, and the Maya (in present-day Mexico, Peru, and Guatemala, respectively)—made great strides in art, architecture, and science, contributing medicines and foods still in use today. The Incas were especially adept engineers, having built a complex and wide-ranging system of roads, bridges, and aqueducts. The Aztec capital of Tenochtitlan was by the year 1500 more populous than any European city. The Maya used advanced mathematics and astronomy to develop one of the most accurate calendars ever created.

In pre-Columbian North America, maize cultivation spread into what is now the **Southwest** United States. That sort of cultivation requires irrigation systems (to nourish the plants) and settlements (to tend the fields), so civilizations arose there. The Anasazi developed the Chaco Canyon into a center of trade and religion. Replacing the "ancient ones" would be the Pueblo people, who developed multistory buildings and sophisticated systems of dams and canals for irrigation. by a sophisticated system of dams and canals. They spoke different languages, relied on the three sisters, and performed intricate ceremonies for blessing crops. Tribes of the **Pacific Northwest** built civilizations based on hunting, fishing, and foraging. Since much of the food supply, including fish and other sea creatures, was within easy reach of coastal peoples, many of them settled there permanently. They would build extremely long houses made of local cedar and enjoy a culture rich in art.

The people of the **Great Plains** remained mostly nomadic, partly because they subsisted largely on game such as the buffalo (really, the American bison), which themselves migrated in search of food. Even though these tribes were technically nomadic, they still lived in permanent houses and grew each of the three sisters. The introduction of horses would completely transform this area after the Spanish arrived, helping tribes chase the buffalo herds more easily.

Conversely, the Mississippi River system of the **Midwest**, one of the largest on earth, waters a gigantic area; this encouraged a mix of nomadic and settled life in that area by groups that benefited from a diverse array of fishing, hunting, and growing. Inhabited by the Cahokia, it became the largest settlement in North America, with large and wide earth mounds at its center and a temple at the top. After a colder climate removed much of the population around 1350, smaller tribes settled into the territory, building homes and a defensive wood wall.

Finally the five tribes, while facing the challenges of exhausted soil, dominated the **Northeast** and relied on a combination of hunting and farming for sustenance. Like other tribes across the continent, they lived in families as part of a larger community. Overall, Native tribes adapted to their respective environments by hunting, fishing, and farming but were in constant war with surrounding tribes over contested resources within their unique regions. Each tribe had a political structure that supported a leader or chief, warriors, gender-based labor, advanced languages and tools, and religion practiced in forms that could consist of a shaman and spiritual ritual ceremonies.

THE ATLANTIC WORLD

Throughout most of the Middle Ages, most advanced trading societies were non-European. World trade (meaning, Afro-Eurasian trade) was controlled by Mongols and Muslims, and Europeans who wished to engage in trade had to pay middlemen to get goods into and out of Europe. That changed in the early 1400s, when the Portuguese, a seafaring people located close to Africa, linked up with coastal African traders, outflanking the Muslim-dominated trans-Siberian trade routes. The introduction of new maritime technology, such as the caravel and the sailing compass, made travel across the Atlantic easier as the economic motivation of finding new trade routes encouraged more empires to look west and joint stock companies made it financially possible. Prince Henry (the Navigator) of Portugal would launch the first true attempt at establishing a trade route to Asia and others would follow suit. Competition increased the desire of kingdoms to explore, while consolidation of power (nation-states) through marriages, such as **Isabella and Ferdinand** of Spain, would amplify aspiration to find new sources of trade and riches.

America would become a major source of dispute as Spain and Portugal both laid claim to territories, forcing the Pope to create the **Treaty of Tordesillas** as a means of establishing rights of settlement. Columbus sailed under Spanish auspices, and he and the subsequent explorers and **conquistadors** began the process of exchange. Hernan Cortes would search for the legendary city of gold, conquering the mighty Aztec in 1521. Francisco Pizarro would defeat the Inca, Jacques Cartier would explore the St. Lawrence River, Coronado the Southwest. In 1497, Venetian explorer John Cabot would make a British claim to Canada.

It was the Spanish, however, who truly began the movement to America, and their contact with Native Peoples would dramatically alter their worldwide views and culture. Once there, Europeans began to exchange plants, animals, and germs with the Native population as part of the **Columbian Exchange**. Europeans would receive foods that improved their diets and agricultural harvests such as maize, tomatoes, and potatoes (not to mention the mineral gains of gold and silver). This exchange of goods would help transform Europe into a capitalistic society and away from feudalism, while also creating an even stronger desire to continue to extract native resources. In return, Old World crops (such as wheat and sugar) combined with the introduction of horses, cows, and pigs transformed the Native Peoples' world but at a price.

The Spanish brought diseases, such as smallpox, carried by oxen, cattle, and other large, domesticated animals. The Old World explorers had developed a resistance to such diseases, but the Native Peoples had not. This resulted in widespread epidemics among the Native Peoples; smallpox alone is said to have killed up to 90 percent of the Native population. The biological impact of the exchange was intensified by the fact that the Spanish also had access to guns and alcohol, neither of which had ever been seen by the Native Peoples.

It's not too surprising that the Spanish quickly took control of just about all the cultures in their eventual orbit, especially since many conquistadors thought that it was their solemn duty to bring Christianity to the Native Peoples. Even as the Native People tried to resist European infringement of their lands through negotiation and, more often, resistance, they were often unsuccessful. The impact of Spanish exploration on the millions of people in the Americas was nothing short of catastrophic: it resulted not only in massive epidemics, but also in total domination and the near-death of Native culture. Some Europeans were horrified, including the famous sixteenth-century Spanish bishop **Bartolomé de las Casas**, leading to debates over how Native Peoples should be viewed and treated, but stories of Spanish treatment (Black Legend) would continue to spread.

At first, the Spanish enslaved the Indians in what was called the *encomienda* system: the crown granted the conquerors pretty much everything, from land to people, and they were allowed to do what they wanted to extract wealth. The result was the enslavement of the Native population and the eventual establishment of a caste system with purebred Europeans at the top, **Mestizos** (those of mixed European and Native blood) in the middle, and Native Peoples at the bottom. In exchange, the colonists were expected to protect the Native Peoples and to convert them to Catholicism. At the same time, Europeans like the Portuguese began importing African slaves into the New World, in effect promoting the Native Peoples to a form of serfdom, and establishing yet another lucrative (though even at the time, some said immoral) form of trade—this time in human flesh. The issues of land, labor, and conversion had begun to outweigh the discovery of gold. The rest of Atlantic-facing Europe—France, England, and the Netherlands—began exploring the New World. Moreover, European competition between both religions and nations inevitably spilled over into colonial land-grabs, with each side angling to claim land and convert the Native Peoples to Christianity. The **Protestant Reformation** and subsequent English reformation pushed the English into the New World and, after a failed attempt at **Roanoke**, they would forever change North American colonization.

KEY EVENTS IN PERIOD 1: A TIMELINE

Significant Date	Event
750	Moundbuilders in Mississippi River Valley
850-1100	Rise and fall of Anasazi
950-1400	Rise and fall of Cahokia
1325	Rise of Aztecs
1348-1350s	Black Plague in Europe
1415	Portuguese explore Atlantic coast of Africa
1453	End of Hundred Years War
1469	Marriage of Isabella and Ferdinand
1492	Columbus sails
1498	Vasco da Gama reaches India
1513	Ponce de Leon explores Florida
1517	Protestant Reformation in Europe
1519-1521	Cortes conquers Aztecs
1532	Pizarro conquers Incas
1534-1536	Cartier explores St. Lawrence River
1534	King Henry VIII named head of Church of England
1540-1542	Coronado explores the American Southwest
1565	St. Augustine, Florida, founded
1587	Roanoke founded
1598	Spanish settle in New Mexico

PRACTICE

"It appears to me, that the people are ingenious and would be good servants and I am of opinion that they would very readily become Christians, as they appear to have no religion. They very quickly learn such words as are spoken to them. If it please our Lord, I intend at my return to carry home six of them to your Highnesses, that they may learn our language."

—Christopher Columbus, Journal Entry, 1492

1. Which of the following would be the best evidence to support the views regarding religion expressed by Columbus in the passage?
   A. The Spanish use of the encomienda system
   B. The inclusion of rituals in Aztec culture
   C. Native ability to survive the transfer of European diseases
   D. The lack of marriage between Natives and Europeans

2. What misconception is Columbus dispelling in his journal?
   A. The Native peoples were savages who had no political, social, or economic structure.
   B. Religion played a small role in Native culture.
   C. The Native population was not considered as a labor force when Europeans first arrived in the Americas.
   D. Spanish explorers only attempted to extract gold from North America.

3. The transfer of ideas and cultures that were a result of European and Native interactions is best described as which of the following?
   A. The *encomienda* system
   B. The Protestant Reformation
   C. The Atlantic World
   D. The Columbian Exchange

Answer Key and Explanations

1. A	2. A	3. C

1. **The correct answer is A.** The *encomienda* system was a combination of forced Native labor and an attempt to convert them to Christianity. Choice B is incorrect because the Aztec rituals proved there was religion in Native culture. Choice C is incorrect because Native peoples had no immunity to European disease. Choice D is incorrect because some in the Native population did begin to mix with European settlers, particularly the Spanish and French.

2. **The correct answer is A.** Natives were considered uncivilized by many Europeans because of their dress and rituals, but Columbus shared a belief that they were quick learners and had the ability to adapt to European language. Choice B is incorrect because Columbus was unaware of Native religious beliefs, as evidenced by his belief they have "appear to have no religion." Choices C and D are incorrect because the Spanish had a goal of using the Native population as a labor force when exploring the New World (as well as Christianizing them) but would find they were not a suitable workforce.

3. **The correct answer is C.** The exchange of ideas that resulted from exploration and interaction of the Old and New World is known as the Atlantic World. Choice A is incorrect because this was a combination of forced Native labor and an attempt to convert them to Christianity. Choice B is incorrect because it was a religious change and break from the Catholic Church in England. Choice D is incorrect because the exchange of crops between the New World and Old World, that would include a transfer of disease, is the Columbian Exchange.

SUMMING IT UP

- In 1492, the **European and Afro-Eurasian** branches of the human species were no longer isolated from each other; around 1500, these two branches of humanity started to mix, resulting in a transfer of goods, ideas, and cultures.

- The **Aztec** ruled Central America from their "city of gold" Tenochtitlan; they would make great strides in art, architecture, and science and develop medicines and foods still in use today.

- The **Inca** dominated South America and also contributed much in the way of art, architecture, science, medicine, and food while also becoming adept engineers who built a system of roads, bridges, and aqueducts.

- **Pueblos** built settlements around the Rio Grande.

- The **Anasazi** were found in regions around New Mexico.

- The Woodland mound builders known as the **Cahokia** developed around the Mississippi River Valley, benefiting from a diverse array of fishing, hunting, and growing. The Great Plains saw nomadic tribes such as the Sioux, and the Pawnee, who were more sedentary.

- The **Iroquois Confederation** were found around New York.

- In Mesoamerica, extending roughly from mid-Mexico into what is now Central America, settled life was based on the cultivation of **The Three Sisters:** maize (corn), squash, and beans.

- Since maize cultivation requires irrigation systems to nourish the plants and settlements to tend the fields, civilizations spread to what is now the **Southwest** United States.

- Tribes of the **Pacific Northwest** built civilizations based on hunting, fishing, and foraging along the coast.

- Although they still lived in permanent houses and grew each of the three sisters, the people of the **Great Plains** remained mostly nomadic, partly because they subsisted largely on game such as the buffalo.

- Five tribes dominated the **Northeast** and relied on a combination of hunting and farming, lived in families as part of a larger community, divided jobs by gender, formed a political structure led by a chief, and practiced religion that involved a shaman and spiritual ritual ceremonies.

- During the early 1400s, introduction of new maritime technology made travel across the Atlantic easier, which increased competition to explore, while consolidation of power through marriages, such as **Isabella and Ferdinand** of Spain, amplified the aspiration to find new sources of trade and riches.

- America would become a major source of dispute as Spain and Portugal both laid claim to territories, forcing the Pope to create the **Treaty of Tordesillas** as a means of establishing rights of settlement.

- The Spanish were most responsible for the movement to America, leading Europeans to exchange plants, animals, and germs with Native Peoples as part of the **Columbian Exchange**, which would help transform Europe into a capitalistic society and away from feudalism while also creating an even stronger desire to continue to extract Native resources.

- The Spanish brought diseases to America to which the Native population had no resistance, resulting in widespread epidemics; **smallpox** alone is said to have killed up to 90 percent of the Native population.

- Although the Native Peoples tried to resist European infringement on their lands through negotiation and resistance, the Spanish quickly took control of most of the cultures since **conquistadors** believed it was their solemn duty to bring Christianity to the Native population.

- The destruction of Native life and culture horrified some Europeans, such as the sixteenth-century Spanish bishop **Bartolomé de las Casas** and led to debates over how Native Peoples should be viewed.

- The Spanish crown allowed conquerors to do anything they wanted to do to extract wealth, resulting in the enslavement of the Native Peoples in what was called the *encomienda* system, a caste system with purebred Europeans at the top, Mestizos of mixed European and Native blood in the middle, and Natives at the bottom.

- France, England, and the Netherlands began exploring the New World, and European competition between religions and nations spilled over into **colonial land-grabs** with each side angling to convert the Native population to Christianity.

- The **Protestant Reformation** and subsequent English reformation pushed England into the New World, which would forever change North American colonization.

Period 2 (1607–1754)

Chapter 6

OVERVIEW

- Learning Objectives
- Diverse Patterns of European Colonization
- Diverse Patterns of British Colonization
- The Impact of the Atlantic World on Colonization
- Key Events in Period 2: A Timeline
- Practice
- Summing It Up

LEARNING OBJECTIVES

Upon completion of this chapter, you should be able to...

- Identify the differences in imperial goals, cultures, and environments that caused Europeans to develop different patterns of colonization

- Explain how intercultural contact created tensions between Europeans and Native Peoples

- Describe how the development of colonial societies was directly impacted by "Atlantic World" exchanges

DIVERSE PATTERNS OF EUROPEAN COLONIZATION

As the raw materials and resources discovered in the New World became more valuable, more countries looked to colonization as a tool to achieve their imperial goals. Spanish, French, Dutch, and British colonizers all reached the New World with different ambitions and objectives that would ultimately create very different settlements.

Spain

The Spanish had achieved some success in extracting mineral wealth, but overall their settlements had shifted to a focus of strong control and conversion of surrounding Native populations. With settlements confined to areas such as Florida, Texas, and the American Southwest, the Spanish often faced strong resistance to their conversion and exploitation attempts with the most glaring example coming in the form of the **Pueblo Revolt**. The various Pueblo peoples, under threat by the Spanish, put aside their differences and joined forces in 1680, rising up against their conquerors and laying siege to Santa Fe in New Mexico. The rebels killed hundreds of Spanish settlers and drove out the mostly *mestizo* colonial population. The Spanish returned twelve years later, determined to take a more accommodating stance toward the Pueblo people, in order to forestall further conflicts.

The Spanish would promote a rigid class system in their settlements as their population began to mix and intermarry with the Native population (as well as enslaved Africans). With pureblooded Spanish sitting atop the system, there was little room for movement within the tightly controlled society, but attempts to stamp out tribal practices began to subside. As other European nations began to settle in America, Spain looked to establish settlement in California, pushing more conversions and economic development in the process.

France

The French aimed to find a Northwest Passage to East and Southeast Asia. In this, they were not alone, of course—the Dutch and the English, too, searched for this ultimate outflanking of Afro-Eurasian trading routes and regimes. The French found no precious metals in North America, but they did discover an alternate source of wealth: furs. Much like gold had done for the Spanish, the French now had a valuable source of trade that would transform its economy, as well as that of the Native population. Exchanging guns and alcohol for fur led to greater, more lethal intertribal warfare, and, as with other European explorers, the French introduced diseases to the Native population. Of all the European powers, French interaction with Native people was perhaps the least confrontational, as intermarriage was common and conversion to Catholicism by Jesuit priests was more successful than other European attempts.

As French explorers like Samuel de Champlain began to explore the area of present-day Canada, permanent settlements would develop around important trading centers like the St. Lawrence River and eventually the Mississippi River Valley. Fur trappers (*coureurs de bois*) would be able to develop rich trade with the Native population while bringing wealth back to France. The French would eventually introduce slavery to the region as French Louisiana utilized the port of New Orleans, shaping the culture of the area for years to come.

Dutch

The Dutch also sought a Northwest Passage, but under the auspices of the Dutch West India Company, inventors of the **joint-stock company**. In the process of this search, the Dutch founded New Amsterdam, which later became New York City. Like the French, the Dutch were far less interested in settlement; they instead concentrated at home and abroad on a burgeoning international trade. The Native peoples were happy to pit the Dutch and French against each other in trade, and New Amsterdam would become a commercial center of trade (one that also became active in the slave trade). The Dutch carried over to their American colonies their relatively liberal views on religious freedom and even women's rights before King Charles II "gave" the settlement to his younger brother, the Duke of York. Later becoming King James II, the Duke would split the colony in two (New York and New Jersey, "Restoration Colonies").

NOTE

Restoration Colonies is the term given to the English colonies chartered during the restored reign of Charles II and later his brother James II (1660-1688): New York, New Jersey, Pennsylvania (including what later became Delaware), and North and South Carolina.

England

The English were unlike other European powers, as they had very different goals, relationships, and populations. Settling colonies for mostly agricultural purposes (after attempts to find gold proved futile), the English had very hostile relationships with the Native population, while sending large numbers of both men and women to the colonies. While the crown's reasons for granting charters (a document granting special privileges) was focused on mercantilism, the colonies obtaining these charters would all develop very unique characteristics based on factors such as environment, geography, and purpose of colonization.

DIVERSE PATTERNS OF BRITISH COLONIZATION

English domination of coastal settlement would be the result of its defeat of the Spanish Armada and the use of three types of charters (corporate, royal, and proprietary). The geography and environment would greatly shape the development of these colonies, while the people and purpose would ultimately contribute to regional differences.

The South: the Chesapeake (Virginia and Maryland), the Carolinas, and Georgia

In 1607, the Virginia Company received a **corporate charter** to be operated by a joint-stock company in search of wealth for the crown and its investors. Ships arrived at **Jamestown** full of wealthy men seeking riches and indentured servants hoping to escape poverty (few women originally made the voyage to the region). Problems such as malaria, tensions with the Native population, and laziness would soon overtake the colony, leading to near starvation and extinction. John Smith would institute a strict no-work, no-food policy and push the colonists away from a gold-only mentality. However, the crown had established the colony for economic purposes, and it would take another John—John Rolfe—to help it find a new form of gold, the cash crop of tobacco.

The **Chesapeake** colonial economy was based on tobacco. Tobacco cultivation was very labor-intensive; hence, as white indentured servitude waned, reliance on African slaves grew. This led to a greater justification of slavery, upon which the entire socioeconomic structure of the region was based. Moreover, tobacco exhausted the soil more quickly than many other crops, so land hunger was more pitched in these colonies and the pressure to move west was that much higher. (Tobacco is a notoriously addictive drug, so once it caught on in England and Europe, it became quite a profitable cash crop, yet another effect of The Columbian Exchange).

This kind of **monoculture**—reliance on one crop—also marked the economy of the deeper South: the Carolinas and later Georgia, where the growing season is longer. North Carolina, like the Chesapeake, was and is a center of tobacco cultivation; South Carolina moved into rice cultivation, which is a brutally labor-intensive staple crop to cultivate. Labor was a very strenuous topic for those in the Chesapeake, as many indentured servants could not handle the environmental conditions while providing only a temporary solution to the problem. A **headright** system was implemented as well (50 acres of land to each immigrant who paid his or her own way OR to any plantation owner who paid for an immigrant's passage), but, in the end, enslaved Africans emerged as the reliable form of labor. The South would soon become dominated by a small, planter aristocracy that made government decisions and led to social unrest in more backwoods areas.

TIP

The College Board distinguishes Period 2 with a starting date of 1607 to coincide with the British settlement at Jamestown.

While the economy of the Chesapeake was similar, once King Charles I divided the colony, differences became apparent. Virginia would become England's first **royal colony** (a colony under the authority of the king), but their government was relatively similar to that of other colonies. Promising its people the same rights as Englishmen, the House of Burgesses was established as a representative assembly. Religion may have been an afterthought in Virginia (Church of England) but not in Maryland. After Lord Baltimore (Cecil Calvert, son to the first Lord Baltimore) enacted the **Act of Toleration,** Maryland would become a haven for Catholics by granting religious freedom to all Christians. Religion would also have an impact on the creation of the last English colony, Georgia. Created as a buffer to Spanish (and Catholic) Florida as a form of defense, Georgia would become home to many people who had been jailed in England.

New England: Massachusetts Bay, Rhode Island, Connecticut, and New Hampshire

Puritans who had religious motivations for leaving the Anglican Church of England primarily founded the New England region. Both Separatists and Puritans were Protestants who disagreed with the Catholic rituals that remained within the church and they looked to America to start anew. Separatists were the more radical of the two, landing in Plymouth and hoping to completely separate from a church of royal control. These Pilgrims would celebrate the first Thanksgiving and remain a small part of the New England region.

Puritans were the more moderate of the religious dissenters, attempting to "purify" the church while seeking religious freedom by way of a royal charter (under rule of the king's government) in Massachusetts Bay. A close-knit, like-minded group of religious believers, Puritans established a community based on homogenous ideals and the religious beliefs of John Calvin, known as predestination (that God had predetermined salvation before birth). **John Winthrop** and his message of making the colony "A City Upon A Hill" or the example for all others to follow guided this **Great Migration** of people to the colony. The population was well balanced as families mostly settled the region and their dynamic mirrored that of the church, a patriarchy.

The focus on Puritanism did not come without fault—only Puritans were allowed into the church and after a time membership fell. The **Halfway Covenant** was created to increase church (and voter) membership. The plan allowed those who had not yet experienced a conversion to become partial church members. This was an important step in survival for the colony as Puritans were often intolerant of those who did not follow their religious teachings, as in the cases of **Roger Williams** and **Anne Hutchinson**. Both chose to question Puritan leaders and were banished to what would become the liberal religious refuge of Rhode Island. Williams believed civil or church authority could not control an individual's conscience, while Hutchinson believed in antinomianism, the idea that faith alone is necessary for salvation.

The characteristics of Massachusetts Bay mirrored their religious beliefs. Literacy was high as reading the Bible was necessary, creating a culture of education in the colony that would lead to institutions of both elementary and higher education. Religion dominated all aspects of society—the church was at the center of the town, and male practitioners had the right to participate in yearly elections or town hall meetings (seen as the earliest form of democracy in America). Self-government was present with an elected representative assembly and two-house legislature. In Connecticut, arguably the first written constitution was formed, the **Fundamental Orders of Connecticut**, which established greater voting rights and a representative government.

A favorable environment that created a mixed economy of agriculture and commerce aided the colony. Mostly a subsistence farming society, the people of New England had to deal with rocky soil and long winters while using family members as labor. But commercially the colony profited from shipbuilding, fishing, and trade that became important parts of the British mercantile system thanks to natural bays and harbors. In addition, natural fisheries not far off the coast had already been well frequented by Europeans before 1600.

Finally, New England was not without tensions with the Native peoples, such as the Pequot War or King Philip's War. Unlike the French, Dutch, and even Spanish, England fostered a harsh relationship with the Native population. There were no attempts at conversion and relatively few at forced labor; instead the English focused on the Native population's greatest resource, land. Similar to the conflicts in other colonies, those in New England arose when the Native population tried to resist, ultimately unsuccessfully, the colonists' taking their territory.

The Middle Colonies: New York, New Jersey, Delaware, and Pennsylvania

In the so-called Middle Colonies, the economy was a mix of agriculture and trade, but the immigrant population was more culturally varied than in New England. For example, thanks to William Penn, Pennsylvania became Quaker territory; **Quakers** were far more religiously tolerant than the Puritans. Thus, anyone not Puritan, or not English for that matter, who wanted to immigrate to America naturally chose places like Pennsylvania. Increased diversity and tolerance encouraged even more immigration, which in turn expanded the colonies' diversity and tolerance. Because Penn had been granted a proprietary charter (an individual given authority by the king), his "Holy Experiment" saw guaranteed freedom of worship, unrestricted immigration, and attempts to treat Native peoples fairly.

Here, too, existed fantastic harbors, such as that of New Amsterdam (soon to become New York), which begged for trade. However, the land in general was far more arable, so farming was relatively easy for the growing of cereal crops (garnering the area the nickname of "breadbasket"). Additionally, these colonies enjoyed vast forests, which naturally encouraged lumbering; lumber was necessary for maritime trade. Labor was initially provided by white indentured servants and later, increasingly, by African slaves.

THE IMPACT OF THE ATLANTIC WORLD ON COLONIZATION

The exchange of goods from New World to Old and vice-versa yielded not only economic change, but cultural change as well. While trade of human beings created a system of exploitation and discrimination, the movement of ideas would spur a change in thinking for colonists in British America.

The Atlantic Slave Trade

African slave importation spiked as economies both North and South required labor in their different ways. Of course, since the North's economy concentrated more on trade, the slave trade undergirded much of the North's economy, too. For instance, relatively liberal Rhode Island was in fact a major center of the slave trade. Whether as a labor supply or as a source of "goods" to be traded, slavery was a feature of the American economy. However, the South was unable to do without slavery; tremendous manpower was required to run its vast plantations, while the North could carry or trade *anything* profitable without any fundamental change. Excuses were made to justify the practice, including using environmental, biblical, and scientific claims. The southern planters had no other labor source to turn to without revolutionary change.

Attempts at using Native peoples and even indentured servants had yielded undesirable results for plantation owners, and African slavery became the only answer to the cheap labor question. After **Bacon's Rebellion** and the **Stono Rebellion**, owners became increasingly focused on controlling slaves to be sure their power atop the social hierarchy remained. While Bacon's Rebellion scared plantation owners politically as poor whites attempted to overthrow their government, the Stono Rebellion showed how dangerous a slave uprising could be if given the chance. Slavery would become as much a social construct for racism as it was an economic institution for plantation owners. The horrors of the **Middle Passage**, the most horrid aspect of the Triangular Trade, would lead to changes in how slaves were received in the colonies, and eventually the trade would be banned (1808 as part of the Constitutional Compromise).

Influx of New Ideas

In spite of the increasing ethnic diversity of immigrants to the New World, the English remained culturally dominant, and "**Anglicization**" of the colonies proceeded apace. Certain parts of English culture, politics, and society were deemed "English" and fostered, consciously or not, in colonial society. Concrete examples include Protestant evangelism and British notions of political rights and other governing arrangements; concrete resources and influences are expanded through communication: a transatlantic commerce of both goods and (printed) ideas.

The commerce of goods led to paired interests, until those interests later diverged. For a time, economic interests knitted together the two societies. More interesting was the effect of the commerce of *ideas*, which mostly fell into two categories: religious trends in Protestantism known as the **Great Awakening** (the first of many) and the far more secular trends that were part of what was known as **the Enlightenment.**

The Great Awakening was a mostly grassroots religious uprising, a reaction against the dominant hierarchy of the Church of England. It could be seen as a further reformation of the Protestant Reformation, insofar as it took a person's individual, subjective, unmediated experience of faith even further than the Anglican Church. The Great Awakening was a religious movement (aspects of which still echo today) that featured fiery, "hellfire-and-brimstone" preaching by charismatic traveling preachers such as **Jonathan Edwards**; large-scale revival meetings; emotional and enthusiastic responses; and a near-literal reading of the Bible. Much of this form of religion was based on the charismatic leadership of a small number of individuals, such as **George Whitefield**, who was arguably the first transatlantic celebrity and was admired even by deists like Benjamin Franklin, who published Whitefield's sermons.

The Enlightenment, meanwhile, while hardly atheist, was surely secular—according to the standards of the time. Faith was mostly relegated to a kind of calm, rational deism of the Newtonian clockmaker sort; religions and religious institutions, however, were often the target of vicious attack, with no better example than that of Voltaire. The Enlightenment was centered on what was called "man"—on the mundane, not the divine; on experimental science; on rationality; on the belief in progress or at least the possibility of progress in human affairs; on either a kind of enlightened kingship or even an oligarchical, aristocratic republic often based on what was understood to be the Roman model. Most Enlightened churchmen looked askance at the rabble-rousing emotionality of the Great Awakening.

Interest in governance would again prove instrumental in developing colonial identity as these new ideas made their way up and down the coast in newspapers, pamphlets, and even taverns. Examples such as the **John Peter Zenger trial** provided a window to the colonial mindset with the concept of freedom of the press.

The Mercantile System

The basic principle undergirding **mercantilism** was the belief that the basis of economic power was a favorable balance of trade and control of the currency. Interestingly, the seeds of economic and political dissension lay in the very structure of the same mercantilist system that, for a time, welded the colonies to England/Britain.

Britain wanted raw materials from its American colonies. It preferred that those raw materials come *only* to Britain, so that the British could manufacture value-added products and export them, including back to the colonies, which were prohibited from procuring those manufactured products from anyone else or making them for themselves. One key method by which Britain discouraged both competition and independent economic development was through high import tariffs on manufactured goods and subsidized exports of the same. The intended result was a positive balance of trade for the home country and a steady ingress of money (i.e., precious metals) to balance the budget, fund wars with European competitors, finance further colonial imperialism, and so on. Mercantilism was the dominant economic form until Adam Smith's free-trade critique began to actually affect policy formation in the early nineteenth century.

At the beginning of the colonial process, when life was precarious and much depended on the largesse of "the mother country," few colonists would think to complain about this guaranteed market for raw-material export. Colonists benefited economically as shipbuilding and tobacco became viable exports. But as colonial life slowly became easier and as wealth built up, it became clear that mercantile colonialism hindered further development. Closely related to this economic issue was the fact that colonists had no control over home-country policy formation: no representation but plenty of taxation. This struck not only the colonists (at least the powerful merchant class) but also people like Adam Smith and even British statesmen such as Edmund Burke as deeply unfair and even "un-English." The spread of industrialized production in the eighteenth century only made the domineering economic relationship all the more obvious.

Colonists had also become accustomed to the autonomy afforded from living an ocean away while reaping the benefits of trade. Even when attempts were made to control trade, such as with the Navigation Acts between 1650 and 1673, the colonists mostly ignored or violated them. Britain was notorious for lacking the ability to follow through with their acts (or placing agents who were willing to take kickbacks for looking the other way). Known as **salutary neglect**, Great Britain's lack of governance of the colonies was about to end as war with the French and Native populations dominated the colonial landscape.

KEY EVENTS IN PERIOD 2: A TIMELINE

Significant Date	Event
1607	English founding of Jamestown
1608	French founding of Quebec
1610	Spanish founding of Santa Fe, New Mexico
1620	English Pilgrims founding of Plymouth
1626	Dutch founding of New Amsterdam
1630	English Puritans founding of Boston
1634	English (Lord Baltimore) founding of Maryland
1636	Founding of Rhode Island
1639	Fundamental Orders of Connecticut
1660	Charles II begins rule
1662	Halfway Covenant
1663	English founding of Carolina
1664	English claim New Netherlands (rename New York)
1676	Bacon's Rebellion
1680	Pueblo Revolt
1681	English (William Penn) founding of Pennsylvania
1682	French claim Mississippi River
1692	Salem Witch Trials
1704	First colonial newspaper in Boston
1718	French establish New Orleans
1732	Georgia established
1734	First Great Awakening begins
1735	John Peter Zenger trial
1739	Stono Rebellion

PRACTICE

Directions: Choose the correct answer to the following questions.

Questions 1–3 refer to the passage below.

> We shall find that the God of Israel is among us, when ten of us shall be able to resist a thousand of our enemies; when He shall make us a praise and glory that men shall say of succeeding plantations, "may the Lord make it like that of New England." For we must consider that we shall be as a city upon a hill. The eyes of all people are upon us. So that if we shall deal falsely with our God in this work we have undertaken, and so cause Him to withdraw His present help from us, we shall be made a story and a by-word through the world.
>
> — John Winthrop, "A Model of Christian Charity" 1630

1. How does the passage above contrast with those of the people who settled in the Chesapeake?
   A. The people in the Chesapeake created tolerance for all who settled in their community.
   B. The people who settled in the Chesapeake originally settled for individual, monetary gain.
   C. The people who settled in the Chesapeake created a society that focused on tight-knit, homogenous communities.
   D. The people who settled in the Chesapeake had a community centered on the church and its Anglican beliefs.

2. Which of the following was a result of the rigid expectations and requirements placed upon Puritans as implied by the passage?
   A. Town hall meetings
   B. Headright system
   C. Halfway Covenant
   D. Bacon's Rebellion

3. How do examples like Roger Williams and Anne Hutchinson support the ideals implied in the excerpt?
   A. Puritans were unwilling to accept challenges to their beliefs.
   B. Their ideas were focused on material wealth over religious beliefs.
   C. They are examples of religious tolerance, which other colonies looked to for inspiration.
   D. Their resistance to intolerance led to the First Great Awakening.

Answer Key and Explanations

1. B	2. C	3. A

1. **The correct answer is B.** Based on the passage, a difference, or contrast, between the New England and Chesapeake colonies was their purpose and goals. The Puritans in New England hoped to be an example for others to follow, based primarily on their religious beliefs, whereas those in the Chesapeake arrived hoping to become wealthy or obtain individual success. Choice A is incorrect, as Maryland had tolerance only for Catholics; this choice is more in line with Pennsylvania. Choice C is incorrect as it defines the New England colonies, not the Chesapeake. Choice D is incorrect because religion was not the central focus in the Chesapeake; crop cultivation was.

2. **The correct answer is C.** The Halfway Covenant allowed new members into Puritan society after their strict rules for church membership led to declining population. Choice A is incorrect because town halls were a result of a call for democracy, not strict religious guidelines. Choice B is incorrect as it relates to labor shortages and passage to America in exchange for land. Choice D is incorrect because it references a political rebellion in the Chesapeake.

3. **The correct answer is A.** Williams and Hutchinson chose to challenge the religious authority of the Puritans and denied their beliefs about God; those who defied that message would not be tolerated. Choice B is incorrect because they did not look for material wealth, and wealth was not the intent of the message. Choices C and D are incorrect because the message was not intended to inspire tolerance but rather to encourage the Puritans to act in a way that would inspire others to follow their example.

SUMMING IT UP

- During the **Pueblo Revolt** (1680), forces rose up against conquerors to lay siege to Santa Fe, New Mexico, killing hundreds of Spanish settlers and driving out the mostly *mestizo* colonial population.

- While aiming to find a Northwest Passage to East and Southeast Asia, French settlers discovered furs as a valuable source of trade that would transform its economy. Fur trappers (*coureurs de bois*) developed a trading relationship with the Native population while bringing wealth back to France.

- Permanent settlements developed trading centers like the St. Lawrence River and eventually the Mississippi River Valley; the French eventually introduced slavery to the region.

- Seeking a Northwest Passage, the Dutch founded New Amsterdam, which later became New York City. Their focus was on developing a burgeoning international trade. King Charles II "gave" the settlement to his younger brother the Duke of York, who split the colony in two (New York and New Jersey).

- The English settled colonies for mostly agricultural purposes and had hostile relationships with Native peoples.

- In 1607, via a corporate charter, the Virginia Company sent off ships, full of men seeking riches without doing work and indentured servants hoping to escape poverty, to **Jamestown**. John Smith instituted a no-work, no-food policy and pushed the colonists away from a gold-only mentality.

- The **Chesapeake** colonial economy was based on tobacco; as white-indentured-servitude waned, reliance on African slaves grew. This led to a greater justification of slavery, upon which the entire socioeconomic structure of the region was based.

- **North Carolina**, like the Chesapeake, was a center of tobacco cultivation; **South Carolina** moved into rice cultivation.

- A **headright** system was implemented—50 acres of land to each immigrant who paid his or her own way OR to any plantation owner who paid for an immigrant's passage—but in the end, enslaved Africans emerged as the main form of labor.

- **Virginia** became England's first **royal colony** (a colony under the authority of the king); the House of Burgesses was established as a representative assembly.

- After Lord Baltimore enacted the **Act of Toleration,** Maryland became a haven for Catholics by granting religious freedom to all Christians.

- Created as a buffer to Spanish (and Catholic) Florida as a form of defense, Georgia became home to many people who had been jailed in England.

- **Puritans** who had religious motivations for leaving the Anglican Church of England primarily founded the New England region. Separatists, who landed in Plymouth and hoped to completely separate from a church of royal control, celebrated the first Thanksgiving.

- Puritans established a community based on homogenous ideals and the religious beliefs of John Calvin, known as predestination (that God had predetermined salvation before birth). **John Winthrop** guided the **Great Migration** of people to the colony.

- The **Halfway Covenant**, created to increase Puritan church membership, allowed those who had not yet experienced a conversion to become partial church members.

- **Roger Williams** and **Anne Hutchinson** questioned Puritan leaders and were banished to the liberal religious refuge of Rhode Island.

- In Massachusetts Bay, literacy was high—creating a culture of education in the colony that would lead to institutions of both elementary and higher education.

- The **Fundamental Orders of Connecticut** (perhaps the first written Constitution) established greater voting rights and a representative government.

- New England profited from shipbuilding, fishing, and trade, and became an important part of the British mercantile system. There were no attempts at conversion and relatively few at forced labor; instead the English focused on the takeover of land owned by the Native peoples.

- The Middle Colonies had an economic mix of agriculture and trade and a varied immigrant population. Pennsylvania became a landing ground for **Quakers** and anyone else not Puritan; diversity rose and tolerant attitudes persisted.

- William Penn's "Holy Experiment" saw guaranteed freedom of worship, unrestricted immigration, and attempts to treat Native populations fairly.

- African slave importation spiked as economies both North and South required labor in different ways.

- Slavery became a feature of the American economy in both the North and the South, for both labor and trade purposes. Excuses were made to justify the practice, including using environmental, biblical, and scientific claims.

  o After **Bacon's Rebellion** and the **Stono Rebellion**, owners became focused on controlling slaves to be sure their power atop the social hierarchy remained.

  o The horrors of the **Middle Passage** led to changes in how slaves were received in the colonies. Eventually the trade was banned in 1808 as part of the Constitutional Compromise.

- **Anglicization** of the colonies was common; examples include Protestant evangelism and British notions of political rights and other governing arrangements.

- The **Great Awakening** was a reaction against the dominant hierarchy of the Church of England and featured fiery preaching by charismatic traveling preachers such as **Jonathan Edwards**.

- The **Enlightenment** was centered on the mundane, not the divine: experimental science, rationality, progress in human affairs, and the Roman model of a republic.

- **Mercantilism** was the belief that the basis of economic power was a favorable balance of trade and control of the currency. Mercantilism was the dominant economic form until Adam Smith's free-trade critique began to actually affect policy formation in the early nineteenth century.

- **Salutary neglect**, Great Britain's lack of governance of the colonies, would soon end as war with the French and Native peoples dominated the colonial landscape.

Period 3 (1754–1800)

Chapter 7

OVERVIEW

- Learning Objectives
- The French and Indian War/End of Salutary Neglect
- The Road to Revolution
- The American Revolution
- The Constitution Debate
- Governing the New Nation
- Key Events in Period 3: A Timeline
- Practice
- Summing It Up

LEARNING OBJECTIVES

Upon completion of this chapter you should be able to...

- Explain how British attempts to better control their American colonies and the determination of said colonists to remain autonomous led to an independence movement and war

- Relate how democratic and republican beliefs led to new forms of government in America

- Describe how movement within North America and competition over land, materials, and trade led to more conflict between people, cultures, and nations

THE FRENCH AND INDIAN WAR/END OF SALUTARY NEGLECT

France and England had been in almost perpetual warfare during the eighteenth century (with a series of four wars), culminating in a battle for the heart of North America. It began in the **Ohio River Valley**, where longstanding friction between British and French colonists finally ignited a real conflict. British colonial populations were exploding and moving west, right into French territories, disrupting long-established French-Indian trading networks. In fact, rich Virginia planters, including George Washington, arranged for the colony to grant a half million acres to the newly formed Ohio Company—a sort of "East India Company" for the fertile Ohio Valley.

The Ohio Company demanded French recognition of their claims, which sparked the war. When the French built forts in the region, Britain sent troops to support the colonial effort against its long-time rival. The French and Indian War, which began in 1754 and became the North American theater of the Seven Years' War once the British declared war on France, lasted until 1763. This war would create the spark that ignited American independence, even if it didn't always seem that way. In 1754, for example, Benjamin Franklin proposed a plan of inter-colonial government to provide a common defense. The **Albany Plan of Union** would ultimately fail (while its political cartoon "join or die" became one of the most famous symbols in American history), showing the colonists' indifference to a unified government.

Britain was able to remove the French from North America at an enormous financial cost. In the complex negotiations that ended the war in 1763, the Spanish ceded Florida to the British and received the vast tract of Louisiana, to the west of the Mississippi River, from the French. To win the war, the British outspent the French to near financial ruin. Thus, almost as soon as the British had won, they began to turn their attention to the colonies in order to lower their massive national debt. The autonomy that colonists had enjoyed while Britain focused on other parts of its empire was about to end, as their period of **salutary neglect** was over. The British would reorganize its colonial polices with more attention toward repayment for a war fought almost entirely for colonial benefit (while noting those same colonists did very little to support the war effort). With more land to protect, Britain would also send more troops to guard the frontier, leading to an issue other than taxation that would anger the colonists.

THE ROAD TO REVOLUTION

To Parliament and the King, the idea of having to pay for protection made plenty of sense, especially for colonies that were created with a mercantile purpose. Britain believed it was well within its rights to ask for repayment and enforcement of policies meant to better English citizens in the colonies. The first attempt to enforce British policies was directed, not at repayment, but toward protection against hostilities from Native populations with the **Proclamation of 1763**. By prohibiting movement past the Appalachian Mountains, Britain had hoped that they could prevent colonists' interaction (and potential death) by forbidding their westward movement. However, colonists were defiant after years of salutary neglect, and they continued to venture past the boundary in hopes of claiming the new territories. Examples like **Pontiac's Rebellion** would prove Britain correct, and they would end up having to send in troops to save the colonists once again.

Following the Proclamation of 1763, Britain would begin to focus on more revenue-based policies in hopes of lowering its debt while reducing smuggling and corruption in the colonies. Under the direction of Prime Minister George Grenville, a series of acts were placed on the colonies with mixed results and reactions. The first was a familiar focus, the **Sugar Act** of 1764. There had been previous attempts to properly enforce collection, such as the Navigation Acts or Molasses Act, but the Sugar Act was the first after the war created for the purpose of revenue. The colonists, as before, largely ignored or found ways around the act, but it was a step in the wrong direction in their view.

Following the Sugar Act would be two more concerning taxes, each for different reasons. In 1765, both the **Quartering Act** and **Stamp Act** were passed, requiring colonists to provide housing and food for soldiers (in the colonists' eyes, this was considered another form of taxation) while also placing a stamp on most printed paper and legal documents. Unlike the Sugar Act, the Stamp Act was a direct tax on goods people used, meaning more people were affected—and angered. The colonial response was swift as they formed the Stamp Act Congress and organized effective boycotts of goods. The Sons and Daughters of Liberty also formed and used harassment and violence in order to thwart the efforts of tax agents. The tactics worked; Parliament was forced to repeal the act because it was not generating the revenue it was created for.

The larger issue created by this new enforcement of policy by Parliament was not actually the tax itself, as most colonists saw themselves as English; thus, they understood the purpose of taxation. Rather, their point of concern was based on a rather "American" idea of having taxation *with* representation. The colonists believed that they were unfairly underrepresented in Parliament, as no member of a colonial assembly actually sat in Parliament. This idea of "actual" or direct representation seemed foreign to members of the British government, as they believed in "virtual" representation, by which all Englishmen were represented in Parliament, regardless of location.

This difference of opinion would become the central issue in the colonists' anger with Britain and drive their reaction to each additional tax. Soon after, the **Declaratory Act** would be passed, declaring Parliament had the right to tax and make laws for the colonies. The **Townshend Acts** would follow, as duties were placed on imports such as tea, glass, and paper, leading to colonial response in the form of John Dickinson's *Letters from a Farmer in Pennsylvania*. Only the tax on tea would remain after the repeal in 1770, and it seemed as though Parliament would leave the colonists alone for a time.

Events in Boston Unite the Colonies

It would take the aftermath of the **Boston Massacre** (known at the time as the "Bloody Massacre") to get this to happen. Five people, including African American Crispus Attucks, were killed in an incident that could be called many things, including murder or propaganda. Paul Revere's engraving depicting a version of the event made its way through the colonies, the Sons and Daughters of Liberty commemorated the event, and committees of correspondence kept a watchful eye on British activities. It was clear, at least within Boston, that tensions would remain high between colonists and Britain, but it wasn't until 1773 that another conflict would arise. Britain would pass the **Tea Act** in hopes of providing financial support (and in colonists' eyes, a monopoly) for the British East India Company. Instead of being overjoyed that the mother country had provided them with a cheaper alternative for tea, colonists boycotted to reinforce their beliefs on taxation. On the night of December 16, 1773, members of the Sons of Liberty (some dressed as Mohawk warriors) boarded three ships in the Boston harbor and threw 342 chests (approximately 90,000 pounds) of tea overboard, causing financial damage and angering the King.

The dumping of tea into Boston Harbor (later referred to as the **Boston Tea Party**) received swift reaction from the British government, and punishment came in the form of the Coercive Acts, which were known in the colonies as the **Intolerable Acts**. Boston faced the most severe punishment. The Boston port was closed (Port Act), stopping all trade to and from the harbor. The royal government received more power at the expense of the Massachusetts legislature (Massachusetts Government Act). Royal officials would now be able to be tried in Great Britain instead of the colonies (Administration of Justice Act), and a new quartering act was expanded to all colonies. These acts (combined with the passage of the pro-Catholic **Quebec Act**) enraged the colonists and brought them closer together than ever before. Unlike the failure of the Albany Plan, these acts unified the otherwise diverse colonies; they sent supplies and supported Massachusetts defiance of the British government. They saw an attack on one colony's rights as a step toward theirs being denied as well—a very enlightened point of view. The ideas of Locke and other Enlightenment thinkers had led colonies to a breaking point with the mother country.

THE AMERICAN REVOLUTION

Not everyone in America was keen on separating from Britain. Those who remained loyal to King George were called Loyalists; the rest called themselves Patriots. Subjected to public humiliation and violence at the hands of the Patriots, many Loyalists eventually fled either back to England or to Canada during or shortly after the war, leaving what property they couldn't transport to the Patriots. **Committees of correspondence** among colonial revolutionary elites that had originally coordinated resistance to British repression took on greater importance as the revolution got under way. Almost all levels of society—from white men to white women to free blacks—contributed, at least rhetorically, to the revolution. An early version of what would come to be called **republican motherhood**, which was an imitation of the Roman view that the role of good republican women was to conceive and then bring up solid republican men, spread to some still-debated extent. As one would expect, external threat muted much, though far from all, internal conflict.

As delegates of the First, and then Second, Continental Congress met to decide the course of action for the colonies, rebellion would eventually become the cry over reconciliation. Ideological statements were many and varied, but the two most notable were Thomas Paine's *Common Sense* and the **Declaration of Independence**. Paine was an Englishman who played a key role in not only the American but also the French Revolution. *Common Sense* was read by nearly everyone who could read in the colonies, and most agreed that the title was apt: given the widening gap of interests, separation seemed obvious. The Declaration, Jefferson's work in the main, famously gave due respect to the opinions of mankind, something one can usually expect from the relatively powerless, by laying out the bill of complaints that had induced the colonist elite to separate. Perhaps most impressive was Jefferson's replacement of John Locke's inalienable rights to life, liberty, and *property* with those of life, liberty, and *the pursuit of happiness.*

At the outset the colonies were undermanned, undersupplied, and underfunded. It seemed as though the idea of independence overshadowed the actions necessary to support it. Without a navy, uniforms, or much training, the early parts of the war saw constant American defeats and discouragement. After three years, there was little hope for victory until a series of victories at Trenton and **Saratoga** brought encouragement as well as French naval support for the American cause. The last major battle of the war would be fought at Yorktown, Virginia, as Washington's army, coupled with the French naval blockade, forced Lord Cornwallis (actually his subordinate) to lay down his sword in defeat. The Treaty of Paris would see Britain formally recognize American independence in 1783, and the issue of governing would now fall squarely on the thirteen colonies.

Organization of a new government had actually begun during the war when the Articles of Confederation were ratified by the Second Continental Congress in 1781. This government would be the work of colonial ideals and fears of centralized government. A one house (unicameral) legislative body would govern without an executive and allow every state (colony) the same number of votes, one. A unanimous vote would be required for amendments, and there would be no ability to tax or regulate commerce, leaving those powers to the individual states. While true to revolutionary ideals, this government would soon show major weaknesses that needed to be addressed after the war. The debate over keeping a government that was true to the revolution—or one that actually worked—would be the central issue of the late 1780s.

THE CONSTITUTION DEBATE

Amazingly enough, some things actually got done under the Articles: rough rules for westward expansion, which was in everyone's general interest and was, in fact, one main reason for the revolution, were agreed to. Perhaps most important, the **Northwest Ordinance** of 1787 ensured that new states would enter the loose union with powers and rights equal to those of the original states. Slavery was prohibited in these new states (in the upper Midwest), and while positive noises about treatment of the Native population were duly inserted, their obvious fate was to be pushed westward. In addition, the Ordinance guaranteed trial by jury, freedom of religion, and freedom from excessive (what would eventually be called "cruel and unusual") punishment.

However, the Articles' flaws soon became very clear. Wars, even successful ones, cost money and increase debt, both private and public. Former soldiers and current farmers, usually one and the same, were crushed with debt and flush with unredeemable notes with which they had been paid. Each state tried to solve these problems on its own, but British markets were more or less barred from American merchants, and no one state really had the wherewithal (or authority) to resolve such issues. Moreover, states were taxing citizens at comparable or even higher rates than the British had. Unrepresented, intolerable taxation was a core reason for the revolution; now people like Daniel Shays of Massachusetts led debt-ridden farmers in a desperate revolt (**Shays' Rebellion** in 1786–1787) against what seemed to them a worse state of affairs than what had led the colonies to declare independence. The rebellion was crushed, but state legislatures responded to mass pressure and achieved by vote what Shays had tried to achieve by force of arms: more democratic control over property rights. The point had been made: if the new country was to survive, states were going to have to give up some sovereignty to the central government.

Creating the Constitution

Many of the colonies' elites (or their representatives), among whom were some of the most brilliant—and wealthiest—men of the age, gathered in Philadelphia in 1787 for what was ostensibly another attempt to amend the Articles but was soon co-opted for a far grander purpose: an entirely new framework of government, the **Constitution**. While George Washington oversaw the secret negotiations, it was James Madison who would receive the title, "Father of the Constitution." (Thomas Jefferson was in Paris during the convention.) The Constitution created a republic (though led by the wealthy elite) with a strong central government, separation of powers, and many checks and balances, and, under severe pressure to secure ratification, the promise of the immediate adoption of a **Bill of Rights** in the form of ten amendments to check the power of the new central government itself. Compromises were made over representation—in what became known as the Great Compromise, the **Virginia Plan** and **New Jersey Plan** were combined to create a two-house legislature: the Senate with equal representation (two Senators per state) and the House of Representatives based on population. The **three-fifths compromise** determined that for purposes of representation, slaves would count as three-fifths of an actual citizen. An executive branch was created, as well as a judicial branch that would include the Supreme Court.

Neither **Federalists** nor **Anti-Federalists** wanted a democracy or a monarchy. But within the agreed-upon framework of an aristocratic republic, each group (forerunners of today's political parties, in fact) fought over the relative strength of the new central government. Federalists like Hamilton and Madison, who wrote most of the famous *Federalist Papers,* desired greater centralization of power, often with a burgeoning, trade-based, urbanized, and even proto-industrialized economy firmly in mind. Anti-federalists like George Mason and Patrick Henry, who, among many others, wrote counter-editorials, feared over-centralization of power at the expense of states' rights, often with the maintenance of a slave-based, rural, agricultural, and non-industrialized economy firmly in mind. Since people with powerful stakes in different economic systems tend to seek to maintain their power, the compromises they reached are rightly regarded as a triumph. The debate over ratification would move to the states (all of which, except Rhode Island, had representatives present in Philadelphia), and eventually all would accept the new plan for government. While the issue of the form of government was now settled, the larger issue of how to govern still lay before the nation.

GOVERNING THE NEW NATION

The first and perhaps most important decision for the United States under the Constitution would be picking the executive, a position that created much controversy in the years prior. There was no doubt George Washington would be chosen, but if he would choose to accept was up for debate. Washington had a deep understanding of his role in the young country, as proven by his choice not to accept the title of King or his majesty and by his decision to voluntarily give up power after his second term. Washington was unanimously elected President with John Adams as his Vice President, and the **Federalist Party** would begin to build the rest of their staff. Alexander Hamilton was brought in as Secretary of the Treasury, Thomas Jefferson as Secretary of State, and George Knox as Secretary of War. While Washington's cabinet would become his greatest challenge in the years following his election, the young nation would face international and internal tests as well.

Debate Within the Cabinet

The seeds of political parties would be planted as division over foreign support, taxes, and the future of the country were debated between Hamilton and Jefferson. Hamilton, like Washington and Adams, was a Federalist. His ideas supported manufacturing, bankers, and merchants (those found mostly in the north and east), while leaning toward a loose view of the Constitution and pro-British policies. Jefferson, however, believed the future of the country should be placed in the hands of an agrarian society, viewing the Constitution with a strict interpretation, pro-French tendencies, and a states' rights focus. These differences would often force Washington to pick sides, and Hamilton was usually first in his ear.

The largest internal debate was based on Hamilton's financial and economic program, best symbolized by his famous work of 1791, *A Report on Manufactures.* In this report, Hamilton revealed himself to be a far-sighted theorist of economic development. Realizing that only well-developed nations with mature national economies and strong militaries find much faith in free trade—that is, only when they are reasonably sure to profit from free trade—Hamilton recommended what we might call the incubation of infant industry, a plan of national economic development for a still-underdeveloped nation-state based on tariffs and subsidies. That is, he envisioned something not altogether different from the mercantilist policies of Britain against which the colonists had revolted.

Jefferson, along with Madison (in ideas that would eventually form the basis for the **Democratic-Republican Party**), firmly disagreed with aspects of Hamilton's plan, including the creation of a national bank as well as implementation of an excise tax. The Bank would be an issue hotly debated for some time in American politics, but the more pressing issue would become the excise tax on whiskey. Farmers on the western frontier attempted to revolt, causing Washington himself to help quell the **Whiskey Rebellion**. Foreign policy also faced challenges based on party lines as the **Jay Treaty** (1794), the purpose of which was to improve the United States' postwar relations with Britain, bitterly divided Americans, while the French Revolution saw Jefferson and Hamilton firmly planted on separate sides. The European warfare caused so much turmoil at all levels of American society that Washington felt moved in his **Farewell Address** of 1796 to decry "faction" (i.e., political parties) and to warn against "entangling alliances" with European or any other powers.

The Adams Administration

Washington's successor, John Adams, served one tumultuous term during which the United States, almost unimaginably, flirted with war against the far more powerful France, of late the savior of the revolution. Adams insisted on publishing the secret French requests for the usual bribes required to place U.S.-French relations on a basis more permanent than that of the Treaty of 1783 that had ended the Revolutionary War, redacting the actual names of the diplomats involved and substituting X, Y, and Z—hence, the **XYZ affair**. Hamilton, always close to the British, was ready for all-out war, as opposed to the desultory naval skirmishes that marked the **Quasi-War**. Adams, however, managed a reconciliation with the French by the end of his term in 1800.

Domestically, two ominous notes were struck under Adams. The first were the **Alien and Sedition Acts** of 1798. These acts essentially tried to outlaw the Federalist's political opposition. The Alien Act and Alien Enemies Acts allowed the government to deport any foreign national deemed a threat; the Sedition Act essentially authorized the shuttering of any publication or even public assembly deemed annoying by the administration. The allied Naturalization Act aimed to undermine support for the Democratic-Republicans among recent immigrants by extending the time to citizenship from five to fourteen years. The Democratic-Republicans' response boded ill for the future. The **Virginia and Kentucky Resolutions**, the former authored by Madison and the latter by Jefferson, urged federal courts to protect First Amendment rights. But Jefferson's Kentucky Resolution went further: it argued, for the first time in post-Constitutional history, for **nullification**: the right of a state to *nullify*, that is, to simply refuse to recognize, a federal law. That is, Jefferson and Madison argued, the states had the authority to judge the constitutionality of federal laws.

As the nineteenth century loomed, so, too, did the election for the next President with the future of the country at the center of the debate. Americans would be determining if the Federalist policies of the past twelve years would continue or agrarian policies of the Democratic-Republicans would move the nation in a new direction.

KEY EVENTS IN PERIOD 3: A TIMELINE

Significant Date	Event
1754-1763	French and Indian War (Seven Years' War)
1763-1766	Pontiac's Rebellion
1765	Stamp Act
1770	Boston (Bloody) Massacre
1773	Boston Tea Party
1774	Intolerable (Coercive) Acts, Meeting of First Continental Congress
1775	Lexington and Concord, Meeting of Second Continental Congress
1776	*Common Sense* published, Adoption of Declaration of Independence, Washington's capture of Trenton
1777	Adoption of Articles of Confederation, American victory at Saratoga
1781	British surrender at Yorktown
1783	Treaty of Paris
1786	Annapolis Convention
1786-1787	Shays' Rebellion
1787	Constitutional Convention, Northwest Ordinance
1787-1788	*The Federalist* papers published
1789	George Washington becomes first U.S. President
1791	Bill of Rights ratified, First Bank of the United States chartered
1793	Washington reelected President
1793-1794	Whiskey Rebellion
1794	Battle of Fallen Timbers, Jay Treaty
1797	Quasi-War with France
1798	XYZ Affair, Alien and Sedition Acts, Kentucky and Virginia Resolutions
1800	Peace with France, Judiciary Act signed, Jefferson elected President

PRACTICE

Directions: Each of the questions or incomplete statements below is followed by four suggested answers or completions. Select the one that is best in each case.

> If men were angels, no government would be necessary. If angels were to govern men, neither external nor internal controls on government would be necessary. In framing a government which is to be administered by men over men, the great difficulty lies in this: You must first enable the government to control the governed; and in the next place, oblige it to control itself.

> —James Madison, *Federalist Paper* 51

1. What was the main intent of Madison's argument as stated above?
    A. An audience with the King in hopes of reaching an olive branch with Britain
    B. Support for overthrow of Parliament and American independence
    C. Acceptance for a decentralized government under state control
    D. To obtain more power for a centralized government after the failure of the Articles of Confederation

2. Which of the following would be an example of a control that Madison would support giving to the new government?
    A. State-controlled militia
    B. One vote per state
    C. Veto power from an executive
    D. Remove the ability of a central government to tax

3. What would be an argument provided by the opposition to Madison's views?
    A. The revolution was fought to guard against these ideas.
    B. A bill of rights was not necessary to protect against these types of abuses.
    C. The Constitution provided guards against the powers Madison feared.
    D. Americans had an effective government under the Articles of Confederation.

Answer Key and Explanations

1. D	2. C	3. A

1. **The correct answer is D.** Madison, along with Hamilton and Jay, wrote the *Federalist Papers* in an attempt to gain support for ratification of the U.S. Constitution. This document would replace the Articles of Confederation with a stronger and more centralized government that had an executive. Answers A and B are incorrect because the excerpt was written years after the conflict with the British and was focused on an American government. Answer C is incorrect because Madison is arguing for the opposite, a centralized government to fix the problems created by a decentralized government.

2. **The correct answer is C.** Madison believed a system of checks and balances among the three branches (Executive, Legislative, and Judicial) would help to keep a centralized government from abusing its power over the people. Answers A, B, and D are incorrect because they were all powers granted by the failing Articles of Confederation and led to an ineffective government. These powers did not protect the people or the government from an abuse of power but instead created a government that had difficulty providing effective results for its people.

3. **The correct answer is A.** Anti-Federalists, who disagreed with Madison and other Federalists, believed the spirit of the revolution was being lost in the new Constitution. The abusive tyranny that ruled under the King of Great Britain would return under this new government that had a stronger central government than in the Articles. Answer B is incorrect as opponents argued a bill of rights was necessary to protect against a centralized government. Answer C is incorrect as it would be in support of Madison's argument. Answer D is incorrect because most everyone agreed the Articles were not effective; the argument was over how to fix them.

SUMMING IT UP

- The Ohio Company demand that France recognize its land claims sparked the **French and Indian War (1754-1763)** between French and English colonists. This war for the heart of North America was also known as the Seven Years' War and would ultimately lead to American independence. Britain won the war by outspending France to near financial ruin.

- The **Albany Plan of Union (1754)** was Benjamin Franklin's scheme to establish a government for the thirteen colonies, and its failure revealed the colonists' indifference to a unified government.

- Following the French and Indian War, Britain focused on receiving repayment through taxation for a war fought mostly for colonial benefit, while further angering colonists by sending more troops to guard the frontier.

- **The Proclamation of 1763** was enacted to protect against Native American hostilities and prevent interaction among colonies by prohibiting movement past the Appalachian Mountains.

- **Pontiac's Rebellion (1763)** was a Native American attack that seemingly justified the Proclamation of 1763 and caused the British to send more troops to rescue colonists.

- The taxation on molasses imposed by **the Sugar Act (1764)** angered colonists, but they mostly ignored the act or found ways around paying the taxes it required.

- The **Quartering Act and Stamp Act (1765)** required colonists to provide housing and food for British soldiers while also placing a stamp on most printed paper and legal documents. Both acts were regarded as another form of taxation among colonists, who subsequently staged a boycott of goods and attacked tax agents, forcing Parliament to repeal the Stamp Act.

- Colonists fought against new taxes because they demanded representation, but the British government believed in "virtual representation," embodied by the **Declaratory Act (1766)**, which declared Parliament had the right to tax and make laws for the colonies.

- The **Townshend Acts (1767)**, which taxed tea, glass, and paper, were mostly repealed in 1770 following the Boston Massacre, leaving only the tea tax in place.

- The **Tea Act (1773)**, which allowed the British East Tea Company a monopoly on the sale of tea in the colonies, led to a boycott of tea that involved an act of protest in which a group of colonists dressed as Native Americans dumped chests of tea into Boston harbor, causing financial damage and angering the King.

- The **Coercive Acts (1774)**, known by colonists as the Intolerable Acts, were a form of punishment for the Boston Harbor protest in which Boston Port was closed, stopping all trade to and from the harbor.

- The series of acts imposed by the British government in 1774 enraged colonists, brought them closer together, and inspired them to send supplies and support to Boston in defiance of the British government.

- Thomas Paine's influential *Common Sense* (1775) declared that given the widening gap of interests, independence from Britain seemed obvious.

- The **Declaration of Independence (1776)** gave due respect to the opinions of humankind by laying out the bill of complaints that had induced the colonists to separate. In the document, Thomas Jefferson emphasized the inalienable rights to life, liberty, and the pursuit of happiness.

- After three years of revolution, the colonies began to achieve success against Britain with victories at **Trenton and Saratoga (1776-1777)**, which brought French naval support for the American cause. The last major battle of the war was fought at Yorktown (1781).

- The **Treaty of Paris (1783)** saw Britain formally recognize American independence.

- According to the **Second Continental Congress (1781)**, the new government would be a one-house legislative body that would govern without an executive and allow every state one vote. A unanimous vote would be required for amendments, and there would be no ability to tax or regulate commerce, leaving those powers to the individual states.

- The **Northwest Ordinance (1787)** ensured that new states would enter the union with powers and rights equal to those of the original states, slavery was prohibited in these new states, Native Americans were to be pushed westward, and Americans were guaranteed trial by jury, freedom of religion, and freedom from excessive punishment.

- **Shays' Rebellion (1786–1787)** was a revolt against the Articles of Confederation. The revolution was crushed, but state legislatures began responding to such pressure and voted for more democratic control over property rights.

- The **U.S. Constitution (1787)** created a republic with a strong central government, separation of powers, many checks and balances, a Bill of Rights in the form of ten amendments to check the power of the new central government itself, and a legislative branch, an executive branch, and a judicial branch that would include the Supreme Court.

- **Federalists** desired greater centralization of power, while **Anti-Federalists** feared over-centralization of power at the expense of states' rights.

- **George Washington** was unanimously elected President in 1789 with John Adams as his Vice President.

- The **Federalist Party** built the rest of their staff with Alexander Hamilton as Secretary of the Treasury, Thomas Jefferson as Secretary of State, and George Knox as Secretary of War.

- The debate between Alexander Hamilton and Thomas Jefferson over division of foreign support, taxes, and the future of the country planted the seeds of **political parties**.

- Hamilton's financial and economic program, which included the creation of a **national bank** and an **excise tax on whiskey**, prompted intense disagreement from Thomas Jefferson and James Madison and the quickly quelled Whiskey Rebellion.

- **John Adams** succeeded George Washington as president in 1797, serving one tumultuous term during which the United States flirted with war against France as Adams published secret French requests for bribes in a move known as the XYZ Affair. Adams managed a reconciliation with France by the end of his term in 1800.

- The **Alien and Sedition Acts (1798)** attempted to outlaw the Federalist's political opposition by allowing the government to deport any foreign national deemed a threat and essentially authorizing the shuttering of any publication or public assembly deemed annoying by the administration.

- The **Virginia and Kentucky Resolutions of 1798 and 1799** urged federal courts to protect First Amendment rights and argued for the right of a state to refuse to recognize a federal law.

Period 4 (1800–1848)

Chapter 8

OVERVIEW

- Learning Objectives
- Defining Politics in the First Half of the Nineteenth Century
- The Marshall Court
- Cultural Changes and Challenges
- The Market Revolution and Regional Specialization
- Key Events in Period 4: A Timeline
- Practice
- Summing It Up

LEARNING OBJECTIVES

Upon completion of this chapter you should be able to...

- Explain how the United States developed a mass democracy and new American culture

- Describe how developments in technology, agriculture, and commerce led to major changes in numerous aspects of America

- Recognize how foreign policy and government initiatives were influenced by United States interests in foreign trade, territorial expansion, and a focus on the Western Hemisphere

DEFINING POLITICS IN THE FIRST HALF OF THE NINETEENTH CENTURY

Thomas Jefferson's election in 1800 would come to be known as the Revolution of 1800 because it was the first peaceful transition of power between political parties (while also shifting the country from Federalist policies to an agrarian emphasis). The new President would find it was easier to criticize the office than run it as he found himself in situations that would test his resolve on certain issues.

Jefferson had believed Federalists loosely interpreted the Constitution instead of strictly adhering to the document. However, when the opportunity arose to purchase Louisiana from France and double the size of the country (and the farmland for his yeoman farmers), he violated his beliefs on interpretation to fulfill his greater vision of an Empire of Liberty.

He would send explorers Lewis and Clark out to map the territory while also taking note of scientific discoveries. Jefferson also was forced to utilize a loose view of the Constitution in attempting to resist the impressment policies of the French and British during their ongoing war in Europe.

The Embargo of 1807 stopped all exports of goods in an attempt to remain neutral during the conflict by pressuring both foreign powers' economies. Unfortunately, the act did more to damage New England's economy than either nation's economy and after further attempts, such as the Nonintercourse Act and Macon's Bill #2, did nothing to stop the forced enlistment of Americans, warhawks persuaded Congress to go to war with Great Britain in 1812.

The War of 1812 would see the White House burned, the end of Tecumseh's attempts to unite his peoples, and the death of the Federalist Party at the Hartford Convention (thanks in part to Andrew Jackson's decisive victory at New Orleans). The war would result in national pride and the creation of American culture (such as Francis Scott Key's poem that would become the national anthem), as well as a sense of confidence from a second defeat of the British.

This confidence would lead to a declaration of policy regarding the Western Hemisphere written by John Quincy Adams and delivered by President Monroe. The Monroe Doctrine stated that the United States would stay out of the Eastern Hemisphere in return for European powers not interfering in the affairs of the Western Hemisphere. The nation was still too young and weak to actually enforce the doctrine, but it was a symbol of the more aggressive and nationalistic view that America had taken following the war. During this same period, the United States would negotiate a disarmament pact with the British (Rush-Bagot) and purchase Florida from the Spanish as part of the Adams-Onis Treaty. This time would come to be known as the "Era of Good Feelings" because there was little outward unrest and political control by one party, the Democratic Republicans. Even a debate over the extension of slavery into the Louisiana Territory was calmed by Henry Clay's Missouri Compromise. This decision that balanced the number of slave and free states while creating a line that determined where slavery could expand (slavery prohibited above 36°30') would be held sacred for almost thirty years after it was signed.

A major shift in politics would come in the form of new political parties and the rise of the "common man." When Andrew Jackson lost the election of 1824 to John Quincy Adams because of what was deemed a "corrupt bargain," it created a turning point in the political future of the country. Henry Clay agreed to support Adams for President in exchange for support of his American System and in the process made a political enemy in Jackson. When "Old Hickory" Jackson won the election of 1828, it signaled a shift in voting as the removal of property qualifications allowed more, common white men to go to the polls. These men saw Jackson as their hero, and he supported their views by expanding land opportunities (through Indian Removal), attacking northeastern interests (vetoing the charter of the Second National Bank during his all-out political war with Nicholas Biddle and Henry Clay in the 1836 election), and rewarding them with government positions as part of his patronage (spoils) system.

Jackson's rejection of the doctrine of nullification when John C. Calhoun and South Carolina tried to reject a tariff in 1828 (known as the Tariff of Abominations), along with his veto of the bank, would earn him another dubious nickname, "King Andrew." The Whig Party would form almost entirely in an effort to counter all of Jackson's beliefs, and the second party system was born.

The underlying political issue of the period was slavery, however, even if most politicians refused to address the issue, as exemplified by the 1836 gag rule. But the desire of many Americans, especially in the South, to obtain more land would lead to conflicts over territories such as Oregon and Texas (not to mention the effects the discovery of gold would have on California in the late 1840s).

This desire would also negatively affect the Native peoples, as the Indian Removal Act (1830) during Andrew Jackson's presidency forced them further west.

In 1835 the Senate ratified the Treaty of New Echota, which provided the legal basis for the forcible removal of the Cherokee Nation from Georgia. Signed by Jackson, the treaty gave the Cherokee until May of 1838 to leave. In spite of numerous protests against the treaty, the Cherokee were rounded up and driven west under armed guard to Oklahoma on what has become known as "The Trail of Tears." Thousands of Cherokee, including women and children, died of disease and starvation along the way.

Ultimately, Manifest Destiny would push the country into a debate that would eventually lead to political, economic, and physical war by mid-century.

THE MARSHALL COURT

As the Revolution of 1800 brought Democratic Republicans into power, there was only one branch of the federal government that remained in Federalist control: the judiciary. John Marshall, Chief Justice of the Supreme Court, would have a lasting impact on establishing the judicial branch as the final determination on the laws created in the United States. In 1803, Marshall ruled that a law created by Congress was unconstitutional in *Marbury v. Madison*, establishing judicial review and setting a precedent for checks and balances for years to come. Marshall would continue to rule in favor of a strong, central government in most of his cases, and strengthening the power of the court in the process. Future decisions, such as *Fletcher v. Peck* (ruling a state law unconstitutional), *McCulloch v. Maryland* (declaring the National Bank constitutional), and *Gibbons v. Ogden* (Congress only had the power to regulate interstate trade), would all show Marshall did not favor states' rights.

In *Cherokee Nation v. Georgia* (1831), Marshall found in favor of the Cherokee, ruling that the state of Georgia could not deprive them of their rights within its boundaries. A year later, in *Worcester v. Georgia*, Marshall found that the right to regulate Indian land was limited to the federal government, not the states. Both rulings were largely ignored as President Andrew Jackson refused to recognize them, choosing instead to enforce the Indian Removal Act. Marshall served as Chief Justice until his death in 1835. He was succeeded by Roger Taney (after a highly controversial nomination) in March 1836.

CULTURAL CHANGES AND CHALLENGES

The first third of the nineteenth century saw the rise of all kinds of voluntary citizen organizations, what we'd now call "civil society." As much as (and perhaps more than) increasing democracy in the formal political system, civil society, often leavened by religious movements, began somewhat modifying what had been consciously designed to be an aristocratic republic. Many of these associations were of a religious or pietistic bent or were originated or inspired by religion in some fashion, such as the rise of temperance and other evidences of "the reforming impulse," as some historians have

NOTE

The 1838 Trail of Tears relocation involving the Cherokee of Georgia was just one of many forced removals of several tribes, beginning in 1831 (Chocktaw) and continuing in 1832 (Seminole), 1836 (Creeks), and 1837 (Chickasaw). By 1840, tens of thousands of Native Americans had been forced to walk the "Trail of Tears," a term which, to some historians, not only refers to the literal route to the west walked by the Native Americans but also has come to encompass the history of the Native Americans' forced relocation from the south to the Indian Territory.

termed it. Many such associations were led by or mostly composed of people in the upper sections of an increasingly unequal class system.

Many were paternalistic. Some even took the form of utopian socialist communes, such as Robert Owen's New Harmony, Indiana, or the Oneida Community in New York. Transcendentalists like Thoreau and Emerson preached another form of moral self-reliance—hardly atheist, far from entirely secular, but distinct from evangelical Christianity in theory, practice, and cultural form. Both movements arose at least in part in response to the market revolution: both aimed to rehumanize, in their different ways, individual lives seen as increasingly instrumental in the hands of the market. Each was a reminder that human beingswere not means to an end; they were seen as living, free, moral agents, potentially improvable, as was the society they created. People, they believed, were *not* simply another in the increasing set of interchangeable parts that fueled the market and industrial revolutions then radically reshaping society.

Also consequential in the mid- to latter part of the century were the movements for women's rights and the abolition of slavery. As the market revolution increasingly shifted economic production out of the home and into the factory, the economic role of women contracted. To be sure, some women became "factory girls," but most who could afford to remained at home, far from the economic action. Still unable to vote and now shorn of what economic power they'd had, they were even more relegated to the background. Republican motherhood, which, at least in theory, made women active participants in a new revolutionary society, withered away, leaving the far more passive role of "harbor-masters," shielding men from the burgeoning market-storm. This cult of domesticity limited women's power to the home, leaving the rest to the men they were to nurture. Yet not all women were limited to domestic servitude.

The poor had no choice but to work, whether in factories or as part of the putting-out system, by which women could import work to be done at home, while not leaving their domestic domain. The cult of domesticity became, therefore, a measure of class, of social status, and a kind of goal of full femininity, since to work, especially outside the home, was defeminized. A different view emerged and is best symbolized by the Seneca Falls Convention of 1848. Often barred by gender from participating in the abolitionist movement, women such as Elizabeth Cady Stanton and Lucretia Mott gathered in upstate New York to author a Declaration of Sentiments modeled on the Declaration of Independence. Suffrage (i.e., the right to vote) was paramount, but not the only goal: liberation in the social and economic spheres was expected to follow.

During the antebellum period, many reforms took place that changed the course of American society. One of the greatest reforms was known as the Second Great Awakening, a series of religious revivals that attempted to counter rationalism and Puritan teachings of the previous decades. Much like the politics of the time, religion had become diverse and open to new groups and ideas. The movement itself saw many forms with a focus on the democratization of American society, and groups such as the Baptists, Methodists, and Mormons were formed. Perhaps the greatest impact of the Second Great Awakening, however, would be its influence on abolition and the war on slavery. With a renewed focus on religion, many in the North began to speak out against the sins of slavery and use a moral argument for ending the practice.

Slavery had become synonymous with wealth in the South following the introduction of Eli Whitney's cotton gin in 1793. Although most people in the South did not actually own slaves, a degree of wealth and power was measured in land and slaves. Because there was a strict racial hierarchy found both in the North and South as well as an economic advantage to the practice, many people turned a blind eye to the practice for much of the early nineteenth century. However, as the North began to industrialize and manufacturing increased, many in the North no longer saw the economic necessity for slavery. Also, with the aforementioned Second Great Awakening putting a greater emphasis on religion and democracy, abolitionists began to raise the question that had been ignored by the United States Constitution and politicians. Men like John C. Calhoun spoke out about the positives of slavery and it being a "*necessary evil.*" The North had been reaping the benefits of cotton production, and the Union was economically strong because of it (as Southerners believed was validated by the Panic of 1857). There had been an unspoken agreement that slavery benefited both regions of the country for some time, and the South was prepared to defend its labor conditions.

Slave owners started to shift their defense of slavery from being just economically beneficial to using religion, race, and standard of living as support for their "*peculiar institution.*" Slave owners used scripture from the Bible to justify both slavery and racism against blacks. They also looked to "science" to prove that Africans were better suited for slavery and even argued conditions were better for slaves than those working in northern factories. Abolitionists began to speak out more mid-century and two camps developed: gradual abolitionists and immediate abolitionists. Gradual abolitionists believed that slavery should be ended over time and allowed to die its own death, whereas immediate abolitionists wanted an abrupt end to slavery.

All abolitionists began to see slavery as a sin and many took to new media, such as William Lloyd Garrison. Garrison, a white abolitionist, began publishing an antislavery newspaper entitled *The Liberator*. The paper called for immediate, and sometimes radical, abolition of slavery and would remain in publication for over thirty years. Another voice in the movement came from former slave, Frederick Douglass, who published his antislavery newspaper *The North Star*. Perhaps the biggest attack on slavery would come from an unlikely place, a woman living in Connecticut. Harriet Beecher Stowe would write a fictional account of a black slave that would become the second-best-selling book of the century, just behind the Bible. The book, **Uncle Tom's Cabin**, created an even deeper divide between North and South while becoming a major factor in the growing abolitionist movement. The book appalled Southerners, seeing it as highly inaccurate and using falsities to further the abolitionist cause. Finally, an economic attack on the institution of slavery would be seen in Hinton Rowan Helper's book, *The Impending Crisis of the South*. This was a different approach to fighting slavery, using the economy and industrialization as reasons why slavery was hurting the South.

Slaves looking to escape bondage would find allies in members of the Underground Railroad, a network of safe houses and secret passages that helped them find their way to the North or even Canada. This was extremely dangerous, and abolitionists and slaves risked their lives by participating. However, the work of people like Harriet Tubman and others was vital to securing freedom for many slaves. Overall, the abolitionist movement took many forms, as there was no "right" way to defeat slavery. Back-to-Africa movements, political parties, and violence were all attempts to end the Southern practice, but with no success. The thirst for more land consumed slave owners looking for more ways to profit from cotton, and the United States government was happy to oblige as Manifest Destiny dominated the country's agenda for the foreseeable future.

THE MARKET REVOLUTION AND REGIONAL SPECIALIZATION

By 1840, the United States looked very different depending on where you lived. In the South you would still find plantations and farmland reaching across the region, but land was running out, as planting cotton was demanding on the soil. The North had begun transitioning into an industrial society, with factories replacing cottage industries and the transportation revolution steadily evolving. A new, national economy was formed, linking regions and people together. The federal government financed a national road in an attempt to better help the transportation movement west; the Erie Canal would help the Midwest to reach the New York harbor, and by mid-century a new means of transportation would revolutionize travel by utilizing components of steamboat travel: railroads. The railroad would become a key component connecting the North to the West, allowing grains and foods to travel back and forth. This relationship would expand the market economy of the United States as well as create more interdependence between the regions.

In Northern factories, white laborers were competing for jobs with new immigrants arriving from Europe. Between 1820 and 1860 immigrants left Europe, with most attempting to escape famine (Irish) or political unrest (Germans). The Irish had faced starvation due to the loss of potato crops and looked to northeastern port cities. These immigrants, who supported Democrats, worked low-paying, unskilled jobs and practiced Catholicism, leading to an increase in nativism (anti-foreign beliefs). This opposition would manifest itself in the creation of the Know-Nothing Party, as beliefs about religion, politics, and even temperance developed into a resistance to European immigrants. Urbanization was taking over this part of the country, and the industrial growth led to a more diversified economy that would become a large strength for the Union during the Civil War.

The plantation system established in the South had little room for railroads or urban development; King Cotton had taken over both the South and the United States economy, and the region's hunger for more land to grow cotton overshadowed its desire to industrialize. Because of the massive amount of land required for plantation life, the South had a smaller work force but a larger role in the economy. By the start of the Civil War, the cotton industry would account for almost 57 percent of United States exports, so many in the region were eager for new land. Most people living in the region were not plantation owners, however, and worked as small farmers or even subsistence farmers. The South did benefit from the new technology created by industrialization, including the ability to send much of its cotton to Northern factories while also taking advantage of new farming tools.

The United States population had more than doubled during the early half of the nineteenth century, and it would double again leading into the 1850s. Birthrates were high during this period, but immigration from European countries was also a contributing factor. With the addition of new technology, manufacturing, transportation, and commercial agriculture, the United States saw people living longer and enjoying more opportunities. Not only did wages increase, so, too, did the need for labor, leading to a higher standard of living and national economy. The North continued to hold a population advantage due to compact living arrangements created by the new industrial centers.

Factory life was more appealing to immigrants coming to America, if only because it did not require owning land, helping to increase the number of people living in the northeast. The South was fairly spread out, with almost 9 million of the nation's 23 million people living on small farms and larger plantations. Of those people, more than one-third were enslaved Africans who were forced into bondage.

Another key difference between the regions would be their views on tariffs, as those in the North saw high tariffs as a way to protect American industries at the cost of Southern profits. This issue would be raised time and again (most famously in the battle over the Tariff of 1828, otherwise known as the Tariff of Abominations), adding to the tensions that would lead to the Civil War. Tariffs were a key component (along with the National Bank and internal improvements) of Henry Clay's American System, which attempted to promote a national economy and industry. The goal was to connect the country while promoting American products and businesses for advancing growth. This plan would have detractors (specifically President Jackson and his followers, and those in the South who opposed tariffs).

KEY EVENTS IN PERIOD 4: A TIMELINE

Significant Date	Event
1800	Thomas Jefferson elected President
1803	Louisiana Purchase, *Marbury v. Madison*
1804-1806	Lewis and Clark Expedition
1807	Embargo Act
1812-1815	War of 1812
1817	Rush-Bagot Treaty, Erie Canal approved
1819	Adams-Onis Treaty, Financial Panic, *McCulloch v. Maryland*
1820	Missouri Compromise
1823	Monroe Doctrine
1825	Erie Canal
1828	Tariff of Abominations, Andrew Jackson elected President
1830	Congress passes Indian Removal Act
1831	*The Liberator* published, Nat Turner's Rebellion
1832	Veto of the Second Bank of the United States
1833	Compromise Tariff
1836	Texas declares Independence, Gag Rule passed in Congress
1837	Financial Panic
1831-1850	Trail of Tears
1848	Seneca Falls Convention

PRACTICE

Directions: Each of the questions or incomplete statements below is followed by four suggested answers or completions. Select the one that is best in each case.

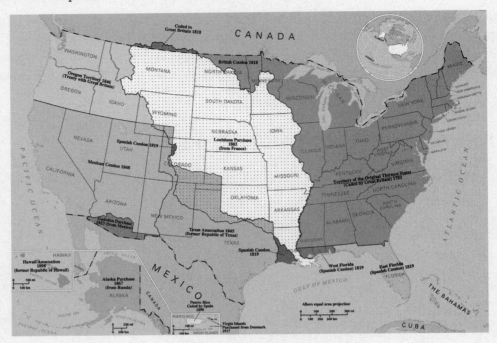

United States Expansion

[Source: *https://en.wikipedia.org/wiki/Louisiana_Purchase#/media/File:UnitedStatesExpansion.png*]

1. Which of the following directly resulted from the purchase of the Louisiana territory?

   A. War broke out between Americans and Mexicans over disputed territory.

   B. Native Americans were forced off their land in the region and into reservations as part of the Trail of Tears.

   C. The territory dispute over the Mississippi River was finally resolved with the Spanish.

   D. Lewis and Clark were sent to explore and map the new territory.

2. How did Jefferson's decision to purchase the territory reflect his greater vision for America?

   A. Jefferson believed in large government that grew the power of the country.

   B. Jefferson believed the land was full of rich farmland for his society of yeoman farmers to benefit.

   C. The removal of the French from North America had been a goal of Jefferson since before his time as President.

   D. Loose construction of the Constitution was a staple of Democratic Republican ideals.

3. What was the political dispute that immediately plagued the purchase?

   A. Expansion of slavery

   B. Interpretation of the Constitution

   C. National defense

   D. Violation of Washington's Farewell Address

Answer Key and Explanations

1. D	2. B	3. B

1. **The correct answer is D.** Jefferson commissioned men like Lewis and Clark to map the territory to find its immediate borders, threats, and address Native relations (scientific discoveries were also made). Choice A is incorrect as war did not break out with Mexico until forty years after the purchase and was not directly caused by the purchase. Choice B is incorrect as the forced migration of Native Americans resulting in the Trail of Tears occurred almost thirty years after the purchase and was not directly caused by the purchase. Choice C is incorrect as the disputes were not solved; they were instead increased and would result in the Adams-Onis Treaty in 1819.

2. **The correct answer is B.** Jefferson believed the future of the country should be tied to an agrarian society because of its ties to the land and the importance of farming to the country. Choice A is incorrect as Jefferson believed the exact opposite about government. Choice C is incorrect because Jefferson had supported the French prior to the war even though removing any foreign threat, not specifically the French, benefited the country. Choice D is incorrect because Democratic-Republicans supported strict interpretation of the Constitution, even if they violated that principle while in office.

3. **The correct answer is B.** The debates over the purchase between parties (and even inside of his own party) centered on Jefferson's liberal interpretation of the Constitution, which did not specifically allow him to purchase the territory; the purchase also violated Jefferson's well-known beliefs on national debt. Choice A is incorrect because even though slavery could expand as a result of the purchase, slavery wasn't the issue of these debates—Jefferson's interpretation of the Constitution was. Choice C is incorrect as the removal of a foreign power from North America did not cause debate. Choice D is incorrect because the United States did not enter into an entangling alliance as part of the purchase. (In his Farewell Address, Washington warned against joining any entangling alliances.)

SUMMING IT UP

- Thomas Jefferson's election in 1800 was known as the **Revolution of 1800** because it was the first peaceful transition of power between political parties.

- In 1803, President Jefferson doubled the size of the United States by arranging the **Louisiana Purchase** from France. He also sent explorers **Lewis and Clark** to map the territory and take note of scientific discoveries.

- The **Embargo of 1807** stopped all exports of goods in an attempt to remain neutral during the conflict between the French and the British by pressuring both foreign powers' economies.

- After the Nonintercourse Act and Macon's Bill #2 did nothing to stop the forced enlistment of Americans, Congress decided to go to war with Great Britain in 1812, and the **War of 1812** would see the White House burned, the end of Tecumseh's attempts to unite Native peoples, the death of the Federalist Party, a rise in national pride, and the creation of American culture.

- The United States negotiated a disarmament pact with the British called the **Rush-Bagot Treaty** (1817) and purchased Florida from the Spanish as part of the Adams-Onis Treaty (1819) during a period known as the "Era of Good Feelings."

- A debate over the extension of slavery into the Louisiana Territory was calmed by Henry Clay's **Missouri Compromise** (1820), which balanced the number of slave and free states while creating a line that determined where slavery could expand.

- When Andrew Jackson, nicknamed Old Hickory, lost the election of 1824 to John Quincy Adams, it created a turning point in the political future of the country as Henry Clay agreed to support Adams for President in exchange for support of his **American System**.

- The **Monroe Doctrine** (1823) stated that the United States would stay out of the Eastern Hemisphere in return for European powers not interfering in the affairs of the Western Hemisphere. Although the nation could not enforce the doctrine, it still served as a symbol of the more aggressive and nationalistic view that American had taken following the war.

- In 1828, the removal of property qualifications allowed more voting by **common men,** who saw Andrew Jackson as their hero because he expanded land opportunities, attacked northeastern interests, and rewarded them with government positions as part of his patronage system.

- President Jackson rejected the doctrine of nullification when John C. Calhoun and South Carolina tried to reject the **Tariff of Abominations** in 1828 and vetoed the Second National Bank.

- The **Whig Party** formed to counter all of President Jackson's beliefs and the second party system was born.

- The desire of many Americans, especially in the South, to obtain more land would lead to conflicts over territories such as Oregon and Texas, and **Manifest Destiny** would push the country into a debate that would eventually lead to political, economic, and physical war by mid-century.

- As the Revolution of 1800 brought Democratic Republicans into power, only the judiciary branch of the federal government remained in Federalist control, and in *Marbury v. Madison* (1803), Chief Justice of the Supreme Court John Marshall ruled that a law created by Congress was unconstitutional, establishing judicial review and setting a precedent for checks and balances for years to come.

- Marshall showed that he did not favor states' rights in such cases as *Fletcher v. Peck* (ruling a state law unconstitutional), *McCulloch v. Maryland* (declaring the National Bank constitutional), and *Gibbons v. Ogden* (Congress only had the power to regulate interstate trade).

- In *Cherokee Nation v. Georgia* (1831), Marshall found in favor of the Cherokee, ruling that the state of Georgia could not deprive them of their rights within its boundaries, and in *Worcester v. Georgia* (1832), he found that the right to regulate Native American land was reserved to the federal government.

- President Jackson refused to enforce Marshall's decisions in *Cherokee Nation v. Georgia* and *Worcester v. Georgia*, forcing thousands of Cherokees to walk under armed guard to Oklahoma and die on what became known as **"The Trail of Tears."**

- The first third of the nineteenth century saw the rise of utopian socialist communes, such as Robert Owen's **New Harmony** in Indiana, and the **Oneida Community** in New York.

- In response to the market revolution, **Transcendentalists** arose, preaching a form of moral self-reliance that was distinct from evangelical Christianity in theory, practice, and cultural form; like the socialists, the transcendentalists believed that human beings are living, free, moral agents, and potentially improvable, as is the society they created and not merely parts that fuel the market and industrial revolutions.

- A measure of class and social status, the **cult of domesticity,** limited women's power to the home, where they could work according to the putting-out system.

- Women such as Elizabeth Cady Stanton and Lucretia Mott gathered in upstate New York to author a **Declaration of Sentiments** intent on attaining suffrage and liberation at the Seneca Falls Convention of 1848.

- The **Second Great Awakening** was a series of religious revivals that attempted to counter rationalism and Puritan teachings of the previous decades, focused on the democratization of American society, championed the moral argument against slavery, and saw formation of the Baptists, Methodists, and Mormons.

- Despite a rise in the abolitionist movement, slavery continued as **John C. Calhoun** described it as a *"necessary evil"* and the North benefited from cotton production.

- To justify slavery, slave owners used biblical scripture, looked to "science" to prove that Africans were better suited for slavery, and argued conditions were better for slaves than those working in northern factories.

- Gradual **abolitionists** believed that slavery should be ended over time and allowed to die its own death, whereas immediate abolitionists wanted an abrupt end to slavery.

- The printed word played an important part in the abolitionist movement:
  - **William Lloyd Garrison** published an antislavery newspaper entitled *The Liberator*, which called for immediate, and sometimes radical, abolition of slavery.
  - Former slave **Frederick Douglass** published an antislavery newspaper called *The North Star*.
  - *Uncle Tom's Cabin* (1852), Harriet Beecher Stowe's fictional account of a black slave, became the second-best-selling book of the century and, by galvanizing the growing abolitionist movement, created an even deeper divide between North and South.
- By 1840, the North began transitioning into an **industrial society** with factories replacing cottage industries and the transportation revolution evolving with use of railroads and the Erie Canal.
- Between 1820 and 1860, many immigrants left Europe to work low-paying and unskilled jobs in the United States, which led to an increase in nativism and led to the creation of the **Know-Nothing Party**.
- By the start of the Civil War, the **cotton industry** was responsible for almost 57 percent of United States exports, even though the North held a population advantage due to compact living arrangements created by the new industrial centers.
- Tariffs were a key component of Henry Clay's **American System**, which attempted to promote a national economy and industry. Northerners saw high tariffs as a way to protect American industries at the cost of Southern profits—a belief that contributed to the tension that would lead to the Civil War.

Period 5 (1844–1877)

OVERVIEW

- Learning Objectives
- Westward Expansion of Free and Slave Territory
- The Political Situation in 1860
- The Civil War
- Reconstruction Plans
- The Southern Response
- The End of Reconstruction
- Key Events in Period 5: A Timeline
- Practice
- Summing It Up

LEARNING OBJECTIVES

Upon completion of this chapter you should be able to…

- Recognize how the United States desire for westward expansion led to more internal conflicts and connections with the world

- Understand how expansion and regional division led to conflicts that would result in war

- Illustrate how Reconstruction in the South created more questions and conflicts within the nation after the Civil War

WESTWARD EXPANSION OF FREE AND SLAVE TERRITORY

The idea of Manifest Destiny and western fever had taken over much of America by mid-century, with James K. Polk's election in 1844 its best example. When the dark-horse candidate was elected on a platform of expansion, thanks primarily to voters from the South and West, America began work on Manifest Destiny. After a brief spat with Great Britain over Oregon, Polk turned his attention to California.

First Polk attempted to buy the land from the Mexican government, while also negotiating the Texas border. However, he was turned away. In response he sent General Zachary Taylor and his army to the Rio Grande border. Tensions were high and fighting broke out, leaving 11 Americans dead. This event led Polk to declare war on Mexico, with a large majority in Congress approving the measure (although there were doubters, specifically Whig Party members such as a young Abraham Lincoln, who declared the decision to go to war was based on "spot resolutions"). Though the Mexican-American War was relatively short, its effects had great consequence in the United States, specifically regarding slavery.

Slavery and the Missouri Compromise

David Wilmot, a Pennsylvania Congressman, proposed that all territories acquired as part of the **Treaty of Guadalupe Hidalgo** (1848) not permit slavery. The measure was defeated in the Senate and what to do with the territory would be settled by the **Compromise of 1850**. Once again, Henry Clay came to the rescue, as the line created by the **Missouri Compromise** (1820) would cut directly through California, which wished to remain a free state. Clay's proposal included the following:

- Admit California as a free state (adding to the North's political power)
- Allow slavery to be decided by popular sovereignty in both Utah and New Mexico
- Settle the Texas border dispute by paying the Mexican government $10 million
- Ban the slave trade in the District of Columbia
- Adopt and enforce a new, stricter Fugitive Slave Law (which was rarely enforced in the North, upsetting Southerners)

In 1854 the Kansas and Nebraska territories were ready to apply for statehood, and both saw the economic benefits of being open to slavery. Senator Stephen A. Douglas also looked to benefit from the territories when proposing the Kansas-Nebraska Act to Congress. Douglas, who had presidential aspirations, needed Southern approval to build a railroad through the central United States. To win over Southern votes, he proposed **popular sovereignty** be used to decide the slavery question in both territories. When the bill passed, political outrage and citizen violence broke out in the territories. By effectively removing the line created by the Missouri Compromise, slavery could now spread into Northern territories.

People on both sides of the argument, proslavery and antislavery, flocked into the territories hoping to swing the vote to their side. Fighting would break out between them leading to violence and bloodshed, termed "**Bleeding Kansas.**" This violence would last more than three years and even make its way into Congress when, during the so-called **Brooks-Sumner Affair**, South Carolina Representative Preston Brooks attacked Massachusetts Senator Charles Sumner with a walking cane on the Senate floor in an act that defended the institution of slavery.

In reaction to the situation created by the Kansas-Nebraska Act, a partnership of different, smaller political parties joined together to form the **Republican Party**. With the goal of stopping the spread of slavery across the country, Republicans would grow stronger as more people began to oppose the "peculiar institution." However, this strength was found almost exclusively in the North.

The final blow to the Missouri Compromise would come in 1857 via a Supreme Court decision made by Roger Taney. The case involved a slave, **Dred Scott**, who had been moved to the free territory of Wisconsin before returning to Missouri two years later. Scott argued this made him free and sued, resulting in a Supreme Court case. Chief Justice Taney ruled against Scott, citing the Fifth Amendment of the Constitution (Taney claimed slaves were property, not citizens). The decision effectively ruled the Missouri Compromise unconstitutional and made all parts of the country open to slavery. This only heightened tensions between regions, and Southerners were excited to end the question forever, as well as to open new territories to the institution. The decision would be hotly discussed and disputed, including during the **Lincoln-Douglas debates** for the Illinois Senate seat in 1858 (won by Stephen A. Douglas).

John Brown had been no stranger to violence in his mission of abolition, as he took part in the fighting of "Bleeding Kansas." After the Dred Scott decision, Brown attempted to arm slaves in Virginia in his greatest example of radical abolitionism. Federal troops ended his attempt after only two days, and Brown was hanged for treason. The country was firmly divided over Brown as Southerners pointed to his attempt as proof the North would do anything, including use violence, to end slavery. Northern abolitionists saw John Brown as a martyr for their cause, even as many others in the region spoke out against his use of violence. The events of the 1850s only further cemented what many in the country had feared: war would be the only answer to the question of slavery.

THE POLITICAL SITUATION IN 1860

In 1860 the country saw four candidates running for the White House, with three drawing votes from each other's base. Northern Democrats hoped to run Stephen A. Douglas, but he wasn't popular in the South, leading to John C. Breckinridge being nominated as well. The Constitutional Party's John Bell and the Republican candidate, Abraham Lincoln, challenged both Democratic Party nominees. The results of the election mirrored the events of the country to that point; the North voted for Lincoln, and he carried every free state. Breckinridge and Bell held the South, and Douglas received twelve electoral votes, meaning, that due to the population advantage in the North, Abraham Lincoln would be elected sixteenth President without obtaining a single Southern vote.

This confirmed what the South had long feared—no matter what they did, they were still at a political disadvantage and their voices would go unheard. A last-ditch effort was made to calm the fears of Southern slave owners by Senator John Crittenden, but to no avail (the *Crittenden Compromise* sought to restore the Missouri Compromise line). Following Lincoln's election, South Carolina voted to secede from the Union, with seven states leaving before he had even taken office. Citing the Virginia and Kentucky Resolutions as support for their decision to protect states' rights, the President-elect would address preserving the Union during his first inaugural address.

> *"I am loath to close. We are not enemies, but friends. We must not be enemies. Though passion may have strained it must not break our bonds of affection. The mystic chords of memory, stretching from every battlefield and patriot grave to every living heart and hearthstone all over this broad land, will yet swell the chorus of the Union, when again touched, as surely they will be, by the better angels of our nature."*

Secession and the Path to War

After the election of Abraham Lincoln, with no electoral votes coming from the South, the President faced a crossroads in dealing with the **secession** of South Carolina and other Southern states. As the Confederate States of America created their own constitution (one similar to the United States but with provisions on tariffs and slavery) under President Jefferson Davis, Union President Lincoln faced a tough decision with regard to a federal fort in Charleston, South Carolina. **Fort Sumter** was in desperate need of supplies but had been blocked by Southern forces. Lincoln had to decide: would he send reinforcements and risk starting a conflict, or would he let the troops suffer? The President formally announced he would send supplies and provisions to the fort, placing the burden of what to do next on South Carolina. The response was thundering, as South Carolina fired its guns on the fort. The Civil War had begun.

THE CIVIL WAR

The original enlistment for Union troops was only ninety days, as Lincoln showed optimism his army would easily defeat their Confederate brothers. The Union Army had many advantages, including a much larger population (almost four times as many free whites) and a strong navy that dominated the waters during the war. Economically, the Union had control of the banking centers, factories, railroads, and their provisions and weapons were never in danger of being in short supply. Perhaps the greatest strength for the Union would be their President, as Abraham Lincoln would show his leadership throughout the war. Although there were struggles with his leadership style, including his tireless control of every decision as evidenced by his shuffling of generals, Lincoln would show great vision and strength. His ability to retain the Border States through martial law (and later the Emancipation Proclamation) was not without criticism, but overall he was seen as a strong and legitimate President.

Jefferson Davis, on the other hand, seemed ill equipped for the position of President. Perhaps his biggest downfall had nothing to do with him, but the position of the Confederate States. Secession had been based on the idea of states' rights, so any attempt to create a stronger central government in the South during the war was met with resistance. Davis had little to give in terms of military leadership, and the Confederate States lacked supplies, money, and a navy, instead placing much of their hope on using cotton exports to bring foreign support to their side. What would turn out to be the greatest advantages for the Confederate States, however, would be their heart and their generals. The South had a cause they were fighting for, and they had the best-trained generals leading that charge on their own land. Many of the generals leading the South, including Robert E. Lee, had graduated from West Point and fought in the Mexican-American War. This experience, coupled with the ability to fight a defensive war on home soil, gave the South hope they could hold out long enough for the Union to tire of the war. This had been the original Southern strategy: wait the North out until they tired of war and simply let the Confederacy leave the Union. The Confederate Army did not actually have to win the war, only protect their land—it was the North that was fighting to save the Union. President Jefferson Davis himself believed the best strategy for the Confederacy was simply to "survive."

However, as victories mounted, General Lee led his army into enemy territory hoping to gain an even greater advantage: support from Great Britain and, more important, their navy. Most of the South's cotton exports had been purchased by Britain, and the Confederacy thought they could leverage those exports into foreign aid. A victory in enemy territory would most assuredly prove to Europe that the Confederacy was a legitimate threat to defeat the Union, weakening the Union in the process.

Unfortunately for the Confederacy, the victory they so desperately needed would not come, and the consequences would forever end their chances of gaining foreign support. The battle at **Antietam** would not only go down as the single bloodiest day of the war (with more than 22,000 soldiers injured or killed), but the Union "victory" (which actually was a military draw) would keep foreign powers from supporting and supplying the Confederacy.

The Emancipation Proclamation

While Great Britain had found a new source to import cotton (from India and Egypt), they were more concerned with President Lincoln's newly announced **Emancipation Proclamation**, which put the focus of the war squarely on slavery. President Lincoln realized the war could no longer continue simply with the goal to "save the Union." Northerners began to tire of the war and volunteer numbers were down, and more important, morale in the field was waning. Lincoln was also receiving pressure from more radical members of his party to take a stance on slavery. He was wary of losing the important Border States, where slavery was still in practice, so he had resisted calls for emancipation.

With the military draw at Antietam, Lincoln saw his chance to change the course of the war and give the Union a greater purpose for fighting. On January 1, 1863, President Lincoln officially issued the Emancipation Proclamation, which freed all enslaved people in the rebellious states. While the declaration had no legal effect on the war (Confederate States ignored the proclamation as Lincoln was not *their* commander-in-chief), the morale of the Union was immediately improved—and the Border States were able to keep their slaves. Soldiers had a moral purpose for the war, and former slaves were free to fight for the Union. The proclamation also kept Great Britain's government (which had already banned slavery) from recognizing the Confederacy due to pressure from its citizens.

Following the Emancipation Proclamation, almost 200,000 African Americans would come to serve in the Union Army. Freedmen, as they were known, had escaped the perils of slavery and the South to come and fight for the Union in an attempt to right the social wrong of the "peculiar institution." This added number of soldiers would help the Union gain an even greater advantage on the battlefield. When joining the Northern cause, freedmen would still face discrimination, however, as racism still existed above the Mason-Dixon Line. Black soldiers were segregated into all-black units, had only white commanders, and initially earned less pay for their service. They would find more support in Western Campaigns under General Grant (something that would not be forgotten in his election as President in 1868), but generally they saw less action than white units. The most famous example of their commitment and skills would be the 1,000 men of the Massachusetts 54th, who fought most famously in the Battle of Fort Wagner under General Robert Gould Shaw. They helped to rescue white troops and proved their bravery as the Army of Freedom.

The decision to turn the Civil War into a campaign against slavery was not popular in all areas of the North, as proven by Draft Riots that broke out in New York City during July 1863. Whites, primarily Irish Americans, were upset that the poor were being sent to die in a war for African Americans. Blacks, along with wealthy whites, were attacked during the riots that led to property damage and the deaths of over 100 people. The violence proved that racism continued to exist even in the North and that not everyone was pleased with the course the war had taken.

Eastern and Western Theaters

Perhaps the only bright spot for the Union in the Eastern Theater would be at sea, as their superior navy was able provide an effective blockade on Southern ports. The Union successfully countered a Confederate **ironclad**, the *Merrimac*, with their own ironclad, the *Monitor*, in a battle that was the first of its kind. Prior to the *Merrimac*, ships had been constructed with wood for speed but after this battle, naval engagement would never be the same, as ironclads easily tore through their wooden counterparts. The Union blockade would remain intact, and the Confederacy would continue to struggle to obtain supplies from to their ports. The Union would have better success in their Western campaigns under General Ulysses S. Grant. Their goal was to gain control of the Mississippi River and the port at New Orleans as part of their **Anaconda Plan**.

The **Battle of Gettysburg** is perhaps the most famous Civil War battle because of its bloodshed and President Lincoln's famous speech afterwards. The Confederacy had hoped a victory at Gettysburg would turn the war back in their favor while also forcing the Union to finally end the war. General Lee's Army of Northern Virginia, flanked by Generals James Longstreet and George Pickett, made what would be their greatest challenge to the Union Army in the Eastern Theater. President Lincoln had decided that the Union would make its stand at Gettysburg, and by the second day the Army of the Potomac would hold its ground. On the third day, Pickett led a fatal charge directly into Union lines, which devastated the Confederacy militarily and psychologically. Lee and his troops would be pushed back after the battle, never regaining the offensive or the confidence they had when the year began.

In the Western Theater, General Grant of the Union was continuing his successful push to control the Mississippi at the **Battle of Vicksburg**. This would be the start of Grant's strategy of **attrition**, which would become the key to his victories moving forward. The Union General would surround and starve the city for almost a year, resulting in full control of the Mississippi River for Lincoln's forces and the position of General-in-Chief of all Union armies for Grant.

Weapons and Women's Roles During the War

At the start of the Civil War, traditional practices were still being used, as many of the generals had trained at West Point. Focusing on a limited war and battles, fighting with muskets, and attacking in close-order formations seemed the basic plan for war in 1861. However, as technology improved and the war dragged on, so did the strategies for both sides. The war would transition into one of attrition in an attempt to kill as many men as possible. This was made easier with the advent of deadlier weapons such as the rifle (which was more accurate at close range, could be used to identify targets at longer ranges, and inflicted more damage). The rifle would end up being a key advantage for the Union, as the Confederacy could not match the production or speed in which they were produced in the North. Minié balls were also introduced—cylindrical bullets with a hollow base that expanded when fired, shredding through the bodies of soldiers and increasing casualties. Finally, cannons were used in a new, defensive way, to take down bullets and also to shoot down lines of attackers. With all of the new destruction created by technology, strategies had to adapt and generals began changing how they approached battles.

Women, too, found a place in the war as men needed support both on the battlefield and back home. In the South, women took over the family farms and continued to take care of the fields; the North saw women work in factories. The greatest impact women would have on the Civil War, however, would be found directly on the battlefield. Inspired by women like Florence Nightingale, whose work in England encouraged the likes of Dorothea Dix and Clara Barton, the medical profession in America was forever changed. The Sanitary Commission was created in 1861 to provide medical care for troops while other women helped wherever they could. Women took on the role of military nurse, tending to injured soldiers on and off the battlefield. While medicine itself was not always effective (and in fact sometimes more deadly than the wounds created by war), the introduction of women as nurses would be a bright spot for the profession even though they had very little medical training. Barton, specifically, took her experiences from the battlefield and began the American Red Cross after the war. The war, along with the rights given to African Americans after it ended, would be a catalyst for the women's rights movement.

Northern Demoralization

It seemed that everything was stacking up against Abraham Lincoln in 1864. The economy, the number of casualties, and political support were all moving in the wrong direction. The effects of emancipation had worn off, and it was replaced with war fatigue on numerous fronts that were not confined to the battlefield. Economically, the war had a huge financial cost that forced Congress to pass the **Morrill Tariff** as well as the first income tax. These attempts to raise money would not be enough, and the Union would resort to printing paper money, known as Greenbacks. Because this legal tender could not be redeemed in gold, the North would see inflation hit incredible peaks (it would also lead to a rise in "shoddy millionaires" who became rich selling poorly made products to the Union army) even with an established Treasury Department in place. Workers did not see much in terms of wage increases, but the North did see a large increase in manufacturing.

There were also great benefits to the war that would not be seen until well after its conclusion, such as the Homestead Act, Morrill Land Grant Act, and the Pacific Railway Act. However, the North still struggled with the continuing war, as the number of deaths grew to totals never seen before, or since. Cities and families looked vastly different as so many men left to fight. The toll expressed itself politically. Northern Democrats saw a split within their party between the ideas of war and peace as Copperheads, or Peace Democrats, started a greater push to end the war. While their primary motive focused on "King Lincoln" and his war on slavery, many were drawn to the idea of ending a war that caused so much death and destruction to society. Volunteerism declined, and the draft riots proved support for the war was waning. This division would be seen as the next Presidential election began to take shape.

Reelection and the Unionist Party

Lincoln ran for reelection in 1864 but made some noticeable changes that included a new party name and Vice President. The Republican Party had made its name ten years earlier disputing the Kansas-Nebraska Act and the expansion of slavery. But as the war continued on, and many in the

North began to question why they continued to fight (and lose countless lives), Lincoln needed to find a way to unite his party while growing his support base. Republicans renamed their party the Unionist Party and selected War Democrat Andrew Johnson as Lincoln's Vice President in an attempt to combat the growing strength of the Copper Democrats. Running against Lincoln was a familiar face, former General George B. McClellan, with a strong platform of making peace and ending the war. Many in the North, including Lincoln himself, thought McClellan had a strong chance of winning, and those in the Confederacy saw it as their last hope. It would be the events that led up to the election, specifically the campaign of William T. Sherman, which changed not only the election but also the war itself.

President Lincoln's greatest hope in being reelected in 1864 was a string of decisive victories that would prove the Union's decision to continue with the war. Those victories would come courtesy of William T. Sherman, Grant's replacement as General in charge of the West. Sherman had a different vision for the war and his 100,000 men who followed him on campaign across the Confederacy. Destroying and burning everything in his path, Sherman gave a new meaning to the term *total war*. His scorched earth approach destroyed the homes, farms, cities, and infrastructure of the South and its effects would be felt for years to come. (Sherman told his men to bend the rail lines so they could not be used to transport supplies to the Confederates, effectively stunting their ability to advance their economy.) Not only did Sherman's men destroy everything in their path but they also destroyed what morale the Confederates had left. When Sherman took **Atlanta** in September of 1864 the Confederates evacuated the city, seeing the flames rise as they left. This victory, coupled with another naval success by Admiral Farragut at Mobile Bay, was more than enough to secure reelection for Lincoln. The writing was on the wall; the Union was closing in on a triumph.

Surrender at Appomattox

While Sherman was heading up the East Coast, Ulysses S. Grant had forced the Army of Northern Virginia into retreat. Losing control of Petersburg and its accompanying railroad, Lee and the Confederacy had essentially given their capital of Richmond to the Union. All the Confederate leaders, including government officials and President Jefferson Davis, left the city and took their records and valuables. As the Union forces arrived, they were greeted not by soldiers but by angry Southern white men who had gathered to burn the city in anger. There was nothing left of for the Confederacy, and Lee would be forced to surrender in Virginia at **Appomattox Court House** within the Wilmer McLean home. His men had no supplies and were dangerously close to starvation. As a sign of peace, General Grant allowed them to return home (even allowing them to keep their horses and giving them rations). While President Davis attempted to keep the war alive, it was painfully obvious to everyone else this was the end of the Confederacy.

Costs of the War

The Civil War would go down as the deadliest war in American history, with more than 800,000 casualties before the Union was restored. The South was a shell of its former self, as its entire economic institution of slavery had been dismantled, its infrastructure destroyed and burned to the ground, and its government now at the mercy of Northern Republicans. The North had more people, more industry and technology (including rail access), and, most important, more power.

The costs of the war were great on both sides, but the cost of losing was even greater for the Confederacy. It would take over twenty years for the South's economy and infrastructure to recover from the war and its population even longer. Their political structure would also face changes in light of the newly found freedom and citizenship of African Americans (while there would be very few Southern Democrats elected to the Oval Office over the next century).

The period following the Civil War saw a divided nation attempting to heal from the wounds of a devastating war as well as the death of their President. The Union was whole in theory but far from it in practice, as both sides of the conflict faced rebuilding after a devastating war. For the South it would be more difficult; much of the fighting had taken place on their soil and, especially after Sherman's March, civilization would need to catch up to the industrial world of the North. Not only did the South need to recover physically, but also politically, as Congress was dominated by "Radical" Republicans who wished to punish the South. African Americans had also been given the right to vote, and few would forget the Democrats' role in starting the conflict, as Republicans were "waving the bloody shirt" before each election. As African Americans faced a new day following the Reconstruction Amendments, the South would eventually return to many of its prewar practices, if only under another name.

RECONSTRUCTION PLANS

Before Lincoln was assassinated, he had begun to formulate a plan that would allow the South back into the Union as early as 1863. Lincoln did not believe the South had actually left the Union (believing in contract theory over compact theory) and instead saw them in a state of "rebellion." He was piecing together a way to heal the nation from the Confederate "rebellion" when John Wilkes Booth, a Confederate sympathizer and former actor, shot and killed the President at Ford's Theater on April 14, 1865. The President knew it was important to return the Union to whole as quickly as possible and did not believe the people within a rebellious state should be punished for what their government officials had done (but he did believe strongly those officials should not regain power). Lincoln's plan for Reconstruction was called the Proclamation of Amnesty and Reconstruction, or the 10% plan, because when 10 percent of a rebellious state's voter population took a loyalty oath, their state government could be returned. Under this plan most Confederates would be given a pardon by taking this oath and also accepting the Thirteenth Amendment (acceptance would also have to be part of the state constitution). The assassination of the Republican leader would change the course of Reconstruction as a Democratic Vice President from Tennessee clashed with Radical Republicans.

Republicans in Congress had contested Lincoln's 1863 plan, and the **Wade-Davis Bill** was introduced the next year in an attempt to challenge the leniency of the President's proposal. The Wade-Davis Bill countered with 50 percent of the state population needing to take a loyalty pledge while refusing to allow any Confederate to vote on the bill for fear power would return to previous leaders. Lincoln had refused to sign the bill and, when Congress was away, the President had used a **pocket veto** to stop it. Everything would change after Lincoln's death, however, as former War Democrat and new President Andrew Johnson attempted to implement his plans for Reconstruction. Although similar to Lincoln's 10% plan, President Johnson made use of a pardon that would eventually allow many of the planter aristocracy that ruled the South before the war back into power. The President's plan took away the right to vote and hold office to all former leaders and government officials of the

Confederacy, as well as those with over $20,000 in taxable property. But because of Johnson's use of the pardon, by the end of his first year, the South's political lineup looked eerily similar to pre-secession.

Internal Struggles Challenge Reconstruction

During the war, the North saw a large shift toward Republican power, as the Democrats were blamed for slavery and the Civil War (***waving the bloody shirt***). With a larger population and the ability to work with the President to determine how to readmit the Confederate states, the Republican Party did everything it could to protect its political power. A group within the Republican Party, including Senators Charles Sumner of Massachusetts (the same Sumner involved in the Brooks-Sumner Affair) and Thaddeus Stevens of Pennsylvania, pushed to give African Americans more civil rights following the war. The goal was not only to help blacks, especially in the South, but strengthen the Republicans' base in the region as well. It was clear that few within the South supported the Republican platform, but the passage of the Fifteenth Amendment would increase the voting population to include blacks, who would most assuredly vote Republican.

The **Radical Republicans,** as they were labeled, saw their opportunity to push a stronger civil rights agenda, while punishing the South, following Lincoln's assassination. Congressional leaders butted heads with his successor, President Johnson, but had the ability to go around him on many issues. The greatest achievement would be the passage of the Reconstruction Amendments, the **Thirteenth, Fourteenth, and Fifteenth Amendments**. These were the first steps in granting African Americans freedom, rights, and suffrage (while also being a catalyst for a stronger women's rights movement). These amendments were part of the Congressional plan that included a rejection of President Johnson's plan for Reconstruction.

- The Thirteenth Amendment ended slavery in the United States.
- The Fourteenth Amendment granted citizenship to African Americans by declaring all persons born or naturalized in the United States were citizens.
    - It also forced states to respect the rights of citizens and provide them with "equal protection" and "due process of the law."
    - Finally it disqualified former Confederate leaders from holding state or federal offices while renouncing the debt of their defeated governments.
- The Fifteenth Amendment granted suffrage to African American males by prohibiting any state from denying a citizen's right to vote "on account of race, color, or previous condition of servitude."

Congress followed up their rejection of the President's plan with another tremendous victory in the 1866 elections. Johnson toured the country in an attempt to attack Republican candidates in hopes they would lose their seats in Congress. The "swing around the circle" tour backfired and not only did more Republicans win, creating majorities in both the House and Senate, but the President was largely relegated to a bystander role in governing. The Radicals were able to override his numerous vetoes to create three **Reconstruction Acts** in 1867.

- The former Confederate South was divided into five military districts with each being placed under control of the Union army.

- Readmission to the Union would now require not only ratification of the Thirteenth Amendment, but the Fourteenth Amendment as well.

- State constitutions had to include guarantees for all citizens to be *franchised* regardless of race.

This military Reconstruction placed an Army General as Governor of the region and attempted to help procure the newly minted rights of African Americans. With the South being placed under martial law, troops remained in the region until the states met the Reconstruction requirements. During this time, Congress also passed the **Tenure of Office Act**, which prohibited the President from removing a federal official or military commander without the approval of the Senate. This was an obvious attempt by Republicans to prevent President Johnson, a Democrat, from removing key Radical Republicans from the cabinet he inherited from President Lincoln. A key member of that cabinet was Secretary of War Edwin Stanton, the man in charge of Southern military governments.

Johnson was well aware of the true motivations behind the act, and he tested its merits by promptly firing Stanton. The House would bring impeachment articles against Johnson in 1868; the trial ended with Johnson remaining President by one vote (it was obvious to all that the act and trial were politically charged and not constitutionally based). Johnson would remain powerless for the remainder of his term, and Union war hero Ulysses S. Grant would be nominated and then elected President in 1868. The Republican President would owe much of his victory to large support from African American voting population.

THE SOUTHERN RESPONSE

While all of the Reconstruction requirements were met, the harsh reality saw few actually being followed, as many in the South found ways to continue to push racism and segregation. Black Codes, sharecropping, and Jim Crow laws all crept into Southern society while Congressional leaders turned their attention to the economy in the North.

Black Codes developed as states began to restrict the rights of freedmen. These codes had devastating consequences on African Americans and placed them in a position of economic disadvantage. Black codes included the following:

- Blacks were not allowed to testify against whites in court.

- Blacks could not rent or borrow money to buy land, leading to many having to resort to signing work contracts, known as sharecropping.

Sharecropping was a new form of slavery in many ways. Following the war, most African Americans in the South could not read or write and knew only one job: working with crops. Because they had no money, homes, or employment, they looked to what they knew—and a field that had recently lost all of its work force. Sharecropping allowed a worker (black or white) to plant and farm on someone else's land. In exchange for use of the land, the sharecropper would then pay the landowner in crops. Most of these workers needed money for the crops, food, or homes so they would exchange more of what they yielded to the landowner. As the system continued, it began to replicate a key element of slavery: dependency.

Jim Crow laws were Southern states' attempt to legally deny blacks the right to vote guaranteed by the Fifteenth Amendment while also segregating them (most often a violation of their Fourteenth

Amendment rights). In Southern states, laws were passed that became voting "qualifiers" such as the following:

- **Poll Taxes:** Any citizen wishing to vote had to pay a poll tax, or fee. While this was effective in stopping many black voters, it also denied many poor whites the right to vote.

- **Literacy Tests:** Any citizen wishing to vote had to pass a literacy test. Again, however, many poor, illiterate whites were also disenfranchised.

- **Grandfather Clause:** This was the most effective way of disenfranchising black voters only, as only those individuals whose grandfather had been able to vote could also vote. While almost no blacks could navigate this clause, many poor whites could.

Segregation: The Fourteenth Amendment required that all people born or naturalized in the United States be given due process as citizens. This meant that blacks were to be given the same rights as whites, but in the South this ceased to be the case, especially after the landmark Supreme Court case of 1896, *Plessy v. Ferguson*. The decision in this case ruled that citizens could be separated as long as they received equal services or amenities. This legalized the Southern practice of creating two separate societies, one black and one white. There were separate schools and, later, separate water fountains and dining areas. The biggest issue with this ruling (as was the case with much of Reconstruction) was the lack of enforcement of the requirement for equal facilities. Once troops left the South, there were few reasons for the ruling to be followed, leading African Americans to face greater challenges with less support and fewer resources. *Plessy v. Ferguson* would be overturned in 1954 by *Brown v. Board of Education of Topeka, Kansas*.

Racism and the Struggle for Civil Rights

As governments in the South essentially restored the old ways of the past while "legally" oppressing African Americans, there was another challenge blacks faced in obtaining their rights. Racism and anger following the Confederate loss had caused new terrorist societies to form. One such group was the **KKK**, or **Ku Klux Klan**, composed of mostly lower-class white males who attempted to use violence and fear tactics to keep blacks from voting, among other things. These groups wore all white with hoods and used torches to light their way. The KKK was responsible for using many different tactics to oppress blacks, including public lynching. The KKK targeted not only African Americans but also anything they felt challenged white power or kept white males from taking their proper place in society (such as women's rights, Prohibition, or Catholicism). The focus on blacks was much more apparent, however, following the increase of federal rights during Reconstruction, as KKK members believed blacks were taking their job opportunities.

In an attempt to combat all the discrimination and disadvantages African Americans were up against, Congress created the **Freedmen's Bureau** (Bureau of Refugees, Freedmen, and Abandoned Lands). This agency was the first unemployment or welfare office and often the only place that blacks could find assistance following the war. The Freedmen's Bureau gave food, shelter, medical aid, and education to freedmen. As many had no formal schooling, education assistance would become important in helping them become literate, while also providing a chance to escape the South for jobs elsewhere. Some blacks would try to move North for factory jobs or even West in hopes of taking advantage of the Homestead lands offered by the federal government. Overall, the majority was forced to stay in the South and work as sharecroppers, however, as the Bureau received little support (especially from President Johnson, who used his veto against it) and ceased to exist after 1870.

There were some political successes for African Americans, including two Southern blacks being elected to the Senate (Blanche K. Bruce and Hiram Revels) and a small number being elected to the House of Representatives. The majority of Congress remained white, but the presence of blacks and of the Radical Republicans who moved from the North caused much anger in the South. The term *scalawag*, given to white Southerners who collaborated with northern Republicans during Reconstruction (often for personal profit), was used derisively by white Southern Democrats who opposed Reconstruction legislation. The term *carpetbagger* was given to northerners who came to the South looking to profit from postwar situations. These derogatory terms reinforced that fact that the divide in the South was based not only on race but also political gain. Other attempts were also made to politically assist African Americans, such as the Civil Rights Act of 1875, but there was little support or enforcement, and politicians would begin to move their attention to a different focus. There would be no new civil rights legislation introduced to Congress until the 1950s.

THE END OF RECONSTRUCTION

As historians look back on Reconstruction, they do so with a divided view. On the one hand, the federal government not only reintegrated the South following the Civil War but also rebuilt it. When President Grant took office, his administration quickly made Reconstruction its focus (amid myriad scandals).

Redeemers, or Southern conservatives, had gained control of the South's government, and many in the North had become tired of the Radical Republicans' mission in favor of a focus on the growing Northern economy. Redeemers brought back much of the previous South, including a hatred for taxes, a stronger focus on states' rights, and, most devastating for Reconstruction, white supremacy.

Democrats reclaimed control of Southern states and, by 1876, they created a battle for the office of President. Samuel J. Tilden of New York received a victory in the popular vote but missed winning the Electoral College by a single vote. The Republican nominee, Rutherford B. Hayes of Ohio, was awarded a series of disputed Electoral College votes because of the Republicans' majority in Congress. This prevented Tilden's victory. The resulting compromise, known as the **Compromise of 1877**, would give the Republican Party the White House but at the cost of ending Reconstruction, as Hayes removed the remaining federal troops from the South. Hayes also agreed to build a Southern transcontinental railroad, turning the economy and infrastructure into a powerhouse that would be realized during the Gilded Age.

While African Americans were given federal amendments that would define them as citizens and give them suffrage, the record is murkier when discussing the ability of blacks to obtain and use those rights as the racial divide that grew before the war continued to deepen. As generations continue to see segregation, discrimination, and racial tension, the failure of Reconstruction to address the real problems of the divide is seen in a clearer light.

KEY EVENTS IN PERIOD 5: A TIMELINE

Significant Date	Event
1845	Manifest Destiny coined
1846	War with Mexico
1848	Treaty of Guadalupe Hidalgo ends Mexican War
1850	Compromise of 1850 passed
1852	*Uncle Tom's Cabin* published
1854	Kansas-Nebraska Act
1855-1859	"Bleeding Kansas"
1857	Dred Scott decision
1858	Lincoln-Douglas debates
1859	John Brown's raid on Harpers Ferry
1860	Abraham Lincoln elected, South Carolina secedes
1861	Fort Sumter
1862	*Monitor v. Merrimac*, Battle at Antietam
1863	Emancipation Proclamation, Battle of Gettysburg, New York City Draft Riots
1864	Sherman's March to the Sea, Lincoln reelected
1865	Thirteenth Amendment, Lee surrenders, Lincoln assassinated
1866	Civil Rights Act passed
1867	Reconstruction Act passed
1868	Fourteenth Amendment, Impeachment of President Johnson
1869	Grant takes office as President
1870	Fifteenth Amendment
1873	Slaughterhouse Cases
1877	End of Reconstruction

PRACTICE

Directions: Each of the questions or incomplete statements below is followed by four suggested answers or completions. Select the one that is best in each case.

Source: *https://en.wikipedia.org/wiki/Origins_of_the_American_Civil_War#/media/File:Southern_Chivalry.jpg*

1. How does the image express the larger issues surrounding the Civil War?

   A. Abolitionists mounted a violent campaign against the institution of slavery in an attempt to end the practice.

   B. The Southern defense of slavery was based solely on the use of violence instead of being grounded in political argument.

   C. The enthusiasm for territorial expansion and support of slavery was so strong that people were willing to resort to violence to protect their values.

   D. Loyalty within party lines was lost after Lincoln was elected and the end of slavery was near.

2. What did the response to the event portrayed in the image highlight about the state of the nation at the time?

   A. The nation was highly divided as proven by both men being celebrated as heroes in their respective regions.

   B. Compromises were no longer attempted as even members of Congress were resorting to violence.

   C. Members of Congress had become tired of Presidential inaction on the subject of slavery.

   D. The South was visibly upset with the election of Abraham Lincoln and lashed out as they voted to secede from the Union.

3. How could the image represent the Southern attitude following the war?

   A. The violence and aggression shown would give those in the South justification for continued violence against blacks during Reconstruction.

   B. Efforts by Radical Republicans like Sumner would continue to be met with violence in the face of compromise in Congress.

   C. The wounds would lead to punishment and resentment toward the South for their actions.

   D. It shows a deeply rooted ideology that Southerners were willing to fight for and maintain, regardless of the laws passed during Reconstruction.

Answers and Explanations

1. **The correct answer is C.** The Sumner-Brooks caning on the Senate floor showcased the larger issue that slavery had become. People were so divided by their ideology that violence became a viable form of expressing beliefs. Choice A is incorrect, as it was not an abolitionist perpetuating the violence but a supporter of slavery. Choice B is incorrect, as there were other defenses of slavery, including ones using the Bible and science. Choice D is incorrect, as the men involved in the incident were not members of the same political party, and Lincoln's election was well after the event.

2. **The correct answer is A.** The sectionalism that had been growing as a result of regionalization and territorial expansion reached a height as Brooks was given parades in the South for standing up for slavery; Republicans and others in the North rallied around Sumner and against slavery. Choice B is incorrect because compromise was still attempted even after violence erupted as many tried to keep both sides satisfied. Choice C is incorrect because inaction was not at the root of the beating nor was the President the focus of inaction as the Senate had yet to find a suitable answer to the question of slavery. Choice D is incorrect because Lincoln had yet to be elected and was not a factor in the beating.

3. **The correct answer is D.** Following the war, the South would continue the discrimination and segregation it had practiced prior to the war while preserving an ideology that their position was justified. Choice A is incorrect, as violence was not necessarily justified after the war in the South but was more accepted in some circles; the caning did not have any impact on this ideology. Choice B is incorrect, as violence did not continue in Congress and attempts were made to compromise after the war, even if those compromises were not always equal. Choice C is incorrect because this answer would not support a Southern position, but a Northern view on how to address the South postwar.

SUMMING IT UP

- David Wilmot, a Pennsylvania Congressman, proposed that all territories acquired as part of the **Treaty of Guadalupe Hidalgo** (1848) not permit slavery, but the measure was defeated in the Senate.

- Drafted by Senator Henry Clay, **The Compromise of 1850** proposed that:
  - California be admitted as a free state
  - Popular sovereignty should decide whether slavery should be allowed in Utah and New Mexico
  - A payment of $10 million be made to the Mexican government to settle the Texas border dispute
  - Slave trade should be banned in the District of Columbia
  - A stricter Fugitive Slave Law should be enforced

- Following the proposal of the Kansas-Nebraska Act (1854), which called for popular sovereignty to decide the local legality of slavery, years of violent clashes between proslavery and antislavery advocates ensued, becoming known as **"Bleeding Kansas."**

- Small political parties joined together to form the **Republican Party** as a reaction to the situation created by the Kansas-Nebraska Act and to stop the spread of slavery across the country.

- In the 1857 **Dred Scott Decision**, Supreme Court Chief Justice Roger Taney ruled against Scott, citing the Fifth Amendment of the Constitution. The decision ruled the Missouri Compromise unconstitutional, made all parts of the country open to slavery, heightened tensions between regions, and caused heated discussions and disputes, including during the **Lincoln-Douglas debates** (1858) for the Illinois Senate seat.

- The nation was further divided by an attempted revolt led by **John Brown**, an abolitionist who attempted to arm slaves in Virginia; Federal troops ended the effort after only two days and Brown was hanged for treason.

- After the election of Abraham Lincoln with no electoral votes coming from the South, South Carolina decided to **secede** from the United States in 1860; other southern states followed to form the Confederate States of America, which created its own constitution under President Jefferson Davis.

- Amid the desperate need for supplies and blocking by Southern forces at **Fort Sumter** in Charleston, South Carolina, (1861) President Lincoln decided he would send supplies and provisions to the fort, a move that angered the Confederates and officially started the Civil War.

- The battle at **Antietam** (1862) was the single bloodiest day of the Civil War, with over 22,000 soldiers injured or killed. It was considered a Union "victory," and it kept foreign powers from supporting and supplying the Confederacy.

- President Lincoln's **Emancipation Proclamation** (1863), which freed all enslaved people in the rebellious states, had no legal effect on the war since Confederate states ignored the proclamation, but it improved the morale of the Union and kept Great Britain's government from recognizing the Confederacy.

- In 1864, the Union successfully defeated a Confederate **ironclad**, the *Merrimac*, with their own ironclad, the *Monitor*, in the first battle to involve ironclad ships.

- The **Anaconda Plan** (1861) was a Union plan to gain control of the Mississippi River and the port at New Orleans under General Ulysses S. Grant.

- The Confederacy hoped a victory at the **Battle of Gettysburg** (1863) would turn the war back in their favor, but the Union made its stand at Gettysburg. On the third day of the battle, George Pickett led a charge directly into Union lines, which devastated the Confederacy.

- During the **Battle of Vicksburg** (1863), Union troops under General Ulysses S. Grant surrounded and starved the city for almost a year, which resulted in full control of the Mississippi River for Lincoln's forces and the position of General-in-Chief of all Union's armies for Grant.

- Union General William T. Sherman led a string of victories that involved destroying and burning everything in his path throughout the South, which ultimately destroyed morale in the Confederacy. Sherman's taking of **Atlanta** (1864) was decisive in the Union winning the war.

- In 1865, General Robert E. Lee was forced to surrender in Virginia at **Appomattox Court House** and send his men home because they had no supplies and were close to starvation, effectively marking the end of the Confederacy and the Civil War.

- Before the end of the Civil War, President Lincoln had begun to formulate a plan that would allow the South back into the Union, refusing to punish the people within rebellious states for what their government officials had done. Lincoln's plan for Reconstruction was called the **10% plan** (1863), because when 10 percent of a rebellious state's voter population took a loyalty oath, their state government could be returned. Under this plan most Confederates would be given a pardon by taking this oath and accepting the Thirteenth Amendment.

- Republicans in Congress contested the 10% plan and introduced the **Wade-Davis Bill** (1864) to challenge the leniency of the President's proposal by countering with 50 percent of the state population needing to take a loyal pledge while refusing to allow any Confederate to vote on the bill for fear power would return to previous leaders, but Lincoln refused to sign the bill.

- During the war the North saw a large shift toward Republican power as Democrats were blamed for slavery and the Civil War in emotional efforts ridiculed as "**waving the bloody shirt.**"

- The **Thirteenth Amendment** to the U.S. Constitution (1864) ended slavery in the United States.

- The **Fourteenth Amendment** to the U.S. Constitution (1868) granted citizenship to African Americans by declaring all persons born or naturalized in the United States were citizens, forced states to respect the rights of citizens and provide them with "equal protection" and "due process of the law," and disqualified former Confederate leaders from holding state or federal offices while renouncing the debt of their defeated governments.

- The **Fifteenth Amendment** to the U.S. Constitution (1870) granted suffrage to African American males by prohibiting any state from denying a citizen's right to vote "on account of race, color, or previous condition of servitude."

- The **Reconstruction Acts** (1867) divided the former Confederate South into five military districts with each being placed under control of the Union army, required ratification of the Thirteenth and Fourteenth Amendments for readmission to the Union, and required state constitutions to place guarantees for all citizens to be *franchised* regardless of race.

- The **Tenure of Office Act** (1867) prohibited the President from removing a federal official or military commander without the approval of the Senate and was recognized as an attempt by Republicans to prevent President Johnson, a Democrat, from removing key Radical Republicans from the cabinet he inherited from President Lincoln.

- Southern states passed **Black Codes** (1865-1866), laws that placed African Americans into a position of economic disadvantage by banning them from testifying against whites in court and renting or borrowing money to buy land.

- **Sharecropping** allowed a worker to plant and farm on someone else's land and pay the landowner in crops. It was regarded as another form of slavery, since it left the workers dependent on the landowners.

- **Jim Crow** laws were Southern states' attempt to legally deny blacks the right to vote guaranteed by the Fifteenth Amendment by use of poll taxes, literacy tests, and the Grandfather Clause, which denied the right to vote to men whose grandfathers had not been allowed to vote.

- The Fourteenth Amendment required that blacks were to be given the same rights as whites, but, in the South, this ceased to be the case after the 1896 Supreme Court case *Plessy v. Ferguson* decided that blacks and whites could be **segregated** as long as they received equal services or amenities.

- The **KKK**, or **Ku Klux Klan**, was a racist group composed of mostly lower-class white males who used violence and fear tactics to keep blacks from voting, among other things.

- In an attempt to combat all the discrimination and disadvantages African Americans were up against, Congress created the **Freedmen's Bureau** (Bureau of Refugees, Freedmen, and Abandoned Lands) (1865), which was the first unemployment or welfare office and often the only place that blacks could find assistance in the form of food, shelter, medical aid, and education following the war.

- The presence of Radical Republicans (who moved from the North) and blacks in Congress caused much anger in the South, and Southerners nicknamed Southern Republicans **scalawags** and Northerners who came to the South looking to make a profit **carpet-baggers**.

- **Redeemers** was the name for Southern conservatives who gained control of the South's government and brought back such Southern "ideals" as a hatred for taxes, a stronger focus on states' rights, and, most devastating for Reconstruction, white supremacy.

- The **Compromise of 1877** awarded a series of disputed Electoral College votes to Republican Rutherford B. Hayes, effectively making him President of the United States and preventing Democrat Samuel J. Tilden from winning the election.

- Reconstruction ended in 1877, when President Hayes withdrew the last federal troops from the South.

Period 6 (1865–1898)

OVERVIEW

LEARNING OBJECTIVES

Upon completion of this chapter you should be able to...

- Discuss how the rise of big business led to a positive and negative reshaping of the nation and national identity

- Explain how the new industrial culture led to opportunities and restrictions for minorities, and immigrants

- Recognize how politics, economics, and society were reshaped by cultural and intellectual movements

THE RISE OF BIG BUSINESS

The massive **"second industrial revolution"** had begun before the Civil War, and, encouraged by Lincoln's reformation of the country into a centralized nation-state, exploded after war's end. By 1877, with both the war and what many considered the postwar distraction of Reconstruction were over, the recently acquired continent's resources were ripe for exploitation. America had the perfect recipe—natural resources, an abundance of labor, government support, and men who were willing to work (or invent) for wealth.

Republican tariff policy followed Hamilton's recommendation to incubate infant industry until it was ready to compete with more mature versions abroad. The railroads, though built with private wealth by what would soon be referred to as "railroad barons," benefited massively from dirt-cheap **grants of land** by the government—an early form of subsidy help to create new economic markets. Production shifted definitively out of the home and into factories that were themselves increasingly owned by corporate trusts: vertically and/or horizontally integrated mega-corporations that became near-monopolies.

In this increasingly industrialized system, economic efficiency required that workers specialize in a small number of repetitive tasks and be always under the tyranny of the clock, as production time was wages, and wages were lost profit. Technological developments, such as the spread of coal-fired steam power (and later, electricity generation, telephones, airplanes, and automobiles), created both markets and jobs, shifting Americans far from their Puritan roots. A consumer society was at least half-formed by the end of the century.

At the forefront of the reshaping of the United States was a divisive group of men who both helped to create the infrastructure of the country while also widening its economic inequality. **U.S. Steel** and **Standard Oil** saw men like **Andrew Carnegie**, **J.P. Morgan**, and **John D. Rockefeller** become rich beyond their imagination. By bringing new methods (like the Bessemer Process) and materials such as steel and oil to U.S. markets, these men completely transformed the United States into an industrial powerhouse. Even so, their management techniques would shine a bright light on inequalities in society. Steel frames, stronger, more durable and now cheaper than iron thanks to Carnegie Steel, helped to build the skyscrapers that towered over newly formed urban centers. Oil, refined and monopolized by Rockefeller's Standard Oil through horizontal integration, fueled the railroads. However, the lack of competition in these industries would lead to price gauging and collusion known as pools. These captains of industry were making extreme amounts of profit but doing so with questionable hiring practices, lack of safety protocols, and support from government officials. The debate over whether their practices were justified soon garnered the men the nickname, "**robber baron**."

In 1899, the economist and social critic Thorstein Veblen noted the anthropological value of what seemed to him and many others a wasteful economic system: "**Conspicuous consumption** of valuable goods is a means of reputability to the gentleman of leisure." Aside from the ostentation of great wealth concentrated in the hands of the few, the basis upon which that ostentation was made possible was itself the subject of widespread moral debate. On the side of justification were those who preached a perversion of Darwinian evolutionary theory that came to be known as **Social Darwinism**. Social Darwinism held that in business, as in nature, unrestricted competition allowed the "fittest"—and *only* the fittest—to survive. This perspective fit nicely into the ancient and seemingly indelible point of view that held the poor entirely responsible for their state. The rich earned their position solely through vigorous bootstrap-pulling, just as **Horatio Alger** had written in his widely popular series of "self-made man" stories.

A more beneficent vision of society was known as the **Gospel of Wealth**, after an 1889 article by Andrew Carnegie. Carnegie believed in the redistribution of wealth, but crucially by the philanthropic actions of the wealthy, *not* by government action. He agreed to a large extent with Veblen; he decried conspicuous consumption and urged his wealthy fellows to earn social status (and entrance to heaven) through conspicuous philanthropy instead. To Carnegie, the hard work and character that created wealth shouldn't be allowed to atrophy once wealth was gained; rather, he urged the continuance of character through the mostly voluntary redistribution of great wealth for social benefit. In fact, the Carnegie Foundation still exists, and many universities, public libraries, and hospitals in America owe their existence to the philanthropy of men like Rockefeller or Vanderbilt. However, the battle inside the arena of social inequality raged on, as workers found a new weapon with which to defend themselves.

LABOR'S RESPONSE

One effect of more efficient production was a drop in the cost of goods and services. As long as wages stayed ahead of these lowered costs, standards of living increased. However, wages paid meant profits lost; hence, the long battle between capital and labor over the spoils of their joint efforts took on new importance as the American economy radically shifted toward greater centralization of production.

Trusts themselves were a method by which profits were raised: why pay for transfers of products within a supply chain or tolerate profit-reducing competition among producers when one could simply absorb them? No redistributive taxation system existed at the time; the wartime income tax was seen merely as a wartime necessity. Naturally, as wealth concentrated, so did power. Moreover, when the economy contracted, as occurred with regularity, as financial panics in 1873 and 1893 led to depressions, those with power tended to suffer least.

Labor was doing the heavy lifting for the country, and it was beginning to take its toll. Ten plus hours a day, six days a week, and unsafe conditions created a vacuum that labor unions attempted to fill. With different ways of achieving goals, these unions were all dedicated to helping organize labor. The **Knights of Labor** focused on attempting to combine wages of workers with open membership and the use of strikes. Unfortunately for their members, this led to misrepresentation as radicals, and they were blamed for the Haymarket Square riot and bombing in the late 1890s. This would all but end their charge for workers leaving the IWW and AFL to fight for workers in distinctive ways.

The **Industrial Workers of the World** were "One Big Union" that, similar to the Knights of Labor, united skilled and unskilled workers. They hoped to achieve a socialist economic system but, like the Knights of Labor, were seen as too radical for mainstream America. The **American Federation of Labor** behind **Samuel Gompers** would see the greatest and longest lasting success of all unions because of their use of collective bargaining and focus on "**bread and butter**" issues. Because the AFL only accepted skilled workers, they were able to demand higher wages and could not be replaced by immigrant labor.

Management used several different approaches to handling labor discontent. They would close the factory, "**locking out**" the workers, keeping them from obtaining their day's pay (however, this also meant no work was being completed). **Blacklists** were created with names of pro-union workers, **yellow-dog** contracts were forced upon workers to keep them from joining unions, and **Pinkerton agents** were hired to infiltrate unions. **Strikes** were often the only tool unions could utilize to force their issues, but the government seemed to be firmly behind management in all instances. President Hayes ended the **Great Railroad Strike of 1877**, the National Guard was brought in to protect the **Homestead** plant in 1892, and President Cleveland used federal troops to crush the **Pullman Strike** organized by **Eugene Debs**. Labor would have to wait until the next century to find support from the federal government and success with the private sector.

Farming, too, had become centralized and financialized, numbering if not the days then at least the decades of the Jeffersonian family farm—a feature naturally not lost on farmers, who would soon flock to a new political party. Increasing mechanization of agriculture increased per capita productivity, and thus supply, which lowered the price of foodstuffs while raising the cost of production. But farmers, always exposed to the vagaries of the weather, required loans as profit margins fell and were bound to commodity markets that increasingly defined prices; to successive administrations that insisted on paying down the national debt and a "tight money supply," which further squeezed both available credit and lowered prices; and to large agricultural corporations, as they bought up smaller farms and centralized production.

Financial panics in both **1873** and **1893** saw farmers hit the hardest, and the federal government responded with a laissez-faire attitude that did little to ease the burden. Small farmers were also forced to deal with the new reality that the railroads had created: the railroads had indeed opened up new markets, but they charged high freight rates and had also integrated American farmers into a world market stuffed with competition. They faced challenges not only from the railroad companies but also the government, and attempts to regulate the system resulted only in more struggles. The creation of an **Interstate Commerce Commission** and passage of the **Sherman Anti-trust Act** (coupled with the repeal of the **Sherman Silver Purchase**) did more to harm farmers (and labor in general) than help. When the favorable decision of *Munn v. Illinois* was essentially nullified by the *Wabash v. Illinois* decision, farmers had to look elsewhere for support.

Farmers fought back with cooperative farms soon bolstered by the **Farmers' Alliance**, which organized cooperative efforts to provide financing and marketing to farmers as a whole. However, farmers themselves lacked the collective wealth the Alliance needed. Eastern banks were not interested in helping those who were mostly debtors (that is, hurting themselves, the creditors), so the Alliance proposed that the federal government provide low-interest loans and also help farmers to warehouse excess crops for future sale. Thus the Alliance morphed in 1892 into the **Populist Party,** a "people's" party that spread throughout rural America via outdoor meetings with a rhetoric reminiscent of the Great Awakenings.

The Populists demanded silver money under government, not banker, control; freer credit; the right to unionize; the nationalization of the railroads as a kind of public utility; direct election of federal Senators; women's suffrage; and a graduated income tax (much of which was taken from the **Omaha** or **Ocala Platform**). By the end of the century, they were on the verge of taking real, national power behind the **Cross of Gold** speech of William Jennings Bryan and a combined ticket with the Democrats. Every economic downturn gained them more support. However, the Populists were driven by racial and other divisions, which were usually widened by conscious effort of their opponents. Ultimately, the divergent interests of city and countryside—higher food prices helped farmers but hurt factory workers—limited the party's reach. Moreover, the Protestant-revival nature of their rhetoric held little appeal for mostly Catholic urban workers.

THE AMERICAN WEST

While industrial growth did touch those in the West and South, it primarily was found near larger populations and transportation (Northeast and Midwest). The movement west, however, deserves special note both for what it created and for what it destroyed. Government policies (such as the **Homestead Act**), the spreading railroads, and the lure of gold and other mineral riches turned the West wild. Boomtowns and bonanza ranches arose almost overnight. Some grew, prospered, and survived; many did not. Fortunes were made and lost with equal speed as a vast, nearly pre-modern expanse was within a generation dragged into modernity.

The impact of the **transcontinental railroad** cannot be overstated: it cut travel time for goods and people, helped to create time zones, transported goods freely (helping to create a national market and economy), and shifted population to the West. People of the West were resourceful—they built homes of sod or mud, adopted **dry farming**, and handled extreme weather conditions. However, change would also have an impact on the old ways of the West, including cowboys and farmers. Open ranges would become a thing of the past, and, with the introduction of **barbed wire**, the vast stretches of grassland would be no more. The historian Frederick Jackson Turner's **frontier thesis** noted that the frontier was essentially gone and that the massive safety valve provided by that frontier was soon to be shut off.

Left out of Turner's thesis were Native Americans, as Patricia Nelson Limerick would note. Native Americans were consistently herded into ever-smaller spaces and finally onto reservations, usually on the most inhospitable lands available—that is, lands undesired by the settler-colonists. Both the Plains Indians and the bison that formed the basis of their economy and way of life were steadily exterminated (in part due to the railroad).

The federal government led the way with the **Dawes Act** of 1887, which broke up tribal lands into parcels: some reserved for Native Americans, who were to be "civilized," and the rest for white settlers who poured in. Education was provided at places such as the Carlisle Indian school, but, as Helen Hunt Jackson noted in her work, *A Century of Dishonor*, the United States government actions would actually have an adverse effect. Intended as a humane solution to the "Indian problem," the Act's aim of more closely integrating Native Americans into society was met with resistance, and many Native Americans ended up both landless and poverty-stricken.

Added to failed acts of Congress (or outright ignoring of treaties) were brutal disputes or **Indian Wars** that sometimes ended in outright massacre, such as at **Wounded Knee** (1890), where confusion among cavalry troops who wished to disarm the Lakota at South Dakota's Pine Ridge Indian Reservation ended with their killing more than 150 Lakota men, women, and children. Subsequent actions, such as the banning of the tribal ritual the **Ghost Dance,** coupled with the previous discovery of mineral wealth in the **Black Hills** meant that Native Americans would continue to be treated as second-class citizens in the United States.

THE NEW SOUTH

The South remained primarily focused on agriculture after the Civil War, even as industry slowly crept its way into their practices of farming. As the North continued to dominate the economic landscape, the South looked for ways to diversify its crop holdings. Segregation continued to be found on southern farms in the form of sharecropping, but it was seen at even greater heights within the new southern society.

The Fourteenth Amendment required that all people born or naturalized in the United States were to be given due process as citizens. This meant that blacks were to be given the same rights as whites, but in the South this was not the case. The biggest issue with this ruling (as was the case with much of Reconstruction) was the lack of enforcement. Once troops left the South, there were few reasons for the ruling to be followed, leading African Americans to face greater challenges with less support and resources.

The laws and social codes that undergirded **segregation** were collectively known as **Jim Crow,** and they governed black life for almost a century after the fall of Reconstruction. In Southern states laws were passed that became voting "qualifiers" such as the following:

- **Poll Taxes:** Any citizen wishing to vote had to pay a poll tax, or fee. While this was effective in stopping many black voters, it also denied many poor whites the right to vote.

- **Literacy Tests:** Any citizen wishing to vote had to pass a literacy test designed to stop freedmen from voting. Again, however, many poor, illiterate whites were also disenfranchised.

- **Grandfather Clause:** This was the most effective way of disenfranchising black voters only: those whose grandfather had been able to vote could also vote. While almost no blacks could navigate this clause, many poor whites could.

The Jim Crow laws were codified by the landmark Supreme Court case of 1896, **Plessy v. Ferguson**. The decision in this case ruled that citizens could be separated as long as they received equal services or amenities. This legalized the ability for the South to create two separate societies: one black and one white. There were separate schools, and later separate water fountains and dining areas. The Plessy v. Ferguson ruling would later be overturned in 1954 by **Brown v. Board of Education of Topeka Kansas**. Northern racism flared up as thousands of African Americans fled the increasingly inhospitable South, attracted by the demand for labor in burgeoning Northern cities, bringing a hybrid music, the blues (the precursor of jazz and rock), with them.

URBAN REFORMS AND MOVEMENTS

The second industrial revolution drove many millions to move: from Europe and even Asia to America; from the still-underdeveloped, quasi-feudal South to the North (especially African Americans); from the countryside into the rapidly growing cities; from the East to the West; and from inside the home to factories. Standard of living and life expectancy both increased as better products and improvement of mechanization led to better diets and lower prices. It was truly revolutionary, and thus reactions abounded. Know-Nothingness ended as a party but nativism remained a feature of American politics.

Prejudice was stoked by the **mass immigration** of foreigners from Southern and Eastern Europe (as opposed to previous immigration that stemmed from Western Europe), often through New York's **Ellis Island**. Many of these immigrants were not welcomed and were seen, rightly or not, as yet more competition for jobs and other resources. Not only did they willingly take less pay and long hours for their unskilled work in the industrial economy, but they lived in crowded **tenement** housing, often held strong to their cultural ties, and were Roman Catholic or Jewish. Neighborhoods saw a mix of people looking to escape persecution, find employment, and assimilate to the national culture while remaining true to their heritage. Discrimination against immigrants would be found all over the country, as the **Chinese Exclusion Act** was passed in 1882 to restrict the immigration from Asia that had been instrumental in building the western railroads. Much like in the East, competition for jobs was the issue. Even as the West Coast closed its doors, more and more immigrants were passing the **Statue of Liberty** and making their way to the land of opportunity. These new immigrants in the Northeast were politically raw and looking for something or someone to help them survive.

This led in some cases to corrupt **machine politicians** in the big cities, such as New York City's **Tammany Hall**, gaining power; in order to maintain that power, politicians redistributed a little of what they stole from the public back to those who supported them in elections in the form of social services and perks. With no real countervailing force and lobbyists in control of state, and sometimes federal, legislatures, the poor were left to fend for themselves; so, they were almost grateful to people like **Boss Tweed**. While Tweed would suffer a great fall at the hands of political cartoonist **Thomas Nast,** other political machines continued the corruption.

Different forms of support would be found in the growth of public schools, U.S. colleges, the statistical methods of **W.E.B. Du Bois**, and the **Social Gospel**, which extended Carnegie's ideas to religious institutions and individuals who were not wealthy. Both Protestant and Catholic (and other) congregations were urged to follow New Testament injunctions to help the poor and downtrodden. There were plenty of opportunities to do so, and many religious organizations allied with labor and other social reformers of the day, such as Jane Addams, to urge progressive action on housing, health, and the ongoing practice of child labor, among other goals. (Among other endeavors, Addams founded **Hull House**, which provided English lessons for immigrants and daycare and playgrounds for the children of working mothers. Addams was the first woman to win the Nobel Peace Prize.)

Exposés of appalling urban living conditions did much to open the public's eyes to the underside of the second industrial revolution. What probably had even greater impact were photographic essays, such as those of **Jacob Riis,** a Danish-American social reformer who used photography to document the plight of the poor during a period of literature and the arts that was focused on **realism**. The essays of Riis and others depicted just how poorly "the other half" lived and utilized the popular press to spread their works through printing technology like magazines. These interventions helped shape a growing progressive attack on what was called the **Gilded Age**.

The attempts at political, economic, and social reform would all struggle to gain traction during this period, but, by the end of the century, more people were advocating for equity and honesty in all parts of the nation. The first decade of the twentieth century would see great challenges—to industry, government corruption (at federal, state, and local levels), minority rights, and the environment while America stepped onto the world stage.

KEY EVENTS IN PERIOD 6: A TIMELINE

Significant Date	Event
1862	Homestead Act
1869	Transcontinental Railroad completed
1870	Standard Oil created
1873	Financial Panic
1874	Black Hills Gold Rush
1876	Battle of Little Big Horn; Alexander Graham Bell patents telephone
1877	Compromise of 1877; Nez Perce surrender; Great Railroad strike
1879	Carlisle Indian School; Edison invention of incandescent lamp
1882	Chinese Exclusion Act
1883	Buffalo Bill's Wild West Show debuts
1886	Haymarket Square bombing
1887	Dawes Act
1889	Hull House founded
1890	Massacre at Wounded Knee
1892	Ellis Island opens
1893	Financial Panic; *McClure's* Magazine published
1894	Coxey's Army; Pullman strike
1896	*Plessy v. Ferguson* decision

PRACTICE

Directions: Each of the questions or incomplete statements below is followed by four suggested answers or completions. Select the one that is best in each case.

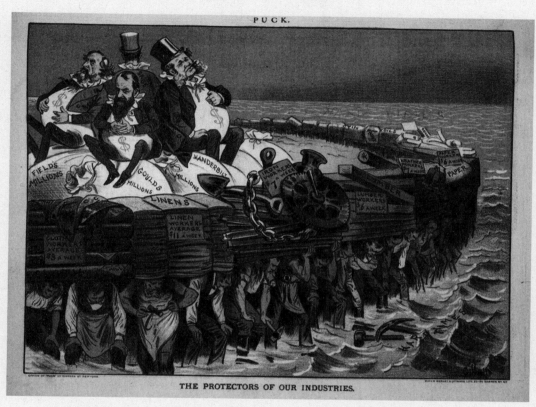

[Source: *https://en.wikipedia.org/wiki/Robber_baron_(industrialist)#/media/File:The_protectors_of_our_industries.jpg*]

1. Which of the following men would support the point of view depicted in the image above?
   A. John D. Rockefeller
   B. J.P. Morgan
   C. Andrew Carnegie
   D. Samuel Gompers

2. What evidence would be used to support the point of view of the image above?
   A. The men referenced helped to build the infrastructure of the United States.
   B. The men referenced donated millions of dollars to charities.
   C. The men referenced influenced government officials and decisions.
   D. The men referenced created employment for millions of workers.

3. What defense would the men in the picture give as support for their actions during the Gilded Age?

   A. Immigration created competition in the workforce, which led to lower wages and the necessity to hire unskilled workers.

   B. Labor organized into unions, leading to confrontations with management and uneasy feelings between the two.

   C. Social Darwinism and the works of Horatio Alger supported the lifestyles and hard work of these men.

   D. They provided necessary social services to lower class citizens in exchange for support.

Answer Key and Explanations

1. D	2. C	3. C

1. **The correct answer is D.** Gompers was the leader of the American Federation of Labor and would view the men in the boat as "robber barons" who abused their power and wealth. Choices A, B, and C are incorrect because these men were given the label of "robber baron."

2. **The correct answer is C.** The point of view is negative and the "robber barons" of the Gilded Age used their wealth to influence members of the Congress and persuade government decisions in their favor. Choices A, B, and D are all examples of a positive view of the "captains of industry" and would not support the point of view.

3. **The correct answer is C.** The captains of industry/robber barons used the ideas of Social Darwinism (that humans are subject to the survival of the fittest) and Alger's "self-made man" stories to support their actions. Choice A is incorrect because hiring unskilled laborers would not help support these men in proving their actions were just. Choice B is incorrect because the battle between unions and management does not justify low wages or poor working conditions. Choice D is incorrect because this is inaccurate; it was political machines that provided these services.

SUMMING IT UP

- The **second industrial revolution** that began in the middle of the nineteenth century was the result of America's abundant natural resources, labor, government support, and men willing to work or invent for wealth.

- During the second industrial revolution, production shifted out of the home and into factories increasingly owned by corporate **trusts:** vertically and/or horizontally integrated mega-corporations that became near-monopolies.

- At the forefront of the reshaping of the United States were men such as **Andrew Carnegie, J.P. Morgan,** and **John D. Rockefeller,** who brought new methods and materials such as steel and oil to U.S. markets, completely transforming the United States into an industrial powerhouse. However, such men were also guilty of questionable hiring practices and the failure to meet safety protocols, which garnered them the nickname "robber barons."

- In 1899, economist and social critic Thorstein Veblen criticized the wasteful economic system and the fact that just a few men possessed the majority of the wealth when he wrote, "**Conspicuous consumption** of valuable goods is a means of reputability to the gentleman of leisure."

- **Social Darwinism** held that in business, as in nature, unrestricted competition allowed the "fittest"—and *only* the fittest—to survive, which supported the point of view that held the poor entirely responsible for their state.

- The **Gospel of Wealth** was a vision of society based on an 1889 article by Andrew Carnegie that championed the redistribution of wealth without government action, decried conspicuous consumption, and urged the wealthy to earn social status through conspicuous philanthropy.

- That many people worked ten-plus hours a day, six days a week, under unsafe conditions gave birth to labor unions such as the **Knights of Labor,** which focused on combining wages with open membership and the use of strikes; the radical **Industrial Workers of the World,** which united skilled and unskilled workers and hoped to achieve a socialist economic system; and Samuel Gompers's **American Federation of Labor,** the most successful union because of its use of collective bargaining and focus on "bread and butter" issues.

- Management handled **labor discontent** by "locking out" workers by closing factories, keeping workers from obtaining their day's pay, creating blacklists with names of pro-union workers, forcing yellow-dog contracts upon workers to keep them from joining unions, and hiring Pinkerton Agents to infiltrate unions.

- **Strikes** were often the only tool unions could utilize to force their issues, but the government was firmly behind management in all instances: President Hayes ended the Great Railroad Strike of 1877, the National Guard was used to protect the Homestead plant in 1892, and President Cleveland used federal troops to crush the Pullman Strike organized by Eugene Debs.

- During the **financial panics of 1873 and 1893,** the federal government responded with a laissez-faire attitude that did little to ease the burden; small farmers were forced to deal with the railroads' high freight rates in a world market stuffed with competition, as well as new regulations imposed by the Interstate Commerce Commission, the Sherman Anti-trust Act, and the *Wabash v. Illinois* decision.

- Farmers fought back against their financial woes with cooperative farms bolstered by the **Farmers' Alliance**, which organized cooperative efforts to provide financing and marketing to farmers as a whole.

- Their lack of collective wealth caused the Farmers' Alliance to morph into the **Populist Party** (1892), a "people's" party that demanded silver money under government, freer credit, the right to unionize, the nationalization of the railroads, direct election of federal Senators, women's suffrage, and a graduated income tax. Divergent interests limited the party's reach.

- New government policies, the transcontinental railroad, and the lure of gold and other mineral riches found **boomtowns** and bonanza ranches arising in the American West where people built homes of sod or mud, adopted dry farming, and handled extreme weather conditions.

- As open ranges became a thing of the past, historian Frederick Jackson Turner's **frontier thesis** noted that the frontier was essentially gone and that the massive safety valve provided by that frontier was soon to be shut off.

- The **Dawes Act** (1887) broke up tribal lands into parcels with some reserved for Native Americans and the rest for white settlers.

- In *A Century of Dishonor* (1881), Helen Hunt Jackson noted that the Dawes Act's aim of integrating Native Americans into society was met with resistance, and many Native Americans ended up both landless and poverty-stricken.

- At **Wounded Knee** (1890), confusion among cavalry troops, who wished to disarm the Lakota at South Dakota's Pine Ridge Indian Reservation, ended with their killing more than 150 Lakota men, women, and children.

- The banning of the tribal ritual the **Ghost Dance** and the discovery of mineral wealth in the **Black Hills** were factors in the continued treatment of Native Americans as second-class citizens in the United States.

- According to the Fourteenth Amendment, all people born or naturalized in the United States were to be given due process as citizens, but this was not the case in the South, especially after the *Plessy v. Ferguson* (1896) decision legalized segregation between blacks and whites.

  - Any citizen wishing to vote had to pay a **poll tax**, which was a Jim Crow law that not only stopped many black voters but also denied many poor whites their right to vote.

  - Any citizen wishing to vote had to pass a **literacy test**, which was a Jim Crow law designed to stop freemen from voting.

  - The **Grandfather Clause**, which allowed voting rights only to those whose grandfather had been able to vote, was the most successful Jim Crow law since almost no blacks could navigate this clause while many poor whites could.

- During the second industrial revolution, prejudice was stoked by the **mass immigration** of people from Southern and Eastern Europe to Ellis Island. These Roman Catholic or Jewish immigrants were largely willing to perform low-paying, unskilled work in the industrial economy for long hours; lived in crowded tenement housing; and often held strong to their cultural ties.

- The **Chinese Exclusion Act** (1882) restricted the immigration from Asia that had been instrumental in building the western railroads.

- The desire of new immigrants for government support led to corrupt **machine politicians**, such as Boss Tweed of New York City's Tammany Hall, gaining power and redistributing a little of what they stole from the public back to those who supported them in elections in the form of social services and perks.

- The **Social Gospel** extended Andrew Carnegie's ideas to religious institutions and non-wealthy individuals, as Protestant and Catholic congregations were urged to follow New Testament injunctions to help the poor and downtrodden: many religious organizations allied with labor and other social reformers to urge progressive action on housing, health, and the ongoing practice of child labor.

- In 1889, Jane Addams co-founded **Hull House**, which provided English lessons for immigrants and daycare and playgrounds for the children of working mothers.

- **Jacob Riis** was a Danish-American social reformer who used that photography to document the plight of the poor during a period of literature and the arts focused on realism: this helped shape a growing progressive attack on what was called the **Gilded Age**.

Period 7 (1890–1945)

OVERVIEW

LEARNING OBJECTIVES

Upon completion of this chapter you should be able to...

- Describe how the impact of industrialization, urbanization, and mass migration created problems for governmental, political, and social organizations

- Recognize how a new mass culture developed out of technological, communication, and transportation revolutions while increasing conflicts between multiple groups and values

- Relate how conflicts over resources, territories, and ideologies across the globe created national debates as well as catapulted the United States into a world power

PROGRESSIVISM

As the twentieth century began, there was a changing attitude toward the social and economic gaps that had dominated the Gilded Age, producing a **Progressive movement** out of the ashes of the reform-minded Populist Party. It would start at local and state levels as corruption, Social Darwinism, and laissez-faire policies were rejected by a growing group of middle class reformers exposing the ills of society while calling for **initiative, referendum, and reform**. **Muckrakers** published investigative reports that mirrored Jacob Riis; John Muir and the **Sierra Club** pushed for new environmental regulations that promoted preservation; women became greater activists pushing for and achieving temperance (**Eighteenth Amendment**) and suffrage (**Nineteenth Amendment**); and corporations were held accountable for fair and safe practices by labor unions and the federal government. Perhaps the Progressives'

155

greatest allies would come in the form of presidents, as a succession of men were instrumental in trust-busting and reforms.

The first true supporter of the Progressive movement came about as result of consequence instead of purpose. **Theodore Roosevelt** was selected as President McKinley's vice president during his second term—mostly to keep the former Rough Rider out of Republicans' hair. Unlike the rest of his party, Roosevelt believed the government could help solve the nation's problems and wanted to have an imperial voice in office. When an assassin took the life of McKinley just six months into his second term, Republicans were in a panic over their new commander-in-chief.

Roosevelt wasted no time and helped settle the **Anthracite Coal Strike**, marking the first time that a sitting president did not immediately side with management. He would continue to be a thorn in the side of corporations with the proper enforcement of the Sherman Antitrust Act that led to the breakup of would-be monopolies like the **Northern Securities Company**. Roosevelt's promise of a **"Square Deal"** for all and his focus on the three Cs (Corporations, Consumers, and Conservation) would garner him the nickname "**trustbuster.**"

After Upton Sinclair's novel *The Jungle* exposed the horrors of the food packing industry, the **Meat Inspection Act** and the **Pure Food and Drug Act** were passed. Progressive action had begun to transform American society, and the federal government was enforcing a new wave of protectionist regulations. Regulation would make its way to the environment as forests, wildlife, and wilderness were being destroyed in the name of industry, hunting, and westward migration. The Roosevelt administration would advocate for **conservation** of these lands and, combined with the **preservationist** work of Muir, numerous acts were created to protect monuments, parks, and preserves.

After Roosevelt's groomed successor William Howard Taft began to turn his back on some of Roosevelt's policies (though it should be noted that Taft actually "busted" more trusts than Roosevelt), a wild election took place in 1912. The incumbent, Taft, received the nomination for the Republican Party and was pitted against Progressive Democrat **Woodrow Wilson**. Roosevelt, unsatisfied with Taft and the Republicans, ran as a third-party candidate, Progressive (**Bull Moose**). Rounding out the ballot was Independent (and Socialist Party) candidate Eugene Debs. When the dust settled, Wilson was elected due to the split Republican ticket.

The true winner of the election of 1912, however, was the Progressive movement—Wilson continued to regulate business (**Clayton Antitrust Act**) while lowering tariffs and passing the **Federal Reserve Act**, reforming the nation's banking industry. Unfortunately, even as these men helped to address key political and economic issues and as women saw greater gains in society, African Americans were largely left to continued discrimination. The likes of **Booker T. Washington** and his **Atlanta Compromise** speech had attempted to address the economic inequality, but an increase in **lynching** coupled with the continued legal nature of segregation meant that leaders like **W.E.B. Du Bois** and his **NAACP** needed to work even harder to overcome a federal blind eye to their plight (Wilson reflected this when screening *The Birth of a Nation* at the White House). The Progressive movement would ultimately take a back seat to American interests in promoting democracy abroad.

IMPERIALISM AND THE GREAT WAR

The Progressive movement was happening concurrently with another shift in American policy, and domestic policies focused on supporting equal rights would bleed into desires for foreign land and markets, otherwise known as **imperialism**. America would find many reasons to enter the imperialist race, including dollars, deity, Darwinism, defense, and destiny. Business leaders needed new consumers for their products; **Alfred T. Mahan** (*The Influence of Sea Power Upon History*) influenced the buildup of a powerful navy, fueling the desires of the United States to be a world power; and expansionists feared falling behind in the race for world power, while using **"White Man's Burden"** as justification for spreading their political and economic systems around the globe.

Prior to his death, President McKinley had shown a willingness to expand across the world by **annexing Hawaii**, and he agreed to an **Open Door Policy** of trade in China (which pleased many of his supporters, including wealthy businessman Mark Hanna). After sensational stories of **yellow journalism** focused on Spain, coupled with the sinking of the **U.S.S.** *Maine*, the United States declared war on Spanish forces in both **Cuba** and the **Philippines**. This "splendid little war" ended quickly, and the United States received Puerto Rico, Guam, and the Philippine Islands as part of the treaty. The **Teller Amendment** and **Platt Amendment** would muddle the issue of Cuban independence, while the **Anti-Imperialist League** attempted to block the annexation of the Philippines.

After McKinley's death, President Roosevelt pushed American expansion to greater levels with his rhetoric of **"speak softly and carry a big stick."** Construction on the **Panama Canal** began a period of investment in Latin American markets that would continue with Taft (**dollar diplomacy**) and finally end as part of the **Good Neighbor Policy** with Roosevelt's distant relative Franklin D. Roosevelt. However, Theodore Roosevelt's addition to the Monroe Doctrine, known as the **Roosevelt Corollary**, would become justification for intervention in Latin America during the first half of the twentieth century.

Imperialism, along with military buildup, formation of alliances, and extreme growth in nationalism, had created tensions around the world. While the United States was not directly involved in European competition that had been escalating, it was keeping a close eye on the results. After Archduke Francis Ferdinand was assassinated, sparking World War I, U.S. President Woodrow Wilson declared **neutrality**. However, he also believed it was imperative that America be present at the negotiating table in what he saw as the "war to end all wars."

Subsequent events, such as the sinking of the British *Lusitania* (with more than 100 Americans onboard), resumption of unrestricted submarine warfare by Germany (breaking the *Sussex* Pledge), and interception of the **Zimmermann telegram** (attempting to form a union between Germany and Mexico against the United States), led Congress to approve of the United States' entry into the Great War in an effort to—in Wilson's words—**"make the world safe for democracy."**

While the United States would see little fighting under the likes of General John J. "Black Jack" Pershing's **American Expeditionary Forces**, at home the **Committee on Public Information** combined muckrakers and yellow journalism to spur wartime mobilization. Victory gardens, anti-German propaganda, and even attacks on civil liberties with the creation of the **Espionage and Sedition Acts** were of greater consequence to the American public. After victory was declared by the **Allies** in 1918, Wilson personally made the trek to Versailles in an attempt to implement his vision of the **Fourteen Points**. Angering members of the opposing party with his singular and uncompromising vision, the United States Congress would be the greatest threat to Wilson's plan for a worldwide peacekeeping organization, known as the **League of Nations**. Men like **Henry Cabot Lodge** referenced Washington's warning against entangling alliances and, after much debate, the treaty was never approved by the Senate. **Warren G. Harding** would be elected soon after, and America would **"return to normalcy."**

THE ROARING TWENTIES

The 1920s were a period of cultural clash that saw battles between religion and science (as seen in the **Scopes Trial**), tradition and modernization (women's rights, technology, crime), and even between capitalism and socialism. As the decade began, the **Bolshevik Revolution** in Russia, coupled with a postwar recession, led to Americans being cautious of any ties to communism. As a result of the **Red Scare** in America, several postwar strikes were received negatively, while anarchist violence, such as the bombing on Attorney General A. Mitchell Palmer's home, created a massive attempt to find anyone with ties to communism as part of the **Palmer Raids**.

This was only one example of a growing nativism in the country, as the influx of immigrants had continued from the late nineteenth century. Italian-born anarchists **Sacco and Vanzetti** were sentenced to death (with little evidence to support the ruling, many believed that prejudice was a key factor), immigration restriction passed through Congress (**National Origins Act of 1924**), and the **Ku Klux Klan** expanded its targets to include immigrants as part of its mission to achieve Anglo-Saxon white supremacy. As discrimination increased across the country, African Americans took part in a "great migration" to the North in an attempt to escape the sharecropping of the South by obtaining factory jobs or assembly work for Henry Ford.

Harlem would emerge as a popular landing spot for many African Americans, and it would become a hotspot for black writers and artists to create a unique and celebrated culture. **Langston Hughes** described the "new Negro" of hope and pride while men like Louis Armstrong brought the sound of the Jazz Age to white America. Even so, African Americans were still facing racism in the North leading some, like **Marcus Garvey**, to advocate for a "back to Africa" movement. This attempt was largely unsuccessful. By the end of the 1920s, the **Harlem Renaissance** was creating new opportunities for African Americans while infusing their culture into every white society before the Great Depression drew away its resources.

The jobs that immigrants, blacks, and whites alike all hoped to find were now heavily concentrated in the urban centers around factories that employed principles of mass production and Frederick W. Taylor's scientific management. **Henry Ford's automobile** and its use of the **assembly line** revolutionized not only the workplace but society as well. Because they were more affordable to produce, Ford's vehicles were also more affordable to purchase (the Model T would cost under $300 in 1924). These principles would be applied to other technologies, creating a transformation in everyday life that included more efficient products for home use.

Consumerism would boom as credit made buying easier, while also helping to stimulate an economy that had been built on **Mellon-omics** (or trickle-down economics). A "**lost generation**" of writers like **F. Scott Fitzgerald** and **Sinclair Lewis** would criticize this ideology, as well as the mass culture that had been created by radio, movie "palaces," and pop culture icons such as Babe Ruth or Charles Lindbergh. However, the public enjoyed traveling in cars and using products that gave them more free time to enjoy a developing nightlife that had been built out of a rebellious generation that challenged traditional values. **Flappers** (women who expressed themselves with a new, independent spirit resulting from the successful passage of the **Nineteenth Amendment**) cut their hair short, wore heavy makeup, smoked cigarettes, and danced the Charleston. They did so in clubs or even in **Speakeasies** as they drank bootlegged alcohol with men in spite of the passage of the **Volstead Act** and **Eighteenth Amendment**. **Bootlegging** became a valuable business (which also helped to spur the creation of auto racing) that stimulated the crime industry with the likes of crime boss **Al Capone** becoming one of the wealthiest men in America.

All of these new changes to American society excited some while scaring others, but they could all agree on one thing: Americans were living in a prosperous time. However, that prosperity had been built on speculation, credit, and overproduction, which would create disastrous results.

THE GREAT DEPRESSION AND THE NEW DEAL

Even though the stock market crash did not directly impact the lives of everyday Americans, the multiplier effect that resulted from the crash did. **Unemployment** rose to the highest levels the country had ever seen, with 1 in 4 people out of work at the height of the **Great Depression**. Banks ran out of money and would seemingly close overnight; mortgages for homes and farms were foreclosed at a rapid rate; malnutrition and even suicide spread throughout the country at alarming rates; and the **Dust Bowl** destroyed agriculture in the Great Plains. (It should be noted that crop yields actually increased during this period in most areas of the country but this, too, created a negative effect as prices dropped dramatically.)

Americans, upset with the **Nye Committee** findings of World War I, had advocated for isolationism and a focus on America First, leading the government to create high tariffs (**Smoot-Hawley**) that essentially cut off trade with the rest of the world. **Under-consumption** at home, coupled with **overproduction,** meant that many businesses were failing and would close their doors and end employment for millions of Americans.

President **Herbert Hoover**, former head of the Food Administration during World War I, leaned on local and state organizations in hopes that the bust cycle was temporary and that Americans' ability to sacrifice like they had during the Great War would be enough to get them through these tough times. **Volunteerism** was not enough, however, and the public started using Hoover as a symbol of their despair. Shantytowns that had become the new communities for those who had lost their homes were labeled "**Hoovervilles**." Soldiers who had served during WWI marched on Washington, protesting for their pensions or **bonuses**, in an embarrassing low point for the administration. By the 1932 election, Hoover attempted to intervene with steps like establishing the **Reconstruction Finance Corporation (RFC)**, but it was too little, too late, and he stood virtually no chance in defeating the reform-minded heir to the Progressive party, **Franklin D. Roosevelt**.

Roosevelt proposed a "**New Deal**" for Americans based on the three R's—relief, recovery, and reform—and promoted it with weekly "fireside chats" to restore the confidence of the American people. FDR immediately began working for Americans and, with the support of Congress, passed an unprecedented amount of social and economic legislation during his first "**hundred days**" in office in an effort to spur relief. Roosevelt created a bank holiday that closed all banks in an attempt to reassure the public that only strong banks would reopen (**Emergency Banking Relief Act**) and then turned his attention to help unemployment (Civilian Conservation Corps, or the **CCC**, and the Public Works Administration, or the **PWA**). His wife, **Eleanor**, used the position of First Lady to push a social agenda supporting African Americans and women that would actually lead to a shift in voting patterns for both groups toward the Democratic Party.

Policies revolving around agriculture (Agricultural Adjustment Act or **AAA**), industry (National Industrial Recovery Act or **NIRA**), and infrastructure (Tennessee Valley Authority or **TVA**) were all attempts to help the United States recover from the devastation of the Great Depression. But by the end of FDR's first term, these three acts specifically came under attack, and the criticism of welfare socialism and massive deficit spending had grown louder. Father Charles Coughlin, the "radio priest" from Michigan; Francis E. Townsend, a retired physician from California; and Huey Long, a Senator from Louisiana, attacked the President for doing too much or not doing enough. Long announced his intention to run against FDR in the 1936 election with a more socialized "**Share Our Wealth**" program before being assassinated in September 1935.

It was clear that Roosevelt was having the federal government make a greater attempt at helping Americans through the Depression, but by 1937 a recession had returned, and the President promoted a "**Second New Deal.**" The **WPA** (Works Progress Administration), the Social Security Act (**SSA**), and the National Labor Relations Act (**Wagner Act**) all addressed new areas of concern for Americans. The problem for FDR was that Congress no longer rubber-stamped all his legislation, and the Supreme Court had ruled the AAA and NIRA unconstitutional. The President responded by attempting to **court-pack**, or add new members to the Supreme Court who would support his programs. While his attempts were rebuffed, the Court began to become more responsive to his agenda.

Overall, the New Deal is a great source of debate, as it shows a clear divide between Democrats and Republicans, the role of the federal government, the merits of **John Maynard Keynes** economic strategy of deficit spending, and the power of the Presidency. What cannot be debated, however, are the effects of the New Deal, which did improve the plight of many but did not actually end the Great Depression. Instead, the horrible atrocities in Europe would stimulate and catapult a struggling economy into the strongest in the world.

NOTE

The WPA was renamed Work Projects Administration in 1939.

Major New Deal Programs, 1933–1938

Name	Acronym	Purpose	Year of Passage
Federal Deposit Insurance Corporation	FDIC	To protect citizen assets against bank failure	1933
National Recovery Administration	NRA	To regulate business output, labor practices, and prices; part of the National Industrial Recovery Act of 1933	1933
Glass-Steagall (Banking) Act	n/a	Erected a wall between commercial and investment banks	1933
Agricultural Adjustment Act	AAA	To set quotas for agricultural output as well as price supports	1933

Name	Acronym	Purpose	Year of Passage
Public Works Administration	PWA	Government employment program aimed at infrastructure; part of the National Industrial Recovery Act of 1933	1933
Civil Works Administration	CWA	To create millions of manual labor jobs for the winter of 1933-34	1933
Civilian Conservation Corps	CCC	Government employment program aimed at conservation	1933
Home Owners Loan Corporation	HOLC	To refinance mortgages in default in order to avoid foreclosure	1933
Tennessee Valley Authority	TVA	To improve conditions for Tennessee Valley residents through economic development, energy production, and environmental stewardship	1933
Federal Housing Administration	FHA	Set standards for home-building, stabilize mortgage market, insure mortgages	1934
Works Progress Administration	WPA	Government employment program that included projects to employ white-collar workers, professionals, and even artists, of all races	1935
Social Security	n/a	Unemployment insurance, pensions, aid to the poor and elderly	1935
Wagner Act	n/a	Protect union organizing rights	1935
United States Housing Authority	USHA	Aimed at funding low-cost public housing and eradicating slums (a replacement for the PWA)	1937
Fair Labor Standards Act	n/a	Set a minimum wage and maximum number of work hours	1938

WORLD WAR II

America had been focused on isolating itself from the rest of the world in an attempt to crawl out of the Great Depression. Leaning once again on Washington's Farewell Address, the United States declared neutrality as its allies in Europe began to see **Nazi aggression** increase across the continent and the Japanese invade Manchuria. Following the agreements of the 1920s (**Washington Naval Conference, Kellogg-Briand**), America had strong support for staying out of war with an America First mentality. President Roosevelt, serving his third and soon-to-be fourth terms, understood the totality of war and that the United States could not remain neutral forever. Declaring America the "**arsenal of democracy**," he pledged to support all those rejecting fascist aggression.

His **quarantine** and **four freedoms speeches** made clear where American support lay, and subsequent acts such as **Destroyers for bases, Lend-lease**, and **cash and carry** (while also instituting the **Selective Service Act**) inched the United States closer to war while angering the **Axis powers**. December 7, 1941, would push the country into war as Japan retaliated against the last of a series of economic sanctions and embargoes the United States had placed on Japan by launching a surprise attack on **Pearl Harbor**. More than 2,000 Americans were dead after the attack, and the next day the President received Congress's (and Americans') support to go to war with Japan. By the next year, American forces were stationed in the Pacific fighting the Japanese, while more were sent to support the **Allies'** battle against Nazi Germany.

At home, America entered into total wartime production in a way that had never been seen before or matched since, and by the end of the war the United States had produced twice as much as all the Axis powers *combined*. Every aspect of the country was working toward victory, as unions made no-strike pledges, workers took on extra "victory" shifts, war bonds sold at high rates, women rallied behind the iconic "**Rosie the Riveter**" to take men's places in factories, and minorities aided in the war effort in numerous areas. Mexican Americans worked on farms as **braceros**, and Native Americans served as **code talkers**. African Americans also fought for the United States and saw Executive Order 8802 produce the **Fair Employment Practices Committee** as part of the **Double V** campaign. Japanese-Americans faced discrimination at home in response to the attacks at Pearl Harbor, as FDR placed them in **internment camps** (Executive Order 9066), violating their civil liberties in an attempt to keep them "safe" (*Korematsu v. United States*). But they still joined the war effort in an attempt to prove their loyalties. The country experienced overwhelming nationalism in support of a war supporting democracy but also continued discrimination against many of its citizens.

Once the United States joined the war, the decision was made to defeat Germany first because it was a greater threat, leaving the Soviet Union to fight on the Eastern front alone while U.S. Marines attempted to control the Pacific. The "**Big Three**"—FDR, **Winston Churchill** of Great Britain, and **Joseph Stalin** of the Soviet Union (after their nonaggression pact with Nazi Germany was violated)—met at **Tehran** and **Yalta** to discuss the fate of the war. The Allied invasion of Normandy, France (**D-Day**), would be a major turning point, and **Adolf Hitler** of Germany, faced with a two-front war, would surrender less than a year later (Victory in Europe Day or **VE Day**).

The United States would turn its full attention to Japan and, after months of **island hopping**, was ready to invade the mainland. However, **Operation Olympic** would cost millions of American lives and stretch the war even longer; after almost four years at war, the thought of continued fighting seemed less than desirable for Americans and their government. The **Manhattan Project** had begun under the direction of President Roosevelt, but, after his death, the decision on what to do with atomic weapons would be left to **Harry S Truman**. The debate continues today on the necessity of using the bombs, but Truman decided to do so: one on **Hiroshima** (August 6) and the other on **Nagasaki** (August 9). Only after the second bomb did Japan formally surrender (**VJ Day** or Victory in Japan Day).

Following the war, much of Europe was ravaged; the Soviet Union controlled much of the eastern portion as the rest of the Eastern Hemisphere tried to climb out of war and debt. However, the United States was largely unharmed domestically and was economically the only country able to produce for the rest of the world. As the world entered the atomic age, the race for markets, political supremacy, and even the moon would come to dominate global headlines.

KEY EVENTS IN PERIOD 7: A TIMELINE

Significant Date	Event
1890	Mahan's *The Influence of Sea Power Upon History* published
1892	Sierra Club founded
1893	*McClure's* published; Hawaii annexation blocked by President Cleveland
1898	Hawaii annexed
1901	Theodore Roosevelt becomes President after assassination of President McKinley
1904	Panama Canal Treaty; Ida Tarbell's *History of Standard Oil Company* published; Northern Securities Case
1906	Upton Sinclair's *The Jungle* published
1907	Gentlemen's Agreement
1911	Triangle Shirtwaist Factory Fire
1912	Woodrow Wilson elected President
1913	Federal Reserve established
1914	Clayton Antitrust Act, WWI begins in Europe
1915	British vessel *Lusitania* sunk
1917	United States enters WWI
1919	Treaty of Versailles rejected by United States; Palmer Raids; Steel Strike
1920	Eighteenth and Nineteenth Amendments ratified; Harding elected President
1921	Margaret Sanger's Birth Control League; Washington Naval Conference
1925	*Great Gatsby* published; Scopes Trial

Significant Date	Event
1927	Sacco and Vanzetti convicted; Kellogg-Briand Pact
1928	Herbert Hoover elected President
1929	Stock Market Crash
1930	Smoot Hawley Tariff
1932	Bonus March; Franklin D. Roosevelt elected President on New Deal platform
1933	Bank Holiday; Fireside Chats; CCC and NRA
1935	Social Security Act; Wagner Act
1936	FDR reelected
1937	Court Packing; Quarantine Speech
1939	Germany invades Poland beginning WWII
1940	America First Committee Established; Destroyers for Bases deal; Service Draft enacted; FDR reelected for third term
1941	Lend Lease deal; Four Freedoms Speech; FEPC established; Attack on Pearl Harbor
1942	Japanese Internment; Battles of Coral Sea, Midway, and Guadalcanal
1943	Invasion of Italy; Tehran Conference
1944	D-Day invasion; FDR reelected for fourth term
1945	Battle of Iwo Jima; FDR dies (Truman becomes President); Victory in Europe; Dropping of two atomic bombs on Hiroshima and Nagasaki, Japan; Victory in Japan

PRACTICE

Directions: Each of the questions or incomplete statements below is followed by four suggested answers or completions. Select the one that is best in each case.

> In the future days, which we seek to make secure, we look forward to a world founded upon four essential human freedoms.
>
> The first is freedom of speech and expression—everywhere in the world.
>
> The second is freedom of every person to worship God in his own way—everywhere in the world.
>
> The third is freedom from want—which, translated into world terms, means economic understandings which will secure to every nation a healthy peacetime life for its inhabitants—everywhere in the world.
>
> The fourth is freedom from fear—which, translated into world terms, means a world-wide reduction of armaments to such a point and in such a thorough fashion that no nation will be in a position to commit an act of physical aggression against any neighbor—anywhere in the world.
>
> That is no vision of a distant millennium. It is a definite basis for a kind of world attainable in our own time and generation. That kind of world is the very antithesis of the so-called new order of tyranny which the dictators seek to create with the crash of a bomb.
>
> — Franklin D. Roosevelt, excerpted from the State of the Union Address to the Congress, January 6, 1941

1. How does the context of the period directly relate to the four freedoms?
   A. The issues of the Progressive Era had spread into the country, and FDR wished to see a nation no longer divided by social, political, and economic inequality.
   B. Imperialistic ventures by the United States had created extreme tensions between the United States and other European nation states that were compounded by domestic conflicts over "modern" values.
   C. The Great Depression placed the United States in economic dependence on trade with other countries, and that trade was being threatened by European powers.
   D. Germany's continued push into Europe had put America's allies into a dire situation that required support that directly conflicted with the current isolationist climate in the United States.

2. Which of the following would best relate to one of the four freedoms?
   A. First Freedom—Jacob Riis's publishing of *How the Other Half Lives*
   B. Second Freedom—Scopes Trial
   C. Third Freedom—The Bank Holiday
   D. Fourth Freedom—Kellogg-Briand Pact

3. Which of the following would most likely oppose the intentions of this speech?
   A. Winston Churchill
   B. The America First Committee
   C. Woodrow Wilson
   D. Supporters of the "arsenal of democracy"

Answer Key and Explanations

1. D	2. D	3. B

1. **The correct answer is D.** FDR understood the need to support allies like Britain both for trade and for protection against the advancing Nazi threat across the world, but he faced extreme challenges from isolationists who were still upset with the United States' entry into WWI. The speech was an attempt to make the war about greater issues that could directly impact American lives. Choice A is incorrect, as the issues of Progressive reformers were not directly related to the war in Europe. Choice B is incorrect because United States imperialism in the early twentieth century had given way to isolation in America and lack of interaction with other world powers. Choice C is incorrect because the United States had removed itself from trade during the Great Depression and was slowly working itself back into a relationship during this period. However, the threat of Nazi takeover was a more direct cause of the speech than trade.

2. **The correct answer is D.** The Kellogg-Briand Pact was a worldwide agreement of peace and repudiation of war. While it was not followed, the ideas established in this pact are similar to the fourth freedom. Choice A is incorrect because although publishing a work is an act of free speech, there were no problems with photographing economic inequality in the slums; thus, it is not the best choice. Choice B is incorrect because the Scopes Trial was a decision on teaching evolution in school in Tennessee but not on how one should be able to practice his or her own religion. The trial was focused on Tennessee law and is not the best choice. Choice C is incorrect because the ability of people to put their money in banks, while helpful to their economic safety, is not the best choice of a connection to the four freedoms speech, which was referring to protecting world trade.

3. **The correct answer is B.** Members of the America First Committee would oppose this speech because it put the United States in a position to defend these declarations, especially as Nazi Germany was violating them across the Atlantic. Choice A is incorrect as Churchill, Prime Minister of Great Britain, would echo the ideas and welcome United States support in protecting them. Choice C is incorrect because Wilson would support these ideas, as they mirrored his vision for a postwar world as outlined in his Fourteen Points speech. Choice D is incorrect because FDR wanted to make the United States an "arsenal of democracy" to supply others fighting tyranny the support they needed to be victorious.

SUMMING IT UP

- At the beginning of the twentieth century, middle-class reformers intent on exposing the ills of society while calling for initiative, referendum, and reform led a new **Progressive movement** that championed environmentalism, women's activism, and the accountability of corporations.

- The first true supporter of the Progressive movement was President **Theodore Roosevelt**, who helped settle the Anthracite Coal Strike, promised a "Square Deal" for all, and focused on the three C's of Corporations, Consumers, and Conservation, which garnered him the nickname "trustbuster".

- After Upton Sinclair's novel *The Jungle* exposed the horrors of the food packing industry, the **Meat Inspection Act** and the **Pure Food and Drug Act** were passed.

- As forests, wildlife, and wilderness were destroyed in the name of industry, hunting, and westward migration, the Roosevelt administration advocated for **conservation** of these lands, and, combined with the preservationist work of John Muir and his Sierra Club, numerous acts were created to protect monuments, parks, and preserves.

- After President William Howard Taft turned his back on some of Roosevelt's policies, a wild election took place in which Progressive Democrat **Woodrow Wilson** was elected due to the Republican ticket being split between Taft and former President Roosevelt, who was running as a member of the Bull Moose party.

- President Wilson regulated business with the **Clayton Antitrust Act** while lowering tariffs and passing the Federal Reserve Act, reforming the nation's banking industry.

- Booker T. Washington's Atlanta Compromise speech attempted to address the economic inequality between blacks and whites, but an increase in lynching and segregation forced W.E.B. Du Bois and his **NAACP** to work harder to overcome a federal blind eye to African Americans' plight.

- Desires for land and markets in the name of dollars, deity, Darwinism, defense, and destiny led America into an **imperialist** race.

- **Alfred T. Mahan's** *The Influence of Sea Power Upon History* influenced the buildup of a powerful navy fueling the desires of the United States to be a world power, as expansionists feared falling behind in the race for world power.

- President William McKinley annexed Hawaii and agreed to an **Open Door Policy** of trade in China.

- After the sinking of the **U.S.S. *Maine***, the United States declared war on Spanish forces in both Cuba and the Philippines. The United States received Puerto Rico, Guam, and the Philippine Islands as part of the treaty.

- After McKinley's death, President Theodore Roosevelt pushed American expansion to greater levels with his rhetoric of **"speak softly and carry a big stick."**

- Construction on the **Panama Canal** began a period of investment in Latin American markets, but President Theodore Roosevelt's addition to the Monroe Doctrine, known as the Roosevelt Corollary, became justification for intervention in Latin America during the first half of the twentieth century.

- After the assassination of Archduke Francis Ferdinand sparked World War I, President Woodrow Wilson declared **neutrality** while also believing that America should be present at the negotiating table in what he saw as the "war to end all wars."

- Following the sinking of the British *Lusitania*, resumption of unrestricted submarine warfare by Germany, and interception of the **Zimmermann telegram**, Congress approved the United States' entry into World War I in an effort to, in Wilson's words, "make the world safe for democracy."

- Victory gardens, anti-German propaganda, and attacks on civil liberties with the creation of the **Espionage and Sedition Acts** had great consequences for the American public.

- After the **Allies** declared victory in 1918, President Wilson trekked to Versailles in an attempt to implement his vision of the Fourteen Points.

- The 1920s were a period of cultural clash that saw battles between religion and science (as seen in the **Scopes Trial**), tradition and modernization (women's rights, technology, crime), and even between capitalism and socialism.

- The **Bolshevik Revolution** in Russia and a postwar recession caused Americans to be cautious of any ties to communism, resulting in the Red Scare in America.

- A growing nativist movement saw Italian-born anarchists **Sacco and Vanzetti** sentenced to death, immigration restrictions passed through Congress in the form of the **National Origins Act of 1924**, and the **KKK** expanding its targets to include immigrants as part of its mission to achieve Anglo-Saxon white supremacy.

- By the end of the 1920s, the **Harlem Renaissance** created new opportunities for African Americans while infusing their culture into every white society.

- **Henry Ford's** use of the assembly line revolutionized the workplace and society by making automobiles more affordable, and consumerism boomed as credit made buying easier while also helping to stimulate an economy built on Mellon-omics, or trickle-down economics.

- Following passage of the **Volstead Act** and **Eighteenth Amendment,** bootlegging became a valuable business that stimulated the crime industry with the likes of crime boss Al Capone becoming one of the wealthiest men in America.

- During the **Great Depression**, unemployment rose to the highest levels the country had ever seen, with 1 in 4 people being out of work, banks running out of money, mortgages for homes and farms being foreclosed, malnutrition and suicide spreading throughout the country at alarming rates, and the Dust Bowl destroying agriculture in the Great Plains.

- Herbert Hoover was viewed as a symbol of American despair during the Great Depression, and he was soundly defeated by the reform-minded Franklin D. Roosevelt, who proposed a "**New Deal**" for Americans and passed an unprecedented amount of social and economic legislation during his first hundred days in office.

- As its allies in Europe began to see Nazi aggression increase across the continent and the Japanese invade Manchuria, the United States declared **neutrality** and championed an America First mentality, but President Roosevelt pledged to support all those rejecting fascist aggression and made speeches and enacted legislation that inched the United States closer to war while angering the Axis powers.

- The United States' total embargo of Japan resulted in Japan's surprise attack on **Pearl Harbor** on December 7th, 1941, an act that left over 2,000 Americans dead and caused the U.S. to enter World War II.

- Every aspect of America worked toward victory as unions made no-strike pledges, workers took on extra "victory" shifts, war bonds sold at high rates, women rallied behind the iconic **"Rosie the Riveter"** to take men's places in factories, and minorities aided in the war effort in numerous areas as Mexican Americans worked on farms as braceros and Native Americans served as code talkers.

- African Americans fought for the United States and saw Executive Order 8802 produce the **Fair Employment Practices Committee** as part of the **Double V** campaign.

- Japanese Americans faced discrimination in response to the attacks at Pearl Harbor as President Roosevelt placed them in **internment camps**, violating their civil liberties in an attempt to keep them "safe," but they still joined the war effort in an attempt to prove their loyalties.

- The **"Big Three"** of FDR, Winston Churchill of Great Britain, and Joseph Stalin of the Soviet Union discussed the fate of the war during meetings at Tehran and Yalta.

- The allied invasion of Normandy, France (**D-Day**), was a major turning point in the war, and Adolf Hitler of Germany, faced with a two-front war, surrendered less than a year later, on what would be known as Victory in Europe Day or **VE Day**.

- Following the defeat of Germany, the United States focused on Japan, and President Harry S Truman approved the dropping of atomic bombs on **Hiroshima** and **Nagasaki**, after which Japan formally surrendered on what would be known as **VJ Day** or Victory in Japan Day.

Period 8 (1945–1980)

Chapter 12

OVERVIEW

- **Learning Objectives**
- **The Golden Age of America**
- **The Civil Rights Movement**
- **The Cold War**
- **The Great Society and The Vietnam War**
- **America in Fluctuation**
- **Key Events in Period 8: A Timeline**
- **Practice**
- **Summing It Up**

LEARNING OBJECTIVES

Upon completion of this chapter you should be able to...

- Explain how the United States became a global power as a result of its responses to the postwar world and the effects these responses had on a national and international scale

- Relate how civil rights and liberal control of the government created numerous political and social responses

- Recognize how the postwar economy and demographic changes impacted society, politics, and culture

During this period in American history, many things were happening at the same time. Instead of a chronological approach, in this chapter we will use a thematic approach to help you better understand the topics in context. It is important as you read to remember that while a foreign issue is being discussed, other issues may be happening domestically.

THE GOLDEN AGE OF AMERICA

As men returned home from war, they would enter a world that looked extremely different in every walk of life. **Teenagers** were rebelling, thanks to pop culture influences like James Dean movies and the **Beat** movement. Women were challenging their domestic roles by attempting to remain in the workplace, and men hoped to direct their return to the home in a revitalization of the **cult of domesticity**. The **GI Bill** sent more people to college, and incomes rose from a combination of the United States being a producing power with more jobs and the success of **unions** following World War II.

This economic boom of sustained economic growth led to a population "**baby boom**" (which, in turn, helped to fuel the economic boom via a new market), and consumer spending spread to new products—credit allowed people to purchase their first homes, cars, and televisions. They moved to **suburbs** in homes that were mass-produced like those in **Levittown**, traveled to the West on highways (as part of the **Interstate Highway Act**) in search of vacations or defense jobs created by Cold War spending, and consumed the new culture of **Jackson Pollock** and **Elvis Presley**.

Everyone continued to spend in hopes of promoting capitalism in the fight against communism, which hit home through the **McCarthy** trials, loyalty oaths, Hollywood Ten, **HUAC**, and hearings against Alger Hiss and the Rosenbergs. The **Red Scare** had returned and sparked a desire to repudiate all things anti-American, even in space—NASA was created to compete with the Soviet launching of *Sputnik*. Americans bought bomb shelters and feared atomic and hydrogen bombs could end their existence any day, again leading to a boom in economic spending fueled by **anticommunism**. Even as exiting President Eisenhower warned against a **military-industrial complex**, it became increasingly clear that the United States had learned that its best protection against another depression would be increased government spending and new jobs springing from the glut of wartime spending.

THE CIVIL RIGHTS MOVEMENT

All was not golden, however, as African Americans looked to build from their Double V campaign and confront the hypocrisy of democracy within the United States. The doctrine of separate but equal was challenged in the Supreme Court and, as a result of the *Brown v. Board of Education* case, overturned. While this represented a political victory, African Americans still faced real discrimination, racism, and segregation at state and local levels via Jim Crow, the **dixiecrat** party, and "massive resistance" as part of the **Southern Manifesto**'s rejection of the ruling. President Eisenhower was called on to enforce the desegregation order at **Little Rock High School**, and future Presidents John F. Kennedy and Lyndon B. Johnson would make legislative attempts to protect civil rights.

At the ground level, a movement for civil rights was growing out of repeated and blatant discrimination. The **Montgomery Bus Boycott** was effective in addressing the issues brought to light by **Rosa Parks**; **Dr. Martin Luther King, Jr.**, gave speeches and created writings recognizant of Thoreau's message of **civil disobedience** (the **Letter from a Birmingham Jail** and, most famously, his "**I have a dream**" speech during the **1963 March on Washington**). Through founding the Southern Christian Leadership Conference (**SCLC**), he inspired students across the nation to form a sit-in movement and undertake **Freedom Rides** that stretched across the South. **Birmingham** was the center of discrimination; "**Bull**" **Connor**'s strategy of using police dogs and water hoses forced action by President Kennedy, including a televised address on civil rights and a call for stronger protective legislation.

As nonviolence was ineffective at securing immediate change, a more militant group began to embrace the civil rights movement. **Malcolm X** and the Black Muslim movement, the Student Nonviolent Coordinating Committee (**SNCC**) under **Stokely Carmichael**, and the **Black Panthers** under Bobby Seale and Huey Newton advocated different modes of achieving the same ideal: black power, pride, and self-rule. The tension between whites and blacks would manifest in many ways, later highlighted by the **Kerner Commission**, including movement (white flight to the suburbs) and violence (race riots in cities such as L.A. and Detroit). Several movements in the political arena also came about: the **Civil Rights Act of 1964**, the Equal Employment Opportunity Commission, the **Voting Rights Act of 1965**, the **Southern strategy**, and the rise of **George Wallace**. As African Americans entered the 1980s, they had seen many gains but also many continued barriers to total equality.

THE COLD WAR

Following World War II, tensions were extremely high between the Soviet Union and the United States due to heavy Soviet war causalities and atomic warfare looming on the horizon. The Soviet Union under Joseph Stalin was, like much of Europe, devastated and hoped to utilize **satellite nations** to create a **buffer** between itself and the threat of invasion. Their communist regime had built, as Churchill put it, a figurative "**iron curtain**" that would soon result in creation of a **wall in Berlin**, dividing not only East and West Berlin but also East Germany (communist) and West Germany (capitalist).

America's answer was a doctrine of **containment** recommended by **George Kennan**. President Harry Truman had come out of his meeting at **Potsdam** with Stalin prepared to stop the threat of communist expansion in an effort to protect U.S. markets in Europe (and keep the United States from falling into another depression). Under the Truman administration, numerous attempts were made to stop the advances: issuing the **Truman Doctrine**, creating the **Marshall Plan**, joining **NATO** (in retaliation, Stalin formed the **Warsaw Pact**), ordering the **Berlin Airlift** to counter the Berlin blockade, and supporting the **UN Security Council** resolution to assist in the **Korean conflict**.

U.S. Army General Douglas MacArthur's challenge of Truman's position in Korea, combined with lingering effects of being "soft" on China, led America to look to a former war hero to lead it into the next decade. **Dwight D. Eisenhower**, Supreme Commander of the Allied forces in Europe during WWII, was elected and immediately made his military presence felt. Supporting the ideas of his Secretary of State **John Foster Dulles**, the President declared a strategy of massive retaliation, and the world was drawn into a period of **brinksmanship**, where nuclear war was possible at any moment. Eisenhower also pursued American involvement in the Middle East as well as Vietnam, as his position on communism would come to be known as the **Domino Theory**. Future Presidents Kennedy, Johnson, and Nixon would all be subject to the fear that Asia could fall to communism if South Vietnam were allowed to collapse.

When the 1960 election catapulted the television into a key medium, it helped to shape the future of the country and its ideas. **John F. Kennedy** won the election, marking a sharp transition from his predecessor, Eisenhower, as their difference in age and political philosophy was apparent. JFK also would use TV to make important speeches on civil rights, as well as his declaration of "quarantine" (naval blockade of Cuba) in response to discovering missiles in Cuba that had been secretly approved by Soviet Premier **Nikita Khrushchev**. The **Cuban Missile Crisis** would end peacefully. It was the closest the two countries had ever come to nuclear war, and it gave Kennedy new public support that he had lost during the **Bay of Pigs** invasion. As he spoke out against the spread of communism in places like **Berlin**, at home America was changing drastically, as culture and the economy each became issues he hoped to address. He would push his **New Frontier** agenda with a focus on civil rights, healthcare, and education for Americans. Education would be primary, as the space race continued to dominate headlines after JFK promised to put a man on the moon by the end of the 1960s.

Unfortunately, tragedy would strike before the President could see his dream become reality—Kennedy was assassinated in Texas in November 1963 during a campaign stop. His Vice President **Lyndon B. Johnson** would attempt to continue not only the Kennedy policies but also those of the New Deal by implementing his own "**Great Society**" for America.

THE GREAT SOCIETY AND THE VIETNAM WAR

Presidents from Truman through Nixon added to the New Deal's legacy. Truman, and later LBJ, argued for something Teddy Roosevelt had proposed as early as 1912—the kind of universal health coverage that was then being provided by most developed nations. LBJ got Medicare and Medicaid out of the appeal as part of his social agenda, the so-called "Great Society," which included several other key pieces of legislation: a public television and radio network (today's PBS and NPR); increased funding for education and urban development; a new, quota-abolishing immigration regime; and new departments and agencies including Transportation, Housing and Urban Development, the Equal Employment Opportunity Commission, and the National Endowment for the Arts. Above all, Johnson's Great Society declared a **War on Poverty,** points of which were the introduction of food stamps, Head Start, and a domestic version of JFK's Peace Corps, VISTA. The combination of LBJ's legendary mastery of parliamentary and other forms of political power and a sense of national shock over the assassination of JFK allowed this latter-day extension of the New Deal to make it through Congress.

The problem for LBJ was that his war on poverty could not continue to be funded as long as the war in Vietnam continued to escalate. Believing that the fight against communism was too important to lose, America continued to pour resources into a war that gave Johnson a "**blank check**" to compensate for the **Gulf of Tonkin** attack. At the start of the war, most Americans firmly supported the President but, as television continued to show the increase in deaths that correlated with the escalation in number of troops, many (especially on the left) became more disillusioned with the war. As **hawks** supported the war, a counterculture movement combined with **doves** to protest against it at teach-ins, in song and at festivals such as **Woodstock,** and in groups such as the Students for a Democratic Society (**SDS**).

After the **Tet Offensive** convinced many the war was unwinnable, President Johnson announced he would not seek reelection, leaving the Democratic nomination up for grabs. Senator **Robert Kennedy** was seen as the popular antiwar choice to take over as head of the party, but, like his brother (and Dr. King earlier in the year), he was assassinated in what would be an incredibly unstable year of **1968**. The Democrats would remain divided, and Republican **Richard Nixon** would appeal to the **Silent Majority** with his 1950s views on communism, society, and the failing economy.

Nixon's position on Vietnam was muddled at times; he ran on a proposal of ending the war by training those in South Vietnam to fight for themselves (known as **Vietnamization**) but declared there would be "**peace with honor.**" At the same time, he continued to escalate the war by sending troops to **Cambodia** and approving secret bombings. In response, protests erupted at **Kent State**, expressing the frustration many Americans had with not only the war but also tests at home.

Nixon would shift focus away from Vietnam and follow the foreign policy advice of National Security Advisor **Henry Kissinger** by visiting China and the Soviet Union in an attempt to ease Cold War tensions (**détente**). However, a growing energy crisis due to the **OPEC** embargo was followed by revelations that Nixon had been behind the Watergate break-in. His firing of officials and attempt to cover it up would lead to **impeachment** proceedings that demonstrated the mistrust in politics for most Americans. Nixon resigned before he could be impeached, leaving the first unelected President, **Gerald Ford**, in office. A **pardon** of Nixon coupled with an economy that could not "whip" **stagflation** led to the election of political outsider **Jimmy Carter** in 1976. His one term in office was filled with increased stagflation, an energy crisis, the **Iran hostage crisis,** and success in the Middle East in completing the **Camp David Accords**.

AMERICA IN FLUCTUATION

After the civil rights movement made considerable strides in the 1960s, other minority groups looked to find equity during the late sixties and early seventies. Many women rejected the housewife label that had returned following World War II. Inspired by Betty Friedan's *The Feminine Mystique*, a feminist movement made gains as a result of **Title IX** and the Civil Rights Act of 1964 but still faced opposition. The National Organization for Women (**NOW**) attempted to combat low pay and discrimination while the ruling in *Roe v. Wade* protected a woman's right to privacy. Attempts at an **Equal Rights Amendment** outlawing discrimination based on sex were defeated thanks to the efforts of **Phyllis Schlafly**.

During this same period, a movement surrounding sexual identity grew into the **Gay Liberation Movement**. Following riots at the **Stonewall Inn**, greater attention was given to the cause; today, its effects on the acceptance of the **LGBTQ** community can be found all over the country.

Hispanic Americans were a growing population following World War II and, with help from immigration reform as part the Great Society, more were living in the United States. A key event in organization of the Hispanic movement came in 1962 when **Cesar Chavez** helped found the National Farm Workers Association (**NFWA**) that would become the **UFW** (United Farm Workers). Leading a strike that led to a national boycott of grapes, Chavez united people behind protest and a hunger strike.

Native Americans also organized during this period in an attempt to draw attention to their treatment by the United States government. The **AIM** (American Indian Movement) would see success in achieving education funding and changes to reservation management.

Finally, the environment was the focus of changes after years of neglect due to urbanization, industrialization, and even pesticides. Rachael Carson's *Silent Spring* helped to project a focus on the environment that would lead to Earth Day, the **Clean Air Act**, and creation of the Environmental Protection Agency (**EPA**).

KEY EVENTS IN PERIOD 8: A TIMELINE

Significant Date	Event
1945	FDR dies, Truman becomes President; United Nations charter approved; Potsdam Conference; Atomic bombs dropped on Japan
1946	Kennan's "long telegram"; Iron curtain speech
1947	Marshall Plan proposed; Levittown opens
1948	Berlin airlift
1949	Senate ratifies NATO membership; Soviet Union tests atomic bomb
1950	Alger Hiss convicted; North Korea invades South Korea
1952	Eisenhower elected President; United States tests H-bomb
1953	Soviet Union tests H-bomb
1954	*Brown v. Board of Education* ruling; Defeat of French at Dien Bien Phu; Senate censures Joseph McCarthy
1955	Rosa Parks arrested
1956	Interstate Highway Act; Suez Canal crisis; Montgomery bus boycott ends
1957	Riots at Central High School in Little Rock, Arkansas; Soviet Union launches *Sputnik*
1960	U-2 plane shot down over Soviet Union; JFK elected President
1961	Bay of Pigs invasion fails; Berlin Wall is built
1962	SDS Port Huron statement; *Silent Spring* published
1963	March on Washington for Civil Rights; JFK assassinated; *The Feminine Mystique* published
1964	Civil Rights Act passed; Great Society announced; Free Speech Movement; LBJ defeats Goldwater for Presidency
1965	Malcolm X assassinated; LBJ signs Medicare-Medicaid, Voting Rights Act; Immigration Reform Act; Elementary and Secondary Education Act
1968	Tet Offensive; Martin Luther King, Jr. and Robert Kennedy assassinated; Democratic National Convention riots; Richard Nixon elected President
1969	Neil Armstrong walks on the moon; Woodstock festival
1970	U.S. invasion of Cambodia; Kent State demonstration; First Earth Day
1972	Nixon visits China; Title IX signed; Watergate break-in; Phyllis Schlafly launches STOP ERA

1973	Last U.S. combat troops leave Vietnam; *Roe v. Wade* decision; AIM occupies Wounded Knee; Gerald Ford named Vice President, replacing Spiro Agnew
1974	Richard Nixon resigns, Gerald Ford becomes President
1976	Jimmy Carter elected President
1978	Camp David peace talks and Camp David Accords
1979	Three Mile Island nuclear accident; American hostages taken in Iran; Soviet invasion of Afghanistan
1980	Ronald Reagan elected President

PRACTICE

Directions: Each of the questions or incomplete statements below is followed by four suggested answers or completions. Select the one that is best in each case.

Perhaps the more tragic recognition of reality took place when it became clear to me that the war was doing far more than devastating the hope of the poor at home. It was sending their sons, and their brothers, and their husbands to fight and die in extraordinarily high proportion relative to the rest of the population. We were taking the black young men who had been crippled by society and sending them eight thousand miles away to guarantee liberties in Southeast Asia which they had not found in Southwest Georgia and East Harlem. So we have been repeatedly faced with a cruel irony of watching Negro and white boys on TV screens as they kill and die together for a nation that has been unable to seat them together in the same school room. So we watch them in brutal solidarity, burning the huts of a poor village. But we realize that they would hardly live on the same block in Chicago or Atlanta. Now, I could not be silent in the face of such cruel manipulation of the poor.

—Martin Luther King, "Why I Am Opposed to the War in Vietnam"
April 30, 1967, Riverside Church, New York

1. What is the context surrounding the speech Dr. King is giving about Vietnam?
   A. The removal of segregation in the military after the Korean War has led to more African American deaths in combat.
   B. The Civil Rights movement had yet to see significant gains in American society, yet African Americans were being sent overseas to fight for others' freedom.
   C. The Great Depression negatively impacted African Americans more than any other group in society, and economically they continued to struggle.
   D. Vietnam was not this country's war to begin with, and sending troops only compounds the problems America was having with the rest of the world.

2. Which of the following leaders might echo the sentiments of Dr. King?
    A. Robert Kennedy
    B. Lyndon B. Johnson
    C. Richard Nixon
    D. Hubert Humphrey

3. Which would be the best evidence to support the views expressed by Dr. King in the excerpt?
    A. The creation of Medicaid and Medicare
    B. The passage of the Civil Rights Act and 26th Amendment
    C. The ruling in *Brown v. Board of Education*
    D. The sit-in and bus boycott movements

Answer Key and Explanations

1. B	2. A	3. D

1. **The correct answer is B.** The civil rights movement was still attempting to find equity domestically as America turned away from the Great Society and focused on the foreign policy in Vietnam. Instead of fighting for an end to segregation at home, the United States was attempting to prevent communism from spreading in Asia by using African American troops, among others. Choice A is incorrect because King's issue was not with blacks and whites fighting together but rather that blacks were being forced to fight for freedom they did not have at home. Choice C is incorrect because the Great Depression occurred too far in the past to have an effect on the war in Vietnam, and issues of the Great Society not being funded were a greater problem. Choice D is incorrect because King's issue was not with American perception around the world but its lack of focus on equity at home.

2. **The correct answer is A.** Kennedy was a noted peace (dove) Democrat who wished to continue the work of his brother on civil rights while ending the conflict in Vietnam; he would be assassinated the same year as King. Choices B and D are incorrect, as Johnson instituted the policy of escalation in Vietnam with Humphrey serving as his vice president. Humphrey would run in Johnson's place for President in 1968 and advocated similar goals and platform. Choice C is incorrect because Nixon (while advocating for an end to the war) continued the war and pushed back against the civil rights movement domestically.

3. **The correct answer is D.** The sit-in and bus boycott movements were reactions to the inequality that African Americans faced in society and would support Dr. King's view that America was not protecting their rights. Choices A, B, and C are incorrect because these were all attempts to create better protections, support, and equality for African Americans.

SUMMING IT UP

- During the 1950s, teenagers were rebelling, women were challenging their domestic roles by attempting to remain in the workplace, men hoped to direct a return home in a revitalization of the **cult of domesticity**, and the GI Bill sent more people to college.

- As incomes rose, there was sustained economic growth that led to a population **"baby boom"**, and consumer spending spread to new products of leisure and affluence as credit allowed people to purchase their first home, car, and television.

- People moved to **suburbs** in homes that were mass-produced like those in Levittown, traveled to the West on the highway in search of vacations or defense jobs, and consumed the new culture of Jackson Pollock and Elvis Presley.

- **Anticommunism** resulted in the McCarthy trials, loyalty oaths, the Hollywood Ten, HUAC, and hearings against Alger Hiss and the Rosenbergs.

- Amidst the Soviets' launch of *Sputnik*, Americans bought bomb shelters and feared atomic and hydrogen bombs.

- The doctrine of separate but equal was overturned in the Supreme Court as a result of the *Brown v. Board of Education* case, but African Americans faced discrimination at state and local levels via Jim Crow laws, the dixiecrat party, and "massive resistance" as part of a Southern Manifesto rejecting the ruling, forcing President Eisenhower to enforce the desegregation order at Little Rock High School.

- Civil Rights efforts included the **Montgomery Bus Boycott** inspired by Rosa Parks and Dr. Martin Luther King, Jr.'s, message of civil disobedience and his "I have a dream" speech during the 1963 March on Washington.

- "Bull" Connor's use of police dogs and water hoses against African Americans in **Birmingham** forced President John F. Kennedy to call for stronger protective legislation.

- **Malcolm X** and the Black Muslim movement, the Student Nonviolent Coordinating Committee (**SNCC**), and the **Black Panthers** promoted black power, pride, and self-rule in a more militant form of the civil rights movement.

- Issuance of the **Truman Doctrine**, the Marshall Plan, the United States' joining of NATO, the Berlin Airlift, and support of the UN Security Council resolution to assist in the Korean conflict were among the efforts to stop the advances of communism.

- President **Dwight D. Eisenhower** was drawn into a period of brinksmanship where nuclear war was possible at any moment and pursued American involvement in the Middle East and Vietnam as his position on communism came to be known as the Domino Theory.

- President Lyndon Johnson's social agenda, the so-called **"Great Society,"** included a War on Poverty, Medicare and Medicaid, a public television and radio network, increased funding for education and urban development, and a quota-abolishing immigration regime, as well as new departments and agencies, such as Transportation, Housing and Urban Development, the Equal Employment Opportunity Commission, and National Endowments for the Arts and the Humanities.

- The fight against communism gave President Johnson a "blank check" to compensate for the **Gulf of Tonkin** attack, and he escalated U.S. involvement in Vietnam amid firm support from the public, but a counterculture movement that protested the war arose.

- After the **Tet Offensive** convinced many the Vietnam War was unwinnable, President Johnson announced he would not seek reelection, and Senator Robert Kennedy was seen as the popular antiwar choice to take over as head of the Democratic Party, but he was assassinated in 1968, leaving Democrats divided and allowing Republican Richard Nixon to appeal to the Silent Majority with his 1950s views on communism, society, and the failing economy.

- Nixon had campaigned for President on a proposal of ending the Vietnam War and "**peace with honor,**" but, as President, he escalated the war by sending troops to Cambodia and approving secret bombings.

- Nixon's attempt to cover up the **Watergate** break-in led to impeachment proceedings, but Nixon resigned before he could be impeached, leaving the first unelected President Gerald Ford, in office, but Ford's pardon of Nixon and stagflation led to the election of Jimmy Carter in 1976.

- President Jimmy Carter's one term in office included increased stagflation, an energy crisis, the **Iran hostage crisis,** and success in the Middle East in completing the Camp David Accords.

- In the 1960s, the feminist movement made gains as a result of Title IX and the Civil Rights Act of 1964, the National Organization for Women attempted to combat low pay and discrimination, and the ruling in *Roe v. Wade* protected a woman's right to privacy, but attempts at an **Equal Rights Amendment,** outlawing discrimination based on sex, were defeated due to the efforts of Phyllis Schlafly.

- Following riots at the Stonewall Inn, greater attention was given to the **Gay Liberation Movement**.

- With help from immigration reform as part the Great Society, more Hispanic Americans were living in the United States, and, in 1962, **Cesar Chavez** helped found the National Farm Workers Association and united people behind protest and a hunger strike.

- Native Americans organized in an attempt to draw attention to their treatment by the United States government, and the **AIM** would see success in achieving education funding and changes to reservation management.

- After years of urbanization, industrialization, and pesticides, Rachael Carson's *Silent Spring* helped to project a focus on the environment that would lead to Earth Day, the Clean Air Act, and creation of the Environmental Protection Agency (**EPA**).

Period 9 (1980 to Present)

Chapter 13

LEARNING OBJECTIVES

Upon completion of this chapter you should be able to...

- Relate how views of tradition and government led to a new conservative wave
- Explain how the United States redefined itself in a post-Cold War world
- Recognize the challenges that the United States faces in the twenty-first century

Before we begin this chapter, which reviews the most important concepts of the most recent years in history, it is important to note that history needs time to be digested and discussed years after the fact. Judging events, reactions, and programs without the opportunity to fully understand their consequences is not only difficult, but also unsound. The latter part of this chapter deals with current-day issues that are yet to have the luxury of time—so, as a reader, try not to form opinions but rather understand the reasons behind the actions in the context of the period.

THE NEW RIGHT

During the 1960s, a new faction and focus of the Democratic Party led to a more liberalized view of society and government called the "New Left." This counter-revolution would create new policies, views, and values within the country at a time when the United States was experiencing changes politically, economically, globally, and socially. This new movement challenged the traditional values and roles of society, including the conservative values of the 1950s.

A decade of turmoil in Vietnam and social unrest within America, combined with an economy that was struggling, led to a conservative counter-counter revolution that gained momentum. This revolution focused on limited federal government, free-market economic policies, stronger military presence, and a return to traditional values. The New Deal and Great Society programs, movements of radical feminism and gay rights, and a growth in crime, drugs, and HIV/AIDS alarmed members of this "**New Right**." With strong support from evangelical Christians, they began to mobilize. While Barry Goldwater was unsuccessful in achieving a platform to implement his message, it survived nonetheless—and in 1980 a former Democrat and actor would use it to become President.

Ronald Reagan used his previous career as an actor to his advantage as his wit, charm, and public speaking ability drew people to his message. Unlike some candidates, Reagan had the ability to draw people outside of his party into his camp (such as the Reagan Democrats). It was his optimistic view of America coupled with support from the **Moral Majority** that helped him soundly defeat Jimmy Carter in the 1980 election. This **Religious Right** (led by men such as Pat Robertson, Oral Roberts, Jim Baker, and Jerry Falwell) believed the country was in a state of moral decay. They called for the removal of liberal members of Congress who supported rulings such as *Roe v. Wade*. Reagan would address the ideology of the Supreme Court while appointing the first female to the bench (conservative-leaning **Sandra Day O'Connor**), along with William Rehnquist. (Reagan's vice president and future President George H.W. Bush would continue this conservative push with his appointment of Clarence Thomas).

The economy was another major factor in Reagan's election, as he promised tax cuts (which brought in former blue staters and New Deal supporters) and a continued deregulation of business to promote free markets and competition. As the country was in an economic downturn, with stagflation and high unemployment, Reagan unveiled a plan that would attempt to remove government from the equation. Nicknamed "**Reaganomics**," his plan of supply-side or "trickle down" economics mirrored policies of the 1920s. He sharply reduced the federal government funding of New Deal and Great Society programs in an attempt to decrease spending and inflation. The combination of the removal of regulations on businesses coupled with the tax cut would eventually (as there was an immediate recession) create one of the greatest stretches of economic growth in American history, while also eventually being a major cause of the Great Recession years later. However, by 1985 Americans were confident in the dollar, engaging in **conspicuous consumption** of products and the latest fashions, using credit cards (and racking up debt) in new shopping malls, and purchasing homes they would eventually not be able to afford. Spending not only helped the economy but also served another purpose: it reinforced the ideas of capitalism during a period of heightened Cold War tensions.

One area that President Reagan did not cut back on was defense, as his budget rose to levels never seen before in America. Reagan believed this spending was necessary to build confidence in the American military while also helping to defeat the ailing Soviet Union under **Mikhail Gorbachev**. Referring to the Soviet Union as "**The Evil Empire**," Reagan had created a villain for the country to vanquish, and the Soviet Union's economy made it impossible for it to keep up. The **Reagan Doctrine** increased military spending and attempted to create a space-based missile defense system (**SDI**) nicknamed "Star Wars."

Again using speeches to gain support for his vision, Reagan's message outside the Berlin Wall echoed a feeling that Americans needed to be more aggressive toward the Soviets and reject the ideas of détente, especially after Soviet action in **Afghanistan**. Although he tripled the national debt with his programs and had some questionable results in foreign policy (**Nicaragua, Grenada,** and **Iran-Contra**), Reagan was president for two terms and even to this day politicians on the right invoke his name and message when running for office.

Following Reagan's terms in office, his vice president and former challenger **George H. W. Bush** would take office for one term. His tenure included the official fall of the Soviet Union (which ended the Cold War), domestic troubles with the economy that resulted in an unpopular tax increase (despite his campaign pledge of "no new taxes"), and a war in the **Persian Gulf** that unsuccessfully attempted to unseat Iraq's dictator, Saddam Hussein (but did defeat Iraq as part of **Operation Desert Storm**).

THE GLOBAL WORLD

As the twenty-first century drew near, America was one of many countries experiencing an overhaul in almost every aspect of its society. Race riots and violent attacks seemed to be found in every region of the country, from the Rodney King beating in Los Angeles, to suicides and killings in Waco, Texas, to the Oklahoma City bombing. New **technology,** such as computers, the Internet, and cellular telephones had transformed how people interacted with each other. The global markets that had been strengthened after World War II now had new leaders and saw the United States lagging behind in areas such as manufacturing.

Society looked vastly different than it had even twenty years before, with a large increase in Hispanic population, growth in the Sunbelt region of America, and the **"graying"** of America, as more people than ever before in the country were over the age of 65. However, a new generation of voters was eager to cast their ballots at the polls to have their issues addressed. **William (Bill) Jefferson Clinton** used this MTV generation to his advantage and defeated Bush in 1992. Clinton, a Democrat, took on issues of healthcare reform, crime, deficit reduction, and trade as part of the highly controversial **NAFTA.** This agreement between Mexico, Canada, and the United States removed trade barriers but also saw jobs moved to factories that hired inexpensive workers. But the budget was balanced, the economy was thriving, and there was a federal surplus—it seemed as if Clinton could do no wrong (even though his attempts at humanitarian missions under the direction of **Madeleine Albright** in the **Balkans** were mixed at best). Yet, Republican control of Congress highlighted ideological differences between branches of the government that led to political conflicts (as well as impeachment proceedings due to Clinton's handling of the Monica Lewinsky scandal). The Republicans' **"Contract with America"** forced the President to rethink how he would handle welfare programs, and by the end of his second term the country seemed more politically divided than ever before.

The Supreme Court would decide the contested **election of 2000** between George W. Bush and Al Gore. As the second Bush to hold the presidency turned his attention to a slowing economy, disaster struck. On the morning of **September 11, 2001,** terrorist members of Al-Qaeda, under the direction of Osama bin Laden, attacked America. The lives lost as a result of the plane hijackings would lead to drastic changes in domestic and foreign policy. As the country began its War on Terror (first in Afghanistan and then in Iraq), President Bush signed the **USA Patriot Act** and **Homeland Security Act of 2002** into law to strengthen national security while combating terrorism domestically. President Bush would also have to deal with **Hurricane Katrina** and the aftereffects of FEMA's mismanagement.

The election of 2008 would focus on the lingering effects of the war on terror and its continued strain on the U.S. economy. While the federal government was spending itself into greater national debt during years of fighting in the Middle East, the domestic economy had fallen into the **Great Recession** because of years of housing speculation, lackluster regulations, and soaring gas prices. A Democratic junior Senator from Illinois would defeat Hillary Clinton in the primaries to run against Republican (and Vietnam War hero) John McCain in the presidential election. **Barack Obama** promised change via a New Deal-like stimulus program for the economy (and the automobile industry), an end to the war in the Middle East, and creation of a Universal Health Care system as part of the Affordable Care Act (labeled "**Obamacare**" by his opponents). The first African American President in United States history would see his party face challenges from the growing **Tea Party** movement in the midterm elections of 2010 and continued struggles with the economy, gun violence, and his healthcare program. He would win a second term in 2012. By the end of his time in office, the economy had improved and U.S. forces had killed Osama Bin Laden. Lingering issues of race, same-sex marriage, and immigration would all come to dominate the 2016 election cycle.

THE POLITICAL CLIMATE IN 2016

In 2016, the election cycle highlighted a growing divide within the country as true political outsider and business mogul **Donald Trump** secured the Republican nomination over an extremely large field of candidates using a Populist-like campaign and a message of "America First." His defeat of former First Lady, Senator, and Secretary of State **Hillary Clinton** (the first woman to head a major party campaign) was a product of Reagan-like shifts in voting. The candidates debated topics that continued to be discussed after his election, including taxes, trade, gun control, healthcare, race relations, border security, and even nationalism. Concepts like a border wall between the United States and Mexico, the slogan "Make America Great Again," "Black Lives Matter," and even kneeling for the national anthem were all hotly debated during his first year in office. Looming questions about the role and firing of FBI Director James Comey, Russia's influence in the presidential election, the notion of "fake news," and immigration policy seemed to continue with no end.

However, historians are unable to truly judge the impacts or even the importance of certain events in the actual moment. Looking ahead, America will continue to redefine its place in the world as social media changes how we view it; as the global economy changes what products are needed and how those products are delivered; and as the country moves in different political directions in response to world events.

KEY EVENTS IN PERIOD 9: A TIMELINE

Significant Date	Event
1980	Reagan elected President
1981	HIV/AIDS recognized by U.S. Centers for Disease Control; Reagan tax and budget bill passed; PATCO strikers fired by Reagan
1982	Boland Amendment
1983	Reagan declares Soviet Union "Evil Empire"; SDI announced; U.S. invasion of Grenada
1984	NSC begins what will become Iran-Contra Scandal; Reagan reelected
1986	Chernobyl explosion
1987	Report on Iran-Contra released
1988	George H.W. Bush elected President
1989	Tiananmen Square protest; Berlin Wall falls
1990	East and West Germany unified
1991	Operation Desert Storm; Rodney King beaten by Los Angeles police; Clarence Thomas appointed to the Supreme Court; Soviet Union disbands
1993	Waco, Texas, assault and suicide; Military "don't ask, don't tell" policy begins; U.S. troops Somalia, NAFTA approved
1995	Newt Gingrich (Republican) elected Speaker of the House; Oklahoma City federal building bombed
1996	Welfare Reform Act
1998	Clinton impeachment; Google founded
1999	Clinton acquitted; Columbine shooting
2001	George W. Bush inaugurated and signs tax-cut legislation; terrorist attacks on the United States; Apple iTunes and Wikipedia launched
2002	No Child Left Behind legislation
2003	United States invades Iraq and overthrows Saddam Hussein
2005	Hurricane Katrina
2008	Financial crisis; Barack Obama elected President
2010	Affordable Health Care Act
2011	Death of Osama Bin Laden
2012	"Dreamers" Act (Immigration Reform)
2016	Donald Trump elected President

PRACTICE

Directions: Each of the questions or incomplete statements below is followed by four suggested answers or completions. Select the one that is best in each case.

> The search is underway for those who were behind these evil acts. I have directed the full resources of our intelligence and law enforcement communities to find those responsible and to bring them to justice. We will make no distinction between the terrorists who committed these acts and those who harbor them.
>
> —George W. Bush, 9/11 Address to the Nation

1. Which previous event had the most similar impact as the one described in the excerpt above?
   A. Boston Massacre
   B. Sinking of U.S.S. *Maine*
   C. Pearl Harbor
   D. Watergate

2. Which of the following best reflects the changes in American domestic life brought about by the event described in the excerpt?
   A. Civil liberty rights were tested as new acts and security attempted to protect Americans.
   B. Military spending increased the size of the U.S. forces in the Middle East.
   C. Production in factories increased to create a wartime boom in the economy.
   D. The United States entered into alliances with European powers to combat terrorism abroad.

3. Which of the following Presidents would have disagreed with the actions of President Bush after 9/11?
   A. Abraham Lincoln
   B. Woodrow Wilson
   C. Franklin D. Roosevelt
   D. None of the above

Answer Key and Explanations

1. C	2. A	3. D

1. **The correct answer is C.** The attack on Pearl Harbor by the Japanese not only brought the United States into World War II but also created nationalism in the country directed at those responsible for the attack. Choice A is incorrect because after the Boston Massacre there was a relative lull in British and American conflict (although it must be noted that Americans were upset with the event, just not enough to insight direct war). Choice B is incorrect as this event (which was later found to be incorrectly connected to the Spanish) did cause America to become involved in conflict with Spain but nationalism was largely fabricated by yellow journalism. Choice D is incorrect because this scandal did not lead to war or a renewed sense of nationalism.

2. **The correct answer is A.** Changes to airline security as well as legislation such as the Patriot Act infringed on the civil liberties of Americans by violating some of their rights of freedom in order to better protect against terrorist attacks. Choice C is incorrect, as the economy did not improve but instead began to decline with military spending increasing federal debt. Choices B and D are incorrect because they are not domestic issues.

3. **The correct answer is D.** Choices A, B, and C are incorrect, as all these men took similar actions during wartime: Lincoln suspended habeas corpus during the Civil War, Wilson enacted the Espionage and Sedition Acts during WWI, and FDR sent Japanese Americans to internment camps during WWII.

SUMMING IT UP

- The turmoil in Vietnam, social unrest within America, and the struggling economy of the 1960s and 1970s inspired a conservative counter-counter revolution that focused on limited federal government, free-market economic policies, stronger military presence, and a return to traditional values known as the **"New Right"** that survived into the 1980s.

- Republican **Ronald Reagan**, with support from the Moral Majority, defeated Jimmy Carter in the 1980 presidential election.

  ○ Reagan unveiled a plan nicknamed **"Reaganomics"** that reduced federal government funding of New Deal and Great Society programs in an attempt to reduce spending and inflation.

  ○ Reagan's tax cuts and removal of regulations on businesses created one of the greatest stretches of economic growth in American history, while also eventually causing the Great Recession years later.

  ○ The **Reagan Doctrine** increased military spending and attempted to create a space-based missile defense system nicknamed "Star Wars" to build confidence in the American military and defeat Mikhail Gorbachev's Soviet Union, which Reagan labeled "The Evil Empire."

- Reagan's Vice President **George H.W. Bush** took office for one term that included the official fall of the Soviet Union and the end of the Cold War, economy troubles, and a war in the Persian Gulf that unsuccessfully attempted to unseat Iraq's dictator, Saddam Hussein, but did defeat Iraq as part of **Operation Desert Storm**.

- President **William (Bill) Jefferson Clinton**, a Democrat, took on issues of healthcare reform, crime, deficit reduction, and trade as part of NAFTA, which removed trade barriers but also saw jobs moved to factories that hired inexpensive workers.

  ○ During the Clinton administration, the national budget was balanced, the economy was thriving, and there was a federal surplus, though the President's attempts at humanitarian missions in the Balkans under the direction of Madeleine Albright were mixed at best.

  ○ Republican control of Congress highlighted ideological differences between branches of the government that led to political conflicts, and by the end of Clinton's second term, the country seemed more politically divided than ever before.

- The Supreme Court decided that Republican **George W. Bush** was President in the contested election of 2000.

  ○ On **September 11, 2001**, terrorist members of Al-Qaeda under the direction of Osama bin Laden attacked America, which led to a War on Terror in Afghanistan and Iraq and President Bush's signing of the **USA Patriot Act** and **Homeland Security Act of 2002** to strengthen national security and combat terrorism domestically.

  ○ While the federal government was spending itself into greater national debt during years of fighting in the Middle East, the domestic economy had fallen into the **Great Recession** because of years of housing speculation, lackluster regulations, and soaring gas prices.

- The first African American President in United States history, President **Barack Obama**, promised change with a stimulus program for the economy, an end to the war in the Middle East, and creation of a Universal Health Care system as part of the Affordable Care Act labeled "Obamacare" by his opponents.

  ○ Although President Obama would see Democrats face challenges in the midterm elections of 2010 from the growing Tea Party movement, the continually struggling economy, and gun violence, He would win a second term in 2012, and by the end of his time in office, the economy had improved and Osama Bin Laden had been killed by U.S. forces.

- In 2016, political outsider and business mogul Donald Trump secured the Republican nomination using a Populist-like campaign and a message of "America First" and defeated former Secretary of State and First Lady Hillary Clinton to become President of a drastically divided nation.

PART IV
THREE PRACTICE TESTS

Practice Test 1

Chapter 14

ANSWER SHEET PRACTICE TEST 1

Section I, Part A: Multiple-Choice Questions

1. Ⓐ Ⓑ Ⓒ Ⓓ 15. Ⓐ Ⓑ Ⓒ Ⓓ 29. Ⓐ Ⓑ Ⓒ Ⓓ 43. Ⓐ Ⓑ Ⓒ Ⓓ
2. Ⓐ Ⓑ Ⓒ Ⓓ 16. Ⓐ Ⓑ Ⓒ Ⓓ 30. Ⓐ Ⓑ Ⓒ Ⓓ 44. Ⓐ Ⓑ Ⓒ Ⓓ
3. Ⓐ Ⓑ Ⓒ Ⓓ 17. Ⓐ Ⓑ Ⓒ Ⓓ 31. Ⓐ Ⓑ Ⓒ Ⓓ 45. Ⓐ Ⓑ Ⓒ Ⓓ
4. Ⓐ Ⓑ Ⓒ Ⓓ 18. Ⓐ Ⓑ Ⓒ Ⓓ 32. Ⓐ Ⓑ Ⓒ Ⓓ 46. Ⓐ Ⓑ Ⓒ Ⓓ
5. Ⓐ Ⓑ Ⓒ Ⓓ 19. Ⓐ Ⓑ Ⓒ Ⓓ 33. Ⓐ Ⓑ Ⓒ Ⓓ 47. Ⓐ Ⓑ Ⓒ Ⓓ
6. Ⓐ Ⓑ Ⓒ Ⓓ 20. Ⓐ Ⓑ Ⓒ Ⓓ 34. Ⓐ Ⓑ Ⓒ Ⓓ 48. Ⓐ Ⓑ Ⓒ Ⓓ
7. Ⓐ Ⓑ Ⓒ Ⓓ 21. Ⓐ Ⓑ Ⓒ Ⓓ 35. Ⓐ Ⓑ Ⓒ Ⓓ 49. Ⓐ Ⓑ Ⓒ Ⓓ
8. Ⓐ Ⓑ Ⓒ Ⓓ 22. Ⓐ Ⓑ Ⓒ Ⓓ 36. Ⓐ Ⓑ Ⓒ Ⓓ 50. Ⓐ Ⓑ Ⓒ Ⓓ
9. Ⓐ Ⓑ Ⓒ Ⓓ 23. Ⓐ Ⓑ Ⓒ Ⓓ 37. Ⓐ Ⓑ Ⓒ Ⓓ 51. Ⓐ Ⓑ Ⓒ Ⓓ
10. Ⓐ Ⓑ Ⓒ Ⓓ 24. Ⓐ Ⓑ Ⓒ Ⓓ 38. Ⓐ Ⓑ Ⓒ Ⓓ 52. Ⓐ Ⓑ Ⓒ Ⓓ
11. Ⓐ Ⓑ Ⓒ Ⓓ 25. Ⓐ Ⓑ Ⓒ Ⓓ 39. Ⓐ Ⓑ Ⓒ Ⓓ 53. Ⓐ Ⓑ Ⓒ Ⓓ
12. Ⓐ Ⓑ Ⓒ Ⓓ 26. Ⓐ Ⓑ Ⓒ Ⓓ 40. Ⓐ Ⓑ Ⓒ Ⓓ 54. Ⓐ Ⓑ Ⓒ Ⓓ
13. Ⓐ Ⓑ Ⓒ Ⓓ 27. Ⓐ Ⓑ Ⓒ Ⓓ 41. Ⓐ Ⓑ Ⓒ Ⓓ 55. Ⓐ Ⓑ Ⓒ Ⓓ
14. Ⓐ Ⓑ Ⓒ Ⓓ 28. Ⓐ Ⓑ Ⓒ Ⓓ 42. Ⓐ Ⓑ Ⓒ Ⓓ

Section I, Part B: Short-Answer Questions

Question 1

_____

_____

_____

_____

_____

_____

_____

_____

answer sheet

Question 2

_____

_____

_____

_____

_____

_____

_____

_____

_____

_____

_____

_____

_____

_____

Question 3 or 4

_____

_____

_____

_____

_____

_____

_____

_____

_____

_____

_____

_____

_____

_____

_____

Section II, Part A: Document-Based Question

_____

_____

_____

_____

_____

_____

_____

_____

_____

_____

_____

_____

_____

_____

_____

_____

_____

_____

_____

_____

_____

_____

_____

_____

_____

answer sheet

answer sheet

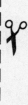

answer sheet

Section II, Part B: Long Essay Question

PRACTICE TEST 1

Section I, Part A: Multiple-Choice Questions

Time: 55 Minutes • 55 Questions

> **Directions:** Each question set is organized around two to five questions that focus on a primary or secondary source. After reading the document, choose the best answer and fill in the correct oval on the answer sheet.

Questions 1–3 refer to the excerpt below.

"And now you have an extraordinary opportunity, a day wherein Christ has thrown the door of mercy wide open, and stands in calling and crying with a loud voice to poor sinners; a day wherein many are flocking to him, and pressing into the kingdom of God. Many are daily coming from the east, west, north and south; many that were very lately in the same miserable condition that you are in, are now in a happy state, with their hearts filled with love to him who has loved them, and washed them from their sins in his own blood, and rejoicing in hope of the glory of God. [...] God seems now to be hastily gathering in his elect in all parts of the land; and probably the greater part of adult persons that ever shall be saved, will be brought in now in a little time, [...] and the rest will be blinded. If this should be the case with you, you will eternally curse this day, and will curse the day that ever you was born, to see such a season of the pouring out of God's Spirit, and will wish that you had died and gone to hell before you had seen it."

—Excerpt from *Sinners in the Hands of an Angry God*, Jonathan Edwards, 1741

Source: *https://en.m.wikisource.org/wiki/Sinners_in_the_Hands_of_an_Angry_God*

1. This style of evangelical preaching was typical of the 1730s and 1740s and inspired which of the following movements?
   A. The First Great Awakening
   B. The Second Great Awakening
   C. The Conservation Movement
   D. Bacon's Rebellion

2. In which of the following settings would a sermon such as this most likely be preached?
   A. A century-old, conservative New England church on Sunday, to the usual congregation
   B. Out of doors, nearly impromptu, to thousands of people
   C. Private homes, and to small groups
   D. Factories, during work, to small groups

3. Some historians argue that the movement typified by the excerpt above helped lay the groundwork for American democracy for which of the following reasons?

   A. The movement existed outside of established social, political, and religious structures and appealed directly to citizens.

   B. The movement held quite liberal interpretations of scripture.

   C. The center of power during such meetings was the congregation itself, not a charismatic preacher.

   D. Interest in the movement increased literacy, as colonists wanted to read published versions of sermons.

Questions 4–7 refer to the figure below.

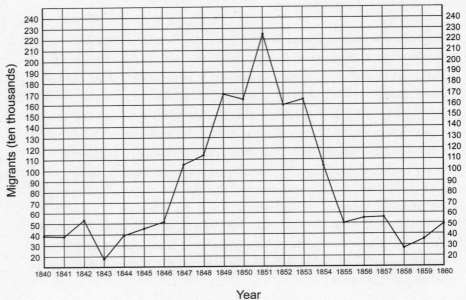

IRISH MIGRATION TO THE UNITED STATES, 1840–1860

Source: U.S. Census Bureau

4. Which of the following caused the spike in Irish immigration pictured above?

   A. The Black Plague

   B. Famine

   C. Influenza

   D. Genocide

5. Increased immigration such as that shown in the figure above gave rise to which of the following political parties?

   A. Democratic-Republicans

   B. Whigs

   C. Federalists

   D. Know-Nothings

6. Aside from Ireland, which of the following countries contributed the most to American immigration during this period?

   A. Mexico

   B. Italy

   C. China

   D. Germany

7. The immigrants represented in the graph would most likely have settled in which of the following?

   A. New York City

   B. San Francisco

   C. New Orleans

   D. Atlanta

Questions 8–10 refer to the excerpt below.

"When, in the course of human events, it becomes necessary for one portion of the family of man to assume among the people of the earth a position different from that which they have hitherto occupied, but one to which the laws of nature and of nature's God entitle them, a decent respect to the opinions of mankind requires that they should declare the causes that impel them to such a course."

—From The Declaration of Sentiments, Seneca Falls Convention, 1848

Source: *https://en.m.wikisource.org/wiki/Declaration_of_Sentiments*

8. Which of the following founding documents does this excerpt echo?
   A. The Articles of Confederation
   B. The Declaration of Independence
   C. The Constitution
   D. The Declaration of the Rights of Man

9. All of the following were goals of the movement exemplified by this document EXCEPT:
   A. abortion.
   B. suffrage.
   C. property rights.
   D. access to education.

10. Which of the following did this movement most directly attack?
    A. Republican motherhood
    B. The putting-out system
    C. Slavery
    D. The cult of domesticity

Questions 11–13 refer to the excerpt below.

"Much has been said of the united strength of Britain and the colonies; that in conjunction they might bid defiance to the world. But this is mere presumption: the fate of war is uncertain. Neither do the expressions mean anything, for this continent would never suffer itself to be drained of inhabitants to support the British arms in either Asia, Africa, or Europe.

Besides, what have we to do with setting the world at defiance? Our plan is commerce, and that, well attended to, will secure us the peace and friendship of all Europe because it is the interest of all Europe to have America become a *free port*. America's trade will always be a protection, and her barrenness of gold and silver secure her from invaders.

I challenge the warmest advocate for reconciliation to show a single advantage that this continent can reap by being connected with Great Britain. I repeat the challenge: not a single advantage is derived. Our corn will fetch its price in any market in Europe, and our imported goods must be paid for, buy them where we will."

—Thomas Paine, *Common Sense*, 1776.

Slightly modernized from: **Source:** *https://en.m.wikisource.org/wiki/Common_Sense*

11. Against which of the following economic systems does this passage argue?
    A. Socialism
    B. Protectionism
    C. Mercantilism
    D. Free trade

12. Which of the following events and its aftermath had already dissuaded most colonists from participating in the British military machine at this point?
    A. The French and Indian War
    B. The Napoleonic Wars
    C. The Thirty Years' War
    D. The Articles of Confederation

13. Appeals to world opinion in favor of the American Revolution drew primarily from which of the following traditions?
    A. The Reformation
    B. The Counter-reformation
    C. Romanticism
    D. The Enlightenment

Questions 14–16 refer to the passage below.

"We consider the underlying fallacy of the plaintiff's argument to consist in the assumption that the enforced separation of the two races stamps the colored race with a badge of inferiority. [...] The argument also assumes that social prejudices may be overcome by legislation, and that equal rights cannot be secured to the negro except by an enforced commingling of the two races. We cannot accept this proposition. [...] Legislation is powerless to eradicate racial instincts or to abolish distinctions based upon physical differences[.] [...] If the civil and political rights of both races be equal, one cannot be inferior to the other civilly or politically. If one race be inferior to the other socially, the Constitution of the United States cannot put them upon the same plane."

—Excerpt from the Opinion of the Court by Justice Henry Billings Brown,
Plessy v. Ferguson, 1896

Source: *https://en.m.wikisource.org/wiki/Plessy_v._Ferguson/Opinion_of_the_Court*

14. Which of the following was upheld by the Supreme Court in this opinion?
    A. Judicial review
    B. Segregation
    C. Desegregation
    D. Corporate personhood

15. Which of the following periods in American history drew to a symbolic close with this ruling?
    A. Reconstruction
    B. Jim Crow
    C. The Progressive Era
    D. The Gilded Age

16. Which of the following decisions reversed *Plessy v. Ferguson*?
    A. *Dred Scott v. Sanford*, which denied citizenship to slaves
    B. *Regents of the University of California v. Bakke*, which restricted affirmative action programs
    C. *Marbury v. Madison*, which established judicial review
    D. *Brown v. Board of Education of Topeka*, which found racial segregation laws unconstitutional

Questions 17–20 refer to the excerpt below.

"I think we now have sufficient population in our country for us to shut the door and to breed up a pure, unadulterated American citizenship. [...] I would like for the Members of the Senate to read that book just recently published by Madison Grant, *The Passing of a Great Race*. Thank God we have in America perhaps the largest percentage of any country in the world of the pure, unadulterated Anglo-Saxon stock; certainly the greatest of any nation in the Nordic breed. It is for the preservation of this splendid stock that has characterized us that I would make this not an asylum for the oppressed of all countries but a country to assimilate and perfect that splendid type of manhood that has made America the foremost Nation in her progress and in her power[.]"

—Senator Ellison Smith in the *Congressional Record*, April 9, 1924, discussing the Immigration Act passed that year

Source: *https://archive.org/details/congressionalrec65bunit*

17. Which of the following intellectual trends most influenced Smith's comments?
    A. The Gospel of Wealth
    B. The Social Gospel
    C. Eugenics
    D. Genetics

18. The Immigration Act of 1924
    A. required immigrants to take a literacy test.
    B. introduced a quota system based on race, ethnicity, and national origin.
    C. restricted only Asian immigration.
    D. placed harsh restrictions on Canadian and Mexican immigration quotas.

19. Which of the following most accurately places the Immigration Act of 1924 in historical context?
    A. It reflected one instance of the periodic xenophobia that rises to the surface during economic downturns or foreign wars.
    B. It reflected solely the specific, unique context of the early 1920s.
    C. It was entirely due to then-current eugenic theories.
    D. It stemmed directly from the aftermath of the collapse of Reconstruction.

20. Following passage of the Immigration Act, immigrants from which of the following regions of the world were least likely to be admitted?
    A. Southern and Eastern Europe
    B. Asia, minus the Philippines
    C. Mexico and Central America
    D. Sub-Saharan Africa

Questions 21–23 refer to the excerpts below.

"At the present moment in world history nearly every nation must choose between alternative ways of life. The choice is too often not a free one. One way of life is based upon the will of the majority, and is distinguished by free institutions, representative government, free elections, guarantees of individual liberty, freedom of speech and religion, and freedom from political oppression. The second way of life is based upon the will of a minority forcibly imposed upon the majority. It relies upon terror and oppression, a controlled press and radio; fixed elections, and the suppression of personal freedoms. I believe that it must be the policy of the United States to support free peoples who are resisting attempted subjugation by armed minorities or by outside pressures."

—President Harry S. Truman requesting aid for Greece and Turkey from a joint session of Congress (The Truman Doctrine), 1947

Source: *https://www.ourdocuments.gov/doc.php?doc=81*

"The risks we face are of a new order of magnitude, commensurate with the total struggle in which we are engaged. [...] It is quite clear from Soviet theory and practice that the Kremlin seeks to bring the free world under its dominion by the methods of the cold war. [...] At the same time the Soviet Union is seeking to create overwhelming military force[.] [...] [I]t is seeking to demonstrate to the free world that force and the will to use it are on the side of the Kremlin, that those who lack it are decadent and doomed. In local incidents it threatens and encroaches both for the sake of local gains and to increase anxiety and defeatism in all the free world. [...] The possession of atomic weapons at each of the opposite poles of power [...] puts a premium on [...] piecemeal aggression against others, counting on our unwillingness to engage in atomic war unless we are directly attacked."

—Paul Nitze, National Security Council Report 68 (Top Secret), 1950

Source: *https://en.m.wikisource.org/wiki/NSC-68:_VII._Present_Risks*

21. Based on the documents above and your knowledge of American history, which of the following best characterizes the alliance between the United States and the Soviet Union during the Second World War?
- **A.** It was typical of American policy since 1917.
- **B.** It was hardly a real alliance.
- **C.** It was a brief exception to a century of confrontation.
- **D.** It was due to Soviet infiltration of the FDR administration.

22. Which of the following geopolitical theories is most closely represented in the excerpted passages?
- **A.** The domino theory
- **B.** Mutual assured destruction
- **C.** Détente
- **D.** Isolationism

23. The position toward the Soviet Union noted in the Truman Doctrine relied upon which of the following strategies?

A. Mutual coexistence, cooperation, and de-escalation of international tensions

B. Turning back to traditional American isolationism

C. Containment of Soviet influence to its immediate postwar sphere of influence

D. Preparation for an inevitable nuclear and conventional war

Questions 24–27 refer to the following image.

Photograph by Lewis Hine, National Child Labor Committee, of a twelve-year-old spinner in the North Pownal Cotton Mill, Vermont, 1910.

Source: *http://metmuseum.org/art/collection/search/285844?sortBy=Relevance&who=Hine%2c+Lewis%24Lewis+Hine&ft="&offset=0&rpp=100&pos=63*

24. Photographs such as this one are most closely related to which of the following?

    A. The use of Pinkerton and other private police forces to break strikes

    B. Yellow journalism that propagandized for the Spanish-American War

    C. Committees of Correspondence that helped organize the American Revolution

    D. Muckraking journalism that helped build support for Progressivism

25. Which of the following best captures the core problem symbolized by the photograph?

    A. Increasing economic inequality and lack of a countervailing force to the growing power of capital

    B. Insufficient follow-through on the freedom of the press guaranteed by the First Amendment

    C. The partial success of machine politicians to ameliorate the worst excesses of the industrial revolution

    D. The triumph of the federal government's intervention into the worst abuses of industrial society

26. Which of the following most likely played the largest role in ending child labor?

    A. Voluntary action on the part of those who employed children

    B. Concerted action by the Supreme Court prior to 1932

    C. State requirements on school attendance

    D. An increased sense of patriotism during and after the First World War

27. The creation and distribution of images such as this depended upon all of the following EXCEPT:

    A. The willingness of for-profit newspapers to publish such images

    B. The existence of the freedoms of speech and press that protected the publication of such images

    C. The good will of those businesses exposed by such images

    D. The production, marketing, and distribution of inventions like photography by the very industrial system that also created the conditions exposed in images such as this

Questions 28–30 refer to the excerpt below.

"Imagine yourself in Hetch Hetchy. It is a sunny day in June, the pines sway dreamily, and you are shoulder-deep in grass and flowers. Looking across the valley through beautiful open groves you see a bare granite wall 1800 feet high rising abruptly out of the green and yellow vegetation and glowing with sunshine, and in front of it the fall, waving like a downy scarf, silver bright, burning with white sun-fire in every fiber. [...] It is a flood of singing air, water, and sunlight woven into cloth that spirits might wear. [...] As will be seen by the map, I have thus briefly touched upon a number of the chief features of a region which it is proposed to reserve out of the public domain for the use and recreation of the people. [...] Unless reserved or protected the whole region will soon or late be devastated by lumbermen and sheepmen, and so of course be made unfit for use as a pleasure ground."

—John Muir, "Features of the Proposed Yosemite National Park," *Century Magazine*, 1890

Source: *https://archive.org/details/centuryillustrat40newyuoft*

28. After camping with John Muir in Yosemite, President Roosevelt took all of the following actions EXCEPT:
    A. Set aside 150 million acres of federal land as a national reserve for conservation
    B. Lobbied Congress successfully to provide money from the sale of public land to fund irrigation projects
    C. Established the Environmental Protection Agency
    D. Established a national commission to promote conservation and the creation of U.S. Forest Service

29. Based on your knowledge of American history, which of the following technological developments was most directly supportive of Muir's goals during the early twentieth century?
    A. Photography
    B. Electricity
    C. Air travel
    D. Antisepsis

30. In addition to conservation, President Theodore Roosevelt promoted all of the following Progressive Movement measures EXCEPT:
    A. Anti-trust laws
    B. Oversight of telephone, telegraph, and cable companies
    C. Civil rights reform
    D. Consumer protection laws

Questions 31–33 refer to the excerpt below.

"[N]othing is more essential than that permanent, inveterate antipathies against particular nations and passionate attachment for others should be excluded, and that, in place of them, just and amicable feelings towards all should be cultivated. The nation which indulges towards another an habitual hatred, or an habitual fondness, is in some degree a slave [...] to its animosity, or to its affection, either of which is sufficient to lead it astray from its duty and its interest. [...] As avenues to foreign influence in innumerable ways, such attachments are particularly alarming to the truly enlightened and independent patriot. How many opportunities do they afford to tamper with domestic factions, to practice the arts of seduction, to mislead public opinion, to influence or awe the public councils! Such an attachment of a small or weak, towards a great and powerful nation, dooms the former to be the satellite of the latter."

—George Washington's Farewell Address, 1796

Lightly modernized from: **Source:** *https://www.congress.gov/congressional-record/1998/02/23/senate-section/ article/S801-1*

31. Washington's Farewell Address warned Americans of all of the following EXCEPT:
A. Forming political parties
B. Forming foreign alliances
C. Advocating for the abolition of slavery
D. Forming sectional alliances

32. Which of the following was a primary concern of Washington in his Farewell Address?
A. The persistence of slavery
B. Westward expansion
C. The formation the Democratic-Republican Party
D. The creation of a national bank

33. What was one of the long-range consequences of Washington deciding to leave office after two terms?
A. Later presidents followed his example, as they voluntarily left office after finishing their tenure of two terms.
B. Most subsequent presidents ran for only one term.
C. Most subsequent presidents often switched political parties so they could run for additional terms.
D. The popularity of third-party candidates increased.

Questions 34-37 refer to the excerpt below.

They called out to us loudly to come to land, but I was apprehensive on account of a reef of rocks, which surrounds the whole island, although within there is depth of water and room sufficient for all the ships of Christendom, with a very narrow entrance. There are some shoals withinside, but the water is as smooth as a pond. It was to view these parts that I set out in the morning, for I wished to give a complete relation to your Highnesses, as also to find where a fort might be built. I discovered a tongue of land which appeared like an island though it was not, but might be cut through and made so in two days; it contained six houses. I do not, however, see the necessity of fortifying the place, as the people here are simple in war-like matters, as your Highnesses will see by those seven which I have ordered to be taken and carried to Spain in order to learn our language and return, unless your Highnesses should choose to have them all transported to Castile, or held captive in the island. I could conquer the whole of them with fifty men, and govern them as I pleased.

—Christopher Columbus, *The Journal of Christopher Columbus*
(During His First Voyage, 1492–93)

34. How does Columbus's account agree with that of other Europeans regarding their views on the Native people they encountered?
    A. Native people were a large threat that needed to be neutralized in order to colonize.
    B. Native people were seen as being uncivilized and in need of conversion.
    C. Europeans were more interested in material wealth than anything else.
    D. Europeans were unsuccessful in defeating the Native people in battle.

35. Which of the following scenarios best corresponds with the passage?
    A. European attempts to Christianize the Native peoples
    B. European attempts to force the Native population into labor
    C. European attempts to decimate the Native population
    D. European attempts to trade with the Native people

36. What most benefited Europeans like Columbus in their subjugation of the Native population?
    A. Superior weapons and technology
    B. Advanced understanding of the land
    C. Diseases such as smallpox
    D. Threat of suspension of the Columbian Exchange

37. Which of the following groups would be least likely to engage in similar interactions with Native populations as that described in the passage?
    A. The English
    B. The French
    C. The Spanish
    D. The Dutch

Questions 38–41 refer to the image below.

EUROPEAN POWERS IN NORTH AMERICA 1750

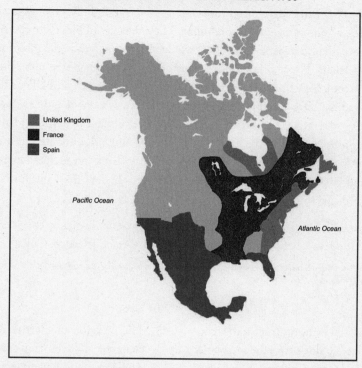

38. This map indicates which of the following concerns of the American colonists at the time?
   A. That North America should remain under the control of European powers
   B. That North America should be freed from the control of European powers
   C. That expansion beyond the colonies' current boundaries would make self-government impossible
   D. That foreign powers allied with local Indians blocked westward expansion

39. Given your answer to the previous question, was that concern of the American colonists permanently removed after the French and Indian War?
   A. Yes, because the British removed only the French but not the Spanish from North America.
   B. Yes, because the British victory removed both the French and the Spanish from North America.

   C. No, because after helping Britain remove the French from the territory noted on the map, the British simply took their place and continued to restrict westward movement.
   D. No, because European powers still remained on the North American continent.

40. Which of the following important North American ports was held by the French at this time?
   A. Puget Sound
   B. Boston
   C. The Chesapeake
   D. New Orleans

41. The major territorial expansions of the nineteenth century were taken from
   A. Britain, France, Mexico, and the American Indians.
   B. Britain, France, and Spain.
   C. Britain, France, and Mexico.
   D. France, Mexico, and the American Indians.

Questions 42–45 refer to the passage below.

"The history of the negro race proves them to be wonderfully adapted to all countries, all climates, and all conditions. Their tenacity of life, their powers of endurance, their malleable toughness, would almost imply especial interposition on their behalf. The ten thousand horrors of slavery, striking hard upon the sensitive soul, have bruised, and battered, and stung, but have not killed. The poor bondman lifts a smiling face above the surface of a sea of agonies, *hoping on, hoping ever.* His tawny brother, the Indian, dies under the flashing glance of the Anglo Saxon. *Not* so the negro; civilization cannot kill him. He accepts it -- becomes a part of it. In the Church, he is an Uncle Tom; in the State, he is the most abused and least offensive. All the facts in his history mark out for him a destiny, united to America and Americans."

—Frederick Douglass, "The claims of the Negro, ethnologically considered: an address before the literary societies of Western Reserve College," 1854

Lightly updated from: **Source:** *http://memory.loc.gov/cgi-bin/query/r?ammem/rbaapc:@field(DOCID+@lit(rbaapc07900div2))*

42. Which of the following most accurately captures Douglass's argument for the acceptance of African Americans in American society?

    A. Like the Indians, "the negro race" has proven itself equal to the Anglo-Saxons.

    B. Unlike the Indians, "the negro race" requires the protection of the Anglo-Saxons.

    C. An accurate understanding of the innate constitution of "the negro race" shows that they, unlike the Indians, deserve to be fully integrated into American society.

    D. Racial characteristics are beside the point: African Americans deserve equal treatment under the law and in society.

43. The mention of Harriet Beecher Stowe's character "Uncle Tom" is important for which of the following reasons?

    A. It proves that Stowe's character was ill-known in the 1850s.

    B. It shows that Stowe's portrayal of the character was considered complimentary by some African Americans at the time.

    C. It proves that views of Stowe's character have been uniform since the publication of her novel of the same name.

    D. It shows how confused Douglass's rhetoric typically was.

44. The passage LEAST supports which of the following conclusions?
    A. Racial prejudice existed even in members of a group that were targeted by it.
    B. Abolitionist arguments do not always match widely held contemporary views on racial equality.
    C. All African-American abolitionists fully rejected the racial categories and explanatory tropes of the day.
    D. Soon after its publication, Harriet Beecher Stowe's novel *Uncle Tom's Cabin* had a wide enough appeal to be referenced before a literate audience.

45. Which of the following best describes the one part of Douglass's argument for racial coexistence as expressed in this passage?
    A. Unlike the Indians, who were too defiant for their own good, African Americans required the protection of whites.
    B. African Americans had proven more than able to assimilate to the dominant white culture.
    C. Like the Indians, African Americans had proven themselves more than able to assimilate to the dominant white culture.
    D. African Americans were superior to whites and would much improve the dominant culture.

Questions 46–48 refer to the excerpt below.

"In the name of God, amen. We, whose names are underwritten, the loyal subjects of our dread sovereign lord, King James by the grace of God of Great Britain, France, and Ireland, King, Defender of the Faith, &c. Having undertaken for the glory of God, the advancement of the Christian faith, and the honor of our king and country a voyage to plant the first colony in the northern parts of Virginia do by these presents, solemnly and mutually, in the presence of God and one another, covenant and combine ourselves together into a civil body politic for our better ordering and preservation and furtherance of the ends aforesaid and by virtue hereof do enact, constitute, and frame such just and equal laws, ordinances, acts, constitutions, and officers from time to time as shall be thought most meet and convenient for the general good of the colony unto which we promise all due submission and obedience. In witness whereof we have hereunto subscribed our names at Cape-Cod the eleventh of November, in the reign of our sovereign lord King James, of England, France, and Ireland, the eighteenth, and of Scotland the fifty-fourth, *Anno Domini*, 1620."

—The Mayflower Compact, 1620

Modernized from: **Source:** *https://archive.org/details/mayflowercompact00bowm*

46. The Mayflower Compact is important for which of the following reasons?
  A. It formed the basis for all subsequent written frames of government in America.
  B. It proves that separation from England was on the minds of the colonists from the start.
  C. It demonstrated how unimportant a religious sanction for self-government was to the original colonists.
  D. It is the first example of a written frame of government in American history.

47. Based on your knowledge of the Pilgrims and Puritans, which of the following best reflects the group of people empowered by this compact?
  A. White adult men of property
  B. All adults regardless of race or gender
  C. White adult men
  D. All white adults

48. All of the following were evidence that the colonies were headed toward self-rule after the Mayflower Compact EXCEPT:
  A. A representative government of male church-goers in the Massachusetts Bay colony
  B. The House of Burgesses, a representative assembly in Virginia
  C. Elections of colonial leaders
  D. Colonial autocratic leadership who answered to the crown

Questions 49–51 refer to the image below.

"**Crowds outside the Lafayette Theatre in Harlem at the opening of** *Macbeth* **produced by the Federal Negro Theatre,**" **Federal Theatre Project, Works Progress Administration, 1936**.

Source: *https://digitalcollections.nypl.org/items/314d8080-3bc9-0134-b3fd-00505686a51c*

49. Based on this image and your understanding of American history, which of the following statements is most likely accurate?
  A. New Deal programs attempted to improve the lives of African Americans as well as whites.
  B. New Dealers were free from racial prejudice.
  C. The Harlem Renaissance launched because of New Deal initiatives.
  D. By the 1930s, racial segregation was a thing of the past in most parts of the country.

50. Which of the following most directly influenced the Harlem Renaissance?
  A. Reconstruction
  B. *Plessy v. Ferguson*
  C. The Great Migration
  D. Prohibition

51. Federal government support for the arts
  A. existed only during the New Deal.
  B. has been significant since the founding of the country.
  C. only began in the twentieth century and has lagged behind that of most other Western countries.
  D. has always existed in great measure.

Questions 52–53 refer to the excerpt below.

"All the pomp and splendor of naval warfare are gone by. Henceforth there must come up a race of enginemen and smoke-blackened cannoneers, who will hammer away at their enemies under the direction of a single pair of eyes; and even heroism—so deadly a gripe is Science laying on our noble possibilities—will become a quality of very minor importance when its possessor cannot break through the iron crust of his own armament and give the world a glimpse of it. [...] The inaccessibility, the apparent impregnability, of this submerged iron fortress are most satisfactory; the officers and crew get down through the little hole in the deck, hermetically seal themselves, and go below; and until they see fit to reappear, there would seem to be no power given to a man whereby they can be brought to light. A storm of cannon shots damages them no more than a handful of dried peas. We saw the shot marks made by the great artillery of the Merrimack on the outer casing of the iron tower; they were about the breadth and depth of shallow saucers, almost imperceptible dents, with no corresponding bulge on the interior surface."

—Nathaniel Hawthorne, "Chiefly about War Matters," Harper's, 1862

Source: *https://www.theatlantic.com/magazine/archive/1862/07/chiefly-about-war-matters/306159/*

52. Hawthorne's view of the new ironclad warships of his day are best understood as a reaction to which of the following?
    A. The Gilded Age's effect on warfare
    B. The changes already being brought about by the second industrial revolution
    C. The effect of the secession of the Southern states on Union military morale
    D. The staleness of Gothic romance in the age of the machine

53. Hawthorne's position would most accurately be characterized as most akin to which of the following?
    A. Populism
    B. Puritanism
    C. The Enlightenment
    D. Romanticism

Questions 54–55 refer to the excerpt below.

"I don't want to present myself as some sort of singular figure. I think part of what's different are the times. I do think that, for example, the 1980 election was different. I think Ronald Reagan changed the trajectory of America in a way that, you know, Richard Nixon did not and in a way that Bill Clinton did not. He put us on a fundamentally different path because the country was ready for it. I think they felt like, you know, with all the excesses of the 60s and the 70s, and government had grown and grown, but there wasn't much sense of accountability in terms of how it was operating. I think people just tapped into—he tapped into what people were already feeling, which was, we want clarity, we want optimism, we want a return to that sense of dynamism and entrepreneurship that had been missing."

—Barack Obama to the Editorial Board of the *Reno Gazette-Journal*,

January, 2008

Source: *http://www.nytimes.com/ref/us/politics/21seelye-text.html*

54. Obama's comments above best support which of the following conclusions?
   A. Obama's presidency marked the return of New Deal-Great Society policies and rhetoric.
   B. Since around 1980, conservative ideas have dominated politics.
   C. Unlike FDR before him, Ronald Reagan failed to significantly reshape the political discourse.
   D. Since 1980, Democrats have refused to adapt their rhetoric and policies to what they perceived to be a general shift to the political right.

55. In order to help contextualize Obama's remarks, all of the following would be most directly relevant EXCEPT:
   A. Reagan's view of the Democratic Party during his presidency
   B. All of Obama's public comments on Reagan
   C. The political and ideological profile of the Democratic voters of Nevada, where Reno is located
   D. The general political positions of the *Reno Gazette-Journal*'s editorial board

STOP.
IF YOU FINISH BEFORE TIME IS OUT, YOU MAY CHECK YOUR WORK ON THIS SECTION ONLY.
DO NOT TURN TO ANY OTHER SECTION IN THE TEST.

Section I, Part B: Short-Answer Questions

Time: 40 Minutes • 3 Questions

Directions: The following section consists of four short-answer questions—you must answer **both** Question 1 and Question 2. You will then choose to answer **either** Question 3 or Question 4. Use the answer sheet provided to respond to the questions.

1. Based on your knowledge of American history, answer both A and B.
   A. Explain why ONE of the following intellectual trends most directly contributed to colonial notions of self-government using at least ONE piece of evidence to justify your selection.
      • The Great Awakening
      • The Enlightenment
   B. Give ONE reason why you didn't select the other option.

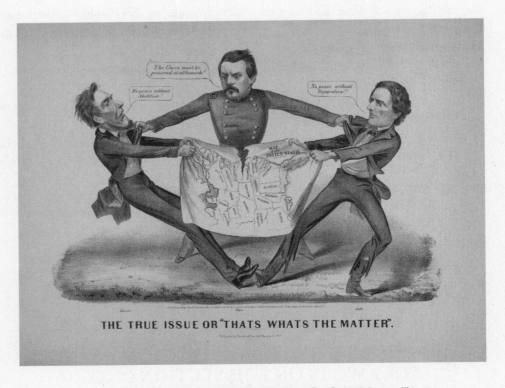

"The True Issue or 'Thats [sic] Whats [sic] the Matter,'"
Currier and Ives, 1864.

On the left of a tearing map of the United States, Abraham Lincoln says, "No peace without Abolition!" while on the right, Jefferson Davis says, "No peace without Separation!!" In the middle, George McClellan, the former Union general and Northern Democratic candidate for the presidency in 1864, tries to pull the two together, saying, "The Union must be preserved at all hazards!"

Source: *http://metmuseum.org/art/collection/search/430812?sortBy=Relevance&when=A.D.+1800-1900&where=United+States&ft=United+States+political+cartoons&offset=0&rpp=100&pos=24*

2. Refer to the image above in answering parts A, B, and C.
   A. Interpret the position of one of the cartoon's key players: Lincoln, McClellan, or Davis.
   B. Give ONE reason why you DISAGREE with the image's depiction of the position of the key player you selected in part A.
   C. Give ONE reason why you AGREE with the image's depiction of the position of the key player you selected in part A.

Directions: Answer *either* Question 3 or 4.

And that claim is by the right of our manifest destiny to overspread and to possess the whole of the continent which Providence has given us for the development of the great experiment of liberty and federated self-government entrusted to us.

—John L. O'Sullivan *New York Morning News, December 27, 1845*

3. Based on your knowledge of American history, and the quote above, answer parts A, B, and C.
   A. Briefly describe what O'Sullivan meant when he used the phrase "entrusted to us."
   B. Briefly describe a person, or group of people, who would oppose O'Sullivan's notion of manifest destiny and the reason for their opposition.
   C. Provide one piece of evidence and explain how it supports either A or B.

"If, as Mr. Kidd's hypothesis assumes, progress was most marked where the struggle for life was keenest, the European people standing highest in the scale would be the South Italians, the Polish Jews, and the people who live in the congested districts of Ireland. As a matter of fact, however, these are precisely the people who have made least progress when compared with the dominant strains among, for instance, the English or Germans. [...] The race existing under conditions which make the competition for bare existence keenest, never progresses as fast as the race which exists under less stringent conditions. There must undoubtedly be a certain amount of competition, a certain amount of stress and strain, but it is equally undoubted that if this competition becomes too severe the race goes down and not up[.] [...] A perfectly stupid race can never rise to a very high plane; the negro, for instance, has been kept down as much by lack of intellectual development as anything else; but the prime factor in the preservation of a race is its power to attain a high degree of social efficiency. Love of order, ability to fight well and breed well, capacity to subordinate the interests of the individual to the interests of the community, these and similar rather humdrum qualities go to make up the sum of social efficiency. [...] In other words, character is far more important than intellect to the race as to the individual. We need intellect, and there is no reason why we should not have it together with character; but if we must choose between the two we choose character without a moment's hesitation."

—Theodore Roosevelt reviewing Benjamin Kidd's *Social Evolution* in *The North American Review*, vol. 161, July 1895.

Source: *https://archive.org/details/northamreview161miscrich*

4. Based on the excerpt above and your knowledge of American history, answer parts A, B, and C.

   A. Supply ONE example of how Roosevelt's argument ALIGNS WITH the traditional understanding of Social Darwinism.

   B. Provide ONE example of how Roosevelt's argument DIVERGES FROM the traditional understanding of Social Darwinism.

   C. Tie any feature of the argument presented in the excerpt to ONE feature of the Progressive Movement.

STOP.
IF YOU FINISH BEFORE TIME IS OUT, YOU MAY CHECK YOUR WORK ON THIS SECTION ONLY.
DO NOT TURN TO ANY OTHER SECTION IN THE TEST.

Section II, Part A: Document-Based Question

Time: 60 Minutes • 1 Question

> **Directions:** The following question asks you to write a cohesive essay incorporating your interpretation of Documents 1 through 7 and your knowledge of the period stated in the question. To earn a high score, you must cite key evidence from the documents and use your outside knowledge of United States history. Take 15 minutes to read all documents and 45 minutes to write your essay on the answer sheet provided.

1. Compare and contrast the nature of the arguments for and against imperialism in the years surrounding the Spanish-American War.

Document 1

Source: *https://archive.org/details/in.ernet.dli.2015.43141*

In these three things—production, with the necessity of exchanging products, shipping, whereby the exchange is carried on, and colonies, which facilitate and enlarge the operations of shipping and tend to protect it by multiplying points of safety—is to be found the key to much of the history, as well as of the policy, of nations bordering upon the sea. [...] If a [Central-American] canal be made, and fulfill the hopes of its builders, the Caribbean will be changed from a terminus, and a place of local traffic, [...] into one of the great highways of the world. Along this path a great commerce will travel, bringing the interests of the [...] European nations close along our shores as they have never been before. With this it will not be so easy as heretofore to stand aloof from international complications. [...] The fact of England's unique and wonderful success as a great colonizing nation is too evident to be dwelt upon [.] [...] If there be in the future any fields calling for colonization, it cannot be doubted that Americans will carry to them all their inherited aptitude for self-government and independent growth.

—Alfred T. Mahan, *The Influence of Sea Power upon History: 1660–1783*, 1918 [reprint of original published in 1890].

Document 2

Source: *https://archive.org/details/republicorempire00smit*

Heretofore our government has been solely charged with the execution of powers conferred by the governed. It is now seriously proposed that within the States it shall continue in the exercise of this authority; and, in addition, that it shall assume and exercise despotic power over the territories and such colonial dependencies as it may choose to acquire. It is to represent democracy in the States and stand for absolutism in its dependencies. With one hand it will administer for a "superior race" the blessing of free government; with the other it will bestow upon "lesser breeds without the law" such measures of good government as it deems them fit to enjoy. In its capacity as an agency of a free people, it will conserve rights guaranteed to them by the Constitution; as the vanguard of returning despotism, it will confer favors on "inferior races." The undisguised basis of this policy is inequality among men. Its purpose is to stay the hands of progress, to escape from the consequences of democracy.

—Edwin Burritt Smith, "Republic or Empire with Glimpses of 'Criminal Aggression,'" Speech delivered at the American Anti-Imperialist League Conference, Philadelphia, 1900

Document 3

"When you have prayed for victory you have prayed for many unmentioned results which follow victory—*must* follow it[.] [...] [God the Father] commandeth me to put it into words. Listen!

"O Lord our Father, our young patriots, idols of our hearts, go forth to battle—be Thou near them! With them—in spirit—we also go forth from the sweet peace of our beloved firesides to smite the foe. O Lord our God, help us to tear their soldiers to bloody shreds with our shells; help us to cover their smiling fields with the pale forms of their patriot dead; help us to drown the thunder of guns with the shrieks of the wounded, writhing in pain; help us to lay waste their humble homes with a hurricane of fire; help us to wring the hearts of their unoffending widows with unavailing grief; help us to turn them out roofless with their little children to wander unfriended the wastes of their desolated land in rags and hunger and thirst, sports of the sun flames of summer and the icy winds of winter, broken in spirit, worn with travail, imploring Thee for the refuge of the grave and denied it—for our sakes who adore Thee, Lord, blast their hopes, blight their lives, protract their bitter pilgrimage, make heavy their steps, water their way with their tears, stain the white snow with the blood of their wounded feet! We ask it, in the spirit of love, of Him Who is the Source of Love, and Who is the ever-faithful refuge and friend of all that are sore beset and seek His aid with humble and contrite hearts. Amen."

(*After a pause.*) "Ye have prayed it; if ye still desire it, speak! The messenger of the Most High awaits."

It was believed afterward that the man was a lunatic, because there was no sense in what he said.

—Mark Twain, "The War Prayer," written in 1904 in reaction to the
Spanish-American War but unpublished until 1916.

Document 4

Source: *https://archive.org/details/jenningsbryanwill02bryarich*

If the Republicans are prepared to censure all who have used language calculated to make the Filipinos hate foreign domination, let them condemn the speech of Patrick Henry. When he uttered that passionate appeal, "Give me liberty or give me death," he expressed a sentiment which still echoes in the hearts of men. Let them censure Jefferson; of all the statesmen of history none have used words so offensive to those who would hold their fellows in political bondage. Let them censure Washington, who declared that the colonists must choose between liberty and slavery. [...] Those who would have this Nation enter upon a career of empire must consider not only the effect of imperialism on the Filipinos, but they must also calculate its effects upon our own nation. We cannot repudiate the principle of self-government in the Philippines without weakening that principle here. Lincoln said that the safety of this Nation was not in its fleets, its armies, or its forts, but in the spirit which prizes liberty as the heritage of all men, in all lands, everywhere, and he warned his countrymen that they could not destroy this spirit without planting the seeds of despotism at their own doors.

—William Jennings Bryan, "Imperialism," Speech Accepting the
Democratic Nomination, Indianapolis, 1900.

Document 5

Lightly modernized from: **Source:** *https://archive.org/details/in.ernet.dli.2015.123677*

In 1898 we could not help being brought face to face with the problems of war with Spain. All we could decide was whether we should shrink like cowards from the contest or enter into it as beseemed a brave and high-spirited people; and, once in, whether failure or success should crown our business. So it is now. We cannot avoid the responsibilities that confront us in Hawaii, Puerto Rico, and the Philippines. All we can decide is whether we shall meet them in a way that will redound to the national credit or whether we shall make of our dealings with these new problems a dark and shameful period in our history. [...] The timid man; the lazy man; the man who distrusts his country; the over-civilized man, who has lost the great, fighting, masterful virtues; the ignorant man; and the man of dull mind, whose soul is incapable of feeling the mighty lift that thrills "stern men with empires in their brains"—all these, of course, shrink from seeing the nation undertake its new duties; shrink from seeing us build a navy and an army adequate to our needs; shrink from seeing us do our share of the world's work by bringing order out of chaos in the great, fair tropic islands from which the valor of our soldiers and sailors has driven the Spanish flag. These are the men who fear the strenuous life, who fear the only national life which is really worth leading.

—Theodore Roosevelt, "The Strenuous Life," Speech before the
Hamilton Club, Chicago, 1899.

Document 6

Take up the White Man's burden—
Send forth the best ye breed—
Go bind your sons to exile
To serve your captives' need;
To wait in heavy harness,
On fluttered folk and wild—
Your new-caught, sullen peoples,
Half-devil and half child.

—Rudyard Kipling, "The White Man's Burden," 1899.

Document 7

"The Survival of the Fittest," cartoon from the satirical magazine *Puck*, 1898. The caption has "Uncle Sam" saying, "By Jingo! I'm sorry for the poor fellow; but he made me do it." Written on Uncle Sam's sword is, "19th Century Enlightenment." On Spain's broken sword is written, "Misrule"; Spain, in armor, is also labeled "Medievalism." Austria and Germany hold up Spain as France, garbed as a doctor, rushes in to help. Behind Uncle Sam stand Japan and "John Bull," or Britain.

WHEN YOU HAVE COMPLETED ANSWERING YOUR DOCUMENT-BASED QUESTION, YOU MAY CONTINUE AND BEGIN WORKING ON PART B, THE LONG ESSAY.

Section II, Part B: Long Essay Question

Time: 40 Minutes • 1 Question

> **Directions:** Answer ONE question from this group. State a thesis, cite relevant evidence, and use logical, clear arguments to support your generalizations.

2. Assess the degree to which the Compromise of 1877, which settled the contested presidential election of 1876, represented continuity as well as change in the social, economic, and political history of African Americans.

3. Assess the degree to which the Korean War (1950–1953) represented continuity as well as change in U.S. foreign policy.

4. Assess how rivalries among European powers helped shape the American colonies from First Contact through the American Revolution.

STOP.
IF YOU FINISH BEFORE TIME IS OUT, YOU MAY CHECK YOUR WORK ON THIS SECTION ONLY.
DO NOT TURN TO ANY OTHER SECTION IN THE TEST.

ANSWER KEY AND EXPLANATIONS

Section I, Part A: Multiple-Choice Questions

1. A	12. A	23. C	34. B	45. B
2. B	13. D	24. D	35. A	46. D
3. A	14. B	25. A	36. C	47. C
4. B	15. A	26. C	37. A	48. D
5. D	16. D	27. C	38. D	49. A
6. D	17. C	28. C	39. C	50. C
7. A	18. B	29. A	40. D	51. C
8. B	19. A	30. C	41. A	52. B
9. A	20. B	31. B	42. C	53. D
10. D	21. C	32. C	43. B	54. B
11. C	22. A	33. A	44. C	55. A

1. **The correct answer is A.** This sermon is typical of the first Great Awakening of evangelical Protestantism, which occurred in both England and the American colonies. George Whitefield, for example, another fiery preacher of this movement, was arguably the first transatlantic celebrity. None of the other options work, as Edwards was a figurehead of the First Great Awakening.

2. **The correct answer is B.** Most, if not all, of Great Awakening preaching took place outside in makeshift campgrounds. As a rule, the establishment churches on both sides of the Atlantic were against such "enthusiasm" in religion, so choice A is incorrect. Choices C and D also mistake the most typical social setting for this style of preaching; moreover, factories were mostly in America's future at this time.

3. **The correct answer is A.** The Great Awakening was directed, for theological reasons, at individual people; it was a kind of radical Protestantism that necessarily outflanked existing social, political, and religious structures. As you can see from this excerpt, the theological opinions were not in themselves necessarily liberal or progressive, even by the standards of the time, so choice B is incorrect. Moreover, the revival meetings were indeed focused upon a charismatic leader, the preacher himself, under one of whom (George Whitefield) even deist Benjamin Franklin felt himself sway, so choice C is incorrect. Finally, the vast majority of people went to hear these traveling preachers, not to read their sermons, which lacked the charismatic power of the live performances.

4. **The correct answer is B.** Ironically, one result of the Columbian Exchange of the seventeenth century was the importation of the potato to Ireland, where it quickly became a subsistence crop. When crops failed in the late 1840s, a wave of Irish fled starvation by coming to the United States. Choices A and C are incorrect because these New World crops were not Irish staples; choice D is incorrect because barley is an Old World crop that was introduced to the Americas.

5. **The correct answer is D.** The Know-Nothings were a nativist party set against continuing immigration, especially of European Catholics. The Whigs were focused on "internal improvements," or what we'd call infrastructure, and economic development in general, whereas the Federalists and Democratic-Republicans were long gone by the mid-nineteenth century.

6. **The correct answer is D.** The 1840s and 50s saw hundreds of thousands of Germans fleeing economic hardship and political unrest, both prior to and following the revolution of 1848. Choice A may be tempting, given the Mexican War, but conquered people are not immigrants; moreover, far fewer Mexicans were "captured" in the new United States than the number of Germans who immigrated from Germany. Italy (choice B) was soon to make a huge contribution, but had yet to do so during this period. And finally, China (choice C) was also soon to lose many, mostly to the American West, serving as a main source of labor for the burgeoning railroad system.

7. **The correct answer is A.** Most mid-century immigrants settled in the Northeast, closest to Europe and where most of the manufacturing jobs were. San Francisco (choice B) was far from Europe, not yet connected by rail to the East, and far from a manufacturing center. Both New Orleans (choice C) and Atlanta (choice D) lay in the South, further from Ireland and still running a feudal, slave-based, agricultural economy.

8. **The correct answer is B.** Finding rhetorical force in closely following Jefferson's Declaration, the authors of this document, primarily Elizabeth Cady Stanton, aimed to convince both American men and the world of the justice of their cause, the right of women to be independent from men. Choice D is a founding document of the French, not American, Revolution; neither the Articles (choice A) nor the Constitution (choice C) contain this language.

9. **The correct answer is A.** Nineteenth-century feminists, including the authors of the Declaration, tended to be anti-abortion, although abortions, which were widespread, were blamed on feminists by conservatives. All the other choices reflect top priorities of nineteenth-century feminism reflected in the full document.

10. **The correct answer is D.** The cult of domesticity relegated women to the home, which was seen as a haven from burgeoning market society and the industrial revolution. Republican Motherhood (choice A) was a feature of the Revolutionary period: women were seen as contributing to the raising of austere, moral, Republican men. The putting-out system (choice B) refers to work often done by women inside the home that could be imported from a central location, worked upon, and then exported out when value had been added. Shoemaking is one example. Slavery (choice C) was never explicitly applied to women, though as a rhetorical resource, feminists did make many comparisons.

11. **The correct answer is C.** Paine, like many others at the time—including Adam Smith in his *Wealth of Nations* published the same year as *Common Sense*—decried the colonial-mercantilist system that relegated America to a provider of raw materials solely to Britain, which added value via manufacture and shipped some of the products back to its captive market, America. Free trade (choice D) was in fact far closer to what Paine wanted: America as a "free port." Socialism (choice A) was yet to be conceived. Protectionism (choice B), if referring to Britain's mercantilist self-protections, was decried. If referring to a future American nation, that was indeed soon to be recommended

by Hamilton and others, but was not what Paine was arguing against in this passage.

12. **The correct answer is A.** Having fought alongside Britain against France and those Indian tribes allied to her only to be squeezed hard for revenue after the war's successful end, Americans in the mid-1770s were hardly impressed by the supposed advantage being part of Britain's developing military might. The Napoleonic Wars (choice B) were yet to come; the Thirty Years' War (choice C) had long since occurred without American involvement. Finally, the Articles of Confederation (choice D) followed the separation with Britain.

13. **The correct answer is D.** Paine, Jefferson, and the rest of the founders drew primarily from the Enlightenment philosophy of Montesquieu, Locke, and others. The sixteenth-century Protestant Reformation did form the background of not only most colonists' specific religions (almost all of which were Protestant) but also of notions of individual worth that underlay democratic ideals, but these notions were further removed from the specifics of political freedom found in Paine's and others' views, so choice A is incorrect. The Catholic Counterreformation was associated with political absolutism, so choice B is incorrect. Finally, Romanticism (choice C) is anachronistic: the first murmurings of that movement were just beginning in 1776.

14. **The correct answer is B.** *Plessy v. Ferguson* upheld virtually all segregationist state laws until it was overturned by *Brown v. Board of Education of Topeka* in 1954, which forced desegregation upon still-segregated states. Therefore, choice C is incorrect. Choice A is incorrect because judicial review was established by John Marshall early in the nineteenth century (in *Marbury v. Madison*). Corporate personhood (choice D) was an

entirely separate creation of many Courts over at least a century of rulings.

15. **The correct answer is A.** While formal Reconstruction ended with the Bargain of 1877, *Plessy v. Ferguson* was the final nail in the coffin, giving constitutional cover to a raft of laws designed to enforce a kind of apartheid—not only in the South. Those laws are collectively referred to as Jim Crow, so choice B is incorrect. The Progressive Era didn't really begin until later in the early twentieth century, so choice C is incorrect. Finally, the Gilded Age may well have been closing by 1896, but it indicated a highly unequal economic system, not primarily legalized racism, so choice D is incorrect.

16. **The correct answer is D.** *Plessy* endorsed state segregation laws; *Brown* overturned them. None of the other cases overturned *Plessy*. *Dred Scott* and *Marbury* preceded it; *Bakke* came almost a century later.

17. **The correct answer is C.** Eugenics was a pseudo-science popular on both the left and the right in the early decades of the twentieth century, and Madison Grant was one of its most recognizable popularizers. As Social Darwinism warped Darwinian evolution, eugenics perverted the new science of genetics—in both cases, despite the fact that many (though not all) Darwinians and geneticists lent their support. Thus, choice D is incorrect. Neither gospel—of wealth, as Carnegie argued, or of social action, as many Christians argued—bears much relation to Smith's comments.

18. **The correct answer is B.** The literacy test was a requirement implemented by the Immigration Act of 1917 (which was replaced by the 1924 Act because it wasn't restrictive enough), so choice A is incorrect. Choice C is incorrect because the Act was discriminatory against more than just Asians. Choice D is incorrect because the law did not restrict Mexicans and Canadians.

19. **The correct answer is A.** From the first immigrants to North America in the seventeenth century to the present day, xenophobic nativism recurs throughout American history, usually in the wake of some kind of socioeconomic dislocation. Therefore, choice B is incorrect. Though eugenics did play a key role, it was not the sole cause; rather, it provided a new bottle for some very old wine, so choice C is incorrect. Finally, choice D is incorrect because of all the features of Reconstruction's collapse, including the cementing of anti-black racism until it began to be broken down in the 1950s, immigration policy, particularly this one that arose half a century later, was not high on the list.

20. **The correct answer is B.** Among the many ethnicities limited by this act's quota system, only non-Filipino Asians were entirely barred. (Filipinos were severely restricted but allowed in due to fact that the Philippines had been U.S. territory since the Spanish-American War.) While none of the other choices work, it's worth noting that quotas were not applied to Mexicans, or indeed all those originating in the Western Hemisphere, given the reliance of Californian agriculture on seasonal Mexican labor. Africans, sub-Saharan or not, were the second most severely limited group.

21. **The correct answer is C.** Since sending troops in 1918 as part of an international counter-revolutionary force, bipartisan American policy has been generally anti-Soviet (and, post 1991, with another brief hiatus during Yeltsin's presidency, generally anti-Russian). Therefore, choice A is incorrect. Choice B is also incorrect; despite all kinds of stresses and intramural positioning, the U.S.-British-Soviet alliance, both military and political and despite much wariness, was indeed real. There was no Soviet infiltration into FDR's administration, making choice D incorrect.

22. **The correct answer is A.** Containing the Soviet Union, it is argued, requires meeting its perceived challenges to the United States in various nation-states around the world. Not to do so risks giving the advantage to the Soviets; once one country, such as Greece, falls, that inevitably increases the chances that others will follow. Note that the theory only holds, logically, if the USSR both leads a monolithic international communism that aims inevitably to expand its influence. If the USSR (or any nation-state to which this notion is applied) is primarily concerned with self-defense or, despite a shared political ideology not free from long-standing national interests, the theory falls apart. Choice B refers to a nuclear-weapons strategy not much noted in these documents, whereas choice D is the opposite position to what is urged in both documents. Finally, choice C came about much later as the costs of containment, in all senses, became clear even to former cold warriors like Nixon and Kissinger.

23. **The correct answer is C.** Choice B is the opposite of the proposed strategy, whereas choice D, though always a minority opinion, never fully captured policy, despite a few attempts over the postwar decades. Even the arms race was justified, rightly or not, as a way to *prevent*, not to prepare to win, an innately unwinnable nuclear war. Finally, choice A, to the extent it was ever attempted, and it was, came much later than this period.

24. **The correct answer is D.** Like the photos of his more famous contemporary, Jacob Riis, Hine's photos brought the plight of working-class people to a broad audience, thus spurring on progressive reform. Choice A doesn't refer to acts of publication, intent to undermine working-class people aside. Choice B is similar in general intent; one could consider these photos "propaganda" in a "public relations" sense, but not in specific intent, so it's incorrect. Finally, the workings

of the Committees of Correspondence were indeed often public, but were aimed at a cross-class revolution or overthrow of a system, not reform within a system on behalf of a particular class. So, choice C is incorrect.

25. **The correct answer is A.** Whether one admires or deplores (or both admires and deplores) unfettered capitalism, it commodifies all, including children, whose labor is then rented on the market just like that of adults. Virtually no pro-capitalist in 2017 would urge the return of child labor; the most deregulatory conservative agrees that *that* regulation is beyond question; a century ago, however, this was not the case. Choice B is contraindicated; only a relatively free press could get away with undermining powerful interests in this way, which was quite widespread. Choice C may well be true, but it had little to no effect on child labor, widely agreed to be one of the worst excesses of industrial society. Moreover, it was photos like this that attempted to force the federal government to intervene in the economy on the direct behalf of working people, something it had rarely, if ever, done up to that point. So, choice D is also incorrect.

26. **The correct answer is C.** Only in 1937 was child labor outlawed. The Supreme Court was in the habit of striking down any limitation on economic activity until well into the New Deal period, so choice B is incorrect. Choice A was also not the case; as Upton Sinclair once said—and it applies to everyone, not just defenders of child-labor in times long past—"It is difficult to get a man to understand something, when his salary depends on his not understanding it." Finally, choice D, while accurate, played no role in curbing child labor.

27. **The correct answer is C.** From the founding of the country on, the existential importance of a free press that enjoyed free speech (along with everyone else, at least in theory) has been widely held. Choices A and D are true, and are therefore representative of two of the many ironies of history.

28. **The correct answer is C.** President Roosevelt, after camping with John Muir in Yosemite, set aside federal lands for conservation, lobbied Congress to fund irrigation projects from the sale of federal lands, and established the U.S. Forest Service while also implementing a national commission for conservation oversight. Choice C is the exception because the EPA was not established until Nixon was president in 1970.

29. **The correct answer is A.** Photography in one form or another had been around since mid-nineteenth century; following a very long tradition of landscape painting, photographers like Ansel Adams took to the wilderness (or what was taken to be wilderness) to record its beauty. Air travel didn't become widespread until well into the 1930s, if not later, so choice C is incorrect. Neither electricity (choice B) which spread throughout the early twentieth century, nor antisepsis (choice D) an undoubted triumph of nineteenth-century medicine, played as direct a role in conservation as photography.

30. **The correct answer is C.** Under President Theodore Roosevelt, and in conjunction with the Progressive Movement, Congress took measures to break up trusts; oversee telephone, cable, and telegraph companies; and pass laws that protected consumers, such as the Meat Inspection Act. While Roosevelt did invite Booker T. Washington to the White House (the first president to ever invite a black leader to the presidential home), he took no stance on civil rights,

let alone attempt to implement reform, so choice C is the exception.

31. **The correct answer is C.** Washington did not, in his farewell address, advocate for the abolition of slavery, though he was personally troubled about the issue. Washington urged a kind of political, though not commercial, isolation from the intrigues of foreign powers (in his day, European but, in later days, any foreign power), so choice B is incorrect. Answer choices A and D were two of Washington's major concerns: he warned against party systems specifically and sectional alliances by extension, as they could "open the door to foreign influence and corruption" and lead to what Washington would have labeled "entanglements" in the affairs of foreign nations, whatever their ideological intent.

32. **The correct answer is C.** Parties—or what were called "factions"—were an ever-present concern of Washington, who had hoped that the American polity would avoid this ever-present feature of republics. Washington may have been concerned about slavery's effect on the prospects of the newly formed union, but not nearly to the extent of his concern about foreign entanglements, so choice A is incorrect. Westward expansion was not particularly considered an issue in Washington's day, with the British just defeated and seeming room aplenty for the burgeoning but still relatively small population; thus, choice B is incorrect. Finally, Washington was an advocate of Hamilton and the creation of a national bank, so choice D is incorrect.

33. **The correct answer is A.** Washington chose to step down from the presidency after two terms to avoid the creation of monarch-like leadership in the fledgling nation. Subsequent presidents, like Jefferson and Monroe, followed suit. It wasn't until FDR that a president sought out a third (and fourth) term. The answer cannot be choice B because many presidents, with some exceptions, ran for a second term after their first. Choice C is incorrect because most presidents, with few exceptions, remained loyal to their parties. Third-party candidates have nothing to do with Washington's choice to step down after two terms, so choice D is incorrect.

34. **The correct answer is B.** Columbus's account is similar to other Europeans of the period in that he labels the Native people as "simple" and wants those captured to be sent back to be civilized in Spanish language. Choice A is incorrect because the account does not label the Native people as hostile or capable of being a threat. Choice C is incorrect because the account relates purposes other than material wealth, such as civilizing the Native population. Choice D is incorrect because the account relays success in capturing the Native people.

35. **The correct answer is A.** Attempts to Christianize the population would be similar to that of "civilizing" them, which was another goal of many Europeans, specifically the Spanish. Choice B is incorrect because, while Europeans did use the Native population as a source of labor, there is no mention of this practice in the passage. Choice C is incorrect because Columbus does not relay a message of genocide towards the population. Choice D is incorrect because the account does not discuss economic interaction with the Native people.

36. **The correct answer is C.** The Native people had no immunity to European diseases, and the result was a 90 percent reduction in their population that left them easily conquered by Europeans. Choice A is incorrect because, although the Europeans had superior weapons and technology, having them was not the key factor in their subjugation of the Native peoples, and due to trade, many

Native people were able to acquire weapons themselves. Choice B is incorrect because Europeans were not as apt to understand the land as their Native counterparts, who had been living there for many years. Choice D is incorrect because there was no threat of ending this mutually beneficial exchange.

37. **The correct answer is A.** The English were more hostile towards the Native people and had little interest in converting or civilizing them. Choices B, C, and D are incorrect, as these explorers made more attempts to civilize and convert the Native people with trade, intermarriage, and cohabitation.

38. **The correct answer is D.** Whether Native American or European, whoever stood in the way of westward expansion soon became a problem. Whether it was the French, Spanish, British, it didn't matter, except insofar as how the problem was dealt with. At this time, the problem was the French, allied with local tribes. It was certainly not a current concern of the colonists that *European* powers control North America (choice A); Choice B is trickier, given the Monroe Doctrine, but note that that came 75 years after this period. The colonists didn't even want Britain off the continent at this point. Finally, choice C was never much of a concern among the vast majority of American elite.

39. **The correct answer is C.** The British soon took France's role of hedging in westward expansion, one of many reasons for the revolution. Choice D gets the answer right but the reason wrong: the concern was to expand westward, regardless of what Adams and Monroe said 75 years later, and long before the United States was in any position to back them up. Choices A and B are incorrect, not only because it wasn't the primary concern of the United States but also because France stuck around for a while; Spain, even longer.

40. **The correct answer is D.** The United States finally acquired New Orleans in the Louisiana Purchase and successfully retook it at the end of the War of 1812. The outlet of the continental Mississippi-Missouri river system, New Orleans was a crucial port. France did not hold any of the other ports at this time.

41. **The correct answer is A.** Choice C may have been tempting, but recall that the actual inhabitants of the land were the American Indians. Land taken from any theoretical grant of Indian land by Pope or King may well count, but so, too, does the practical capture of land from its actual inhabitants.

42. **The correct answer is C.** Interestingly, Douglass uses a racialist argument typical of the mid-nineteenth century against those who would downgrade "the negro race." Choices A and B are incorrect because Douglass considered the Indians weak in the face of Anglo Saxons, as he terms it, unlike "the negro race." Choice D is what a twenty-first-century anti-racist might suggest, but that's not what Douglass did in this speech.

43. **The correct answer is B.** Be careful: The modern meaning of "Uncle Tom" differs from that of the 1850s: the long-suffering, Christlike figure of Tom is actually quite well-chosen by Douglass, given his argument about "negro" racial resiliency. Thus, choice C is incorrect. The character was well-known, so choice A is incorrect. Choice D can't be upheld once a common contemporary interpretation of the character of Tom is taken into account.

44. **The correct answer is C.** This shouldn't be too surprising; the nineteenth century was probably the height of racialist and racist thinking, at least in the United States and Europe. Just about everyone accepted that frame (though not all). All the other choices are supported by the passage.

In general, any exam question that implies that *all* people did or thought something or that something is *always* true, is suspect.

45. **The correct answer is B.** Again, don't project our current, twenty-first-century notions onto people in the past, even generally laudable ones like Douglass. He was a person of his time, as all of us almost certainly are. He was urging acceptance of blacks precisely because they were ready, willing, and able to adopt the dominant white culture. He didn't argue superiority, so choice D is incorrect. Choice C is incorrect because nowhere does it note that Indians were equally able to assimilate; choice A is incorrect because Douglass claims that the Indians were too passive, not too defiant.

46. **The correct answer is D.** Written on the ship itself, we're told, prior even to landfall, the future United States already had a rudimentary frame of government indicative of the kind of limited self-rule typical of the society. The Compact did not, however, have much specific influence on future frames of government, so choice A is incorrect. Nor does it even hint at separation; such was unthinkable in the early seventeenth century, so choice B is incorrect. Finally, and unsurprisingly given who wrote it, the Compact is full of religious references and sanction, so choice C is incorrect.

47. **The correct answer is C.** This is a slightly tricky question. Normally, one would think that choice A would be correct, but since there was no property yet to hold, all adult males were of equal political standing. Women and nonwhites would not have been considered as political individuals at this time.

48. **The correct answer is D.** After the Mayflower Compact and the arrival of colonists in the North American colonies, there was substantial evidence that the colonies were headed toward self-rule. In Massachusetts Bay, there was a participatory annual election, albeit for white male landowners, so the answer cannot be choices A or C. Virginia formed the House of Burgesses as a means to create representation in the lawmaking process, so choice B cannot be correct. Some colonial governors served year after year and answered only to the crown, so choice D is an exception to any evidence that the colonists were heading toward self-rule.

49. **The correct answer is A.** The New Deal attempted to improve the lives of African Americans; however, New Dealers were not all free from racial prejudice, so choice B is incorrect. Choice C is anachronistic: the Harlem Renaissance began in the early 20s and was coming to an end by the mid-30s. Choice D is incorrect because legal/political segregation wasn't rooted out until well into the 60s or, in some areas, the 70s.

50. **The correct answer is C.** That great migration had many effects, the development of jazz and blues not the least of them. Reconstruction (choice A) was long dead; *Plessy* was in 1896 and didn't have as direct an effect as the migration; and prohibition (choice D), other than annoying drinkers and enriching organized crime, played no direct role in the Renaissance.

51. **The correct answer is C.** Since the New Deal, the federal government has supported the arts in its comparatively desultory way (compared to most developed countries, that is), so choice A is incorrect. Prior to the twentieth century, there was virtually no federal support for the arts, so choice B is incorrect; nor has there been much support except possibly in the past several decades, so choice D is also incorrect. Incidentally, the director of this version of *Macbeth* was the roughly twenty-year-old Orson Welles, soon to go on to be perhaps the nation's finest film director.

52. **The correct answer is B.** To the writer of gothic romances, the metal-clad *Monitor* had sucked all the romance out of naval warfare. Thus, choice D is incorrect. While industry was typical of the Gilded Age, the name refers to massive economic inequality and the conspicuous consumption of the one percent of the day, not to the technical advances of the second industrial revolution that made such fortunes possible, so choice A is incorrect. Hawthorne's comments indicate a certain decrease in his morale, but not in that of the Union's army or navy, let alone due to secession, so choice C is incorrect.

53. **The correct answer is D.** Recall that transcendentalism was essentially the American branch of European Romanticism which, while complicated, often deplored the march of technical and economic progress as then understood. An Enlightenment thinker (choice C) would have been more likely to laud the advance, and even see it as progress, whereas Populism (choice A) was still a bit in the future and Puritans (choice B) long in the past—so long before Hawthorne that it's hard to predict just what they would have made of the *Monitor*.

54. **The correct answer is B.** Reagan did indeed reorient American politics in a fashion akin to FDR; no Democratic president since has harkened to the New Deal and Great Society model of government outside of rhetoric, and not much of that, in fact. Therefore, the other choices are incorrect. Many historians consider the shift in the late 70s and early 80s to be from the liberal New Deal postwar consensus to a neoliberal view in favor of deregulation, financialization, and a particular kind of globalization, regardless of relatively minor policy differences between the parties. Moreover, this shift has been virtually global; much of current politics stems from this important shift in political economics.

55. **The correct answer is A.** It wouldn't help much to learn what Reagan thought of the pre-Obama (and pre-Clinton) Democratic Party that, with Carter, was only just beginning to shift away from New Deal policies. All the rest surely would help the historian of tomorrow (or today) to assess Obama's comments, made during his first presidential campaign.

Section I, Part B: Short-Answer Questions

1. For part A, if one chooses the Great Awakening, one could argue that though it was technically an extra-political movement, it did wrest control away from established religious hierarchies, locating Godliness and the organization of religious life in individuals. Moreover, it attracted the less powerful parts of society, though not exclusively; it was a "revolution" in religion that one could argue bled over into the political realm. If one chooses the Enlightenment, one could argue that not only was its effect direct since elite colonial thinkers had read both English and French Enlightenment writers, but also indirect, as even those who could not read were exposed (often secondhand) to pamphlets like Paine's *Common Sense* that were themselves directly inspired by Enlightenment thought.

   For part B, if one chose the Great Awakening, one could argue that Enlightenment thought was too far distant from the masses to have made much impact. Moreover, even pamphlets like *Common Sense* spent time arguing for a Biblical justification for colonial self-rule. If one chose the Enlightenment, one could argue that The Great Awakening in both content and form was hardly in favor of self-rule: charismatic, usually elite preachers used fear to undermine the average person's reason, which is hardly the basis of enlightened self-rule.

2. Given all the possibilities, it's best to use a chart:

Personage	A. Position as per the cartoon	B. Disagreement	C. Agreement
Lincoln	An abolitionist fighting for the end of slavery, not for the Union.	Lincoln was hardly an abolitionist, certainly at first but rather exactly what McClellan is claiming to be, a Unionist.	By 1864, after the Emancipation Proclamation, Lincoln was seen as an abolitionist, even though that Proclamation banned slavery only in captured Southern territory.
McClellan	A Unionist above all, slavery and secession aside.	It's hard to see McClellan's middle position, as to be a real Unionist, one must reverse and defeat secession.	McClellan and the Northern Democrats were trying to stem the bloody tide of war by finding some mutually agreeable basis for armistice.

Personage	A. Position as per the cartoon	B. Disagreement	C. Agreement
Davis	A secessionist above all; not fighting for slavery primarily.	It's very difficult to separate secession from slavery: the South seceded *because* it wanted to preserve its long-standing economic system.	Though defenses of slavery were many and varied, Confederates attempted to justify their secession on the loftier grounds of Jeffersonian nullification and the long tradition of anti-federalism, one interpretation of the "true legacy" of the American Revolution.

3. A top answer will reference John L. O'Sullivan; he coined the term "manifest destiny," and when he used the phrase "entrusted to us," he believed it was the God-given right of Americans to pioneer the settling of the West. People or groups who would have opposed manifest destiny are: abolitionists, Native Americans, Mexico, Northerners, and free-soilers. Evidence can include: the Mexican-American War; the Treaty of Guadalupe Hidalgo; the annexation of Texas; the Gadsden Purchase; "Fifty-four forty or fight!"; the election of James K. Polk; the Wilmot Proviso; or the Aroostook Wars.

4. For part A, one could mention the acceptance of biological argumentation in the social, human sphere in general; that progress is unquestioningly the goal of biological, and thus of social, evolution; that progress is defined as reflecting the real or supposed accomplishments of favored "races," which are nearly coterminous with nation-states or ethnic groups; and much besides, including the (to a modern reader) obvious racism itself.

For part B, and perhaps more interestingly, Roosevelt does not accept that competition always leads to progress. In fact, he posits a ceiling above which further competition harms the "race." One might also argue about his concluding remarks on the primacy of what he calls "character," not intellect, in creating the "social efficiency" by which a race rises. Much of that efficiency seems to reside in subsuming the needs of the individual to those of society, the corporate entity.

For part C, one could select many reasonable points. One could note that the kind of managed competition Roosevelt saw as necessary for social efficiency, and thus racial progress, underlay both trust-busting, which increased competition, as well as paternalistic, if well-intentioned, "character-building" efforts by progressive reformers. Options are numerous and can legitimately be pulled from both the formal political system and the larger society.

Section II, Part A: Document-Based Question

1.   First, make sure your response refers to all or all but one of the documents. That's why they're there, after all: this item tests your ability to synthesize information from several documents of varying types. You have plenty to compare and contrast among the documents.

Second, your thesis should note the two or three most important arguments for and against overseas imperialism around 1900. Good candidates are the racialist/racist "white man's burden" argument for imperialism as well as the geopolitical/economic argument best exemplified in Document 1 and the gendered language that comes up in more than one document in favor of imperialism. Also, note that, as always, the definition of what is truly American—for or against imperialism and colonies—is also in play. You'll want eventually to extend the analysis either to other time periods or to other cultures and societies at the time.

Third, you'll want to go in depth in your analysis of at least four of the documents, addressing one of the following for each of the four in-depth analyses: the historical context, the intended audience, the author's purpose, and the author's point of view. The minimum, mind you, is to discuss one of those four aspects for each of the four: feel free to expand beyond that as your thesis requires, but remember that you'll want to draw connections between the documents, not just analyze each in relative isolation. For example, you could point out the racialist/racist nature of many of the pro-imperialism pieces, noting for even more credit how one of the documents itself makes that very point (Document 2). Note, too, that Document 7 must be read carefully; it's a satire.

Make sure to show how the different kinds of documents—speeches and addresses; satirical cartoon; poem; written satire (Document 3); and work of history and policy (Document 1)—vary in point of view, intended audience, authorial purpose, and so on. You will want (and have) to bring in outside knowledge to contextualize the documents. One fruitful avenue would be to tie domestic economic and political concerns to this supposedly foreign-policy debate. Why would Populists be against imperialism, for example? Go behind the surface rhetoric, without simply dismissing it or its likely intended effect.

As noted earlier, your response should be extended to another time, another place, or another mode of historical writing and argumentation. If, for example, you concentrated on a race-and-gender analysis, make sure to address, say, the geopolitical or economic underpinnings of the debate. Or you could compare and contrast with another society's imperialism, either during this period or in the past.

Section II, Part B: Long Essay Question

Note: Whichever essay you picked, consider not reading the guideline responses to the other two—save them for further practice!

The first two essays require you to determine whether the noted event was indeed a turning point in history. The third essay asks about the role of European rivalries in the shaping of the American colonies. As you would expect, one can either agree or disagree and do just fine: the point is not to choose the "right" answer, but to create a reasonable thesis and back it up. Specific feedback for each essay below will deal with both cases, but in general, the more specific and relevant your support for your thesis and any subsidiary points, the better you'll do. Thesis statements may be two sentences, if you prefer, but make sure they address all parts of the question. After you've developed your argument, make sure to extend it to another time period, another culture or society, or to another mode of historical writing and argumentation.

2. Note that the Bargain is widely considered the end of Reconstruction, which means the end of or the beginning of the rollback of voting and other civil rights for African Americans. However, one could argue that since much of daily life remained unchanged, especially in contradistinction to high hopes at the end of the Civil War, perhaps it wasn't much of a turning point after all. The scope you define will help determine whether you find this event to be a turning point or not. Limit it to the ten years before and after, and it sure looks like one; take a longer view—say, fifty years on either side or more—and the relative freedom of the decade following the Civil War looks like the exception to the rule.

   A recap of the Black Codes and rise of Jim Crow in the South would be useful. To show what stayed the same, you could argue how similar daily life often was before the Civil War and after Reconstruction, with little difference existing between slavery and feudal sharecropping. You could argue that Jim Crow was just slavery by another means—pperhaps not as complete but a legal cage built around technically free people. A complete answer would take into account African American life in the North, too, both before and after 1877: did the North change much for black people before and after this date? What did change was the *de jure* or constitutional status of African Americans (but consider *Plessy v. Ferguson*); what did not much change was their lived experience, especially but not only in the South. Which you consider more important is both up to you and will determine much of the rest of your answer.

   Note that you're free to define what "the history of African Americans" means. Is it economic history? Political? Social? The frame you choose will also help determine whether or not you find this even to be a turning point. Feel free to use comparison to a different period, perhaps the 1950s and 1960s, in order to develop your thesis, but make sure you still extend your argument beyond that comparison.

3. One could argue that the Korean War was the first presidential or executive war, at least in the twentieth century; not since WWII has there been a formal declaration of war. Korea set the tone and mode for subsequent wars in Vietnam, Iraq, and elsewhere. Moreover, one could argue that it was the first war prosecuted by the United States as the dominant global power, one finally free from any hint of isolationism and operating under what is essentially a global Monroe Doctrine as the world's policeman. One could even refer to Eisenhower's military-industrial complex speech to help explain our involvement; that, plus the widespread fear that

without "military Keynesianism," the United States would slide back into the depression that was only solved by the entry into WWII. Another seeming change would be that this was the first U.S. war begun after the nuclear age had dawned, a real change that surely affected the foreign-policy calculus.

Or one could argue that the historical norm in the many "police actions" sometimes claimed to have been fought by the United States since clearing out the Barbary pirates in the late eighteenth century has been no formal declaration of war by Congress; thus, the Korean War is not much of a turning point. Likewise, one could frame it as a hot phase of a cold war that had already begun between the U.S./UK and USSR during WWII; that was the turning point, it could be argued. Additionally, it was not the first Asian war the United States had fought. Not including the Pacific theater of WWII, the war in the Philippines preceded Korea by a half-century. Perhaps Korea, and Vietnam after it, along with the many more covert or proxy wars fought since WWII, have been the usual quasi-imperial game the United States has been playing since at least the middle of the nineteenth century, especially after the acquisition of Pacific-facing California.

Much, if not everything, depends on the chosen frame. Pull in close and this first overt contest between democracy and Communism (as then understood: that is, monolithically) may seem a turning point. Pull back, considering it a typical clash of great powers in ancillary states, and it may not. As you've grasped, the key with these essays is that they can be answered equally well pro or con; what gets you a good score is answering all parts of the question with a plausible thesis statement that you go on to fully support, extending your conclusion to another time, place, or historical mode.

4. This question covers everything from Columbus through the Revolution, so one way to organize your response is by major European power. "American colonies," moreover, could be interpreted as any colonies in the Americas, if one so desires. The rise of European navigation in the fifteenth century—stemming from competition with existing global trade routes—could be traced, as it answers the question of why the Europeans bothered with the expense and trouble of exploration and colonization. Beginning in Portugal but spreading, the age of exploration which necessarily preceded the age of colonization and the Atlantic slave trade (and not by much) should be assessed and discussed.

Moving on, one could cover the colonies of Spain and Portugal in South, Central, and North America; of France, Holland, and Britain in North America; and of just about everyone in the Caribbean. Take note not only of different desired products, from gold to sugar, but of differing impetuses for and goals of colonization among the various European powers. For example, the Spanish wanted to extract resources while settling down and mixing with the indigenous population, whereas the French had little interest in actual settlement, preferring to trade, and the English were keen to settle, but at the expense of the indigenous population with whom they hardly mixed. Spanish castes could be contrasted with English separation of populations, and so on.

Many other things could be legitimately discussed. For example, the conflict between Catholic and Protestant colonial powers, with France and Spain on the one hand and England and Holland on the other. Power politics and wars in Europe, up to and including the Seven Years' War conflict between France and Britain (among others), often had their echoes in the New World. One could even argue that the disaster of the Spanish Armada in 1588 allowed for later English colonization in the Americas. Events internal to the mother countries, such as the Puritan and Glorious Revolutions in England, also echoed in the colonies. The Atlantic slave trade and its variants among the colonizing powers—its introduction and varied growth—would also be worth exploring.

Self-Scoring Sheet for Practice Test 1

Directions:

- For the 55 multiple-choice items, tally up the items you answered either incorrectly or omitted—or just guessed on in some fashion—according to the chronological period. This will help you determine what you need to review. (Some question numbers are repeated, as the subject matter may cross chronological periods.)

- For each of the short-answer items (Q1 through Q4), the content area(s) have been noted in the chart to aid with your review.

- For the DBQ and Essays, an asterisk has been placed in the chronological period most at issue, but keep in mind that the essays usually ask about turning points in history, so discussion can range widely from those turning points.

Period	Multiple-Choice Items	Short Answers	DBQ	Essay 1	Essay 2	Essay 3
1 (1491-1607)	34–37	Q3				
2 (1607-1754)	1, 2, 3, 38, 39, 40, 46–48, 51	Q1				
3 (1754-1800)	4, 8, 11, 12, 13, 31, 32, 33, 39, 51	Q3				*
4 (1800-1848)	1, 4, 5, 6, 7, 8, 9, 10, 37, 41, 51	Q3				
5 (1844-1877)	4, 30, 41–45, 51, 52, 53	Q2, Q3		*		
6 (1865-1898)	14, 15, 16, 28, 41, 51	Q3, Q4				
7 (1890-1945)	17, 18, 19, 21, 24–30, 31, 41, 49–51	Q3, Q4	*			
8 (1945-1980)	16, 21, 22, 23, 33, 51, 54, 55				*	
9 (1980-present)	21, 51, 54, 55					

Practice Test 2

Chapter 15

ANSWER SHEET PRACTICE TEST 2

Section I, Part A: Multiple-Choice Questions

1. Ⓐ Ⓑ Ⓒ Ⓓ   15. Ⓐ Ⓑ Ⓒ Ⓓ   29. Ⓐ Ⓑ Ⓒ Ⓓ   43. Ⓐ Ⓑ Ⓒ Ⓓ

2. Ⓐ Ⓑ Ⓒ Ⓓ   16. Ⓐ Ⓑ Ⓒ Ⓓ   30. Ⓐ Ⓑ Ⓒ Ⓓ   44. Ⓐ Ⓑ Ⓒ Ⓓ

3. Ⓐ Ⓑ Ⓒ Ⓓ   17. Ⓐ Ⓑ Ⓒ Ⓓ   31. Ⓐ Ⓑ Ⓒ Ⓓ   45. Ⓐ Ⓑ Ⓒ Ⓓ

4. Ⓐ Ⓑ Ⓒ Ⓓ   18. Ⓐ Ⓑ Ⓒ Ⓓ   32. Ⓐ Ⓑ Ⓒ Ⓓ   46. Ⓐ Ⓑ Ⓒ Ⓓ

5. Ⓐ Ⓑ Ⓒ Ⓓ   19. Ⓐ Ⓑ Ⓒ Ⓓ   33. Ⓐ Ⓑ Ⓒ Ⓓ   47. Ⓐ Ⓑ Ⓒ Ⓓ

6. Ⓐ Ⓑ Ⓒ Ⓓ   20. Ⓐ Ⓑ Ⓒ Ⓓ   34. Ⓐ Ⓑ Ⓒ Ⓓ   48. Ⓐ Ⓑ Ⓒ Ⓓ

7. Ⓐ Ⓑ Ⓒ Ⓓ   21. Ⓐ Ⓑ Ⓒ Ⓓ   35. Ⓐ Ⓑ Ⓒ Ⓓ   49. Ⓐ Ⓑ Ⓒ Ⓓ

8. Ⓐ Ⓑ Ⓒ Ⓓ   22. Ⓐ Ⓑ Ⓒ Ⓓ   36. Ⓐ Ⓑ Ⓒ Ⓓ   50. Ⓐ Ⓑ Ⓒ Ⓓ

9. Ⓐ Ⓑ Ⓒ Ⓓ   23. Ⓐ Ⓑ Ⓒ Ⓓ   37. Ⓐ Ⓑ Ⓒ Ⓓ   51. Ⓐ Ⓑ Ⓒ Ⓓ

10. Ⓐ Ⓑ Ⓒ Ⓓ   24. Ⓐ Ⓑ Ⓒ Ⓓ   38. Ⓐ Ⓑ Ⓒ Ⓓ   52. Ⓐ Ⓑ Ⓒ Ⓓ

11. Ⓐ Ⓑ Ⓒ Ⓓ   25. Ⓐ Ⓑ Ⓒ Ⓓ   39. Ⓐ Ⓑ Ⓒ Ⓓ   53. Ⓐ Ⓑ Ⓒ Ⓓ

12. Ⓐ Ⓑ Ⓒ Ⓓ   26. Ⓐ Ⓑ Ⓒ Ⓓ   40. Ⓐ Ⓑ Ⓒ Ⓓ   54. Ⓐ Ⓑ Ⓒ Ⓓ

13. Ⓐ Ⓑ Ⓒ Ⓓ   27. Ⓐ Ⓑ Ⓒ Ⓓ   41. Ⓐ Ⓑ Ⓒ Ⓓ   55. Ⓐ Ⓑ Ⓒ Ⓓ

14. Ⓐ Ⓑ Ⓒ Ⓓ   28. Ⓐ Ⓑ Ⓒ Ⓓ   42. Ⓐ Ⓑ Ⓒ Ⓓ

Section I, Part B: Short-Answer Questions

Question 1

_____

_____

_____

_____

_____

_____

_____

_____

answer sheet

Question 2

_____
_____
_____
_____
_____
_____
_____
_____
_____
_____
_____
_____
_____
_____
_____

Question 3 or 4

_____
_____
_____
_____
_____
_____
_____
_____
_____
_____
_____
_____
_____
_____
_____

Section II, Part A: Document-Based Question

_____

_____

_____

_____

_____

_____

_____

_____

_____

_____

_____

_____

_____

_____

_____

_____

_____

_____

_____

_____

_____

answer sheet

answer sheet

Section II, Part B: Long Essay Question

_____

_____

_____

_____

_____

_____

_____

_____

_____

_____

_____

_____

_____

_____

_____

_____

_____

_____

_____

_____

_____

_____

_____

_____

_____

_____

_____

answer sheet

answer sheet

PRACTICE TEST 2

Section I, Part A: Multiple-Choice Questions

Time: 55 Minutes • 55 Questions

> **Directions:** Each question set is organized around two to five questions that focus on a primary or secondary source. After reading the document, choose the best answer and fill in the correct oval on the answer sheet.

Questions 1–4 refer to the excerpt below.

> "Rev. George Whitefield arrived in Boston, September 18, 1740, on his first visit to New England. His fame had preceded him. In the afternoon of the next day he preached in Brattle street meeting-house to 'about four thousand people;' the day following, in the Old South, to 'six thousand;' and on the Common, at a later hour of the same day, to 'eight thousand,' -- which out-door assemblies afterwards increased to 'twenty' and even 'thirty thousand.' These numbers are taken from his own published journal[.] [...] From Boston he proceeded east as far as York, in Maine; then west to Northampton; and completed the tour of New England on the 1st of December, having travelled upwards of eight hundred miles in seventy-four days, and 'preached one hundred and seventy-five times in public, besides exhorting frequently in private.'"
>
> —Joseph Sylvester Clark, *A Historical Sketch of the Congregational Churches in Massachusetts: From 1620 to 1858*, 1858.
>
> Source: *https://archive.org/details/ahistoricalsket00publgoog*

1. Whitefield's popularity and preaching tour were part of which of the following movements?
   A. The Social Gospel
   B. The Gospel of Wealth
   C. The First Great Awakening
   D. The Second Great Awakening

2. Which of the following best captures the effect of Whitefield and those preachers and theologians associated with him on American Protestantism?
   A. Minor and limited to New England in the eighteenth century
   B. Minor, limited to New England, but continuing to the present
   C. Crucial, widespread, and continuing to the present
   D. Crucial, widespread, but limited to the eighteenth century

3. That Whitefield's fame preceded his arrival in the colonies from Britain most directly supports which of the following claims?

   A. Cultural development in the American colonies was significantly influenced by trans-Atlantic exchange.

   B. American colonial cultural development was determined by Britain.

   C. Trans-Atlantic cultural exchange between Britain and the American colonies was limited to religion.

   D. Communication links between Britain and its colonies were so weak as to prevent any significant cultural exchange.

4. The outdoor, ecstatic gatherings typical of this movement are most similar to which of the following?

   A. The ceremony at Gettysburg in 1863

   B. Shays' Rebellion in Massachusetts in 1786

   C. The Constitutional Convention held in Philadelphia in 1787

   D. The free concert held near Woodstock in 1969

Questions 5–7 refer to the excerpt below.

...in the cost of tea, two-thirds are, before it reach them, tax; that, in the cost of sugar , three-fourths are tax; that, in the cost of tobacco , nine-tenths are tax; that, in the cost of spirits , seven eighths are tax; that, in the cost of shoes , more than one-half is tax; that, in the cost of other wearing apparel , including the taxes on wool, on cotton, on silk, on dyeing stuff, and on some of the goods themselves, after made full one-half is tax; that, in the cost of pepper , at this moment, the price is 3d. and the tax 2s. a pound! Let me say this in words, lest the world should not believe it. Pepper, at this moment, costs threepence a pound, in the port of London; and the tax on that pounds is two shillings. It is much about the same with all other species, drugs, and the like. Besides those articles, there is the iron , and the leather , and timber , used by farmers and others. In short, we can touch nothing, we can see nothing, that is not taxed; and it is an indisputable fact, that every tradesman and farmer pays, in one way or another, to the government, in taxes, more than one-half of the profits of his business, including the interest of the money employed in that business.

—excerpt from *The Emigrant's Guide*

Source: *https://www.loc.gov/resource/lhbtn.24759/?q=potato+famine+immigration&sp=17&st=text*

5. All of the following were the policies of the mercantilist system EXCEPT:

A. Trade to and from the colonies should be carried only by English of colonial-built ships

B. All goods imported to the colonies had to pass through English ports

C. Colonists could produce finished goods to send to England

D. Enumerated goods could only be exported to England

6. Which of the following was an outcome of the mercantilist system?

A. New England shipbuilding flourished.

B. The tobacco industry began to diminish.

C. Colonists were able to get finished, British-manufactured goods for very low prices.

D. Colonists produced finished goods to send back to England and to use in Africa for slave trading purposes.

7. What did the British monarchy and Parliament use as their main reason to justify their passage of colonial taxes?

A. Mercantilism

B. Protection

C. "They were British, after all"

D. Paying for the importation of more slaves

Questions 8–11 refer to the excerpt below.

"RESOLUTIONS. Whereas the great precept of Nature is conceded to be, 'that a man shall pursue his own true and substantial happiness.' [The eighteenth-century English legal authority William] Blackstone, in his *Commentaries* [*on the Laws of England*], remarks that this law of Nature being coeval with mankind, and dictated by God himself, is of course superior in obligation to any other. It is binding all over the globe, in all countries, and at all times; no human laws are of any validity if contrary to this, and such of them as are valid derive all their force, and all their validity, and all their authority, mediately and immediately, from this original[.]"

—from *The Declaration of Sentiments* cited in "The first convention ever called to discuss the civil and political rights of women, Seneca Falls, N.Y., July 19, 20, 1848," 1848.

Source: *https://www.loc.gov/item/27007548/*

8. The ideas in the passage most closely resemble which of the following?
   A. Romantic belief in the primacy of emotion
   B. Enlightenment views on natural law
   C. Puritan belief in predestination
   D. Socialist views on the secular basis of law

9. In elevating the goal of individual happiness above all others, the passage attempts to align itself with which of the following?
   A. The Constitution
   B. The Articles of Confederation
   C. The Declaration of Independence
   D. The Federalist Papers

10. Which of the following was not a concern of the women at the Seneca Falls Convention?
    A. Education
    B. Divorce rights
    C. Voting rights
    D. Affordable child care laws

11. Which of the following concepts is most directly addressed in this passage?
    A. Political sovereignty
    B. Legal precedent
    C. Social mores
    D. Cultural values

Questions 12–14 refer to the excerpts below.

"We hold these truths to be self-evident: that all men are created equal; that they are endowed by their Creator with certain unalienable rights; that among these are life, liberty and the pursuit of happiness. That to secure these rights, governments are instituted among men, deriving their just powers from the consent of the governed. That whenever any form of government becomes destructive of these ends, it is the right of the people to alter or to abolish it, and to institute new government, laying its foundation on such principles and organizing its powers in such form, as to them shall seem most likely to affect their safety and happiness."

—The Declaration of Independence

"We the People of the United States, in order to form a more perfect union, establish justice, ensure domestic tranquility, provide for the common defense, promote the general welfare, and secure the blessings of liberty to ourselves and our posterity, do ordain and establish this Constitution for the United States of America."

—The United States Constitution

12. All of the following represent similarity between the two passages EXCEPT:
    A. The investing of ultimate desire for good government in a Creator
    B. The emphasis on the central importance of liberty
    C. An unstated agreement that "the people" refer to propertied, adult, white males
    D. The location of political sovereignty in "the people"

13. Which of the following thinkers was most directly influential on both documents?
    A. Hobbes
    B. Rousseau
    C. Machiavelli
    D. Locke

14. Which of the following rights is LEAST directly referred to in both of the passages?
    A. Justice
    B. Safety
    C. Property
    D. Liberty

Questions 15–18 refer to the excerpt below.

"SECTION 1. I hereby authorize and direct the Secretary of Defense to order into the active military service of the United States as he may deem appropriate to carry out the purposes of this Order, any or all of the units of the National Guard of the United States and of the Air National Guard of the United States within the State of Arkansas to serve in the active military service of the United States for an indefinite period and until relieved by appropriate orders.

SEC. 2. The Secretary of Defense is authorized and directed to take all appropriate steps to enforce any orders of the United States District Court for the Eastern District of Arkansas for the removal of obstruction of justice in the State of Arkansas with respect to matters relating to enrollment and attendance at public schools in the Little Rock School District, Little Rock, Arkansas. In carrying out the provisions of this section, the Secretary of Defense is authorized to use the units, and members thereof, ordered into the active military service of the United States pursuant to Section 1 of this Order.

SEC. 3. In furtherance of the enforcement of the aforementioned orders of the United States District Court for the Eastern District of Arkansas, the Secretary of Defense is authorized to use such of the armed forces of the United States as he may deem necessary."

—Excerpt from Executive Order 10730: "Providing Assistance for the Removal of an Obstruction of Justice within the State of Arkansas," Dwight Eisenhower, 1957

Source: *https://www.ourdocuments.gov/doc.php?doc=89&page=transcript*

15. Eisenhower's action is most similar to which of the following?
    A. Grant's mobilization of federal troops to crush the Ku Klux Klan in 1871
    B. Reagan's removal of Marines from Lebanon in 1984
    C. McKinley's sending of armed forces to the Philippines in 1898
    D. Louisiana governor Kathleen Blanco's deployment of the National Guard after Hurricane Katrina in 2005

16. Which of the following Supreme Court decisions was Arkansas defying?
    A. *Dred Scott v. Sanford*
    B. *Regents of the University of California v. Bakke*
    C. *Marbury v. Madison*
    D. *Brown v. Board of Education of Topeka*

17. Arkansas was one of many southern states that had congressional representatives sign which of the following anti-integration manifestos, declaring that the Supreme Court had violated the Tenth Amendment?
    A. The Southern Manifesto
    B. The Jim Crow Manifesto
    C. The Northern Manifesto
    D. Congressional Manifesto on Federal Violations of the Tenth Amendment

18. All of the following were consequences of Eisenhower's decision EXCEPT:
    A. Black students were accompanied to school by armed guards for the entire school year
    B. The governor of Arkansas eventually withdrew the National Guard that was attempting to prevent black students from attending Central High School
    C. Many Americans watched the events unfold on television and began to support racial justice more outwardly
    D. The segregated schools in the South began implementing swift integration policies

Questions 19–22 refer to the excerpt below.

"[A] bill printed by order of the last session of General Assembly entitled "A Bill establishing a provision for Teachers of the Christian Religion," [...] if finally armed with the sanctions of a law, will be a dangerous abuse of power[. We] are bound as faithful members of a free State to remonstrate against it and to declare the reasons by which we are determined. We remonstrate against the said bill [...] because the proposed establishment is a departure from that generous policy which, offering an asylum to the persecuted and oppressed of every nation and religion, promised a luster to our country and an accession to the number of its citizens.

What a melancholy mark is this bill of sudden degeneracy[!] Instead of holding forth an asylum to the persecuted, it is itself a signal of persecution. It degrades from the equal rank of citizens all those whose opinions in religion do not bend to those of the legislative authority. Distant as it may be in its present form from the Inquisition, it differs from it only in degree. The one is the first step, the other the last in the career of intolerance. The magnanimous sufferer under this cruel scourge in foreign regions must view the bill as a beacon on our coast warning him to seek some other haven where liberty and philanthropy in their due extent may offer a more certain repose from his troubles."

—James Madison, "Memorial and Remonstrance against Religious Assessments," 1785

Source: *https://founders.archives.gov/documents/Madison/01-08-02-0163*

19. Which of the following most nearly reflects the position taken in this passage?
   A. The Declaration of Independence's guarantee of life, liberty, and the pursuit of happiness
   B. The Fourth Amendment's guarantee against unreasonable search and seizure
   C. *Marbury v. Madison's* establishment of judicial review
   D. The no religious test clause in the Constitution

20. Madison's argument would most likely be rejected by all of the following EXCEPT the
   A. American Civil Liberties Union.
   B. Know-Nothings.
   C. Puritans.
   D. Ku Klux Klan.

21. Which of the following most directly influenced the position taken by Madison in the passage and widely shared by the founders?
   A. The English Civil War
   B. The debate over the slave trade
   C. The French Revolution
   D. The debate over ratification of the Constitution

22. Which of the following longstanding controversies in American history is most closely related to the issues raised by Madison in this excerpt?
   A. Which branch of government controls war-related powers
   B. States' rights
   C. The teaching of creationism in public-school biology classes
   D. Racial segregation

Questions 23–24 refer to the excerpt below.

"The widespread use of the market reduces the strain on the social fabric by rendering conformity unnecessary with respect to any activities it encompasses. The wider the range of activities covered by the market, the fewer are the issues on which explicitly political decisions are required and hence on which it is necessary to achieve agreement. In turn, the fewer the issues on which agreement is necessary, the greater is the likelihood of getting agreement while maintaining a free society."

—Milton Friedman, *Capitalism and Freedom*, 1962

Source: *https://en.m.wikiquote.org/wiki/Milton_Friedman* (CC BY-SA 3.0)

23. The position taken by Friedman in this passage is closest to which of the following?
   A. The New Deal
   B. The American System
   C. Containment
   D. Neoliberalism

24. Referring to the time in which Friedman made these comments, which of the following was most accurate about their context?
   A. They reflected an entirely new view.
   B. They were immediately embraced by the Democrats.
   C. They foreshadowed future policies.
   D. They reflected the general thrust of policy at the time.

Questions 25–28 refer to the following image.

**"Once a Missouri farmer, now a migratory farm laborer on the Pacific Coast.
California," Dorothea Lange, 1936.**

Source: *https://www.loc.gov/item/fsa1998018480/PP/*

25. Which of the following most likely explains why this family moved to California?
    A. The Dust Bowl
    B. The failure of the Fair Deal
    C. The widespread poverty brought on by World War II
    D. The triumph of the Populist Party

26. During the period when this photograph was taken, which of the following set of economic beliefs was dominant in the federal government?
    A. *Laissez-faire*
    B. Isolationism
    C. governmental intervention
    D. Military Keynesianism

27. Which of the following most directly ended the conditions reflected in this photograph?
    A. American entry into World War II
    B. The New Deal
    C. The Cold War
    D. The Great Migration

28. The migration noted in the photograph's title helped to foster the rise of which of the following sections of the country?
    A. The New South
    B. The Northeast
    C. The Midwest
    D. The Sun Belt

Questions 29–31 refer to the excerpt below.

"We are coming to recognize as never before the right of the Nation to guard its own future in the essential matter of natural resources. In the past we have admitted the right of the individual to injure the future of the Republic for his own present profit. In fact there has been a good deal of a demand for unrestricted individualism, for the right of the individual to injure the future of all of us for his own temporary and immediate profit. The time has come for a change. As a people we have the right and the duty, second to none other but the right and duty of obeying the moral law, of requiring and doing justice to protect ourselves and our children against the wasteful development of our natural resources, whether that waste is caused by the actual destruction of such resources or by making them impossible of development hereafter."

—Theodore Roosevelt, "Conservation as a National Duty," 1908

Source: *http://voicesofdemocracy.umd.edu/theodore-roosevelt-conservation-as-a-national-duty-speech-text/*

29. Ideas such as those in the excerpt most directly shaped which of the following?
    A. Increased emphasis on striking a balance between capital and labor
    B. The rise of antitrust law
    C. The development of the national park system
    D. The building of the Panama Canal

30. Which of the following was NOT a conservation policy of President Roosevelt?
    A. Setting aside federal lands to protect from private investors
    B. Establishing the U.S. Forestry Service
    C. Making Yosemite Park the official park of the United States
    D. Establishing bird sanctuaries

31. Roosevelt's argument is closest to that of which of the following?
    A. Neoliberal appeals for deregulation in the 1990s
    B. Opponents of amnesty for undocumented immigrants in the 2010s
    C. Opponents of the Iraq War in the 2000s
    D. Those who urge action on global warming in the 2010s

Questions 32–34 refer to the excerpt below.

"Let us, then, fellow citizens, unite with one heart and one mind, let us restore to social intercourse that harmony and affection without which liberty, and even life itself, are but dreary things. And let us reflect that having banished from our land that religious intolerance under which mankind had bled and suffered, we have yet gained little if we countenance a political intolerance as despotic, as wicked, and capable of as bitter and bloody persecutions. [...] We have called by different names brethren of the same principle. We are all republicans; we are all federalists."

—Thomas Jefferson's First Inaugural Address, 1801

Lightly modernized from: **Source:** *https://archive.org/details/truerepublicanco00adam*

32. Based on the passage and your knowledge of American history, which of the following most closely reflects the ideas expressed by Jefferson?
    A. The Monroe Doctrine of 1823
    B. Reagan's speech at the Brandenburg Gate in Berlin in 1987
    C. Washington's Farewell Address in 1796
    D. Eisenhower's Farewell Address in 1961

33. Which of the following most intensified inter-party tensions in the decade prior to this address?
    A. The French Revolution
    B. The Haitian Revolution
    C. The ratification of the Constitution
    D. The Louisiana Purchase

34. Which of the following most accurately expresses how much of the Constitution was devoted to discussion of political parties?
    A. A great deal
    B. Some
    C. A little
    D. None

Questions 35–37 refer to the excerpt below.

"The changing pattern of epidemic infection was and remains a fundamental landmark in human ecology that deserves more attention than it has ordinarily received. On the time scale of world history, indeed we should view the 'domestication' of epidemic disease that occurred between 1300 and 1700 as a fundamental breakthrough, directly resulting from the two great transportation revolutions of that age—one by land, initiated by the Mongols, and one by sea, initiated by the Europeans."

— William H. McNeill, *Plagues and Peoples*, 1976.

35. The changing pattern of epidemics noted in the excerpt most directly relates to which of the following long-term historical trends?
  A. The Atlantic slave trade
  B. The shift from land-based to sea-based trading routes
  C. The rise of scientific medicine
  D. The Colombian Exchange

36. The relationship between the spread of the Mongols and of the Europeans is meant to be taken as
  A. Directly related, with the Mongol spread causing the European spread
  B. Analogous
  C. Directly related, with the European spread causing the Mongol spread
  D. Contradictory

37. All of the following epidemic diseases were brought to the Americas by the Europeans EXCEPT:
  A. Cholera
  B. Bubonic plague
  C. Syphilis
  D. Smallpox

Questions 38–41 refer to the image below.

MAP OF THE OHIO AND OTHER RIVERS FROM LAKE ERIE TO THE ALLEGHENY MOUNTAINS,

THE JOURNAL OF MAJOR GEORGE WASHINGTON, 1754

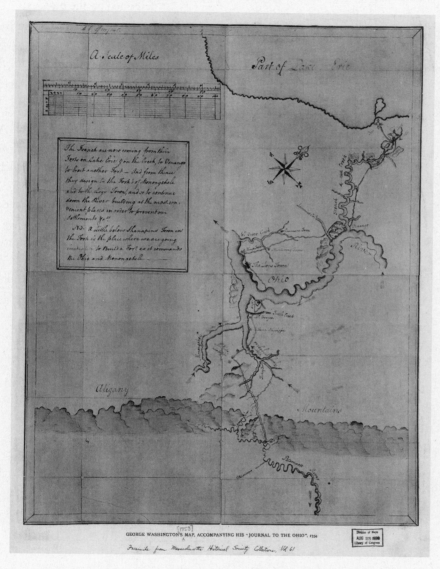

The text in the box on the left is as follows: "The French are now coming from their forts on Lake Erie and on the [French] Creek to [the] Venango [River] to erect another fort. And from thence they design to the forks of [the] Monongahela [River] and to the Logs Town [eighteen miles from present-day Pittsburgh], and so to continue down the River building at the most convenient places in order to prevent our settlements, &c.

NB. A little below Shanapins Town [i.e., present-day Pittsburgh] in the fork is the place where we are going immediately to build a fort as it commands the Ohio and Monongehele."

Source: Library of Congress, Geography and Map Division (*https://www.loc.gov/item/99446116/*)

38. This map indicates which of the following concerns of the American colonists at the time?
   A. Westward expansion
   B. Fear of Indians
   C. Scientific exploration
   D. Preparation for independence

39. Competing claims on this territory were to contribute most directly to which of the following?
   A. The expulsion of the Spanish from North America
   B. The rewriting of the Articles of Confederation
   C. The defeat of Napoleon
   D. The French and Indian War

40. Based on your knowledge of American history, which of the following defined the path by which Washington explored this region?
   A. Canals linking the river system described on the map
   B. Trails blazed by American Indians
   C. Roads laid down by the British colonial government
   D. Roads laid down by the American federal government

41. Based on your knowledge of American history, which of the following was most likely the main benefit the French derived from this territory?
   A. Leverage against Spain in cooperation with Britain
   B. Fertile farmland on which to settle French emigrants
   C. Fur trade with the local Indian tribes
   D. Formal colonies with clear territorial boundaries

Questions 42–45 refer to the excerpt below.

"Mr. [JOHN] CALHOUN [...] declared it as his conviction that, in point of fact, the Central African race (he did not speak of the north or the east of Africa, but of its central regions) had never existed in so comfortable, so respectable, or so civilized a condition as that which it now enjoyed in the Southern States. The population doubled in the same ratio with that of the whites—a proof of ease and plenty—while, with respect to civilization, it nearly kept pace with that of the owners[.] [...] He did not admit [slavery] to be an evil. Not at all. It was a good—a great good."—*Register of Debates*, Senate, 24th Congress, 2nd Session, 1837

Lightly updated from: **Source:** *http://memory.loc.gov/cgi-bin/ampage?collId=llrd&fileName=026/llrd026. db&recNum=362* and *http://memory.loc.gov/cgi-bin/ampage?collId=llrd&fileName=026/llrd026.db&recNum=363*

42. Which of the following groups would have been most likely to disagree with Calhoun's reasoning?
  A. Feminists
  B. Abolitionists
  C. Democrats
  D. Whigs

43. Which of the following is the most direct and warranted inference from Calhoun's argument?
  A. That whites and blacks generally were of equal abilities
  B. That blacks, but not whites, benefited from slavery
  C. That if left to fend for themselves, African slaves would soon enter a condition worse than that of slavery
  D. That if left to fend for themselves, African slaves would soon improve their condition over what had held under slavery

44. Which of the following events would most increase sectional tensions after this speech?
  A. The Mexican Cession
  B. The constitutional ban on the slave trade
  C. The rise of Irish and German immigration
  D. The Missouri Compromise

45. Calhoun's views were of the most direct benefit to which of the following groups?
  A. American Indian tribes
  B. Rich southern plantation owners
  C. Poor southern white family farmers
  D. Northern free blacks

Questions 46–48 refer to the excerpt below.

"For the increase of the shipping and the encouragement of the navigation of this nation [...] be it enacted by this present Parliament, and the authority thereof, that from and after the first day of December, one thousand six hundred fifty and one, and from thence forwards, no goods or commodities whatsoever of the growth, production or manufacture of Asia, Africa or America, or of any part thereof [...] shall be imported or brought into this Commonwealth of England [...] in any other ship or ships [...] but only in such as do truly and without fraud belong only to the people of this Commonwealth [...] under the penalty of the forfeiture and loss of all the goods that shall be imported contrary to this act[.]"

—from the English Navigation Act of 1651

Modernized from: **Source:** *https://en.m.wikisource.org/wiki/Navigation_Act_1651*

46. This and subsequent Navigation Acts had which of the following effects?
    A. They established a free-trade regime among England, its colonies, and the rest of the world.
    B. They were the immediate cause of the French and Indian War.
    C. They were soon extended to the blockade of Napoleonic Europe.
    D. They established a mercantilist colonial system that eventually led to the Revolutionary War.

47. The Navigation Acts were emblematic of which of the following economic philosophies?
    A. Mercantilism
    B. Free trade
    C. *Laissez-faire*
    D. Engrossment

48. The economic philosophy exemplified by the Navigation Acts was most similar to
    A. Jefferson's vision of an agrarian-based republic.
    B. Hamilton's plan for the protection of infant industry.
    C. Southern chattel slavery.
    D. Social Darwinist encouragement of unlimited competition.

Questions 49–51 refer to the excerpt below.

"The Southern States, which had not entered upon an industrial expansion before the Civil War, did not welcome immigrants of the low-grade factory type, hence the South has remained characteristically American. One of the strange results of the Civil War has been that while the victorious North sold its birthright of culture, religion, and racial purity for a mess of industrial pottage, the South, though defeated and impoverished, retained its racial inheritance unimpaired."

—Madison Grant, *The Conquest of a Continent, or, The Expansion of Races in America*, 1933

Source: *https://archive.org/details/conquestofcontin00gran*

49. Based on your knowledge of American history, which of the following statements is most likely accurate about the general attitude expressed in the passage?

   A. It had been popular for some time, but mostly fell out of favor after WWII.

   B. It had never been popular.

   C. It has always been popular in all sections of the country.

   D. It is generally supported by most contemporary historians of the Civil War.

50. Which of the following was most directly influenced by views such as these?

   A. The formation of the United Nations in the 1940s

   B. The rise of the Progressives in the early 1900s

   C. Immigration policy in the 1920s

   D. Isolationism in the 1930s

51. The ideas expressed in the passage are closest to which of the following?

   A. The Gospel of Wealth

   B. The Social Gospel

   C. Darwinism

   D. Eugenics

Questions 52–53 refer to the image below.

"Fairyland Palaces of Our New Multi-Millionaires," Henry Brevoort Eddy, New York Journal, 1900

Source: *http://metmuseum.org/art/collection/search/680838*

52. The image is most closely associated with which of the following periods?
   A. The Gilded Age
   B. The Progressive Era
   C. The Square Deal
   D. Radical Reconstruction

53. The image most likely contains the word *new* because
   A. Populist policies had achieved the goal of a major industrial takeoff that empowered a newly rich class.
   B. the second industrial revolution had engendered much concentration of wealth.
   C. the Gilded Age was noted for a general prosperity unfamiliar to the vast majority it benefitted.
   D. the power of unions during this time had led to many of its leaders becoming newly rich.

Questions 54–55 refer to the excerpt below.

"[I]n a time when our values, when our place in history is so seriously questioned [...] Americans want their sons and daughters to see what is still for them and for so many other millions in the world a city offering the 'last best hope of man on earth!' [...] These visitors to that city on the Potomac do not come as white or black, red or yellow; they are not Jews or Christians; conservatives or liberals; or Democrats or Republicans. They are Americans awed by what has gone before, proud of what for them is still…a shining city on a hill. [...] Let us resolve tonight that young Americans will always see those Potomac lights; that they will always find there a city of hope in a country that is free. And let us resolve they will say of our day and our generation that we did keep faith with our God, that we did act 'worthy of ourselves;' that we did protect and pass on lovingly that shining city on a hill."

—Ronald Reagan, Election Eve Address: "A Vision for America," 1980

Source: *https://reaganlibrary.archives.gov/archives/reference/11.3.80.html*

54. Reagan's harkening back to the language of Puritan sermons was most indicative of which of the following?
    A. A need to counteract the similar rhetoric of the born-again Democratic candidate, Jimmy Carter
    B. His intention to preserve and expand upon the New Deal and Great Society
    C. The importance to Republicans of a newly energized evangelical Christian base
    D. An explicit endorsement of Puritan values

55. To which of the following longstanding beliefs did Reagan directly appeal in this part of his speech?
    A. American Exceptionalism
    B. Manifest Destiny
    C. National malaise
    D. The superiority of American Protestantism

STOP.
IF YOU FINISH BEFORE TIME IS OUT, YOU MAY CHECK YOUR WORK ON THIS SECTION ONLY.
DO NOT TURN TO ANY OTHER SECTION IN THE TEST.

Section I, Part B: Short-Answer Questions

Time: 40 Minutes • 3 Questions

> **Directions:** The following section consists of four short-answer questions—you must answer both Question 1 and Question 2. You will then choose to answer either Question 3 or Question 4. Use the answer sheet provided to respond to the questions.

1. Since the late nineteenth century, mass news media has continually grown in scope and mode. Answer all parts of the following question.
   A. Give ONE reason why any two of the following were SIMILAR in their effect on politics:
      - Mass-circulation newspapers
      - Film
      - Radio
      - Broadcast television
      - Cable television
      - Social media
   B. Give ONE reason why the two you picked in part A were DIFFERENT in their effect on politics.
   C. Give ONE reason why any two in the above list (other than the two you picked in part A) EITHER were similar OR were not similar in their effect on politics.

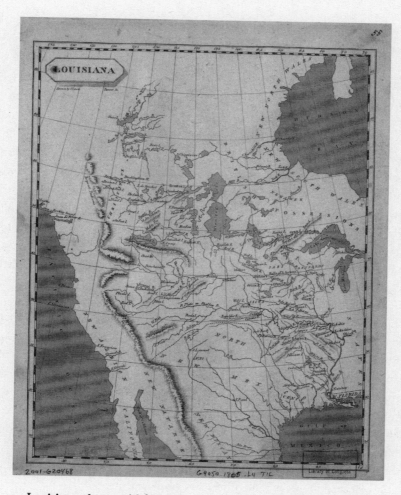

Louisiana, *Arrowsmith & Lewis New and Elegant General Atlas,* **1804.**

Source: Library of Congress, Geography and Map Division (*https://www.loc.gov/item/2001620468/*)

2. Refer to the image above in answering parts A and B.

    A. Explain ONE aspect of the significance of the territorial acquisition depicted in this map and provide ONE piece of evidence in support.

    B. Give ONE reason why any other territorial acquisition by the United States was EITHER similar to OR different from the one depicted in this map.

"[W]herein does this president, invested with his powers and prerogatives, essentially differ from the king of Great Britain[?]

The direct prerogatives of the president [...] are [as follows.] It is necessary, in order to distinguish him from the rest of the community and enable him to keep and maintain his court, that the compensation for his services [...] should be such as to enable him to appear with the splendor of a prince. He has the power of receiving ambassadors from, and a great influence on their appointments to, foreign courts [and] also to make treaties, leagues, and alliances with foreign states, assisted by the senate, which when made, become the supreme law of the land. He is a constituent part of the legislative power, for every bill which shall pass the house of representatives and senate is to be presented to him for approbation. If he approves of it, he is to sign it; if he disapproves, he is to return it with objections which in many cases will amount to a complete negative [i.e., veto].

[Thus] he will have a great share in the power of making peace, coining money, &c. and all the various objects of legislation, expressed or implied in this Constitution. For though it may be asserted that the king of Great Britain has the express power of making peace or war, yet he never thinks it prudent so to do without the advice of his parliament from whom he is to derive his support, and therefore these powers, in both president and king, are substantially the same: he is the generalissimo of the nation and of course has the command and control of the army, navy and militia. He is the general conservator of the peace of the union. He may pardon all offenses, except in cases of impeachment, and is the principal fountain of all offices and employments.

Will not the exercise of these powers therefore tend either to the establishment of a vile and arbitrary aristocracy or monarchy? The safety of the people in a republic depends on the share or proportion they have in the government. But experience ought to teach you that when a man is at the head of an elective government invested with great powers, and interested in his re-election, [...] appointments will be made by which means an imperfect aristocracy bordering on monarchy may be established."

—"Cato" (probably George Clinton), No. 4, November 8, 1787 in the *New York Journal*

Source: *https://www.law.gmu.edu/assets/files/academics/founders/CatoIV.pdf*

"[I]t appears that, except as to the concurrent authority of the President in the article of treaties, it would be difficult to determine whether that magistrate would, in the aggregate, possess more or less power than the Governor of New York. And it appears yet more unequivocally, that there is no pretense for the parallel which has been attempted between him and the king of Great Britain. But to render the contrast in this respect still more striking, it may be of use to throw the principal circumstances of dissimilitude into a closer group.

The President of the United States would be an officer elected by the people for four years; the king of Great Britain is a perpetual and hereditary prince. The one would be amenable to personal punishment and disgrace; the person of the other is sacred and inviolable. The one would have a qualified negative [i.e., veto] upon the acts of the legislative body; the other has an absolute negative. The one would have a right to command the military and naval forces of the nation; the other, in addition to this right, possesses that of declaring war, and of raising and regulating fleets and armies by his own authority. The one would have a concurrent power with a branch of the legislature in the formation of treaties; the other is the sole possessor of the power of making treaties. The one would have a like concurrent authority in appointing to offices; the other is the sole author of all appointments. The one can confer no privileges whatever; the other can make denizens of aliens, noblemen of commoners and can erect corporations with all the rights incident to corporate bodies. The one can pre-scribe no rules concerning the commerce or currency of the nation; the other is in several respects the arbiter of commerce, and in this capacity can establish markets and fairs, can regulate weights and measures, can lay embargoes for a limited time, can coin money, can authorize or prohibit the circulation of foreign coin. The one has no particle of spiritual jurisdiction; the other is the supreme head and governor of the national church!

What answer shall we give to those who would persuade us that things so unlike resemble each other? The same that ought to be given to those who tell us that a government, the whole power of which would be in the hands of the elective and periodical servants of the people, is an aristocracy, a monarchy, and a despotism."

—"Publius" (Alexander Hamilton), *Federalist* Papers, No. 69, March 14, 1788 in
the *New York Packet*

Source: *https://www.congress.gov/resources/display/content/The+Federalist+Papers#TheFederalistPapers-69*

3. Based on the excerpts above and your knowledge of American history, answer parts A, B, and C.
   A. Briefly explain the author's point of view in passage excerpt 1.
   B. Briefly explain the author's point of view in passage excerpt 2.
   C. Provide ONE piece of evidence, not mentioned in either passages and discuss how it relates to either passage.

4. Based on your knowledge of American history, answer parts A, B, and C.

   A. Give ONE example of an American musical form that originated in the South.

   B. Give ONE reason why it originated in the South.

   C. Give ONE reason how it spread out of the South to the rest of the country.

STOP.
IF YOU FINISH BEFORE TIME IS OUT, YOU MAY CHECK YOUR WORK ON THIS SECTION ONLY.
DO NOT TURN TO ANY OTHER SECTION IN THE TEST.

Section II, Part A: Document-Based Question

Time: 60 Minutes • 1 Question

> **Directions:** The following question asks you to write a cohesive essay incorporating your interpretation of Documents 1 through 7 and your knowledge of the period stated in the question. To earn a high score, you must cite key evidence from the documents and use your outside knowledge of United States history. Take 15 minutes to read all documents and 45 minutes to write your essay on the answer sheet provided.

1. Compare and contrast early twentieth-century visions of democracy in America.

Document 1

Source: *https://archive.org/details/EdwardL.BernaysPropaganda*

The conscious and intelligent manipulation of the organized habits and opinions of the masses is an important element in democratic society. Those who manipulate this unseen mechanism of society constitute an invisible government which is the true ruling power of our country. We are governed, our minds molded, our tastes formed, our ideas suggested, largely by men we have never heard of. This is a logical result of the way in which our democratic society is organized. Vast numbers of human beings must cooperate in this manner if they are to live together as a smoothly functioning society. [...] It was, of course, the astounding success of propaganda during the war that opened the eyes of the intelligent few in all departments of life to the possibilities of regimenting the public mind. The American government and numerous patriotic agencies developed a technique which, to most persons accustomed to bidding for public acceptance, was new. They not only appealed to the individual by means of every approach -- visual, graphic, and auditory -- to support the national endeavor, but they also secured the cooperation of the key men in every group -- persons whose mere word carried authority to hundreds or thousands or hundreds of thousands of followers. [...] It was only natural, after the war ended, that intelligent persons should ask themselves whether it was possible to apply a similar technique to the problems of peace. [...] Clearly, it is the intelligent minorities which need to make use of propaganda continuously and systematically. In the active proselytizing minorities in whom selfish interests and public interests coincide lie the progress and development of America.

—Edward Bernays, *Propaganda*, 1928

Document 2

Source: *https://archive.org/details/democracyandsoc02addagoog*

As democracy modifies our conception of life, it constantly raises the value and function of each member of the community, however humble he may be. We have come to believe that the most "brutish man" has a value in our common life, a function to perform which can be fulfilled by no one else. We are gradually requiring of the education that he shall free the powers of each man and connect him with the rest of life. We ask this not merely because it is the man's right to be thus connected, but because we have become convinced that the social order cannot afford to get along without his special contribution. Just as we have come to resent all hindrances which keep us from untrammeled comradeship with our fellows, and as we throw down unnatural divisions, not in the spirit of the eighteenth-century reformers, but in the spirit of those to whom social equality has become a necessity for further social development, so we are impatient to use the dynamic power residing in the mass of men, and demand that the educator free that power. We believe that man's moral idealism is the constructive force of progress, as it has always been; but because every human being is a creative agent and a possible generator of fine enthusiasm, we are sceptical of the moral idealism of the few and demand the education of the many, that there may be greater freedom, strength, and subtilty of intercourse and hence an increase of dynamic power. We are not content to include all men in our hopes, but have become conscious that all men are hoping and are part of the same movement of which we are a part.

—Jane Addams, *Democracy and Social Ethics*, 1915

Document 3

Source: *https://archive.org/details/democracyandedu00dewegoog*

The devotion of democracy to education is a familiar fact. The superficial explanation is that a government resting upon popular suffrage cannot be successful unless those who elect and who obey their governors are educated. Since a democratic society repudiates the principle of external authority, it must find a substitute in voluntary disposition and interest; these can be created only by education. But there is a deeper explanation. A democracy is more than a form of government; it is primarily a mode of associated living, of conjoint communicated experience. The extension in space of the number of individuals who participate in an interest so that each has to refer his own action to that of others, and to consider the action of others to give point and direction to his own, is equivalent to the breaking down of those barriers of class, race, and national territory which kept men from perceiving the full import of their activity. [...] Obviously a society to which stratification into separate classes would be fatal, must see to it that intellectual opportunities are accessible to all on equable and easy terms. A society marked off into classes need be specially attentive only to the education of its ruling elements. A society which is mobile, which is full of channels for the distribution of a change occurring anywhere, must see to it that its members are educated to personal initiative and adaptability. Otherwise, they will be overwhelmed by the changes in which they are caught and whose significance or connections they do not perceive. The result will be a confusion in which a few will appropriate to themselves the results of the blind and externally directed activities of others.

—John Dewey, *Democracy and Education*, 1916

Document 4

Source: *https://archive.org/details/publicopinion00lipp*

That the manufacture of consent is capable of great refinements no one, I think, denies. The process by which public opinions arise is certainly no less intricate than it has appeared in these pages, and the opportunities for manipulation open to anyone who understands the process are plain enough.

The creation of consent is not a new art. It is a very old one which was supposed to have died out with the appearance of democracy. But it has not died out. It has, in fact, improved enormously in technique, because it is now based on analysis rather than on rule of thumb. And so, as a result of psychological research, coupled with the modern means of communication, the practice of democracy has turned a corner. A revolution is taking place, infinitely more significant than any shifting of economic power.

Within the life of the generation now in control of affairs, persuasion has become a self-conscious art and a regular organ of popular government. None of us begins to understand the consequences, but it is not daring prophecy to say that the knowledge of how to create consent will alter every political calculation and modify every political premise. Under the impact of propaganda, not necessarily in the sinister meaning of the word alone, the old constants of our thinking have become variables. It is no longer possible, for example, to believe in the original dogma of democracy; that the knowledge needed for the management of human affairs comes up spontaneously from the human heart. Where we act on that theory we expose ourselves to self-deception, and to forms of persuasion that we cannot verify. It has been demonstrated that we cannot rely upon intuition, conscience, or the accidents of casual opinion if we are to deal with the world beyond our reach.

—Walter Lippmann, *Public Opinion*, 1922

Document 5

Source: *https://archive.org/details/howweadvertiseda00cree*

It was in this recognition of Public Opinion as a major force that the Great War differed most essentially from all previous conflicts. [...] The Committee on Public Information was called into existence to make this fight for the "verdict of mankind," the voice created to plead the justice of America's cause before the jury of Public Opinion. [...] We did not call it propaganda, for that word, in German hands, had come to be associated with deceit and corruption. [...] There was no part of the great war machinery that we did not touch, no medium of appeal that we did not employ. The printed word, the spoken word, the motion picture, the telegraph, the cable, the wireless [i.e., radio], the poster, the sign-board -- all these were used in our campaign to make our own people and all other peoples understand the causes that compelled America to take arms. All that was fine and ardent in the civilian population came at our call until more than one hundred and fifty thousand men and women were devoting highly specialized abilities to the work of the Committee, as faithful and devoted in their service as though they wore the khaki.

While America's summons was answered without question by the citizenship as a whole, it is to be remembered that during the three and a half years of our neutrality the land had been torn by a thousand divisive prejudices, stunned by the voices of anger and confusion, and muddled by the pull and haul of opposed interests. These were conditions that could not be permitted to endure. What we had to have was no mere surface unity, but a passionate belief in the justice of America's cause that should weld the people of the United States into one white-hot mass instinct with fraternity, devotion, courage, and deathless determination. The *war-will*, the will-to-win, of a democracy depends upon the degree to which each one of all the people of that democracy can concentrate and consecrate body and soul and spirit in the supreme effort of service and sacrifice. What had to be driven home was that all business was the nation's business, and every task a common task for a single purpose.

—George Creel, *How We Advertised America*, 1920

Document 6

Source: *http://www.loc.gov/pictures/item/2010652057/*

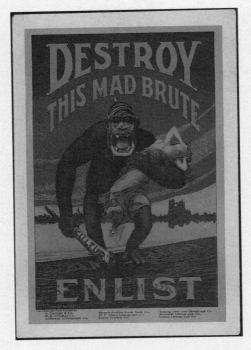

"Destroy this mad brute: Enlist," Harry Hopps, 1918.

Document 7

Source: *https://www.loc.gov/item/2002722580/*

"The combination that will win the war," Adolph Treidler, Committee on Public Information:
Division of Pictorial Publicity, 1917

**WHEN YOU HAVE COMPLETED ANSWERING YOUR
DOCUMENT-BASED QUESTION, YOU MAY CONTINUE AND
BEGIN WORKING ON PART B, THE LONG ESSAY.**

Section II, Part B: Long Essay Question

Time: 40 Minutes • 1 Question

> **Directions:** Answer ONE question from this group. State a thesis, cite relevant evidence, and use logical, clear arguments to support your generalizations.

2. Assess the degree to which the Civil War fostered social, political, and economic change as well as continuity in the United States during the period of 1865–1920.

3. Assess the degree to which the New Deal fostered change as well as continuity in the relationship between government and the economy.

4. Account for the economic differences among the American colonies and how the requisite labor in each of the following regions was secured from initial colonization through the Revolution:
   - New England
   - The Middle Colonies
   - The Chesapeake Colonies
   - The South

STOP.
IF YOU FINISH BEFORE TIME IS OUT, YOU MAY CHECK YOUR WORK ON THIS SECTION ONLY.
DO NOT TURN TO ANY OTHER SECTION IN THE TEST.

ANSWER KEY AND EXPLANATIONS

Section I, Part A: Multiple-Choice

1. C	12. A	23. D	34. D	45. B
2. C	13. D	24. C	35. D	46. D
3. A	14. C	25. A	36. B	47. A
4. D	15. A	26. C	37. C	48. B
5. C	16. D	27. A	38. A	49. A
6. A	17. A	28. D	39. D	50. C
7. B	18. D	29. C	40. B	51. D
8. B	19. D	30. C	41. C	52. A
9. C	20. A	31. D	42. B	53. B
10. D	21. A	32. C	43. C	54. C
11. A	22. C	33. A	44. A	55. A

1. **The correct answer is C.** The Second Great Awakening (choice D) began around 1800; the first took place in the 1740s. The Social Gospel was a religious reform movement that arose during the Gilded Age in the late nineteenth century, so choice A is incorrect. Choice B is incorrect because the Gospel of Wealth, Andrew Carnegie's argument that his class should return its wealth to the general public, also arose in the late nineteenth century.

2. **The correct answer is C.** The First Great Awakening fostered a bottom-up, personal, individual relationship between worshipper and God; an emphasis on being born again; and a thoroughly evangelical mission. This has set the tone for much, if not most, of American Protestantism ever since. Whitefield himself traveled all over the colonies, as well as throughout much of Britain.

3. **The correct answer is A.** Though trans-Atlantic travel was difficult, it was done with increasing frequency in the eighteenth century. Thus, choice D is incorrect. Recall that triangular trade of all kinds was the basis of the mercantilist colonial system; with trade comes ideas. It's a two-way exchange, however; therefore, choice B is incorrect. Furthermore, exchanges were hardly limited to religion; Thomas Paine himself may be seen as an example of political exchange.

4. **The correct answer is D.** This may seem odd, since Woodstock is not thought to have been a religious event, but consider it functionally, as a sociologist would: Woodstock was a free, outdoor, mass event that symbolized a mostly spontaneous, often ecstatic, certainly enthusiastic uprising against perceived Establishment domination. Some observers at the time of the concert and many since have noted how similar it was to the various religious revivals that have marked American history. The Gettysburg ceremony was funereal and consecratory, as well as official—a far cry from calls for rebirth and renewal, so choice A is incorrect. The Constitutional Convention (choice C), while lively and concerned with governmental renewal, was hardly a grassroots revolt; furthermore, it was fully

secular, even to a sociologist. Finally, Shays' Rebellion (choice B) though bottom-up and surely enthusiastic, was violent and political. It was hardly concerned with any kind of spiritual renewal.

5. **The correct answer is C.** According to the mercantilist system, finished goods could be manufactured only by the British. The mercantilist system insisted all imported goods to the colonies pass through British-controlled ports, the transferring of goods had to also be controlled by British ships, and the colonists could send enumerated goods, such as tobacco, only to England.

6. **The correct answer is A.** While most colonists viewed the mercantilist system negatively, New England shipbuilding indeed flourished. The answer cannot be choice B because the tobacco industry was growing. The answer cannot be choices C or D because not only did colonists NOT receive a price break in manufactured goods, but they could not produce their own finished goods either.

7. **The correct answer is B.** The British monarchy used protection to justify taxation against the colonists. They continued to tax colonists under the guise of military protection against the French and the Native Americans. The answer cannot be choice A because the British didn't use mercantilism as an excuse for taxation. The answer cannot be choice C because even though the colonists' British citizenship was a justification, it is clearly not the best answer. The answer cannot be choice D because the monarchy did not use monies collected from taxing the colonists to pay for slaves.

8. **The correct answer is B.** Natural law is a typical feature of Enlightenment thought, and the author's use of the concept to argue against the second-class legal status of women directly appeals to that notion. None of the other choices work, but special note should be made of how unsecular this passage is; like virtually all Enlightenment thinkers, natural law was anchored ultimately in God's authority, He who instilled a moral sense in people.

9. **The correct answer is C.** "The pursuit of happiness" was Jefferson's substitution for "property" in the life-liberty-and part of the Declaration of Independence, not in the other documents.

10. **The correct answer is D.** The women of Seneca Falls were advocating for property and divorce rights, suffrage, and equality in education. While childcare was a concern of these women, there was no discussion of affordable childcare laws.

11. **The correct answer is A.** Political sovereignty can reside in various institutions or individuals—parliament or king, church hierarchy or town meeting—but it must reside *somewhere*. In American history, or at least rhetoric, it has been found to reside in the people and, for a long time (though not in the Constitution itself), in He who created people, that is, natural law. Sovereignty means justification of power and authority; in this document, the authors appeal to God's sovereignty, as exemplified by the common human desire for the pursuit of happiness assumed to have been placed there by the Creator. Choice B is incorrect because legal *precedent*, despite the mention of Blackstone, is not at issue, but rather the justification of the current legal framework itself. However, the issue is legal in the larger sense, so both choices C and D are incorrect as far as the authors of the passage are concerned in this excerpt.

12. **The correct answer is A.** The Declaration mentions the more-or-less deist anchoring of natural rights in a Creator, but the Constitution doesn't mention God at all. The rest of the choices hold.

13. **The correct answer is D.** John Locke was the patron intellectual of the founders, maybe even more so than Montesquieu. Machiavelli did write a much longer and less famous work on republics, but he was nowhere near as central as Locke, so choice C is incorrect. Neither Hobbes (choice A) nor Rousseau (choice B) was as central as Locke.

14. **The correct answer is C.** Interestingly, there's nothing about property in either passage; the closest is "general welfare." Safety, justice, and especially liberty are all quite prominent.

15. **The correct answer is A.** Eisenhower sent federal troops into Arkansas, just as Grant had sent troops eighty years before, in order to assert federal supremacy and protect African-American civil rights. He was not pulling troops out, so choice B is incorrect. He wasn't deploying troops abroad, so choice C is incorrect. Finally, Eisenhower's action was a federal move against state-controlled National Guardsmen, so choice D is incorrect.

16. **The correct answer is D.** *Brown* overturned *Plessy v. Ferguson*, finding separate but equal inherently unequal. None of the other cases overturned *Plessy*. *Dred Scott* was in 1857 and denied African-Americans personhood, whereas *Marbury* established judicial review in the early eighteenth century. *Bakke* limited affirmative action at universities and came much later.

17. **The correct answer is A.** The Southern Manifesto, signed by many southern politicians, cited the Supreme Court's presumed violation of the Tenth Amendment, which they believed protected their states' rights to segregation. The other choices are not possible.

18. **The correct answer is D.** After Eisenhower ordered the 101st Airborne Division to escort the Little Rock Nine to school and federalized the Arkansas National Guard, the African American students continued to be protected for the entire school year. Eventually, then-Governor Orval Faubus gave in to Eisenhower's demand, and some Americans slowly started to support the beginnings of the Civil Rights Movement as they saw images of hatred on television. However, Eisenhower's actions did not seem to force other segregated schools to integrate more expeditiously.

19. **The correct answer is D.** Madison, Jefferson, and most other founders endorsed the separation of church and state, for the good of both. European history had seen much bloodshed from seemingly endless religious wars, and the founders did not want that imported to America. The other choices are not concerned primarily with the separation of church and state.

20. **The correct answer is A.** Founded over a century ago by civil libertarians, the ACLU has played a central role in judicial development and protection of constitutional liberties. The other groups were religiously intolerant, to greater or lesser degrees.

21. **The correct answer is A.** England, like many European countries since the Reformation, had been riven by politicized, sometimes militarized, religious conflict. The founders wanted to avoid that. Choices C and D are incorrect because they post-date Madison's document. The slave trade (choice B) doesn't enter into this question directly.

22. **The correct answer is C.** Even before the 1920s, biological evolution and creationism of one form or another have served as spearheads in the ongoing culture war. The legal issues turn on the separation of church and state. None of the other issues are as directly concerned with the separation of church and state.

23. **The correct answer is D.** Neoliberalism is a classically liberal policy model, emphasizing a kind of *laissez-faire* that amounts to the "discipline" of labor to keep down wages, control inflation, and maintain profit by a global race to the bottom. Among other aspects, it includes deregulation of all kinds, but especially of the financial sector. Containment (Choice C) is a Truman-initiated policy of holding back communism, whereas the New Deal (choice A) is the precise opposite of Friedman's passage. The American System (choice B) was a nineteenth-century, Hamiltonian, protectionist system, It was not well-aligned with later neoliberalism, which was also free-trade.

24. **The correct answer is C.** A minority view in 1962, at least in terms of effect on policy, Friedman's ideas would begin to be ushered into power during Jimmy Carter's presidency and fully implemented during the Reagan administration and those that followed to varying extents. Neoliberalism is not wholly new; it's a market-friendly, mostly *laissez-faire*, free-trade ideology.

25. **The correct answer is A.** The image shows two "Okies" who went west in hope of survival after the Dust Bowl had destroyed so much. The Fair Deal was Truman's program, not FDR's New Deal, so choice B is incorrect. World War II actually ended the Depression in the United States, so choice C is incorrect. The Populists never actually triumphed, though the Democrats did absorb many of their ideas (progressives in general, actually), so choice D is incorrect.

26. **The correct answer is C.** The New Deal was a series of federal programs aimed to intervene in the economic downturn, the very opposite of *laissez faire* (choice A). It was Keynesian, but not military Keynesianism (choice D), by which demand is supported via a large military buildup. Isolationism

(choice B) is a foreign-policy position much more than an economic one.

27. **The correct answer is A.** War material production ended unemployment; demand returned; business boomed. This setup was to some extent continued during the Cold War (choice C), but the cycle itself didn't end the Depression. The New Deal (choice B) failed to end the Depression. Whether this was because of a lack of follow-through or because of the programs themselves has been debated since the 1930s. The Great Migration (choice D) was the movement of African Americans north, usually out of rural Southern areas and into industrialized cities.

28. **The correct answer is D.** Among other movements—especially after the widespread adoption of air conditioning—the Okies helped the Sun Belt's population boom, though it would not take off until the following generation.

29. **The correct answer is C.** Roosevelt's love of nature helped conservation and preservation movements begin to shape policy. Higher wages, work-hour and workday limitations, and less expensive rail travel all combined with a new "strenuousness" of somewhat pietist roots to form a market value for relatively unspoiled land.

30. **The correct answer is C.** After camping in Yosemite with John Muir, Roosevelt made land conservation and wildlife protection a priority. He set aside federal lands to protect them from private interests, established the U.S. Forestry Service, and appointed Gifford Pinchot to head that service. Additionally, he established many wildlife preserves and bird sanctuaries. He did not make Yosemite the National Park, as there is no one national park.

31. **The correct answer is D.** Roosevelt's argument mirrors what campers are taught

as children from their first overnight trip: Leave a campsite as you found it for the next person. Put in effort of your own so others will benefit. Or, to extend that outward, do the work now to aid the generations of the future. The form of the argument is the human-existential one: What to forgo now for future benefit?

32. **The correct answer is C.** Washington's Farewell Address warned about the friction between "factions," as parties were then called. Four years later, Jefferson, in the first American transfer of power between parties, and after the battle over the Alien and Sedition Acts, echoed Washington in trying to remind everyone of their former alliance against Britain and shared goals. Eisenhower's speech referred famously to the military-industrial complex; Reagan's speech asked Gorbachev to "tear down this [Berlin] Wall"; and the Monroe Doctrine warned off European interference in the Western Hemisphere.

33. **The correct answer is A.** The First Republicans aligned with the revolution, at least at first, whereas the Federalists tended toward Britain. Washington saw how foreign entanglements like these exacerbated faction and threatened to make the United States a field for a proxy war between two European powers. The Haitian Revolution was indeed influential but unrelated to faction: all were united in horror. The Constitution had been ratified prior to the decade before this address and the Purchase was to follow it.

34. **The correct answer is D.** Oddly enough, the founders ignored the likelihood that parties would form according to shared interests that would inevitably diverge among the growing population.

35. **The correct answer is D.** The Columbian Exchange featured organisms of all kinds, from microbes and plants to people and other mammals. The gradual global shift of trade routes (choice B) is not as directly related to the introduction of Old World pandemics to the New World, which is specifically a feature of the Columbian Exchange. Neither the Atlantic slave trade nor the rise of scientific medicine (choices A and D) relate to the changing pattern of epidemics.

36. **The correct answer is B.** The analogy is that population mixing, both of disease organisms and of people, was instrumental in spreading general resistance throughout the human species. Neither movement of population directly caused the other; moreover, the point is to show how such movements form the basis for the spread of disease and resistance.

37. **The correct answer is C.** Why such a one-way transfer of epidemic disease? It relates apparently to the greater number of domesticatable large mammals in Afro-Eurasia as opposed to really only one, the llama/alpaca, in the Americas. Close contact between humans and domesticated animals allowed for various diseases to jump to the human population and cause damage, but also raise resistance. Americans avoided all of this until 1500—the effect of the sudden introduction of such organisms was devastating.

38. **The correct answer is A.** American colonists desired new land for farming and general settling for their ever-booming population, as well as for economic and even political reasons: the long-lasting "safety valve" in American history was that of the frontier. Fear of Indians (choice B) was subsidiary to the contact, sometimes unpleasant, that occurred as the Indians were pushed ever-westward. Later, indeed, Lewis and Clark would be sent to explore, partly for scientific reasons (choice C), but

this was not a widespread goal; nor was the idea of independence (choice D) at the time.

39. **The correct answer is D.** Ironically, the British secured their colonists' enthusiastic aid because the colonists desired westward expansion and viewed France as in the way. After the war, the British began limiting American moves west, one of the causes of the American Revolution. Spain was expelled much later; Napoleon's wars lay forty years in the future; and the Articles, even the Revolution, were yet to occur.

40. **The correct answer is B.** Some American roads still trace old Indian pathways, but back then, one can be very confident that Washington would have followed the available trails. This was long before canals or even much in the way of roads existed.

41. **The correct answer is C.** The French lacked the same population pressures at home that supported English emigration, so they were mostly interested in trade, not settler-colonialism beyond that which supported trade, mostly in fur. Thus, choices B and D are incorrect. France and Britain were rivals at this point, so choice A is incorrect.

42. **The correct answer is B.** Abolitionists would have rejected Calhoun's argument out of hand, whereas many Democrats and some Whigs would not. Most feminists would have rejected the argument, too, but not with the unanimity of the abolitionists.

43. **The correct answer is C.** Calhoun, like all pro-slavery figures, had to argue or at least heavily imply that without slavery, Africans would be in a worse situation. The "peculiar institution" was under moral attack; one obvious response was to throw that back in the abolitionists' faces: Not only was abolition an attack on Southern whites, it was destined to worsen the lot of blacks, which Calhoun maintains was hardly as bad as it was made out to be.

44. **The correct answer is A.** A lot of territory of unclear fate—slave or free—entered the delicate compromise all at once. Tensions rose precipitously and didn't really fall until the Civil War. The constitutional ban on the slave trade had been enacted in 1808, whereas the Missouri Compromise was in 1820. Immigration was to boom, but this put less pressure on the issue of slavery and sectional tension per se.

45. **The correct answer is B.** It was primarily the large plantation owners who used and thus benefited from slaves. Poor whites couldn't afford slaves; Indian tribes didn't use them; and Northern blacks were unlikely to do so.

46. **The correct answer is D.** This Navigation Act and the post-restoration acts that replaced it formed the legal basis for the mercantilist system by which colonial development was thwarted so as to enrich the home country. They are anti-free trade, so choice A is incorrect; the French and Indian war was a century later, so choice B is incorrect; and the Napoleonic wars were still later, around the turn of the nineteenth century.

47. **The correct answer is A.** Mercantilism's goal was a net inflow of gold and silver into the mother country, whether directly via mining or indirectly via a sort of captive, raw-material-producing but manufactured-goods-purchasing set of colonies. It is the opposite of free-trade (choice B) and of *laissez faire* (choice C), both of which are post-Smithian economic notions. *Engrossment* (choice D) is a term for cornering a market in monopolistic fashion.

48. **The correct answer is B.** Hamilton's system, later expanded and adopted by the Whigs, was what we'd now call "the incubation of infant industry," using protectionist measures to overcome impossibly high barriers to entry into a market dominated

by mature competitors. Like mercantilism, it is a form of protection or limitation on free, competitive trade.

49. **The correct answer is A.** Grant was a particularly racist eugenicist of his day; few today would hold such extremist views, though milder forms persist. Thus, choice B is incorrect. Few, if any, historians would endorse such claims, and luckily these views have not always been ubiquitous.

50. **The correct answer is C.** The Immigration Act of 1924 was heavily influenced by the racist, eugenic theories then current. Isolation could be racist but was not innately so; its point was more nationalistic than racist. The creation of the United Nations is unrelated, and Progressives, while split on race in many ways, preceded the rise of eugenics, if not of Social Darwinism.

51. **The correct answer is D.** Eugenics was widely popular across the political spectrum during the first forty years of the twentieth century, both in America and around the world.

52. **The correct answer is A.** The Gilded Age made many fortunes, destroyed a few more, and transferred much wealth to the top of the income scale. During this time, Newport, Rhode Island, became a summer home for New York wealth; many mansions, now museums, may be visited to this day.

53. **The correct answer is B.** The second industrial revolution fueled the *nouveau riches* of the Gilded Age, as new fortunes were made. Moreover, old fortunes increased— the multi-millionaires were "new" in that sense as well. Note the commodification of wealth itself that was arising with new forms of media, which brought such evidence of social inequality ever more directly to citizens across a variety of media.

54. **The correct answer is C.** Though Carter was indeed born again, the point of Reagan's much more Christianized rhetoric was to strengthen support among evangelicals. It was not an explicit endorsement of Puritan (choice D); rather, it was more an affirmation of God-ordained American Exceptionalism, in that the renewal and rebirth of America paralleled the evangelical born-again experience to that of the nation itself. Reagan took aim at the New Deal and Great Society, so choice B is incorrect.

55. **The correct answer is A.** Neither particularly American, and thus not all that exceptional among most nation-states, the idea that America is, theologically or "just" historically, an example to all other nations runs very strong in the national psyche and memory. Reagan was arguing against "malaise," referring to Carter's too-honest recent speech, so choice C is incorrect. Manifest destiny is related to, but not the entirely the same as, American Exceptionalism: it has a more limited, territorial connotation. Also, Reagan specifically embraces all faiths; Protestantism may form the rhetorical reservoir, but that is all.

Section I, Part B: Short Answers

1. For part A, some possibilities are grouping by medium. For example, one could say that motion-pictures, whatever the mode (film, television in either form, social media), create a sense of immediacy, even if recorded and not live. As to effect, the debate rages, but one can either argue for the propagandistic effects inherent in motion-pictures—selection of image, editing, juxtaposition of images—or for the potential for increasing empathy. Comparisons to photographs from mass-circulation newspapers may be made.

   For part B, differences also abound. For example, network television was mostly one-way: other than the indirect feedback of advertising success, programs were delivered to an audience. The rise of social media allows for Google-driven suggestions, closed-off Facebook communities, and the rest of the Balkanization to which the internet is argued to have given rise. One could also argue that mass-circulation papers at least engage reading, allowing for more space for argument and evidence and the like, whereas social media outlets like Twitter force discussion into tiny spaces.

   Part C just asks for another pairing of two media, either in how they have had a similar effect or different effects. Possibilities are many; for this kind of item, make sure to create t-charts to organize your work and to make sure you answer all parts of the question with whichever items you select.

2. For part A, recognize that the map shows Louisiana soon after the Purchase. Among the possible significances are increase in sectional tension as the territory's destiny as slave or free had to be worked out; capture of the Missouri-Mississippi river system, soon to be canal-augmented, but as it was then a major economic transportation network that led to now-acquired New Orleans, a critical port; and one of the first stages in westward expansion, with all the effects that was to have on various populations, from American Indian to Mexican.

   For part B, many other territorial acquisitions could be used for comparison, from the Mexican Cession and Texas to Oregon and overseas colonies like Hawaii or the Philippines. One is free to find the imperialism akin, possibly via the mention of the "salt-water fallacy" that limits imperialism to that which occurs via a navy, or different, perhaps insofar as diplomatic purchase of territory differs from its violent conquest both in the event and its downstream effect.

3. For part A, "Cato" gives a range of to him monarchical powers ill-advised to invest in the chief executive, from war powers to vetoing of legislation, that Cato argues would inevitably create intrigue, a court system, and the death of liberties.

   For part B, "Publius" emphasizes the checks and balances on the chief executive, including the sharing of war and treaty powers, and how different he maintains they are from those of the British monarchy.

   For part C, one could discuss the Alien, Sedition, and Naturalization Acts and the Virginia and Kentucky resolutions against them or indeed the Louisiana Purchase itself or the battle between Jefferson and Marshall around *Marbury v. Madison*.

4. Whether jazz, blues, rock, rockabilly, or country, most American music genres emanated from the South. The reasons tend to revolve around the particular ethnic groups—whether Scottish, African, or French or West Indian—that lived amongst each other, even under slavery and Jim Crow, cross-fertilizing each other and budding off into new forms. These forms were often

heavily black-influenced and traveled with blacks during the Great Migration into northern cities. However, from the end of the nineteenth century on, the spread of new modes of communication—from recording techniques to radio and film and even sheet music—spread new music around the country. By the time television came around, let alone social media and the internet, new genres were almost instantaneously available to a large portion of the species.

answers practice test 2

Section II, Part A: Document-Based Question

1. First, make sure your response refers to all, or all but one, of the documents. This item tests your ability to synthesize information from several documents of varying types. You have plenty to compare and contrast among the documents.

   Second, your thesis should note the two or three most important arguments over the vision of democracy presented in these documents and during this time period, the Progressive Era. Good candidates are: what is more likely to provide social stability, top-down or bottom-up control over policy; the role and nature of education in democracy; what propaganda is taken to be and what effects it's understood to have on democracy, however defined; the extent to which democracy is limited to the strictly political realm or not; and the implied role of business or corporations, as well as of government, and especially of the First-World-War effort in what's called "the manufacture of consent." Much of the debate, which rages to this day, turns on precisely what is meant by "democracy," itself a very American question. You'll want eventually to extend the analysis either to other time periods or to other cultures and societies at the time.

   Third, you'll want to go in depth in your analysis of at least four of the documents, addressing one of the following for each of the four in-depth analyses: the historical context, the intended audience, the author's purpose, and the author's point of view. The minimum, mind you, is to discuss one of those four aspects for each of the four: feel free to expand beyond that as your thesis requires, but remember that you'll want to draw connections between the documents, not just analyze each in relative isolation. For example, one could note a chronological trend as PR techniques arise in the Creel Commission and then branch out into both general politics and the larger society—economics, business practices, and so on—by concentrating on Creel, Lippmann, and Bernays, bringing in Dewey and/or Addams for contrast. Certainly one image, if not both, should be used to support any of the points, pro or con, that arise in the documents as well as your knowledge of these practices and events.

   Make sure to show how the different kinds of documents—whether a propaganda poster aimed at the masses or elite discussions aimed at other elites—vary in point of view, intended audience, authorial purpose, and so on. You will want (and have) to bring in outside knowledge to contextualize the documents. One fruitful avenue would be to trace how these techniques spread from political to economic and cultural spheres; another would be to use these documents to discuss different varieties of Progressivism, from the more top-down, paternalistic to the more bottom-up democratic.

As noted earlier, your response should be extended to another time, another place, or another mode of historical writing and argumentation. If, for example, you concentrated on a cultural analysis of the two images in terms of class, race, or gender as a way to enter into the discussion in the texts, then make sure to address, say, the foreign-policy or economic aspects of these practices. Or you could compare and contrast with another society's propaganda and justifications, either during this period or in the past. You always want to extend the argument either in time or space or both as part of your conclusion.

Section II, Part B: Long Essay Question

Note: Whichever essay you picked, consider not reading the guideline response to the other two—save them for further practice!

The first two essays require you to determine whether or not the noted event was indeed a turning point in history. The third option asks for an economic analysis of the labor that supported the main colonial divisions in America in the seventeenth and eighteenth centuries. As you would expect, one can either agree or disagree and do just fine: the point is not to choose the "right" answer but to create a reasonable thesis and back it up. Specific feedback for each essay below will deal with both cases but in general the more specific and relevant your support for your thesis and any subsidiary points, the better you'll do. Thesis statements may be two sentences, if you prefer, but make sure they address all parts of the question. After you've developed your argument, make sure to extend it to another time period, another culture or society, or to another mode of historical writing and argumentation.

2. One would think the Civil War was unquestionably the biggest turning point in American history, and it was, so that position won't be as much exemplified here. Of course, the war helped launch the second industrial revolution, transformed the original republic into a far more centralized (soon to be industrialized) nineteenth-century nation-state, and settled at least the question of slavery that had dogged the original republic.

    The challenge is to show what actually stayed the same. Much did, especially when one considers the collapse of Reconstruction and the relative lack of change for African Americans between slavery and sharecropping and Jim Crow. But American westward expansion kept going; the pushback of Native Americans actually increased in velocity, if not in intent; the actual constitutional framework of the nation did not change, though parts of it did, mostly in expanding personhood and thus rights to African Americans; and the economic system itself, insofar as it was capitalist, could be argued to have remained the same, essentially, though without the semi-feudal inheritance of chattel slavery. Likewise, what could be said to have changed for American women?

    Note how crucial framing is to the assessment of whether any particular feature is to be considered a change or not. That is part of the point: There are no right answers in the mathematical sense to these kinds of questions. They are designed to see how well one can reason out a properly supported answer, regardless of what position is taken. Thus, for example, one can note the end of slavery as a major economic change if one's focus is such that the change within a somewhat capitalist system is the key or as a continuity if the focus is much wider, taking into account whether the society was or was not broadly capitalist.

3. As with the previous essay question, the New Deal is conventionally and rightly seen as a break with the past. For the first time, it is argued, the government took an active role in guiding the economy, forever changing the compact between government and the governed. The New Deal, still partly in operation in 2017, never in a sense went away, despite major changes since then. The entire panoply of New Deal programs is at one's command to show differences both from the immediately preceding administration and from others further in the past.

    But is that unequivocally the case? Perhaps the issue is on whose behalf the government had intervened, not on intervention per se? One could argue that government incentives for corporate or private interest—from railroad construction to tariff systems and even trust-busting and the national park system's limitation on development— had already formed a far-from-*laissez-faire* economic system, PR aside. And yet from Teddy Roosevelt on, presidents have interfered on behalf of labor, so perhaps the New Deal is more a matter of scale-up, not of originality. You will want to compare or at least extend your thesis to other moments in American history or to other nations or societies.

The framing issue, always critical, will come down to matters of degree more than matters of kind, a typical issue in discussions of historical change. To what extent are the aspects of the New Deal differences in degree or differences in kind? Does anything about the specific mode of how the programs operated set them off from previous governmental interventions? Moreover, can the longevity of the New Deal's legacy be limited to itself or is it wrapped up in the effect of World War II? These and other questions illustrate how answerable this and other essay questions are intended to be: here you will demonstrate your historical-reasoning ability, your ability to create and support a plausible interpretation of the facts. As with the previous essay and these turning-point essays recently favored by the test-makers, use of a t-chart is often a big help.

4. This is a question in large part on the origin of sectionalism in the later United States. Three forms of labor predominate: African slave labor; indentured servitude of usually white Europeans; and what would later be called "free labor" of subject/citizens. During most of this period, agriculture is by far the primary economic mode, so one way to organize the essay is to trace the main crops and geographical features of each of the four regions, showing how the climate and crops interacted with cultural practices in each region to form the bulk of labor along slave, indentured, or free lines over the decades covered. For example, rice cultivation in the South was heavily labor-intensive and dangerous due to the subtropical diseases endemic there. That combined with severe racism led to a heavy reliance on imported African slave labor. It would also help to mention the ecological costs of agriculture along the eastern seaboard, and how the resulting "land hunger" as soil was exhausted, put pressure on westward expansion, as well as the bifurcation between a few rich plantation owners and the mass of small family farmers.

And while agriculture was dominant, it was hardly the only economic mode: in fact, without New England's more advanced mercantile and shipping industries, the Atlantic slave trade would not have gotten off the ground. Make sure also to trace any changes in labor supply, such as the move from indentured white servitude to African slave labor. The Atlantic slave trade was a highly capital-intensive effort—from ship-building, to insuring hazardous journeys back and forth, to buying slaves in West Africa, and so on.

Account as much as you can for how such a system became entrenched, concentrating on the biology or natural history as it were of the main crops per region as well as that region's climate and inherited culture. For example, New England stood out for many reasons. First, much of its population came over in families, as Puritans were religious refugees. Unlike the South, there were relatively few young, single, indentured men. Second, agriculture surely existed but in the rocky soil and relatively short growing season, was to be abandoned (probably with joy) given any somewhat reasonable substitute, such as trade or shipbuilding.

Conclusions can and should of course vary, but at the end of this period the invention of the cotton gin, itself a product of a burgeoning industrial revolution, gave rise to a portentous coda, the rise of King Cotton. Finally, to expand your thesis, feel free to move from geographical and economic history out into that of culture and politics as there was, as usual, a delayed cultural reaction to already disappearing economic structures, such as racism itself growing out of African slave labor.

Self-Scoring Sheet for Practice Test 2

Directions:

- For the 55 multiple-choice items, tally up the items you answered either incorrectly or omitted—or just guessed on in some fashion—according to the chronological period. This will help you determine what you need to review. (Some question numbers are repeated, as the subject matter crossed chronological periods.)

- For each of the short-answer items (Q1 through Q4), the content area(s) have been noted in the chart to aid with your review.

- For the DBQ and Essays, an asterisk has been placed in the chronological period most at issue, but keep in mind that the essays usually ask about turning points in history, so discussion can range widely from those turning points.

Period	Multiple-Choice Items	Short Answers	DBQ	Essay 1	Essay 2	Essay 3
1 (1491-1607)	35, 36, 37, 40, 41, 55					
2 (1607-1754)	1–4, 8, 20, 21, 40, 41, 46–49, 54, 55					
3 (1754-1800)	4, 9, 12–14, 19, 20, 21, 22, 32, 33, 34, 38, 39, 40, 41, 48, 49, 54, 55	Q3				*
4 (1800-1848)	5-8, 9, 10, 11, 16, 20, 32, 33, 42–45, 49, 54, 55	Q2				
5 (1844-1877)	4, 15, 18, 20, 44, 49, 54, 55	Q2		*		
6 (1865-1898)	18, 20, 49, 52–55	Q2, Q4				
7 (1890-1945)	18, 20, 22, 25–27, 28, 29, 30, 31, 49, 50–55	Q1, Q4	*		*	
8 (1945-1980)	4, 15, 16, 17, 18, 20, 22, 23, 24, 28, 49, 54, 55	Q1, Q4				
9 (1980- present)	15, 18, 20, 22, 31, 49, 54, 55	Q1				

Chapter 16

Practice Test 3

ANSWER SHEET PRACTICE TEST 3

Section I, Part A: Multiple-Choice Questions

1. Ⓐ Ⓑ Ⓒ Ⓓ   15. Ⓐ Ⓑ Ⓒ Ⓓ   29. Ⓐ Ⓑ Ⓒ Ⓓ   43. Ⓐ Ⓑ Ⓒ Ⓓ
2. Ⓐ Ⓑ Ⓒ Ⓓ   16. Ⓐ Ⓑ Ⓒ Ⓓ   30. Ⓐ Ⓑ Ⓒ Ⓓ   44. Ⓐ Ⓑ Ⓒ Ⓓ
3. Ⓐ Ⓑ Ⓒ Ⓓ   17. Ⓐ Ⓑ Ⓒ Ⓓ   31. Ⓐ Ⓑ Ⓒ Ⓓ   45. Ⓐ Ⓑ Ⓒ Ⓓ
4. Ⓐ Ⓑ Ⓒ Ⓓ   18. Ⓐ Ⓑ Ⓒ Ⓓ   32. Ⓐ Ⓑ Ⓒ Ⓓ   46. Ⓐ Ⓑ Ⓒ Ⓓ
5. Ⓐ Ⓑ Ⓒ Ⓓ   19. Ⓐ Ⓑ Ⓒ Ⓓ   33. Ⓐ Ⓑ Ⓒ Ⓓ   47. Ⓐ Ⓑ Ⓒ Ⓓ
6. Ⓐ Ⓑ Ⓒ Ⓓ   20. Ⓐ Ⓑ Ⓒ Ⓓ   34. Ⓐ Ⓑ Ⓒ Ⓓ   48. Ⓐ Ⓑ Ⓒ Ⓓ
7. Ⓐ Ⓑ Ⓒ Ⓓ   21. Ⓐ Ⓑ Ⓒ Ⓓ   35. Ⓐ Ⓑ Ⓒ Ⓓ   49. Ⓐ Ⓑ Ⓒ Ⓓ
8. Ⓐ Ⓑ Ⓒ Ⓓ   22. Ⓐ Ⓑ Ⓒ Ⓓ   36. Ⓐ Ⓑ Ⓒ Ⓓ   50. Ⓐ Ⓑ Ⓒ Ⓓ
9. Ⓐ Ⓑ Ⓒ Ⓓ   23. Ⓐ Ⓑ Ⓒ Ⓓ   37. Ⓐ Ⓑ Ⓒ Ⓓ   51. Ⓐ Ⓑ Ⓒ Ⓓ
10. Ⓐ Ⓑ Ⓒ Ⓓ   24. Ⓐ Ⓑ Ⓒ Ⓓ   38. Ⓐ Ⓑ Ⓒ Ⓓ   52. Ⓐ Ⓑ Ⓒ Ⓓ
11. Ⓐ Ⓑ Ⓒ Ⓓ   25. Ⓐ Ⓑ Ⓒ Ⓓ   39. Ⓐ Ⓑ Ⓒ Ⓓ   53. Ⓐ Ⓑ Ⓒ Ⓓ
12. Ⓐ Ⓑ Ⓒ Ⓓ   26. Ⓐ Ⓑ Ⓒ Ⓓ   40. Ⓐ Ⓑ Ⓒ Ⓓ   54. Ⓐ Ⓑ Ⓒ Ⓓ
13. Ⓐ Ⓑ Ⓒ Ⓓ   27. Ⓐ Ⓑ Ⓒ Ⓓ   41. Ⓐ Ⓑ Ⓒ Ⓓ   55. Ⓐ Ⓑ Ⓒ Ⓓ
14. Ⓐ Ⓑ Ⓒ Ⓓ   28. Ⓐ Ⓑ Ⓒ Ⓓ   42. Ⓐ Ⓑ Ⓒ Ⓓ

Section I, Part B: Short-Answer Questions

Question 1

_____

_____

_____

_____

_____

_____

_____

_____

Question 2

_____
_____
_____
_____
_____
_____
_____
_____
_____
_____
_____
_____
_____
_____
_____
_____
_____

Question 3 or 4

_____
_____
_____
_____
_____
_____
_____
_____
_____
_____
_____
_____
_____
_____
_____
_____

Section II, Part A: Document-Based Question

answer sheet

answer sheet

_____

_____

_____

_____

_____

_____

_____

_____

_____

_____

_____

_____

_____

_____

_____

_____

_____

_____

_____

_____

_____

_____

_____

_____

_____

_____

Section II, Part B: Long Essay Question

_____

_____

_____

_____

_____

_____

_____

_____

_____

_____

_____

_____

_____

_____

_____

_____

_____

_____

_____

_____

_____

_____

_____

_____

_____

answer sheet

answer sheet

PRACTICE TEST 3

Section I, Part A: Multiple-Choice Questions

Time: 55 Minutes • 55 Questions

> **Directions:** Each question set is organized around two to five questions that focus on a primary or secondary source. After reading the document, choose the best answer and fill in the correct oval on the answer sheet.

Questions 1–4 refer to the excerpt below.

"As I got down before the canoe, I spent some time in viewing the rivers and the land in the fork, which I think extremely well situated for a fort as it has the absolute command of both rivers. The land at the Point is twenty or twenty-five feet above the common surface of the water and a considerable bottom of flat, well-timbered land all around it, very convenient for building. The rivers are each a quarter of a mile or more across and run here very nigh at right angles: Allegheny bearing northeast and Monongahela southeast. The former of these two is a very rapid swift-running water; the other deep and still with scarce any perceptible fall. About two miles from this, on the southeast side of the river, at the place where the Ohio Company intended to erect a fort, lives Singess, King of the Delawares. We called upon him to invite him to council at Logstown."

—George Washington, "Journey to the French Commandant," 1754

Source: *George Washington: Writings*, Library of America, 1997.

1. Tensions over westward expansion would lead most immediately to which of the following?
   A. The Revolutionary War
   B. The French and Indian War
   C. The Louisiana Purchase
   D. The First Great Awakening

2. Based on your knowledge of American history, which of the following best describes the primary purpose of organizations like the Ohio Company?
   A. Westward expansion
   B. Secession
   C. Warfare
   D. Christianization

3. The mention of the Indian chief Singess indicates that
   A. in general, Indians sided with the British and the colonists.
   B. French colonists desired Indian lands and used a variety of means to acquire them.
   C. Americans put steady pressure on Indian territory throughout the eighteenth and nineteenth centuries.
   D. Indian tribes welcomed American westward expansion.

4. The preoccupation with rivers best indicates which of the following?
   A. Washington's noted interest in natural history and geography
   B. The importance during this period of canals that connected rivers
   C. Rivers as the sole mode of transport during this period
   D. Rivers as the main mode of rapid transport during this period

Questions 5–7 refer to the document below.

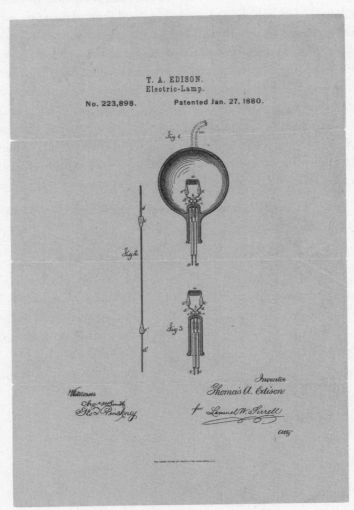

Patent application for incandescent light bulb, Thomas Edison, 1880

Source: *https://www.docsteach.org/documents/document/patent-application-incandescent-light-bulb*

5. This patent application is most indicative of which of the following?

   A. America's long-standing lack of support for intellectual property

   B. The negative impact of high tariffs on the incubation of infant industries

   C. The explosion of inventions during the second industrial revolution

   D. The concentration of wealth during the Gilded Age

6. All of the following were invented between 1865 and 1910, EXCEPT:

   A. Radio

   B. Motion-pictures

   C. The telegraph

   D. The internal combustion engine

7. The wave of inventions during the nineteenth century was

   A. common to both America and Europe.

   B. limited to America.

   C. limited to Europe.

   D. global.

Questions 8–11 refer to the excerpt below.

"From whence originated the idea that it was derogatory to a lady's dignity or a blot upon the female character to labor? And who was the first to say, sneeringly, 'Oh, she *works* for a living?' Surely, such ideas and expressions ought not to grow on republican soil. The time has been when ladies of the first rank were accustomed to busy themselves in domestic employment. [...] Few American fortunes will support a woman who is above the calls of her family; and a man of sense, in choosing a companion to job with him through all the uphills and downhills of life, would sooner choose one who *had* to work for a living than one who thought it beneath her to soil her pretty hands with manual labor[.] [...] To be able to earn one's own living by laboring with the hands should be reckoned among female accomplishments, and I hope the time is not far distant when none of my countrywomen will be ashamed to have it known that they are better versed in useful than they are in ornamental accomplishments."

—"C. B.," republished in *Mind Amongst the Spindles: A Selection from the* Lowell Offering: *A Miscellany Wholly Composed by the Factory Girls of an American City,* 1844.

Source: *https://archive.org/details/mindamongstspind00loweuoft*

8. The ideas in the passage are most opposed to which of the following?

   A. Republican motherhood

   B. The cult of domesticity

   C. Women's suffrage

   D. Abolitionism

9. The rise of the second industrial revolution was accompanied by which of the following changes?

   A. The adoption of slavery

   B. The Great Migration

   C. Urbanization

   D. Full worker rights

10. Which of the following groups, other than women, was most likely to be employed in New England factories of this period?

    A. Children

    B. African American men

    C. Chinese men

    D. Native Americans

11. Which of the following best characterizes the relationship between the mill or factory and its "factory girls," as they were called?

    A. Factory girls lived at home, worked eight hours a day, and had lives separate from the factory.

    B. Factory girls mostly worked at home, receiving raw materials and sending out value-added manufactured goods.

    C. Factory girls lived on site under almost constant surveillance and regimentation but with opportunities for personal development and expression.

    D. Factory girls lived on site out of convenience but were mostly left to themselves when not working.

Questions 12–14 refer to the excerpt below.

"Congress shall make no law respecting an establishment of religion, or prohibiting the free exercise thereof; or abridging the freedom of speech, or of the press; or the right of the people peaceably to assemble, and to petition the government for a redress of grievances."

—the First Amendment to the Constitution, 1791

12. Which of the following represents one of the first challenges to one of the protected rights in the First Amendment?

    A. *Marbury v. Madison*

    B. The Louisiana Purchase

    C. The Nullification Crisis

    D. The Alien and Sedition Acts

13. Which of the following best explains why the Bill of Rights was passed so soon after ratification?

    A. Political parties, or "factions," almost immediately came into existence after ratification.

    B. Quick passage had been promised to Anti-Federalists in order to overcome a major objection to ratification.

    C. Federalists immediately recognized that it was needed.

    D. The French Revolution of 1789 had inspired its passage.

14. Which of the following rights is most directly due to the experience of the English Civil War?

    A. The Establishment Clause

    B. Freedom of speech

    C. Freedom of the press

    D. Freedom of assembly

Questions 15–18 refer to the excerpt below.

"The war in Vietnam is but a symptom of a far deeper malady within the American spirit[.] [...] In 1957 a sensitive American official overseas said that it seemed to him that our nation was on the wrong side of a world revolution. [...] Five years ago [JFK] said, "Those who make peaceful revolution impossible will make violent revolution inevitable." [...] I am convinced that if we are to get on the right side of the world revolution, we as a nation must undergo a radical revolution of values. We must rapidly begin the shift from a "thing-oriented" society to a "person-oriented" society. When machines and computers, profit motives and property rights are considered more important than people, the giant triplets of racism, materialism, and militarism are incapable of being conquered.

A true revolution of values will soon cause us to question the fairness and justice of many of our past and present policies. [...] A true revolution of values will soon look uneasily on the glaring contrast of poverty and wealth. With righteous indignation, it will look across the seas and see individual capitalists of the West investing huge sums of money in Asia, Africa and South America, only to take the profits out with no concern for the social betterment of the countries, and say: "This is not just." It will look at our alliance with the landed gentry of Latin America and say: "This is not just." The Western arrogance of feeling that it has everything to teach others and nothing to learn from them is not just. A true revolution of values will lay hands on the world order and say of war: "This way of settling differences is not just." This business of burning human beings with napalm, of filling our nation's homes with orphans and widows, of injecting poisonous drugs of hate into veins of people normally humane, of sending men home from dark and bloody battlefields physically handicapped and psychologically deranged, cannot be reconciled with wisdom, justice and love. A nation that continues year after year to spend more money on military defense than on programs of social uplift is approaching spiritual death."

—Martin Luther King, Jr, "Beyond Vietnam," 1967

Source: *https://www.commondreams.org/views04/0115-13.htm* (*https://creativecommons.org/licenses/by-sa/3.0/us/*)

15. Which of the following best characterizes the relationship King saw between foreign and domestic policy?
    A. Mostly separate, but rooted in militarism
    B. Mostly separate, but equally rooted in racism
    C. Intimately connected and rooted in moral values
    D. Intimately connected and unrelated to the economic system

16. Which of the following describes Dr. King's biggest issue with the Vietnam War?
    A. It was draining money from social programs helping African Americans.
    B. White people were blaming black soldiers for their lack of headway in the conflict.
    C. African Americans were too pro-Vietnam.
    D. Americans were not winning the war.

17. The Civil Rights Movement's effect can best be summarized as
    A. securing neither political and legal rights nor socioeconomic equality.
    B. securing both political and legal rights and socioeconomic equality.
    C. securing political and legal rights but not socioeconomic equality.
    D. securing socioeconomic equality but not political and legal rights.

18. All of the following were African American leaders who spoke out against the Vietnam War EXCEPT:
    A. Malcolm X
    B. Stokely Carmichael
    C. Muhammed Ali
    D. Medgar Evers

Questions 19–22 refer to the excerpt below.

"But though a funded debt is not in the first instance an absolute increase of capital or an augmentation of real wealth, yet by serving as a new power in the operation of industry, it has within certain bounds a tendency to increase the real wealth of a community in like manner as money borrowed by a thrifty farmer to be laid out in the improvement of his farm may in the end add to his stock of real riches.

There are respectable individuals who from a just aversion to an accumulation of public debt, are unwilling to concede to it any kind of utility, who can discern no good to alleviate the ill with which they suppose it pregnant, who cannot be persuaded that it ought in any sense to be viewed as an increase of capital lest it should be inferred that the more debt the more capital: the greater the burdens, the greater the blessings of the community.

But it interests the public councils to estimate every object as it truly is; to appreciate how far the good in any measure is compensated by the ill, or the ill by the good. Either of them is seldom unmixed."

—Alexander Hamilton, "Report on Manufactures," 1791

Source: *Alexander Hamilton: Writings*, Library of America, 2001

19. Which of the following most nearly reflects the position taken in this passage?
    A. Hamilton extols the benefits of debt-financed investment.
    B. Hamilton appeals to reason and balance over emotion and enthusiasm.
    C. Hamilton decries the dangers of decadence that always arise from debt-financed investment.
    D. Hamilton refuses to take a position on the usefulness or not of debt-financed investment.

20. Later in the nineteenth century, Hamilton's economic plan would be taken up by which of the following political parties?
    A. Democrats
    B. Know-Nothings
    C. Whigs
    D. Populists

21. Which of the following was LEAST associated with Hamilton's general economic program?
    A. Free trade
    B. Tariffs
    C. A central bank
    D. A tax on whiskey

22. Which of the following was the goal of Hamilton's program?
    A. To reunite the United States with its main trading partner, Britain
    B. To maintain an agricultural republic
    C. To replace agriculture with manufacturing
    D. To create a balanced economy of agriculture and manufacture

Questions 23–24 refer to the excerpt below.

"In current discussions of these problems there emerges time and again the conception of counteracting the slump by stimulating *private* investment. This may be done by lowering the rate of interest, by the reduction of income tax, or by subsidizing private investment directly in this or another form. That such a scheme should be attractive to business is not surprising. The entrepreneur remains the medium through which the intervention is conducted. If he does not feel confidence in the political situation, he will not be bribed into investment. And the intervention does not involve the government either in 'playing with' (public) investment or 'wasting money' on subsidizing consumption.

It may be shown, however, that the stimulation of private investment does not provide an adequate method for preventing mass unemployment. There are two alternatives to be considered here, (i) The rate of interest or income tax (or both) is reduced sharply in the slump and increased in the boom. In this case both the period and the amplitude of the business cycle will be reduced, but employment not only in the slump but even in the boom may be far from full, i.e. the average unemployment may be considerable, although its fluctuations will be less marked, (ii) The rate of interest or income tax is reduced in a slump but *not* increased in the subsequent boom. In this case the boom will last longer, but it must end in a new slump: one reduction in the rate of interest or income tax does not, of course, eliminate the forces which cause cyclical fluctuations in a capitalist economy. In the new slump it will be necessary to reduce the rate of interest or income tax again and so on. Thus in the not too remote future, the rate of interest would have be negative and income tax would have to be replaced by an income subsidy. The same would arise if it were attempted to *maintain* full employment by stimulating private investment: the rate of interest and income tax would have to be reduced continuously."

—Michael Kalecki, "Political Aspects of Full Employment," 1943

Source: *http://www.bradford-delong.com/1943/07/michal-kalecki-political-aspects-of-full-employment-policy-political-quarterly-1943.html*

23. During which of the following periods was the program outlined in the passage attempted?

A. After the Crash of 1929 and during the Great Depression

B. After the Crash of 2008 and during the Great Recession

C. During the presidency of Theodore Roosevelt

D. It has never been attempted.

24. Which of the following does Kalecki take for granted?

A. The boom-bust cycle is intrinsic to capitalism.

B. Private investment is the best way out of a slump.

C. Full employment is not worth maintaining.

D. Income subsidies are inevitable, in order to maintain full employment.

Questions 25–28 refer to the following image.

"Migrant agricultural worker's family. Seven hungry children. Mother aged thirty-two. Father is native Californian. Nipomo, California," Dorothea Lange, 1936

Source: *http://www.loc.gov/pictures/item/fsa1998021557/PP/*

25. Which of the following caused the Dust Bowl of the 1930s?

A. An unusually dry period

B. The failure of the Fair Deal

C. An unusually dry period and agricultural practices

D. Agricultural practices

26. The Agricultural Adjustment Act of 1933 had which of the following effects?

A. It raised prices and thus incomes, but it disproportionately benefited property-owning farmers.

B. It raised prices and thus incomes, but it disproportionately benefited tenants and sharecroppers.

C. It helped to alleviate the Dust Bowl and thus encouraged immigration into the formerly affected areas.

D. It helped to cause the Dust Bowl and thus encouraged emigration from affected areas.

27. Which of the following did the most to increase the price of crops?
    A. World War II
    B. Rural electrification
    C. The Agricultural Adjustment Act
    D. The effects of the Dust Bowl itself

28. Which of the following statements is NOT true of New Deal programs?
    A. Federal jobs programs heavily discriminated against African Americans.
    B. The Federal Housing Administration endorsed and even encouraged residential segregation and discrimination.
    C. Southern Democrats insisted on the exclusion of agricultural and domestic workers from Social Security, two sectors in which African Americans were heavily represented.
    D. African Americans were barred from all programs.

Questions 29–31 refer to the following image.

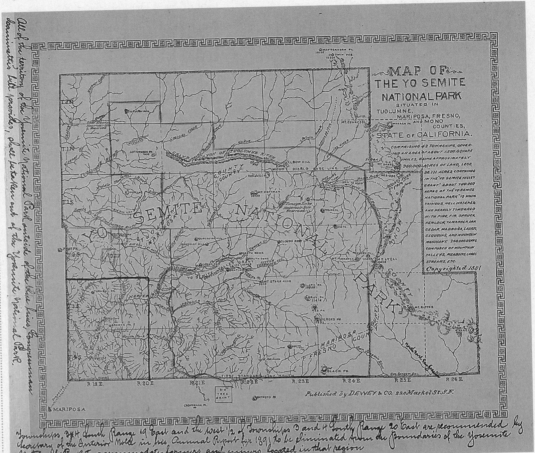

"Petition and Map from John Muir and Other Founders of Sierra Club Protesting a Bill to Reduce the Size of Yosemite National Park," 1893

Text in the left margin reads: "All of the territory of the Yosemite National Park outside of the blue [here, black] lines, [California] Congressman [Anthony] Caminetti's bill provides, shall be taken out of the Yosemite National Park."

Text in the bottom margin reads: "Townships 3 and 4 [?] Range 19 East and the west 1/2 of Townships 3 and 4 [?] Range 20 East [i.e., the black rectangle in the lower-left-hand corner of the map] are recommended by Secretary of the Interior [John W.] Noble in his Annual Report of 1891 to be eliminated from the Boundaries of the Yosemite National Park to accommodate farmers and miners located in that region."

Source: *https://www.docsteach.org/documents/document/petition-and-map-from-john-muir-and-other-founders-of-sierra-club-protesting-a-bill-to-reduce-the-size-of-yosemite-national-park*

29. The national park system was based on which of the following ideas?

- **A.** Government should ban all types of development within natural parks.
- **B.** Government has a responsibility to regulate the development of natural resources.
- **C.** Natural resource management is best left up to the market.
- **D.** Natural resource management is best left up to the states.

30. Conservation is consistent with other Progressive programs and policies insofar as it

- **A.** removed regulatory barriers to economic development.
- **B.** relied on experts and efficiency to regulate economic activity.
- **C.** had no long-lasting effects.
- **D.** ensured racial justice in the pursuit of its goals.

31. The image suggests that even once established, national parks were

- **A.** often still under pressure to be opened up for development or resource extraction.
- **B.** considered inviolate.
- **C.** protected solely through governmental action.
- **D.** defended solely by interested citizens and organizations of civil society.

Questions 32–34 refer to the excerpt below.

"Those then who controvert the principle that the constitution is to be considered, in court, as a paramount law, are reduced to the necessity of maintaining that the courts must close their eyes on the constitution, and see only the law. This doctrine would subvert the very foundation of all written constitutions. It would declare that an act which, according to the principles and theory of our government, is entirely void, is yet, in practice, completely obligatory. It would declare that if the legislature shall do what is expressly forbidden, such act, notwithstanding the express prohibition, is in reality effectual. It would be giving to the legislature a practical and real omnipotence, with the same breath which professes to restrict their powers within narrow limits. It is prescribing limits, and declaring that those limits may be passed at pleasure."

—John Marshall, *Marbury v Madison*, 1803

Source: *https://en.m.wikisource.org/wiki/Marbury_v._Madison*

32. Based on the passage and your knowledge of American history, which of the following most closely reflects the ideas expressed by Marshall?
    A. The Supreme Court has the power to initiate legislation when it strikes down existing laws as unconstitutional.
    B. Congress's powers trump that of the other two branches of government.
    C. Congress's powers subordinate to those of the Supreme Court.
    D. The Supreme Court has the power of judicial review by which it determines the constitutionality of laws.

33. Which of the following persons was most set against Marshall's conception of the power of the federal government?
    A. Hamilton
    B. Adams
    C. Jefferson
    D. Washington

34. The powers claimed by Marshall in this decision were soon extended to which of the following?
    A. Treaties
    B. Impeachment
    C. Federal law
    D. State law

Questions 35–37 refer to the excerpt below.

"America was discovered in 1492, and in the year ensuing inhabited by the Spaniards[.] [...] Such a multitude of people inhabits these countries that it seems as if the Omnipotent God has assembled the major part of mankind in this part of the world. Now this infinite multitude of men are by the creation of God innocently simple, altogether void of and averse to all manner of deceit and malice[.] This is a most tender and effeminate people. [...] They are parsimonious in their diet, as the Holy Fathers were in their frugal life in the desert[.] [...] The natives [are] capable of morality or goodness, very apt to receive the Catholic religion; nor are they averse to civility and good manners, [...] having absorbed the first rudiments of the Christian Faith[.] [...] And to conclude, [...] there was nothing lacking in them for the acquisition of Eternal Beatitude but the knowledge and understanding of the Deity.

The Spaniards first assaulted these innocent sheep, so designed by the Almighty as was earlier mentioned, like the most cruel and hunger-starved tigers, wolves and lions, attempting nothing, for forty years after their first landing, but the massacre of these wretches whom they have so inhumanely and barbarously butchered and harassed with several kinds of torments never before known. [...] Now the ultimate end that incited the Spaniards to destroy these people was solely gold[.] [T]heir ambition and avarice, greater than any which the heart of man has ever entertained, and the vast wealth of those regions, as well as the humility and patience of the inhabitants (which made their conquest easier), did much to promote the destruction. The Spaniards so despicably condemned the inhabitants that they treated them (I speak truly of things I witnessed) not as animals, which I dearly wished they had, but as the most abject dung and filth of the earth[.]"

—Bartolomé de las Casas, *A Brief Account of the Destruction of the Indies*, 1552.

Source: *http://www.gutenberg.org/cache/epub/20321/pg20321-images.html*

35. With which of the following is this text most closely associated?
    A. The Black Legend
    B. The Spanish Armada
    C. English common law
    D. The Transatlantic slave trade

36. In this passage, de las Casas highlights a crucial tension in European colonization of the Americas consisting of which of the following?
    A. Spanish and English claims
    B. Catholic missionary work and Protestant evangelism

C. Christianization and profit
D. Domination of Native Americans and cooperation with Africans

37. Which of the following was de las Casas' initial proposal to alleviate the suffering of the Native Americans?
    A. Indentured servitude of Europeans
    B. The importation of African slaves
    C. The establishment of a caste system in Spanish America
    D. The return of all Spaniards to Spain

Questions 38–41 refer to the excerpt below.

"From the conditions of frontier life came intellectual traits of profound importance. The works of travelers along each frontier from colonial days onward describe certain common traits, and these traits have, while softening down, still persisted as survivals in the place of their origin, even when a higher social organization succeeded. The result is that to the frontier the American intellect owes its striking characteristics. That coarseness and strength combined with acuteness and inquisitiveness; that practical, inventive turn of mind, quick to find expedients; that masterful grasp of material things, lacking in the artistic but powerful to effect great ends; that restless, nervous energy; that dominant individualism, working for good and for evil, and withal that buoyancy and exuberance which comes with freedom—these are traits of the frontier, or traits called out elsewhere because of the existence of the frontier.

Since the days when the fleet of Columbus sailed into the waters of the New World, America has been another name for opportunity, and the people of the United States have taken their tone from the incessant expansion which has not only been open but has even been forced upon them. He would be a rash prophet who should assert that the expansive character of American life has now entirely ceased. Movement has been its dominant fact, and, unless this training has no effect upon a people, the American energy will continually demand a wider field for its exercise. But never again will such gifts of free land offer themselves. [...] And now, four centuries from the discovery of America, at the end of a hundred years of life under the Constitution, the frontier has gone, and with its going has closed the first period of American history."

—Frederick Jackson Turner, "The Significance of the Frontier in American History," 1893

Source: *https://archive.org/details/significanceoffr00turn*

38. According to Turner's thesis, America's move into overseas imperialism was
    A. atypical.
    B. proper.
    C. mistaken.
    D. only to be expected.

39. Based on the passage and your knowledge of American history, the "free land" noted in the passage most likely implies which of the following?
    A. Turner denigrated the military, diplomatic, and settling effort involved in westward expansion.
    B. Turner saw the West as mostly empty before the arrival of white settlers.
    C. Turner acknowledged that the West was granted to America free of charge.
    D. Turner saw America as uniquely free; thus, any territory it acquired was also uniquely free.

40. Based on your knowledge of American history, which of the following was also part of Turner's frontier thesis?

A. The idea of the West as a "safety valve" for social, economic, and cultural tensions in the settled areas of the country

B. A call to engage in widespread overseas imperialism in order to preserve the frontier

C. A condemnation of westward expansion in all its forms

D. A thorough accounting of the cost of westward expansion on Native Americans

41. Based on your knowledge of American history, which of the following is most accurate?

A. Turner's thesis had little impact on historiography.

B. Turner's thesis has been entirely supported by subsequent scholarship.

C. The idea of a "frontier" persisted in American culture long past 1893.

D. American culture has long since dropped the idea of a "frontier."

Questions 42–45 refer to the excerpt below.

"SISTERS AND FRIENDS: As *immortal souls*, created by God to know and love him with all our hearts, and our neighbor as ourselves, we owe immediate obedience to his commands, respecting the sinful system of Slavery, beneath which 2,500,000 of our Fellow-Immortals, children of the same country, are crushed, soul and body, in the extremity of degradation and agony.

As *women*, it is incumbent upon us, instantly and always, to labor to increase the knowledge and the love of God that such concentrated hatred of his character and laws may no longer be so intrenched in *men's* business and bosoms, that they dare not condemn and renounce it.

As *wives* and *mothers*, as *sisters* and *daughters*, we are deeply responsible for the influence we have on the human race. We are bound to exert it; we are bound to urge men to cease to do evil, and learn to do well. We are bound to urge them to regain, defend, and preserve inviolate the rights of all, especially those whom they have most deeply wronged. We are bound to the constant exercise of the only right we ourselves enjoy—the right which our physical weakness renders peculiarly appropriate—the right of petition. We are bound to try how much it can accomplish in the District of Columbia, or we are as verily guilty touching slavery as our brethren and sisters in the slaveholding States: for Congress possesses power 'to exercise exclusive legislation over the District of Columbia in all cases whatsoever,' by a provision of the Constitution; and by an *act* of the *First* Congress, the right of petition was secured to us."

—Address of the Boston Female Anti-Slavery Society, 1836

Source: *https://en.m.wikisource.org/wiki/Address_of_the_Boston_Female_Anti-Slavery_Society*

42. The beginning of the third paragraph is most reminiscent of which of the following?

   A. The cult of domesticity

   B. Republican motherhood

   C. Twentieth-century radical feminism

   D. Eugenics

43. The authors refer to rights guaranteed in which of the following amendments to the Constitution?

   A. The first

   B. The second

   C. The tenth

   D. The fourteenth

44. The first paragraph best supports which of the following statements?

   A. The abolitionist movement was mostly secular.

   B. Abolitionists largely tended to make practical, not ethical, arguments.

   C. The abolitionist movement grew in large part out of deep religious belief.

   D. Abolitionists saw anti-slavery as a moral principle to uphold, even though they found slavery to be mostly benign in practice.

45. Groups like the Boston Female Anti-Slavery Society are most typical of which of the following?

   A. The persistence of Puritan values

   B. The massive increase in voluntary organizations during the Jacksonian period

   C. The widespread acceptance of women into formerly male-dominated domains like politics

   D. Segregationist ideas that penetrated the North during this period

Questions 46–48 refer to the excerpt below.

"But neither the orators nor the contemners are content with the plain record. They must show how the Puritans had all the virtues or all the vices. Once the term Puritanism had fairly definite connotations. Now it has lost them all. By the critics it is used as a term of opprobrium applicable to anything that interferes with the new freedom, free verse, psycho-analysis, or even the double entendre.

Evidently in the midst of much confusion, some definition is necessary, and for that purpose I have run through a dozen eulogiums on the Puritans (not omitting G. W. Curtis's orations) and an equal number of attacks on the Puritans (not omitting Mencken's Prefaces). From these authentic documents I have culled the following descriptive terms applied to Puritans. I append a table for the benefit of the reader. Puritanism means:

Godliness	Principle	Philistinism	Grape juice
Thrift	A free church	Harsh restraint	Grisly sermons
Liberty	A free state	Beauty-hating	Religious persecution
Democracy	Equal rights	Sour-faced fanaticism	Sullenness
Culture	A holy Sabbath	Supreme hypocrisy	Ill-temper
Industry	Liberty under law	Canting	Stinginess
Frugality	Individual freedom	Demonology	Bigotry
Temperance	Self-government	Enmity to true art	Conceit
Resistance to tyranny	The gracious spirit of	Intellectual tyranny	Bombast
Pluck	Christianity	Brutal intolerance	

I look upon this catalogue and am puzzled to find "the whole truth." When I think of Puritan "temperance" I am reminded of cherry bounce and also the good old Jamaica rum which New England used to make in such quantities that it would float her mercantile marine. When I think of "demonology," I remember that son of Boston, Benjamin Franklin, whose liberality of spirit even Mencken celebrates, when he falsely attributes it to French influence, having never in his omniscience read the Autobiography. When I think of "liberty and individual freedom," I shudder to recall stories of the New England slavers and the terrible middle passage which only Ruskin's superb imagination could picture. When I think of "pluck and industry," I recollect the dogged labors of French peasants. Catholic in faith and Celtic in race. When I see the staring words "brutal intolerance" I recall the sweet spirit of Roger Williams, aye, the sweeter spirit of John Milton whose *Areopagitica* was written before the school of the new freedom was established. When I read "hypocrisy" and "canting" I cannot refrain from associating with them the antics of the late Wilhelm II who, I believe, was not born in Boston. So I take leave of the subject. Let the honest reader, standing under the stars, pick out those characteristics that distinctly and consistently mark the Puritans through their long history."

—Charles Beard, "On Puritans," *The New Republic*, 1920

Source: *https://newrepublic.com/article/79396/puritans*

46. Which of the following best characterizes Beard's view of the Puritans?
    A. The Puritans had a wide range of both beliefs and behaviors that can't reasonably be stereotyped.
    B. Puritan beliefs and behaviors were almost entirely positive and laudable.
    C. Puritan beliefs and behaviors were almost entirely negative and deplorable.
    D. Puritan beliefs and behaviors had little long-lasting effect.

47. Which of the following is closest to Beard's point of view?
    A. Since the truth is impossible to ascertain, history is not worth pursuing.
    B. Since any one work of history will be somewhat partial, comparison of many works will yield greater insight.
    C. Historical truth is both obvious and easy to capture and express.
    D. History can never even approach the truth; all that we have to examine are competing narratives.

48. With which of the following statements would you predict Beard to have been most likely to agree?
    A. The wide range of beliefs and behaviors of the Puritans is more typical than not of any large and long-lasting group of people.
    B. For interesting reasons, the variation of Puritan belief and behavior is mostly limited to the Puritans.
    C. Puritans were markedly more hypo-critical than most groups of people.
    D. Puritans were markedly superior to most groups of people.

Questions 49–51 refer to the image below.

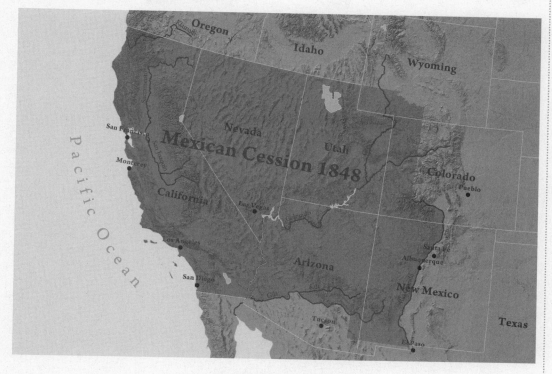

Map of the Mexican Cessions

Source: *https://commons.wikimedia.org/wiki/File:Mexican_Cession.png*

49. The Mexican-American War was a result of all of the following EXCEPT
   A. America's annexation of Texas
   B. Border disputes
   C. Mexico's attack against settlers along the Arizona border
   D. Mexico's refusal to sell California

50. Which of the following marked the formal end of the Mexican-American War?
   A. Gadsden Purchase
   B. Treaty of Guadalupe Hidalgo
   C. The Wilmot Proviso
   D. The Ostend Manifesto

51. Which of the following was NOT a consequence of the Mexican-American War?
   A. Sectional debates heightened over the issue of slavery.
   B. Congress passed the Wilmot Proviso, prohibiting slavery in the cession lands.
   C. Mexico recognized the Rio Grande as the southern border of Texas.
   D. The United States took possession of California.

Questions 52–53 refer to the image below.

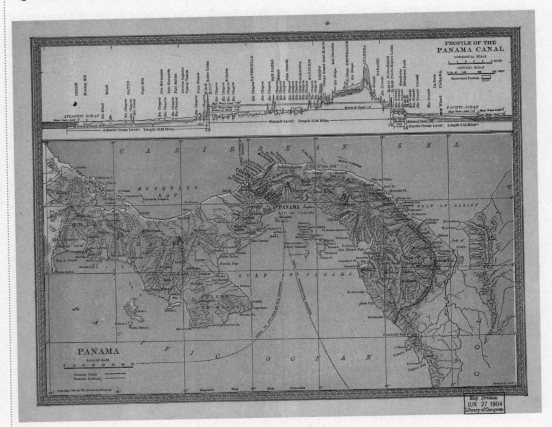

"Panama," Americana Company/Bormay & Co., 1904

Source: *https://www.loc.gov/item/99466711*

52. Which of the following was the primary reason for the construction of the Panama Canal?
    A. The Monroe Doctrine
    B. Control of trade routes
    C. To lower unemployment through public works projects
    D. To demonstrate how racially integrated labor could be successful

53. The construction of the Panama Canal was illustrative of which of the following?
    A. The Roosevelt Corollary
    B. The Era of Good Feelings
    C. The Monroe Doctrine
    D. The Good Neighbor Policy

Questions 54–55 refer to the excerpt below.

"It's morning again in America. Today more men and women will go to work than ever before in our country's history. With interest rates at about half the record highs of 1980, nearly 2,000 families today will buy new homes, more than at any time in the past four years. This afternoon 6,500 young men and women will be married, and with inflation at less than half of what it was just four years ago, they can look forward with confidence to the future. It's morning again in America, and under the leadership of President Reagan, our country is prouder and stronger and better. Why would we ever want to return to where we were less than four short years ago?"

—Transcript of "Morning in America," a television advertisement for the
Reagan campaign, 1984

Source: *https://en.m.wikipedia.org/wiki/Morning_in_America*

54. Advertisements such as these are most indicative of which of the following?
   A. The lack of reliance in modern election campaigns on public-relations and marketing
   B. The ever-declining importance of money in political campaigns
   C. The decline of civility in modern political advertisements
   D. The importance of television advertising in modern election campaigns

55. The magnitude and duration of Ronald Reagan's effect on politics and policy is most comparable to those of
   A. Franklin Roosevelt.
   B. Bill Clinton.
   C. Richard Nixon.
   D. Barack Obama.

STOP.
IF YOU FINISH BEFORE TIME IS OUT, YOU MAY CHECK YOUR WORK ON THIS SECTION ONLY.
DO NOT TURN TO ANY OTHER SECTION IN THE TEST.

Section I, Part B: Short-Answer Questions

Time: 40 Minutes • 3 Questions

> **Directions:** The following section consists of four short-answer questions—you must answer *both* Question 1 and Question 2. You will then choose to answer *either* Question 3 or Question 4. Use the answer sheet provided to respond to the questions.

"A Boxing Match, or Another Bloody Nose for John Bull," William Charles, 1813

In a naval battle in September, 1813, the American "Enterprise" defeated the British "Boxer." The boats themselves, presumably, battle just behind Madison on the right. George III stands on the left, bleeding and battered, saying: "Stop, Stop, Stop, Brother Jonathan, or I shall fall with the loss of blood.—I thought to have been too heavy for you.—But I must acknowledge your superior skill—Two blows to my one!—And so well directed too! Mercy, mercy on me, how does this happen!!!" Standing on the right, James Madison says, "Ha-Ah Johnny! you thought yourself a <u>Boxer</u> did you!—I'll let you know we are an <u>Enterprize</u>ing Nation, and ready to meet you with equal force any day."

Source: *http://www.loc.gov/pictures/item/2002708982/*

1. Use the image above to answer parts A, B, and C.
   A. Explain the image's point of view on American patriotism.
   B. Briefly describe ONE cause of the War of 1812.
   C. Briefly describe ONE effect of the War of 1812.

Why Yankee land is at a stand,
And all in consternation;
For in the South they make a rout,
And all about Nullification.
Sing Yankee doodle doodle doo,
Yankee doodle dandy,
Our foes are few our hearts are true,
And Jackson is quite handy.

These Southern knaves are blustering blades,
Their cash they think is handy,
But we of the North are the right sort,
And the Union is the dandy.
Sing Yankee doodle doodle doo,
Yankee doodle dandy;
Stand to your arms nor fear alarms,
Just play Yankee doodle dandy.

It was the pill at Bunker hill,
For which old Warren fought there,
From Southern boys, though they make a noise,
We can have nought to dread here.
Sing Yankee doodle doodle doo,
Yankee doodle dandy,
They know their slaves the silly knaves,
Will soon find freedom handy.

Nat Turner's plan, the daring man,
May soon reach South Carolina,
Then would the black, their bodies hack,
Caesar, Cato, Pomp, and Dinah,
Sing Yankee doodle doodle doo,
Yankee doodle dandy.
These Southern folks, may crack their jokes,
If northerners are so handy.

When dire oppressed by British laws,
They sent for our protection,
We sent them aid in Freedom's cause,
Nor thought of their nullification.
Sing Yankee doodle doodle doo,
Yankee doodle dandy,
Our hands are strong, the way not long,
And submission is the dandy.

Their cotton bags, may turn to rags,
If Eastern men don't buy them,
For all their gold, they may be sold,
Or their slaves may yet destroy them.
Sing Yankee doodle doodle doo,
Yankee doodle dandy,
If their cotton bags don't find a sale,
Their cash wont be so handy.

When we our glorious Constitution form'd,
These Southern men declined it,
But soon they found they were unarmed,
And petitioned to sign it.
Sing Yankee doodle doodle doo,
Yankee doodle dandy,
Now like the snake torpid in a brake,
They think Nullification it is handy.

Without their trade we are not afraid,
But we can live in peace and plenty,
But if to arms they sound alarms,
They may find it not so handy.
Sing Yankee doodle doodle doo,
Sing Yankee doodle dandy,
For Jackson he is wide awake,
He says the Union is so handy.

Our country's cause, our country's laws,
We ever will defend, Sir,
And if they do not gain applause,
My song was never penned, Sir.
So sound the trumpet, beat the drum,
Play Yankee doodle dandy,
We Jackson boys will quickly come,
And be with our rifles handy.

The Wellington invincibles
At New-Orleans were beat, Sir,
And do the Southerns think their pills,
Will frighten us to a retreat, Sir.
Sing Yankee doodle doodle doo,
Sing Yankee doodle dandy,
We love our friends, but secret foes
May find our courage is handy.

—"Jackson and the Nullifiers," Broadside, 1832.

Source: Library of Congress, Rare Book and Special Collections Division, Printed Ephemera Collection. (*https://www.loc.gov/resource/rbpe.11800800/*)

2. Refer to the text above in answering parts A, B, and C.
   A. Briefly describe ONE cause of the nullification crisis.
   B. Briefly describe ONE consequence of the nullification crisis.
   C. Briefly describe the point of view of the author of the document, mentioning ONE specific portion as evidence.

Directions: Answer *either* Question 3 or 4.

---

3. Based on your knowledge of American history, answer parts A and B.
   A. Briefly explain why ONE of the following periods best represents the beginning of American feminism, mentioning at least ONE piece of evidence:
   - The mid-nineteenth century
   - The 1920s
   - The 1960s to the present
   B. Provide ONE counterargument to your choice.

4. Based on your knowledge of American history, answer parts A, B, and C.
   A. Give ONE example of an act of Native American ethnic cleansing by the United States or its citizens.
   B. Give ONE example of an act of violent Native American resistance.
   C. Give ONE example of an act of nonviolent Native American resistance.

STOP.
IF YOU FINISH BEFORE TIME IS OUT, YOU MAY CHECK YOUR WORK ON THIS SECTION ONLY.
DO NOT TURN TO ANY OTHER SECTION IN THE TEST.

Section II, Part A: Document-Based Question

Time: 60 Minutes • 1 Question

Directions: The following question asks you to write a cohesive essay incorporating your interpretation of Documents 1 through 7 and your knowledge of the period stated in the question. To earn a high score, you must cite key evidence from the documents and use your outside knowledge of United States history. Take 15 minutes to read all documents and 45 minutes to write your essay on the answer sheet provided.

1. Compare and contrast Federalist and Antifederalist legal and philosophical arguments over the ratification of the Constitution in the late 1780s and its impact on recent historical events.

Document 1

Source: *https://www.loc.gov/pictures/item/2008661778/*

Portion of "The looking glass for 1787. A house divided against itself cannot stand,"
Amos Doolittle, New Haven, Connecticut, 1787

Notes: The wagon in the middle, which symbolizes Connecticut, is mired in a swamp of debt. The driver sitting on the wagon says, "Gentlemen, this machine is deep in the mire and you are divided as to its releaf [i.e. "relief"]. Pulling the wagon in opposite directions are the Federalist and Antifederalist factions in Connecticut's Council of Twelve. The Federalists are on the left enjoying sunny weather and stating: "Pay Commutation," "Drive them to it," "I abhor the antifederal Faction," and "Comply with Congress." The Antifederalists on the right, below a stormy sky and on an erupting earth, state: "Tax Luxury," "the People are oprest [i.e. oppressed]" "curses on to Foederal Govermt. [i.e., Federal Government]," "Success to Shays," and "Curse Independence."

Document 2

Source: *https://en.m.wikisource.org/wiki/An_Economic_Interpretation_of_the_Constitution_of_the_United_States/Chapter_VIII*

This whole process was a departure from the provisions of the then fundamental law of the land—the Articles of Confederation—which provided that all alterations and amendments should be made by Congress and receive the approval of the legislature of every state. If today the Congress of the United States should call a national convention to "revise" the Constitution, and such a convention should throw away the existing instrument of government entirely and submit a new frame of government to a popular referendum, disregarding altogether the process of amendment now provided, we should have something analogous to the great political transformation of 1787-89. The revolutionary nature of the work of the Philadelphia Convention is correctly characterized by Professor John W. Burgess when he states that had such acts been performed Julius or Napoleon, they would have been pronounced *coups d'état*.

—Charles Beard, *An Economic Interpretation of the Constitution of the United States*, 1913

Document 3

There is no declaration of rights: and the laws of the general government being paramount to the laws and constitutions of the several states, the declarations of rights, in the separate states, are no security. [...]

In the House of Representatives there is not the substance, but the shadow only of representation [...] The laws will, therefore, be generally made by men little concerned in, and unacquainted with their effects and consequences. The Senate['s ...] great power[s, ...] their influence upon, and connection with, the supreme executive [...], their duration of office, and their being a constant existing body, almost continually sitting, joined with their being one complete branch of the legislature, will destroy any balance in the government, and enable them to accomplish what usurpations they please, upon the rights and liberties of the people.

The judiciary of the Unites States is so constructed as extended, as to absorb and destroy the judiciaries of the several states; thereby rendering laws as tedious, intricate, and expensive, and justice as unattainable by a great part of the community, as in England; and enabling the rich to oppress and ruin the poor.

The President of the United States has no constitutional council (a thing unknown in any safe government)[;] he will therefore be unsupported by proper information and advice; and will generally be directed by minions and favorites -- or he will become a tool to the Senate -- or a council of state will grow out of the principal officers of the great departments -- the worst and most dangerous of all ingredients for such a council in a free country; for they may be induced to join in any dangerous or oppressive measures, to shelter themselves, and prevent an inquiry into their own misconduct in office. [...]

This government will commence in a moderate aristocracy. It is at present impossible to foresee whether it will, in its operation, produce a monarchy, or a corrupt oppressive aristocracy; it will most probably vibrate some years between the two, and then terminate in the one or the other."

—George Mason, "Objections of the Hon. George Mason to the proposed Federal Constitution. Addressed to the Citizens of Virginia," Broadside, Autumn 1787

Document 4

Source: *James Madison: Writings*, Library of America, 1999

I have been this day honored with your favor of the 10th. instant [i.e., a letter from Washington] under the same cover with which is a copy of Col. Mason's objections to the Work of the Convention. [...] What he means by the dangerous tendency of the Judiciary I am at some loss to comprehend. It never was intended, nor can it be supposed that in ordinary cases the inferior tribunals will not have final jurisdiction in order to prevent the evils of which he complains. The great mass of suits in every State lie between Citizen & Citizen, and relate to matters not of federal cognizance. Notwithstanding the stress laid on the necessity of a Council to the President I strongly suspect, tho I was a friend to the thing, that if such an one as Col. Mason proposed, had been established, and the power of the Senate in appointments to offices transferred to it, that as great a clamor would have been heard from some quarters which in general echo his Objections.

—James Madison to George Washington, October 1787

Document 5

Source: *https://archive.org/details/cu31924020874099*

As to the want of a declaration of rights. The introduction of these in England, from which the idea was originally taken, was in consequence of usurpations of the Crown, contrary, as was conceived, to the principles of their government. But there no original constitution is to be found, and the only meaning of a declaration of rights in that country is that in certain particulars specified the Crown had no authority to act. Could this have been necessary had there been a constitution in being by which it could have been clearly discerned whether the Crown had such authority or not? Had the people, by a solemn instrument, delegated particular powers to the Crown at the formation of the government, surely the Crown, which in that case could claim [powers] under that instrument only, could not have contended for more power than was conveyed by it.

So it is in regard to the new Constitution here: the future government which may be formed under that authority certainly cannot act beyond the warrant of that authority. [...] The question then only is whether more power will be vested in the future government than is necessary for the general purposes of the union. This may occasion a ground of dispute—but after expressly defining the powers that are to be exercised, to say that they shall exercise no other powers (either by a general or particular enumeration) would seem to me both nugatory and ridiculous. As well might a Judge when he condemns a man to be hanged give strong injunctions to the Sheriff that he should not be beheaded. It appears to me a very just remark of Mr. Wilson's, in his celebrated speech, that a bill of rights would have been dangerous, as implying that without such a reservation the Congress would have had authority in the cases enumerated, so that if any had been omitted (and who would undertake to recite all the State and individual rights not relinquished by the new Constitution?) they might have been considered at the mercy of the general legislature.

—James Iredell, "Answers to Mr. Mason's Objections to the New Constitution, recommended by the late Convention," early 1788

Document 6

Source: *George Washington: Writings*, Library of America, 1997.

On the prospect of the happy termination of this insurrection I sincerely congratulate you; hoping that good may result from the cloud of evils which threatened not only the hemisphere of Massachusetts but by spreading its baneful influence, the tranquility of the Union. Surely Shays must be either a weak man—the dupe of some characters who are yet behind the curtain—or has been deceived by his followers. Or which may yet be more likely, he did not conceive that there was energy enough in the Government to bring matters to the crisis to which they have been pushed. It is to be hoped the General Court of that State concurred in the report of the Committee, that a rebellion did actually exist. This would be decisive, and the most likely means of putting the finishing stroke to the business. [...] Our Affairs, generally, seem really to be approaching to some awful crisis. God only knows what the result will be. It shall be my part to hope for the best; as to see this Country happy whilst I am gliding down the stream of life in tranquil retirement is so much the wish of my Soul, that nothing on this side Elysium can be placed in competition with it.

—George Washington to Henry Knox, February 1787

Document 7

Source: *https://archive.org/details/cu31924020874099*

The design of a senate is not merely to check the legislative assembly, but to collect wisdom and experience. In most of our constitutions, and particularly in the proposed federal system, greater age and longer residence are required to qualify for the senate than for the house of representatives. This is a wise provision. The house of representatives may be composed of new and unexperienced members—strangers to the forms of proceeding, and the science of legislation. But either positive institutions, or customs, which may supply their place, fill the senate with men venerable for age and respectability, experienced in the ways of men, and in the art of governing, and who are not liable to the bias of passions that govern the young. If the senate of Rhode Island is an exception to this observation, it is a proof that the mass of the people are corrupted, and that the senate should be elected less frequently than the other house. Had the old senate in Rhode Island held their seats for three years; had they not been chosen amidst a popular rage for paper money, the honor of that state would probably have been saved. The old senate would have stopped the measure for a year or two till the people could have had time to deliberate upon its consequences. I consider it as a capital excellence of the proposed constitution that the senate can be wholly renewed but once in six years.

—Noah Webster, "An Examination into the Leading Principles of the Federal Constitution Proposed by the Late Convention Held at Philadelphia. With Answers to the Principal Objections That Have Been Raised Against the System," October 1787

WHEN YOU HAVE COMPLETED ANSWERING YOUR DOCUMENT-BASED QUESTION, YOU MAY CONTINUE AND BEGIN WORKING ON PART B, THE LONG ESSAY.

Section II, Part B: Long Essay Question

Time: 40 Minutes • 1 Question

> **Directions:** Answer ONE question from this group. State a thesis, cite relevant evidence, and use logical, clear arguments to support your generalizations.

2. Assess the degree to which the Mexican War fostered in a social and political change, in addition to continuity in the United States until 1860.

3. Assess the degree to which the advent of nuclear weapons represented a significant change and continuity in United States' foreign policy.

4. Explain how the American colonies came to a break with Britain in the second half of the eighteenth century. Was the Revolution radical or conservative?

STOP.
IF YOU FINISH BEFORE TIME IS OUT, YOU MAY CHECK
YOUR WORK ON THIS SECTION ONLY.
DO NOT TURN TO ANY OTHER SECTION IN THE TEST.

ANSWER KEY AND EXPLANATIONS

Section I, Part A: Multiple-Choice Questions

1. B	12. D	23. B	34. D	45. B
2. A	13. B	24. A	35. A	46. A
3. C	14. A	25. C	36. C	47. B
4. D	15. C	26. A	37. B	48. A
5. C	16. A	27. A	38. D	49. C
6. C	17. C	28. D	39. B	50. B
7. A	18. D	29. B	40. A	51. B
8. B	19. B	30. B	41. C	52. B
9. C	20. C	31. A	42. B	53. A
10. A	21. A	32. D	43. A	54. D
11. C	22. D	33. C	44. C	55. A

1. **The correct answer is B.** Tensions over westward expansion led to the French and Indian War. The Louisiana Purchase was made sixty years after Washington's "Journey to the French Commandant," and the Great Awakening, though contemporaneous, had very little effect on events leading to the French and Indian War. The Revolutionary War would indeed be partly caused by British limitations on expansion, but it was not the most immediate effect of these tensions.

2. **The correct answer is A.** By far, the main driving force behind organizations like the Ohio Company was expansion. Christianization was not nearly as much of a goal as it had been for the Spanish, for example, in South America. Unlike the Spanish, the English had little intention of or desire to mix in any way with the native inhabitants. However, warfare was not a goal but part of the cost of doing business, as it were, while secession didn't arise until independence had been won.

3. **The correct answer is C.** Note that Washington mentions that Singess and his tribe just happened to live where the Company wanted to put a fort. This is emblematic of westward expansion. Indians during this period tended to side with the French, who had no intention of mass settlement (and thus expulsion), which, naturally enough, the Indians did not welcome.

4. **The correct answer is D.** Other than horses, rivers were the primary mode of travel. But they weren't the sole means of transport (choice C). In 1754, no one had built any canals yet (choice B). Choice A is incorrect, as Washington's focus was not the rivers' aesthetic value.

5. **The correct answer is C.** An amazing number of still-used inventions arose during the second industrial revolution. From the first, America protected intellectual property, and high tariffs protect infant industries. Finally, while wealth was indeed concentrated during the Gilded Age, that's not as directly related to inventions as the fact that many inventions arose during this period.

6. **The correct answer is C.** The telegraph was invented during the 1830s and 40s.

7. **The correct answer is A.** Though many inventions occurred in America, many others occurred in Europe, particularly in Germany, which had a very strong university system for science and technology.

8. **The correct answer is B.** The passage is a direct assault on the cult of domesticity, the idea that a woman's sphere was in the home and raising children, period, whereas anything else was deemed unfeminine. Republican motherhood, while still limited to the home, at least allowed for a direct political, external role for home-bound women. The passage is not opposed to either abolition or suffrage; neither comes up.

9. **The correct answer is C.** Urbanization, both in terms of relative share of the population and in the number of cities, boomed with industrialization. Slavery was abolished during this period. Full worker rights have arguably never been achieved, but certainly they were not even partially achieved until the Progressive Era. The Great Migration refers to the northern movement of African Americans from the Jim Crow South, which took place about a century later.

10. **The correct answer is A.** Child labor existed until the New Deal finally eradicated it, and many children worked in the mills and early factories. These factories tended to be segregated, so the other options are incorrect.

11. **The correct answer is C.** In a paternalistic age, letting young girls out of the house was widely agreed to require strict, matronly oversight. However, factory girls did publish newspapers, such as the one this passage comes from, and had other opportunities for personal development. Moreover, since travel was still relatively slow and girls often came from farms, living on site was, for the most part, inescapable. Choice B describes the putting-out system, a system mostly overthrown by industrialization.

12. **The correct answer is D.** The Sedition Act took direct aim at the First Amendment. It led to the Kentucky and Virginia Resolutions, which introduced for the first time the overt idea of state nullification of federal law, but the actual Nullification Crisis came during Jackson's presidency. Neither the Purchase nor *Marbury* had anything to do with First Amendment rights.

13. **The correct answer is B.** We can all thank the Anti-Federalists for the Bill of Rights. James Madison, along with the Federalists, thought it unnecessary. Parties did immediately arise, but that phenomenon wasn't much connected to the Bill of Rights, per se. Although the French Revolution did play a role, especially its Declaration of the Rights of Man, the speed of passage was due to the need to ratify the Constitution.

14. **The correct answer is A.** Centuries of bloodshed over religion, including, crucially, which version of Christianity was to be the state religion in England, led the founders to stay far away from any kind of nationally established church. All the other rights were not nearly as deeply connected to the experience of the English Civil War.

15. **The correct answer is C.** King saw domestic and foreign policy as connected, especially as noted in the famous final sentence of this passage. All three of the "triplets"—racism, militarism, and materialism (i.e., a kind of economic system based on consumerism)—were intimately intertwined, so choice D cannot be true.

16. **The correct answer is A.** King was concerned that all the monies being used for the Vietnam War were being diverted from social programs that were benefiting the

urban poor. While many African American men served in the Vietnam War, they were not blamed for the stalemate, so choice B is incorrect. Most African Americans were not pro-Vietnam, so choice C is incorrect. Finally, Dr. King was concerned with the disproportionate number of young black men dying in the war, not whether they were winning, so Choice D is incorrect.

17. **The correct answer is C.** Though somewhat controversial, it's still safe to say that it's generally accepted that the Civil Rights Movement secured *de jure* and even in some cases *de facto* improvements in political and legal rights—from legalization of interracial marriage to the end of Jim Crow segregation and the reinstatement of voting rights—but fell short of achieving economic parity between African Americans and whites.

18. **The correct answer is D.** Although Medgar Evers was a civil rights leader, he was assassinated before the Vietnam War truly escalated.

19. **The correct answer is B.** Note that Hamilton both criticizes the knee-jerk, moralistic reaction against carrying debt in any situation for any reason and allows for debt's potential danger as well—it's not an "unmixed" good or evil. It is merely useful in certain circumstances for certain goals. This is typical Enlightenment thinking, or at least writing; it was an age that praised moderation.

20. **The correct answer is C.** The Whigs, like Henry Clay and Abraham Lincoln, embraced Hamilton's program, with perhaps more emphasis on the importance of agriculture. Democrats tended not to, whereas Populists were mostly against such things as banks and the power of finance in general. Know-Nothings were mostly anti-Nativist; the Whigs are closest to Hamilton's inheritors.

21. **The correct answer is A.** Like most nations that have successfully developed, protection is fine until one is relatively confident of being able to outcompete, or at least stay in the ring with, one's competition. At that point, typically in modern economic history, free trade is heartily embraced and protectionism decried. Some economic historians refer to this as "kicking away the ladder." So, too, did Hamilton's program, which is sometimes seen as the origin of a form of developmental protectionism.

22. **The correct answer is D.** Hamilton wanted a balanced economy of agriculture and manufacturing, although he was more concerned with national independence through building up domestic manufacturing capacity—why bother to declare political independence if one was to stay a near-mercantilist economic satellite of Britain? Hamilton aimed to support agriculture by increasing its domestic market, not replace it with manufacturing.

23. **The correct answer is B.** In fact, as recently as 2017, almost on Kalecki's cue, people on both the left and right have started talking about income subsidies, while according to some, we already have negative interest rates, if only due to programs like quantitative easing. But ever since the Reagan administration, the main, if not sole, policy tool for countercyclical measures has been monetary. Fiscal fixes are not absent but are few and far between. One need only compare FDR's response to the Depression to Obama's response to the Great Recession—both in terms of what was passed and, more importantly, what was *proposed*, to see how different the conventional economic wisdom had become.

24. **The correct answer is A.** Kalecki presumes that capitalism has always had and always will have cycles of booms and busts. It's clear

from Kalecki's tone that he does not think private investment is the best way to go or that full employment is not worth maintaining; only later on would such notions arise. And income subsidies are inevitable only if private investment support is the chosen pathway.

25. **The correct answer is C.** Though mechanized, topsoil-obliterating agricultural practices were a main cause, nature helped out with a hundred-year-level drought. The Fair Deal was Truman's program, not FDR's, which was the New Deal.

26. **The correct answer is A.** The AAA helped property-owning farmers, for example, by distributing subsidies. Those who didn't own farms weren't much helped; in fact, some historians believe that the AAA as much as the Dust Bowl itself helped shift population west as poor tenant farmers fled in search of better opportunity. The AAA was a mostly financial program that neither caused nor cured the Dust Bowl; other New Deal programs took direct aim at fixing the environment by addressing ecological issues caused by both man and nature, and did so with much success.

27. **The correct answer is A.** The AAA, it seems widely held, did much to support agricultural prices through subsidies, production quotas, and the like, but it was the massive economic mobilization of World War II that really solved the problem. The effects of the Dust Bowl itself—the drop of production—did help to shore up prices, but not as much as WWII. Rural electrification did take off under and via the New Deal, but it didn't directly affect prices—certainly not as much as the war.

28. **The correct answer is D.** To contemporary eyes, much of the New Deal was racist—choices A, B, and C are all accurate—but not to the point of disallowing African American participation. In fact, programs like the WPA theater project directly supported African American participation in the arts.

29. **The correct answer is B.** Typical of the Progressives, the idea was rational regulation, with the government in the role of steward and referee. Conservation—not total preservation—was the goal; some development was allowed, if only to make the parks accessible to the ever-increasing number of tourists that formed the economic basis of and one argument for the park system.

30. **The correct answer is B.** As society grew increasingly complex and specialized, the Progressives championed expertise and efficiency. As with the New Deal, and until the 1950s, racial justice mostly took a back seat, often (but far from exclusively) due to the Solid South's hold on Congress through the Democratic Party.

31. **The correct answer is A.** Choice C is incorrect because organizations like the Sierra Club took a leading role in conservation; however, choice D sells short governmental action of its own accord.

32. **The correct answer is D.** Marshall brilliantly used the case to argue for what some (like Jefferson) considered an unwarranted expansion of and others (like Marshall and many others) considered the natural consequence of Article III of the Constitution. Marshall never argued for the supremacy of any branch, let alone for legislative powers for the Court.

33. **The correct answer is C.** Jefferson was strongly opposed to federal power, whereas Hamilton, Adams, and Washington, all Federalists, were in favor of it.

34. The correct answer is D. This is a tough, little-known-detail question whose answer can be inferred if one understands the point of judicial review. If it were limited only to federal law, states could operate unconstitutionally. Since federal law was understood (by most) to overrule state law—the "supremacy clause" of the Constitution—it was natural to extend judicial review to state law, which Marshall did just as soon as he could (in *Fletcher v. Peck* in 1810).

35. The correct answer is A. Spanish colonization, while brutal, was in general no more so than that of the other European powers. In fact, Spain was at least interested in forming a mixed, if caste-based, society; the English simply wanted the Native population out of the way, one way or another. The other options are not as closely associated with this document, including the transatlantic slave trade; although African slave labor was suggested by de las Casas, it was not the focus of this text.

36. The correct answer is C. The Spanish actually did take Christianization quite seriously, and it did conflict with resource and profit extraction from time to time, as de las Casas notes. None of the other choices were essential tensions noted in this passage, though competition between Catholic and Protestant powers, and later between England and Spain, was certainly a tension.

37. The correct answer is B. It's one of the great ironies of history that one of the most humane documents on behalf of the Native Americans was penned by the same person who suggested African enslavement as its cure. To De Las Casas' credit, he later changed his mind, but the moral of the story is that much in human affairs turns on who is and who is not perceived to be fully and equally human.

38. The correct answer is D. According to Turner, such a restless, ever-expanding society forged on the frontier could hardly be expected to settle down immediately (or perhaps ever), so choice A is incorrect, and Turner is more analytical than either choice B or choice C would allow.

39. The correct answer is B. "Free land" is an odd term for many possible reasons—costs were high—in dollars, in diplomacy, and in war with Mexico and the Native Americans. But most oddly, perhaps, is Turner's intended meaning, one which doesn't take into account the costs to the original inhabitants, which was near-total, a not-just-American notion one tends to find in nations forged by settler-colonialism: that the land they settled and colonized was empty of people—or nearly so. One might consider it in psychological terms as refusing to acknowledge the crime, as it were.

40. The correct answer is A. Turner was not concerned with condemning westward expansion or acknowledging the cost of the expansion on Native Americans, nor did he call for overseas expansion, though he probably found it unsurprising. What concerned him was the increase in tensions at home with no "virgin lands" to act as a safety valve. Again, this is hardly typically American; since time immemorial, nations have "solved" domestic problems abroad, usually by going to war.

41. The correct answer is C. From JFK's "New Frontier" to one perennial justification for manned space exploration to even the ever-popular *Star Trek* franchise, Americans seem enamored of boldly going where no one (or at least no American) has gone before. Turner would have been completely unsurprised.

answers practice test 3

42. **The correct answer is B.** Republican motherhood, following its Roman model, gave much prominence to the importance of properly raising properly republican men and women who would properly raise yet more. Unlike the later notion of the cult of domesticity, which sealed off women from any real engagement with the world outside the home, republican motherhood at least celebrated one external manifestation of women's traditional role. There is no relationship to eugenics, and radical feminists (among others) would be outraged by the notion.

43. **The correct answer is A.** The right to petition the government with grievances is part of the First Amendment. The Second Amendment deals with the right to bear arms, while the Tenth Amendment reserves certain rights to the states. The Fourteenth Amendment wasn't passed until after the Civil War.

44. **The correct answer is C.** Both justifications for and condemnations of slavery emanated from churches—sometimes even churches of the same denominations. None of the other choices are supported by the passage.

45. **The correct answer is B.** Part of Jacksonian democratization consisted of extensions of formal democracy (such as expanding the franchise), but part consisted of an explosion of voluntary associations dedicated to political, social, and cultural issues—what we'd now call "civil society." One could argue that a kind of Puritan pietism had persisted, especially in Boston, and flowed into this group and much of northern abolition, but the general phenomenon of the rise of civil society extended far beyond regions where Puritanism had reigned.

46. **The correct answer is A.** Beard makes the point with humor and grace: beware stereotyping in history. Even useful generalizations are at least partly stereotypes; it's a slippery slope. He neither condemns nor praises, let alone discusses how long Puritanism's effects lasted: His concern is to depolarize depictions and understanding of Puritans.

47. **The correct answer is B.** A question of historiography and even of epistemology, Beard's argument is closest to the usual, modern, scientific notion that approaches to objectivity are best found at the populational, not the individual, level. Scholars may produce less or more objective works, but it's the community of scholars, over time, who progress toward a fuller understanding. None of the other options approach Beard's view.

48. **The correct answer is A.** One is safest presuming that Beard saw the Puritans as human beings; like all human beings in all societies and cultures, they were a mixed bag—much as Hamilton in a previous passage saw debt as a mixed bag. Choice B might be tempting, but it'd be unlikely that Puritans, nearly alone among all analogous human groupings for thousands of years, were somehow unique in this regard. Much in history turns on whether the historian considers people to be roughly the same, at least in the range of potential, if not also in the range of actualization of that potential.

49. **The correct answer is C.** The Mexican-American War started because of border disputes with Mexico, the annexation of Texas, and the Mexican refusal to sell California to the United States. Americans sent in troops after Mexican troops crossed the Rio Grande and captured an American army patrol. While Northern Whigs opposed the conflict, war broke out nonetheless.

50. **The correct answer is B.** The Treaty of Guadalupe Hidalgo formally marked the end of the Mexican-American War. The Gadsden Purchase was a financial transaction with Mexico after the war for the sale of parts of Arizona and New Mexico, but it did not formally end the war, so choice A is incorrect. The Wilmot Proviso was an attempt to prohibit slavery in the Mexican Cession lands, so choice C is incorrect. The Ostend Manifesto was a secret meeting of American diplomats attempting to buy Cuba from Spain, so choice D is incorrect.

51. **The correct answer is B.** After the Mexican-American War, the debate over slavery heightened as the question of whether the Mexican Cession lands should allow slavery. Additionally, the United States took control of California and set clear borders with Mexico south of the Rio Grande. While the Wilmot Proviso was introduced in Congress as a measure to prevent slavery in the Mexican Cession lands, it was never passed.

52. **The correct answer is B.** The French had already tried and failed to set up a canal in the region; whoever succeeded would have control of a new and profitable "choke point" along a new and profitable trading route. Of course, that nation would need to defend trade, which would mean a naval presence. All this starts edging toward choice A, which is intentionally tricky: it was actually the Roosevelt Corollary to the Monroe Doctrine, not the Doctrine itself, that was canal-related. Labor was mostly local, not American, and hardly integrated; quite the contrary.

53. **The correct answer is A.** Again, the Monroe Doctrine is tempting but incorrect, strictly speaking. The Good Neighbor Policy came later; it was FDR's term for his Latin American policy. The Era of Good Feelings occurred after the temporarily unifying War of 1812 and was as transient as all such eras are.

54. **The correct answer is D.** Ever since Kennedy, candidates who aren't "good television" don't do well; moreover, since most people get their news via television (at least until very recently, and even Internet video could be regarded simply as television via another mode of delivery), television advertising (and, now Internet video) play a huge role. Social media in general may be taking over, though: in the 2016 election, both Bernie Sanders and Donald Trump used social media to surprising effect. In 2017, the U.K. Labour Party, led by Jermey Corbyn, pulled off a major advance in parliamentary seats in a very short time due in large part to social media platforms.

55. **The correct answer is A.** The story of the past eighty years could be first the dominance of "the FDR model" and then of "the Reagan model." Nixon added to the New Deal legacy—the last president to have done so, in fact—while Clinton and Obama, in many ways, helped advance the Reagan Revolution.

Section I, Part B: Short-Answer Questions

1. For part A, it's clear that the image is very patriotic. In fact, Americans came together as they hadn't since the Revolution in the face of a renewed war with Britain. Note among other things how upright Madison is, whereas King George is about to keel over. When analyzing images, feel free to play art historian: any aspect of the image is fair game. One could also note the irony of the United States being identified with its president in the same way that Britain is identified with its king: hardly a "republican" notion, but perhaps relevant to patriotism if not merely a visual trope.

   For part B, one could note the blockade of American shipping by the British as they fought Napoleon on the continent and aimed to use its superior navy to hem in France; the impressment of American sailors into the British navy; the retaliatory embargo by the United States, later limited by Madison; and British support for the war Tecumseh launched to prevent American policy of removal of Indians beyond the Mississippi.

   For part C, one could legitimately note that not much at all flowed from this war. Territory remained the same. But one should note the launching of Andrew Jackson's career as the Hero of New Orleans; the consolidation of the United States' sovereignty with the Louisiana Purchase; and of course, the dissolution of Indian power in general east of the Mississippi, which opened up vast regions for expansion.

2. For part A, discuss the effect of the Tariff of 1828, which solidified South Carolina's suspicion that the federal government was growing too powerful and would one day outlaw slavery over state objections. Part of their suspicion stemmed from the series of decisions that had long emanated from Marshall's Court that further bolstered federal power; another part stemmed from the Missouri Compromise of 1820. Another cause was that Jackson came down hard on the side of federal power despite a long commitment to states' rights and limited government.

   For part B, perhaps the most important effect was the reintroduction of nullification as a real threat to federal power. Once raised, the weapon would sooner or later be used, successfully or not. Though Calhoun claimed that nullification prevented secession, Jackson and many others felt it was secession without actually seceding; fault lines that were clear enough during the constitutional convention were becoming ever clearer and more unavoidable. Another important effect was the formation of the Whig Party under Calhoun (who left the Democratic Party), Clay, and Webster.

3. The whole discussion will turn on which "wave" of feminism one considers the real beginning of the movement. As usual, there is no "right answer"—plausible argument is all that is required. If one considers the beginning of the struggle, however protracted, for political rights like suffrage to be the beginning, then the mid-nineteenth century would serve. In fact, one could even point to "factory girls" often "radical" embracing of economic independence—or at least economic participation—as the beginning of economic rights for women, too, however atypical. If one is more concerned with victories, the 1920s serve, as suffrage was then achieved. Also, culturally, women in the twenties began to break out of old domestic roles—the "flapper" was as lauded as vilified, and the kind of urban, relatively freer existence typical of modern urban centers began during this period. Finally, if the criterion is how widespread and relatively major the changes in the culture and economy are, the modern/contemporary period could be considered the beginning. Much turns not only on how one defines feminism but also on

how one ascertains what "beginning" means. It's a question about periodization and historical judgment.

For part B, just apply any of the relevant ideas listed above (or any others) from the periods other than the one chosen.

4.   For part A, there are sadly too many to list. Infamous examples are the Trail of Tears in 1838 and the massacre at Wounded Knee in 1890, but there are many, many examples. Keep in mind, however, that ethnic cleansing is not limited to killing, violence, or even territorial dispossession: any attempt to eradicate existing cultural or social mores or memory is ethnic cleansing. Some examples are the Indian boarding schools that were set up in the nineteenth and twentieth centuries to strip Indians of their ethnic identity, as well as the Dawes Act of 1887, which aimed to assimilate Indians into American culture by undermining Indian traditions of land ownership, tribal loyalty, and family structure. The Indian removal policy of Jackson would be quite appropriate to note.

For part B, one could mention among many possibilities King Philip/Metacom's war against New England colonists in the seventeenth century; Tecumseh's War in the 1810s; the Indian Wars of the 1860s through the 1880s, including the Battle of Little Big Horn in 1876; and many others all the way up to AIM in the 1970s, including the occupation of Wounded Knee in 1973.

For part C, one could also mention Tecumseh and his brother Tenskwatawa, "The Prophet," both of whom decried assimilation to American culture; tribal colleges and universities that began to be set up in the 1960s through which many cultural traditions were revived; and even twenty-first-century attempts to resuscitate Indian languages.

Section II, Part A: Document-Based Question

1. First, make sure your response refers to all or all but one of the documents. That's why they're there, after all: this item tests your ability to synthesize information from several documents of varying types. You have plenty to compare and contrast among the documents.

    Second, your thesis should note the two or three most important arguments about the Constitution presented in these documents as well as the historical context in which they took place. Good candidates for "technical" debates about political power are the power of the executive; the lack of a bill of rights; the danger of aristocracy posed by the Senate; and the role of the judiciary. Much of the debate turned on the balance between centralization and decentralization of power (federal, state, individual) as well as the apportioning of power among the several branches in the federal government itself. However, note the contextual issues among the documents as well: Shays' Rebellion, debt and paper money, and the legality of the Constitutional Convention itself are specifically mentioned. You can also bring in any longer-term context you desire that will fit in with the issues raised in the documents, such as pre-existing models of state constitutions, experiences under the Articles of Confederation, perceptions of governmental power stemming from the revolutionary period, and much besides. Anything that illuminates the technical discussion of the apportionment of power is relevant. Remember, you'll want eventually to extend the analysis either to other time periods or to other cultures and societies at the time, whether formal constitution-making or not.

    Third, you'll want to go in depth in your analysis of at least four of the documents, addressing one of the following for each of the four in-depth analyses: the historical context, the intended audience, the author's purpose, and the author's point of view. The minimum, mind you, is to discuss one of those four aspects for each of the four; feel free to expand beyond that as your thesis requires, but remember that you'll want to draw connections between the documents, not just analyze each in relative isolation. In this case, the fact that some of the documents literally refer to each other might help, but be sure to make conceptual comparisons among those not literally related in that fashion. Some possibilities include a discussion of the lack of a Constitutional Council, the looming threat of Shays' Rebellion's return, and the whole issue of debt and paper money. Take into account the kinds of documents these are: private letters, public broadsheets or "op-eds," and even a political cartoon (the only surviving one, apparently) from the debate. The challenge here is that you'll have to link in-depth reviews of four of the documents to more than one issue, as there are so many represented in the document set and of course in the debate itself, including economic issues. Of course, bring in anything from the *Federalist Papers*.

    Make sure to show how the different kinds of documents—whether a cartoon aimed at the masses or elite private discussions—vary in point of view, intended audience, authorial purpose, and so on. You will want (and have) to bring in outside knowledge to contextualize the documents. One fruitful avenue would be to include classic statements from the *Federalist Papers*, as already noted. Another would be to discuss the public nature of the debate made possible by a vibrant press, or even the issue of slavery, which is not indicated in the documents but is clearly relevant to the subterranean tensions around ratification.

As noted earlier, your response should be extended to another time, another place, or another mode of historical writing and argumentation. If, for example, you concentrated on a technical political-science comparison, you could expand your analysis by relating that to the economic or cultural sphere. Or, alternatively, you could bring in a discussion of the foreign-policy situation in the 1780s or issues of westward expansion and relations with Indians.

Section II, Part B: Long Essay Question

Note: Whichever essay you picked, consider not reading the guideline responses to the other two—save them for further practice!

Two of the essays require you to determine whether the noted event was indeed a turning point in history. As you would expect, one can either agree or disagree and do just fine: the point is not to choose the "right" answer, but to create a reasonable thesis and back it up. The third essay asks you to trace how the colonists broke with Britain.

Specific feedback for each essay below will deal with both cases, but in general, the more specific and relevant your support for your thesis and any subsidiary points, the better you'll do. Thesis statements may be two sentences, if you prefer, but make sure they address all parts of the question. After you have developed your argument, make sure to extend it to another time period, another culture or society, or to another mode of historical writing and argumentation.

2. The Mexican War could be considered a turning point for at least a couple of reasons. First, it was arguably the first aggressive war the nation had fought, but not the last. It was also launched on dodgy grounds and gave rise to an antiwar resistance. Second, the main effect, the Mexican Cession pretty much shattered the Missouri Compromise and arguably brought on the Civil War, while also dooming the Plains Indians and opening up much of the continent for rapid settlement and the introduction of capitalism.

   However, one could see the war as just one of many expansive actions, consistent with the original settlement of the country (and the continent) itself, and forming a historical series. Expansive actions need not be formal wars and needn't rely on justifications for the war, then or in retrospect: the point is to see the Mexican War as a stage of expansion, in which case it's nothing much special. Similarly, its effect on sectional tension over slavery could be seen as valid but relatively unimportant insofar as one presumes that the Civil War was inevitable, built into the economic and political structure of the nation from deep into colonial times.

   Note how crucial framing is to the assessment of whether any particular feature is to be considered a change or not. That is part of the point: There are no right answers in the mathematical sense to these kinds of questions. They are designed to see how well one can reason out a properly supported answer, regardless of what position is taken. Make sure to extend your analysis to other periods, regions, or styles of history. For example, comparison of the Mexican War to the series of land acquisitions that built the country would serve nicely, as would the series of wars of a dicey nature the country has fought, from the Philippines to Vietnam to Iraq.

3. The rise of nuclear weapons may well be the most important turning point in human history, of course, but the specific question is to what extent it changed US foreign policy. That's a more interesting, because more nuanced, question. On the "yes" side would be a limitation on war-making options, given the risks, which ultimately forced a level of negotiation that perhaps would not have otherwise occurred. One could point to the rejection of their use in conflicts like Korea and Vietnam, for example. Another argument is that in a sense nuclear weapons are used all the time by those who have them: as a threat that need never be stated. It's a very risky game to play, but it goes on: the nuclear umbrella could be argued to have encouraged small-scale (relatively speaking) warfare given the confidence that the USSR (or China) would refuse to call the nuclear bluff. Furthermore, one could point to nuclear weapons as the death

of American isolationism: it's hard to be isolated from their effects; hence, NATO and all the rest of the alliances.

On the other hand, did policy change much? What had the record been prior to 1945? Did that change? Short of world wars, which America had resisted entering both times, America's wars tended to be of the Mexican, Spanish-American ilk—smaller, regional wars that seem hardly to have ended after 1945. Quite the contrary, and given the spheres of influence roughly agreed to, the nuclear threat could be argued to have encouraged regional warfare within (or outside, via proxy) each superpower's sphere of influence, whether the USSR disciplining its satellites in Hungary in 1956 or Czechoslovakia in 1968, or invading Afghanistan in 1978, or the U.S. wars in Korea, Vietnam, and Iraq, along with a constant series of supported coups and so on. Surprisingly, perhaps, it's easier to argue that nothing much changed. You will want to compare or at least extend your thesis to other moments in American history or to other nations or societies, which is a challenge with a weapon like nuclear bombs, but not impossible. The long bow had its effects, as did gunpowder and any other game-changing weapon; if you're arguing rather for the new-bottle-for-old-wine side, that the introduction of a weapon doesn't change anything much more than the tactical calculus, show how previous advances did just that.

Ultimately, this is a question of how much technology drives history, as well as an indirect way of asking what, exactly, U.S. foreign policy has been over the years. Has it changed? When? By how much, and why, and to what degree because of nuclear weapons? Again, this is a question that can be plausibly answered in any number of ways, provided one defines the terms that are used, supplies a plausible thesis, and supports it well.

Keep in mind, too, that international economic regimes are part of foreign policy, so feel free to consider what, if any, effects the introduction of nuclear weapons had on Bretton Woods or the later neoliberal consensus. One further point: one could argue that the end of isolation was inherent in WWII and the fact that the United States was utterly dominant after the war, relatively unscathed and with half of the global GDP.

Also fair game would be how the nuclear threat of the Soviets played a cultural role in both elite and popular conceptions of what American foreign policy should be, intersecting with anticommunism from the hysterical, McCarthyite ilk to the more widely accepted kinds. To what extent did the loss of the nuclear monopoly affect the culture, and did that effect play a role in foreign policy? Or was the superpower conflict simply inevitable anyway, even in a non-nuclear world, given simple ideological and national-identity differences?

4. Regardless of whether one considers the Revolution radical or conservative, the data will be the same, but the political character of the Revolution turns on whether one thinks the colonists were creating something new or simply trying to secure longstanding English liberties. Conflict traditionally begins with the aftermath of the French and Indian War, in which colonists thought they'd removed a bar on westward expansion, whereas the British, massively indebted, began to squeeze the colonists through a series of acts. The Royal Proclamation of 1763, as well as the whole series of Acts, from the Stamp Act on, should be mentioned, along with colonial responses.

For example, the Stamp Act gave rise to the Sons of Liberty and sometimes violent resistance to taxation without representation. The Stamp Act Congress in New York City was also the scene of concerted political resistance to the Stamp Act. Similarly, passage of the Townshend

Acts in 1767 led eventually to troop deployments in Boston and, in 1770, the Boston Massacre, just as the Navigation Acts gave rise to the *Gaspee* Affair in Rhode Island. The rise of the more formal Committees on Correspondence in 1772 should be mentioned as well. The Tea Act led in late 1773 to the Boston Tea Party, and finally the Intolerable Acts led to the First Continental Congress and soon to open hostilities and the Declaration of Independence.

Attention should be paid to the economic nature of the break—mercantilist colonialism was falling apart as the colonies became ever-more-complex societies—as one could argue that at least in terms of elites, colonists and Englishmen were culturally unified as perhaps supported by the popularity of the Great Awakening on both sides of the Atlantic. Moreover, some of the debate exemplified in Paine's *Common Sense* could be mentioned, along with British views on the crisis, as exemplified by Adam Smith or Edmund Burke, especially when assessing whether the Revolution was radical or conservative.

Self-Scoring Sheet for Practice Test 3

Directions:

- For the 55 multiple-choice items, tally up the items you answered either incorrectly or omitted—or just guessed on in some fashion—according to the chronological period. This will help you determine what you need to review. (Some question numbers are repeated, as the subject matter crossed chronological periods.)
- For each of the short-answer items (Q1 through Q4), the content area(s) have been noted in the chart to aid with your review.
- For the DBQ and Essays, an asterisk has been placed in the chronological period most at issue, but keep in mind that the essays usually ask about turning points in history, so discussion can range widely from those turning points.

Period	Multiple-Choice Items	Short Answers	DBQ	Essay 1	Essay 2	Essay 3
1 (1491-1607)	35, 36, 37, 39, 50	Q3				*
2 (1607-1754)	1, 2, 3, 4, 14, 36, 39, 40, 46	Q3				*
3 (1754-1800)	3, 12, 13, 14, 19, 20, 21, 22, 39, 40, 42, 43	Q3	*			*
4 (1800-1848)	3, 7, 8, 10, 11, 20, 21, 32, 33, 34, 39, 40, 42, 43, 44, 45	Q1, Q2, Q3, Q4				
5 (1844-1877)	3, 7, 9, 39, 40, 44, 49-51	Q3, Q4		*		
6 (1865-1898)	3, 5, 6, 7, 9, 29, 30, 31, 39, 40	Q3, Q4				
7 (1890-1945)	6, 23, 24*, 25, 26, 27, 28, 29, 30, 31, 38, 39, 40, 41, 46, 47*, 48*, 52, 53	Q3, Q4				
8 (1945-1980)	15, 16, 17, 18, 31, 39, 41	Q3, Q4			*	
9 (1980-present)	17, 23, 31, 39, 41, 54, 55	Q3, Q4				

*mostly conceptual, not chronological